TRADITIONALISM, NATIONALISM, AND FEMINISM

Recent Titles in
Contributions in Women's Studies

As Minority Becomes Majority: Federal Reaction to the Phenomenon of Women in the Work Force, 1920-1963
Judith Sealander

Women in Colonial Spanish American Literature: Literary Images
Julie Greer Johnson

Divorce and Remarriage: Problems, Adaptations, and Adjustments
Stan L. Albrecht, Howard M. Bahr, and Kristen L. Goodman

Women and Death: Linkages in Western Thought and Literature
Beth Ann Bassein

Political Equality in a Democratic Society: Women in the United States
Mary Lou Kendrigan

Fantasy and Reconciliation: Contemporary Formulas of Women's Romance Fiction
Kay Mussell

Three Who Dared: Prudence Crandall, Margaret Douglass, Myrtilla Miner—Champions of Antebellum Black Education
Philip S. Foner and Josephine F. Pacheco

Insatiable Appetites: Twentieth-Century American Women's Bestsellers
Madonne M. Miner

Representations of Women: Nineteenth-Century British Women's Poetry
Kathleen Hickok

Women, Nazis, and Universities: Female University Students in the Third Reich, 1933-1945
Jacques R. Pauwels

Cassandra's Daughters: The Women in Hemingway
Roger Whitlow

The World of Women's Trade Unionism: Comparative Historical Essays
Norbert C. Soldon, editor

TRADITIONALISM, NATIONALISM, AND FEMINISM

Women Writers of
Quebec

EDITED BY
PAULA GILBERT LEWIS

FOREWORD BY
ELAINE MARKS

CONTRIBUTIONS IN WOMEN'S STUDIES, NUMBER 53

GREENWOOD PRESS
WESTPORT, CONNECTICUT · LONDON, ENGLAND

Library of Congress Cataloging in Publication Data

Main entry under title:

Traditionalism, nationalism, and feminism.

(Contributions in women's studies, ISSN 0147-104X ;
no. 53)
    Bibliography: p.
    Includes index.
    1. French-Canadian literature—20th century—History
and criticism—Addresses, essays, lectures. 2. French-
Canadian literature—Women authors—History and criticism
—Addresses, essays, lectures. 3. Nationalism and
literature—Québec (Province)—Addresses, essays, lec-
tures. 4. Feminism and literature—Québec (Province)—
Addresses, essays, lectures. I. Lewis, Paula Gilbert.
II. Series.
PQ3908.T7   1985   840'.9'9287   84-10854
ISBN 0-313-24510-X (lib. bdg.)

Library of Congress Catalog Card Number: 84-10854
ISBN: 0-313-24510-X
ISSN: 0147-104X

First published in 1985

Greenwood Press
A division of Congressional Information Service, Inc.
88 Post Road West
Westport, Connecticut 06881

Printed in the United States of America

10 9 8 7 6 5 4 3 2 1

To Anne, Meredith, and Marian
To Richard

Contents

Foreword
Elaine Marks   xi

Introduction
Paula Gilbert Lewis   3

1. Reflections in the Pool: The Subtext of Laure Conan's
   Angéline de Montbrun
   François Gallays   11

2. Feminism and Traditionalism in the Early Short Stories of
   Gabrielle Roy
   Paula Gilbert Lewis   27

3. *Le Survenant* as Ideological Messenger: A Study of Germaine
   Guèvremont's Radio Serial
   James J. Herlan   37

4. The Pursuit of the Real in Rina Lasnier's ''Présence de
   l'absence''
   James P. Gilroy   53

5. Counter-Traditions: The Marginal Poetics of Anne Hébert
   Susan L. Rosenstreich   63

6. Female Spirals and Male Cages: The Urban Sphere in the
   Novels of Gabrielle Roy
   Paula Gilbert Lewis   71

7. From Feminism to Nationalism: The Theater of Françoise
   Loranger, 1965-1970
   Carrol F. Coates   83

8. Louise Maheux-Forcier and the Poetics of Sensuality
   Maurice Cagnon   95

9. Love on the Rocks: Anne Hébert's *Kamouraska*
   Murray Sachs   109

10. Redefining the Maternal: Women's Relationships in the Fiction
    of Marie-Claire Blais
    Mary Jean Green   125

11. Antonine Maillet and the Epic Heroine
    Marjorie A. Fitzpatrick   141

12. Beyond the Myths and Fictions of Traditionalism and
    Nationalism: The Political in the Work of Nicole Brossard
    Louise H. Forsyth   157

13. A Québécois and an Acadian Novel Compared: The Use of
    Myth in Jovette Marchessault's *Comme une enfant de la terre*
    and Antonine Maillet's *Pélagie-la-Charrette*
    Micheline Herz   173

14. Madeleine Gagnon's Po(e)litical Vision: Portrait of an Artist
    and an Era
    Karen Gould   185

15. Louky Bersianik: Feminist Dialogisms
    Maroussia Hajdukowski-Ahmed   205

16. The Development of a Lesbian Sensibility in the Work of
    Jovette Marchessault and Nicole Brossard
    Marthe Rosenfeld   227

17. Women's Theater in Quebec
    Jane Moss   241

    Bibliography   255

    Index   261

    Contributors   277

Foreword

Elaine Marks ————————————————————————

Feminist discourse assumes that the more numerous the oppressions that inform a writer's situation, the greater the possibility of authenticity in the writing itself and the more "radical" and "political" it will be. Therefore, by virtue of their marginality, women writers of Quebec occupy a privileged position within this discourse. Although contemporary feminist literary critics and theorists are just beginning to describe, interpret, and evaluate their texts, it is clear that they are being represented as exemplary.

I am unable to explain why so much writing of such impressive quality should come from so few. I can only recall a history structured by the Catholic Church, colonialism, and feminism and the adventures of a language that is and is not French, struggling for survival against the dominant English-American presence. In relation to present feminist and avant-garde concerns, it would seem that the most distinguishing mark of women writers of Quebec is their complex relation to language, to the French of France and of Canada, to the English of England and the United States. To the extent that contemporary women writers of Quebec speak and hear four languages, they are aware of the interaction between language and power as it affects questions of national origin, of class, and of gender.

This particular collection of seventeen essays on women writers of Quebec has the advantage of presenting an historical perspective as well as a contemporary analysis, of focusing not only on literary events since 1968, but of going back to the end of the nineteenth century. The three categories that have been used to describe the historical situation—traditionalism, nationalism, and feminism—provide a useful framework for the non-specialists and facilitate their entry into this world.

Indeed this is a new world, in which the exploration of new forms in narrative, in poetry, and in the theater is accompanied by a strong belief that writing by women can bring about social change. Undoubtedly because of the multiple oppressions that weigh on *les Québécoises*, the gap between theory and practice is less noticeable than it is elsewhere.

The essays in this collection are as varied as the writers under consideration. The editor is to be congratulated for having succeeded in bringing together in one volume these substantial and exciting texts. She is also to be thanked for making it possible to journey north, into a contiguous but foreign land, with such expert guides.

University of Wisconsin-Madison

TRADITIONALISM, NATIONALISM, AND FEMINISM

Introduction

Paula Gilbert Lewis ————————————————

[I]ci au Québec, il faudra bien s'expliquer une bonne fois comment il se fait que les femmes aient joué un rôle si important dans notre littérature: Gabrielle Roy, Anne Hébert, Germaine Guèvremont, Marie-Claire Blais. Comment il se fait surtout que leurs oeuvres aient su toucher une vaste partie du public québécois? Sur quelle schizophrénie collective, leurs fantasmes ont-ils eu prise? Sur quelle oppression ont-ils fait le jour?[1]*

This collection of seventeen critical essays on women writers of Quebec does not claim to provide the answers to the above queries made in 1975 by the militant *québécois* feminist writer Nicole Brossard. What it does hope to do is to fill a justifiable need for a literary retrospective that presently exists neither in French nor in English.

Despite a continually increasing international female/feminist consciousness and, concurrently, a growing knowledge of the works of women writers from many countries, the literary production of female (as well as of male) *québécois* writers is not well known outside of Quebec. There are, of course, some exceptions to this widespread unawareness: Anne Hébert, whose 1982 *Les Fous de Bassan* won the Prix Fémina, now lives and publishes her works in France; Madeleine Gagnon has collaborated with the French feminists Hélène Cixous and Annie Leclerc; Antonine Maillet won the prestigious Prix Goncourt in 1979 (and is consistently confused in the United States with Marguerite Yourcenar);

---

*It is for the large group of readers who are not well-versed in French but who may be interested in these writings that each contributor has translated into English all quotations appearing in French. The English texts, placed in the corresponding notes, have been translated solely for the purpose of this book.

and, perhaps, Marie-Claire Blais is remembered for her 1966 Prix Médicis and, even less likely, Gabrielle Roy for her 1947 Prix Fémina. But even these exceptions are limited to a public in France. With a following predominantly in some small academic circles, these women writers of Quebec are practically unknown in the United States.

There has recently developed, however, a slow but clearly apparent growth of an awareness of Quebec throughout the United States, France, and English-speaking Canada. Stemming, most likely, from political and economic concerns over the future of Quebec as part of the Canadian federation, this new awareness has inspired a desire, as well as a need, to learn more about this francophone "nation" on the North American continent. Responding both to feminist consciousness and to this rise in interest in Quebec, therefore, this text will hopefully aid in a deeper understanding of the vibrant and distinctive *québécois* culture.

What is undoubtedly one of the most fascinating aspects of Quebec culture is the fact that it has been marked by a French, American, and English-Canadian presence but has proudly developed its own personality. Women writers on the current Quebec literary scene, for example, have benefited from both the American and French women's movements, theories, and literature. They are as familiar with Adrienne Rich and Mary Daly as they are with Luce Irigaray and Julia Kristeva. And yet with their own long literary tradition of women writers and their own situation as women who have experienced the period of national consciousness of the 1960s but who still live in a colonized society, they have clearly maintained their identity as *Québécoises*.

Only very recently has there been an attempt to begin a true dialogue between American and French literary feminists, in the hope of attaining a better mutual understanding of these two distinctly different movements.[2] In light of this long-awaited communication, it is even more important than ever that the works of women writers of Quebec become better known outside of their own province. With their unique situation at the crossroads of both American and French thought, their works, both traditional and feminist, offer fertile ground for comparative studies of cultures, in general, and of female specificities, in particular.

Speaking of women writers and writing in general, Madeleine Gagnon has stated that "[t]here is no female tradition in literature . . . no female, discursive tradition, literary or otherwise." There is only a "non-tradition."[3] In light of this lack of a female literary tradition in most countries and, especially, in comparison with the universal and centuries-old dominance by a male/patriarchal literature and discourse, Gagnon's words are, indeed, accurate. She does appear, however, to contradict Brossard's aforementioned questions and to ignore, or rather to minimize, the fact that in Quebec there has existed a long and well-established tradition of women writers. *Québécois* dictionaries, manuals, and histories of literature do mention Marie de l'Incarnation, Soeur Marie Morin, and, later, Laure Conan, and no one contests the popularity of Germaine Guèvremont, Gabrielle Roy, Rina Lasnier, and, later, Anne Hébert and Marie-Claire Blais.

One must quickly underscore the reality, however, that this female literary tradition flourished, ironically, because of the institutionalization of both gender roles and sexual repression in Quebec society. It was that patriarchal society, deeply influenced by the Catholic Church, that had traditionally imposed upon women the role of guardians of francophone culture, that is, of religion and of the French language, itself guardian of the faith. Better educated than in many other cultures, therefore, Quebec women often began to write, as their works, along with those of male writers, paradoxically enclosed them even more within the literary archetype of the all-powerful mother, resigned to her destiny.[4]

Contemporary women writers have noted, in addition, that the situation of women in Quebec, especially prior to the 1960s, although deplorable was, in one sense, similar to that of *québécois* men: both groups led a colonized existence under the economic and linguistic dominance of English and the powerful authority of Church and State. Both groups developed signs of feelings of impotency, inferiority, and alienation, characteristic of colonized peoples. The female literary tradition was greatly overshadowed by the necessity of collective survival. Women tended to support men as *Québécois*, rather than to attack them as oppressors. After all, these men have themselves been "humiliated," according to Michèle Lalonde,[5] and forced into "a passivity that one often links to what one can term *femininity*," according to Nicole Brossard.[6] Madeleine Gagnon concludes beautifully: "[H]omme disait vaincu, colonisés et nos hommes des frères beaucoup plus que des maîtres.... Les hommes sont ici plus doux qu'ailleurs.... [D]es solidarités se tissent entre nous et nos frères...."[7]

With the liberalization of the educational system, a decline in the power of the Church, a lower birthrate, and, most importantly, the massive, collective *prise de conscience* that triggered the Quiet Revolution and matured during that decade of the 1960s, one began to observe a significant change on the part of Quebec women in general and women writers in particular: they began to distinguish between their oppression as Quebecers and as women. The development of their national consciousness during the 1960s' *Révolution tranquille* led, during the 1970s and now into the 1980s, to a more clearly focused form of female/feminist consciousness.

This close link between nationalism and feminism in Quebec, however, has never been abandoned. *Québécois* feminists and feminist writers are still concerned with the problems of class struggle, cultural identity, and linguistic rights that plague the average male Quebecer. Their ideology, as reflected in contemporary literature, is, indeed, distinctively francophone and North American, while it is also gender-related and, therefore, international in scope. Michèle Lalonde describes their movement:

Dans son ensemble la contestation féministe me semble, au Québec, moins virulente qu'ailleurs et moins tournée toutes griffes sorties contre le mâle. Peut-être les femmes d'ici ont-elles conscience de leur double exploitation et peut-être savent-elles très bien à quels hommes humiliés elles ont affaire. Cependant le militantisme féministe ne semble pas spontanément désireux de s'intégrer à la lutte de libération nationale. Ce sont deux mouvements singulièrement en affinité, qui évoluent en parallèle et ne se rencontrent qu'occasionnellement.[8]

Traditionalism, Nationalism, and Feminism: Women Writers of Quebec is, therefore, a collection of essays that studies women's writing in Quebec from 1884 to the early 1980s. Its presentation offers a general chronological movement from the pre-1960s (traditionalism) to the 1960s (nationalism) and finally to the 1970s and early 1980s (feminism). Despite differences in time, however, very few writers fall solely under one category: there is an embryonic feminism noticeable even in the works of the most traditional women writers; some traditional values are maintained in more nationalistic and feminist writings; and more recent writers, increasingly concerned with the body/sexual politics and female/feminist *écriture*, remain faithful to their Quebec sovereignty-association leanings.

In the long literary tradition of women writers of Quebec and, in particular, during the almost one hundred years that are studied here, women writers have always expressed a deep concern for other women and for the status of *la condition féminine*; thus, they have most often created female protagonists and voices from their own female perspective. This collection is a study of women's writing, but more specifically of women's writing about women. Even if such a literary focus is not always fully evident, the writings of these women authors can be similarly analyzed from their subtexts, or a female narrative/poetic voice suggests this gender-related concern.

Women's writing in Quebec also inevitably examines and often questions the role of women and of women authors in society. From traditional values and perspectives, to those preoccupied with nationalist concerns, to those essentially involved with gender-specificities, all of these women writers, in diverse ways, manifest some characteristics of feminism, in an embryonic or overt form, consciously or subconsciously. There are no distinct boundaries among traditionalism, nationalism, and feminism in the works of these French-speaking Canadian women writers, merely historically, socially, and personally different ways of viewing many of the same concerns.

It should be noted that certain women writers and their works appear here in more than one study. This choice has been made either because of a distinction between an individual writer's poetry and prose, between early and more mature works, or, finally, because works are treated from a particular perspective in one essay and from another viewpoint in a study of a comparative nature.

In the editing of any collection of essays, one encounters, in addition, inevitable omissions. The works of some important women writers of Quebec will not be studied, therefore, in the following essays simply because of an inability to find scholars who are currently undertaking research on these particular authors. One regrets the omission of Adrienne Choquette, Claire Martin, Madeleine Ferron, Andrée Maillet, Michèle Mailhot, Suzanne Paradis, Monique Bosco,

Geneviève Amyot, Hélène Rioux, Hélène Ouvrard, Carole Massé, France Théoret, Yolande Villemaire, Madeleine Ouellette-Michalska, Alice Parizeau, Anne
Marie Alonzo, and Suzanne Jacob, among others. The list of women writers of
Quebec is indeed long, and if complete, such a study would offer a massive
text. The women writers who are included in this collection do constitute, however, the major beacons of this literary tradition and thus offer a good representation of women's writing in Quebec.

The choice of the order of presentation of these essays has been rendered
somewhat difficult by the fact that only three of the authors studied are deceased,
while all of the others are still writing and continually evolving in their own
ways. From a chronological perspective, of course, it is logical that the collection
open with François Gallays's study of Laure Conan's traditional text. Using a
modern psychoanalytic approach, this essay treats the sub-text of the 1884 work
and convincingly shows the female protagonist's subconscious expressions of
sexual passion, incest, and narcissism. Gabrielle Roy's early short stories, published from 1939 to 1948, are the subject of Paula Gilbert Lewis's article in
which Roy is seen as preoccupied with independent, almost revolutionary female
characters, as manifesting an early feminist consciousness, but as having maintained a duality of traditionalism and feminism in these works. James J. Herlan
examines the 1950s' radio adaptation of Germaine Guèvremont's best-known
novel, *Le Survenant*. This radio serial is analyzed as the popular reflection of
an unstable Quebec society—in which women's traditional roles were already
being questioned—that was slowly and painfully moving toward the Quiet Revolution of the 1960s.

Two important women poets are studied in the following two essays. James
P. Gilroy's analysis of a 1956 *recueil* of poems by Rina Lasnier is the most
traditionally-oriented essay of this collection. Correctly placing Lasnier within
the mainstream of the French Symbolist tradition, he still views her poetic
expression as that of a *Québécoise*, confidently asserting her identity as a woman
and a poet. In the poems of Anne Hébert, published between 1942 and 1960,
Susan L. Rosenstreich sees a powerful female poetic voice that challenges the
power of the past to determine the present, goes beyond nominalism, and expresses a theory of change in order to create new bonds within reality. During
this same period (from 1945 to 1960) Gabrielle Roy wrote three of her major
novels, discussed by Paula Gilbert Lewis in her essay, in which an unusual
combination of female and male circular imagery is used in order to depict the
enticing, claustrophobic structure of the urban metropolis.

With the decade of the 1960s, new concerns appear in the works of Quebec
women writers. Interestingly, the 1965–1970 theater of Françoise Loranger evolves
in a direction counter to that of other women writers. Carrol F. Coates explains
that the feminist awakening of Loranger's theatrical women to their own identity
soon develops into a sense of national identity and a need for revolt. For other
women writers, this decade brought a permissiveness, the possibility of writing
about their innermost feelings and desires. In his essay on Louise Maheux-

Forcier's trilogy of the 1960s, for example, Maurice Cagnon underscores the almost mythical sensuality and intimacy that exudes from and among her female characters. This same search for sensuality and love, however, turns to violence and even greater entrapment in Anne Hébert's 1970 novel about nineteenth-century Quebec. Murray Sachs treats these tragic aspects of the female's rebellion against her traditionally subjugated role in society and in a harsh land.

Three essays on three major contemporary women writers follow. Mary Jean Green examines the relationships among female characters in the 1959 to 1982 fiction of Marie-Claire Blais. She discovers that stemming from relationships that had earlier been the target of the author's attacks, there has evolved a new model of human interaction, based upon reciprocal caring among women and a return to the mother. Although not specifically a *québécois* woman writer, the Acadian, Antonine Maillet, is included in this collection by virtue of the fact that she is a francophone, North American, and Canadian woman writer. Marjorie A. Fitzpatrick treats the heroines of three of Maillet's novels of the 1970s as traditionalists, nationalists, and feminists, while she insists that they also transcend those confines and epically represent Acadia. If the works of Maillet speak for Acadia, then those of Nicole Brossard clearly reflect the development of literary, feminist, and political concerns in Quebec from the 1960s to the present. Louise H. Forsyth traces the career of Brossard, both as a writer and as a feminist activist, and finds that she has radically broken with all traditions and has moved beyond the limiting scope of nationalism to her desired establishment of women at the center of society.

The use of myth, and specifically of a newly rediscovered female mythology, is frequent in the works of many women writers. It is this need to recreate roots for women and for their homelands that Micheline Herz studies in her comparative essay on Antonine Maillet and Jovette Marchessault, as the boundaries of nationalism and feminism, in the 1970s, cross once again. We see a similar journey back toward pre-linguistic origins and a similar merging of politics and feminist poetics in the 1970s' works of Madeleine Gagnon. Karen Gould stresses, in fact, that Gagnon's most important contribution has been precisely this double-voiced discourse on female specificity and socialist solidarity that is peculiar to Quebec.

In her own creation/recreation of a female source, universe, discourse, and text that are all multi-directional and multi-dimensional, Louky Bersianik goes beyond Quebec nationalism and denounces phallic mythology, religion, philosophy, psychoanalysis, history, and language. Maroussia Hajdukowski-Ahmed studies these aspects of Bersianik's works from 1966 to 1980, as she stresses the author's effective use of intertextuality. Her essay is followed by another of a comparative nature, in which Marthe Rosenfeld examines specific works from 1977 to 1980 by Jovette Marchessault and Nicole Brossard in order to illustrate the relationship between lesbian feminism as a way of life and as a revolutionary force in literature. Whether through the use of myths and parables or, predominantly, in terms of woman's access to the linguistic code, the issue of female identity is here explored. The final essay of this collection is a study of the development of women's theater in Quebec from 1969 to the early 1980s. Jane Moss treats the emergence of both the *spectacles de femmes* and the monologue form of this theater, while she sees the plays of the early 1980s as reexaminations of the roles of women in Quebec society and as dramas glorifying female culture.

For those who are familiar with the corpus of writing by women in Quebec, this collection of essays should deepen their existing knowledge by adding new dimensions to it. For those who are, as yet, unfamiliar with these writers and their works, it is the intention of the present collection to introduce them to an exciting and vibrant literature that is distinctly francophone, North American, *québécois*, and—above all—female.

NOTES

1. Nicole Brossard, "La Femme et l'écriture," *Liberté*, 18, Nos. 4-5, année 1976, numéros 106-07 (juillet-octobre 1976), 13.

Here in Quebec, we shall one day have to explain why it is that women have played such an important role in our literature: Gabrielle Roy, Anne Hébert, Germaine Guèvremont, Marie-Claire Blais. Above all, why is it that their works have known how to reach a vast part of the *québécois* public? On what collective schizophrenia have their fantasies taken hold? What oppression have they brought to light?

2. Examples of this recent dialogue include: Elaine Marks and Isabelle de Courtivron, eds., *New French Feminisms: An Anthology* (New York: Schocken Books, 1981); a special issue entitled *Feminist Readings: French Texts/American Contexts*, *Yale French Studies*, No. 62 (1981); a special section on "French Feminist Theory," in *Signs: Journal of Women in Culture and Society*, 7, No. 1 (Autumn 1981), 1-86; and a substantial section on French women writers in *Feminist Studies*, 7, No. 2 (Summer 1981), 247-306. In addition to articles on individual *québécois* women writers that have appeared in journals published in the United States, one can cite three broader studies in this field. See Christiane Makward, "Quebec Women Writers," *Women and Literature*, 7, No. 1 (1977), 3-11; Lucie Lequin, "Les Femmes québécoises ont inventé leurs paroles," *The American Review of Canadian Studies*, 9, No. 2 (Autumn 1979), 113-24; and Karen Gould, "Setting Words Free: Feminist Writing in Quebec," *Signs: Journal of Women in Culture and Society*, 6, No. 4 (Summer 1981), 617-42.

3. Madeleine Gagnon, "La Tradition féminine en littérature," *Revue de l'Université d'Ottawa*, 50, No. 1 (janvier-mars 1980), 27.

4. For an excellent study of women in Quebec, see Le Collectif Clio, *L'Histoire des femmes au Québec depuis quatre siècles* (Montréal: Les Quinze, Editeur, 1982).

5. Michèle Lalonde, "Prose intervenante: Parcours théorique: Anatomie du féminisme," *Défense et illustration de la langue québécoise* (Paris: Editions Seghers Laffont, 1979), p. 212.

6. Brossard, p. 27.

7. Madeleine Gagnon, "Mon corps dans l'écriture," in *La Venue à l'écriture*, with Hélène Cixous and Annie Leclerc, Collection 10/18 (Paris: Union Générale d'Editions, 1977), p. 113.

The word, "man," meant defeated; our men are colonized, brothers much more than masters.... Men here are more tender than elsewhere.... Solidarities are woven between our brothers and ourselves....

8. Lalonde, p. 212.

In its totality, it seems to me that the feminist struggle in Quebec is less virulent than in other countries, less likely to show its claws against the male. It is possible that women here are conscious of their dual exploitation and know very well the kinds of humiliated men with whom they are dealing. Feminist militancy does not seem, however, spontaneously desirous of being integrated into the struggle for national liberation. These are two movements, clearly related, but evolving in parallel directions and meeting only occasionally.

1

Reflections in the Pool: The Subtext of Laure Conan's *Angéline de Montbrun*

François Gallays

Il fait un vent fou. La mer est blanche d'écume. J'aime à la voir troublée jusqu'au plus profond de ses abîmes. Et pourquoi? Est-ce parce que la mer est la plus belle des oeuvres de Dieu? N'est-ce pas plutôt parce qu'elle est l'image de notre coeur? L'un et l'autre ont la profondeur redoutable, la puissance terrible des orages, et si troublés qu'ils soient. . . .

Qu'est-ce que la tempête arrache aux profondeurs de la mer? Qu'est-ce que la passion révèle de notre coeur?

La mer garde ses richesses, et le coeur garde ses trésors. Il ne sait pas dire la parole de la vie: il ne sait pas dire la parole de l'amour, et tous les efforts de la passion sont semblables à ceux de la tempête qui n'arrache à l'abîme, que ces faibles débris, ces algues légères que l'on aperçoit sur les sables et sur les rochers, mêlés avec un peu d'écume.[1]

This splendid text by its metaphoric pattern reproduces quite faithfully the whole essence of the novel: in it, through the parallel established between the sea and the human heart, and by means of the play between surface and depth, the relationship between the conscious and the subconscious is intuitively expressed. For these poor leavings from the sea's depths, these wisps of seaweed to which adhere some flecks of foam, covering the sands and the rocks, do they not constitute, figuratively, a sort of record which reflects the text of the novel? Is not the text itself merely the superficial tracery of the depths of the heart, a veil whose open texture, at once concealing and revealing, even while proffering some fragments of knowledge, succeeds in concealing the heart's depths from the prying eyes of the reader?

This was true, at least, before the advent of Freud. Laure Conan's contemporaries unanimously read her novel as a moral tale, seeing there only an exemplary account of filial devotion, sad perhaps, but so virtuous! It is difficult, nonetheless, to judge these readers harshly. Numerous reasons can be cited if not to justify, yet to explain, what some critics today consider their critical blindness. For one thing, at this time moral example was the major, if not the only, criterion for judging the value of a work. For another—and this seems to me the key—psychoanalytic interpretation was not (for good reason!) yet in vogue. Finally, it seems as if Laure Conan were going out of her way throughout the narrative to camouflage its true nature.

That contemporary readers were taken in by her efforts at camouflage is, quite apart from what is owed to the writer's competence, in no way surprising. One has to remember this basic fact: there was as yet no discussion of incest. Before Freud not merely was incest itself forbidden, but also—and this is essential to an understanding of contemporary readings of the novel—all *discussion* of incest. In Laure Conan's society the subject was taboo. Unthinkable, it was also un-thought of. *Angéline de Montbrun* appeared before the taboo was lifted, before, in other words, the discussion of incest became legitimate. Barred from direct discussion, incest, to provide itself with at least some discursive existence, had, one supposes, to borrow other, more socially acceptable, forms. In *Angéline de Montbrun* it conceals itself behind the virtuous manifestations of filial devotion. But, as though the veil of innocence were threatening at any moment to rend, exposing a less admissible attachment, the text sets up decoys, indicators of innocence and virtue which for the contemporary reader acted as so many limits to interpretation. The double narrative in which the "love story" of Maurice Darville and Angéline de Montbrun is juxtaposed and even sometimes merged, blurring the individual roles, with the story of filial piety is an example. There is no doubt that it was created, as Roger Le Moine has ably demonstrated, with the object of obscuring the incestuous nature of the sentiments uniting father and daughter, and so discouraging any eventually scandalous interpretation of the novel:

However, this story of love between the young man and woman is nothing more than a decoy. Its only purpose is to distract the reader's attention from the real couple, Montbrun and his daughter, the one through which Laure Conan wishes to relive (such as in *Un Amour vrai*) her love affair with Tremblay.[2]

Effective at the time, this narrative redoubling no longer serves to conceal the incestuous aspect of the father-daughter relationship. In addition, the confusion maintained here and there in the text as to the real identity of characters—is it Charles de Montbrun or Maurice Darville?—is extremely suspect in the eyes of the post-Freudian reader:

Si une fois encore, je pouvais l'entendre, il me semble que j'aurais la force de tout supporter. Sa voix exerçait sur moi une délicieuse, une merveilleuse puissance; et, seule, elle put m'arracher à l'accablement si voisin de la mort où je restai plongée, après les funérailles de mon père.

Tant que j'avais eu sous les yeux son visage adoré, une force mystérieuse m'avait soutenue. La main, sa chère main, qui m'avait bénie, reposa jusqu'au dernier moment dans la mienne. . . .[3]

The order of the pronouns in each of these paragraphs creates a momentary confusion in the reader as to the identity of the subject: is it Montbrun or Darville? An earlier passage exhibits the same kind of ambiguity. Angéline has just described the melancholy of her solitude and the unhappiness she feels living in "his home." There is nothing ambiguous here: she obviously refers to her father. In the following paragraph, however, some confusion lingers: "Sans doute, lorsqu'on souffre, rien n'est pénible comme le contact des indifférents. Mais Maurice, comment vivre sans le voir, sans l'entendre jamais, jamais! O l'accablante pensée! C'est la nuit, c'est le froid. C'est la mort."[4]

Because of the preceeding paragraph, it is not immediately clear to the reader to whom the pronoun "le" refers in "vivre sans le voir": to the father, or to Maurice? Such an ambiguity bears precisely the mark of the desire or need to proclaim this incestuous love, to proclaim it despite the censure it would call forth. Unable to proclaim itself openly, demanding imperiously nonetheless to be proclaimed, the sentiment is expressed confusedly. This narrative redoubling, far from being an isolated case, is a part of an imposing series of reduplications, all with one fixed function: to obscure or to exculpate the incestuous relationship.

Along the thread of the narrative, through the play of literary allusions, a paradigm of incestuous couples is developed, couples whom history has enshrined due to the fame of one member or the other. Obviously, the term "incestuous" is understood here in a very broad sense: it refers to all especially close relationships between parent and child, or between siblings. It is an impressive paradigm: it embraces Victor Hugo, Marie de l'Incarnation, Saint Elizabeth, Eugénie de Guérin, Tintoretto, Saint Augustine, and Chateaubriand.[5] All these figures, celebrated in history for various reasons, are known also for the deep emotional tie uniting them to mother, daughter, sister, or brother. Official history, with its moralizing tendency, striving to defend current social values, was quick to elevate the deep emotional attachments of these otherwise justly famous men and women into exemplary relationships for the edification of future generations. This was particularly true of, for example, Marie de l'Incarnation and Saint Augustine. As for Tintoretto, Chateaubriand, and Eugénie de Guérin, their fame, although of diverse origins, conferred on the incestuous tendency of their relationships a quality of tragic necessity which, permitting a transfer of responsibility from the individual to the vague force known as destiny, soon succeeded in effacing completely any moral taint which might originally have been found there.

This paradigm, whose elements are borrowed from real life, is enhanced by the story of the pair of orphans, Paul and Marie, who, living with their grandmother, vow to each other a more than admiring affection:

Ces gentils enfants sont charmants dans leur toilette de première communion. Marie surtout est à croquer avec sa robe blanche, et le joli chapelet bleu qu'elle porte en guise de collier. Paul commence à se faire à la voir si belle, mais les premières fois il avait des éblouissements. Le jour de leur première communion, je les invitai à dîner, et les ayant laissés seuls un instant, je les trouvai qui s'entre-regardaient avec une admiration profonde.[6]

The slightly heavy emphasis on the innocence and purity of the childish couple (the first communion, the white dress and blue rosary of Marie, even her name) has no other object than to assure a morally virtuous interpretation of their love. Moreover, Paul and Marie have, structurally, no role in the novel. Their episodic appearance, their non-participation in the action, reduces them to purely representative figures on the same level as the other couples of the paradigm. And their integration into the fabric of the text on the pattern of others, because, one might say, of their exemplary quality, creates in the reader a particular point of view, a bias against noticing anything more, in short, than a story of filial devotion.

But the insertion of Charles de Montbrun and Angéline in the paradigm confers on this couple, in addition to the plausibility necessary to every fictional character, a particularly exalted status: for, as we have observed, at least one member of each couple is distinguished either by the exemplarity of his or her life (his or her holiness) or by his or her contribution to the arts. Repositories of exceptional qualities and/or virtues, these couples, acting as so many mirrors, are for Angéline and her father, who see themselves in them, the reflection of their own qualities. It is clear: in its disposition of couples—historical couples ranged around a fictitious couple—the novel creates a pattern of profoundly narcissistic relationships. The fictional couple contemplates itself in the historical couple by means of this narcissistic projection:

Lui commença dans l'appartement un de ces va-et-vient qui étaient dans ses habitudes. *La fille du Tintoret* se trouvait en pleine lumière. En passant, son regard tomba sur ce tableau qu'il aimait, et une ombre douloureuse couvrit son visage. Après quelques tours, il s'arrêta devant et resta sombre et rêveur, à le considérer. Je l'observais sans oser suivre sa pensée. Nos yeux se rencontrèrent et ses larmes jaillirent. Il me tendit les bras et sanglota! "O mon bien suprême! O ma Tintorella!"[7]

It remains for the reader only to recognize the resemblances in this confrontation. We will see shortly that the narcissism of the couple which their way of life confirms is no more than the outcome of each partner's individual narcissism.

To this first paradigm of assorted couples we can add a second paradigm which, without being quantitatively as important as the first, is by no means negligible. In it figure the women who loved Charles de Montbrun in his lifetime. First is Mina Darville, the rather worldly sister of Maurice, who at the news of Charles de Montbrun's death discovers quite suddenly in herself a religious vocation. Two other women figure in it: Véronique Désileux and Marie Desroches. Véronique, physically repulsive and repellent to everyone, even her own father, is treated nonetheless with the greatest courtesy by Charles de Montbrun, who is generous enough, moreover, to bail her out when she runs into financial difficulties. As for Marie Desroches, she too, having benefited from Montbrun's generosity, offers him, after his death, a sort of worship usually reserved for divine beings. This is how Angéline describes Marie's room for the reader:

> La charmante statue de la Sainte Vierge que mon père lui donna, lorsqu'elle eut perdu sa mère, y occupe la place d'honneur. Un lierre vigoureux l'entoure gracieusement.
>
> C'est doux à l'âme et doux aux yeux; et j'ai été bien touchée en apercevant, dans cette chambre de jeune fille, la photographie de mon père, encadrée d'immortelles et de mousse séchées.[8]

This passage, obviously, pretends to express the daughterly veneration offered by a young woman to her benefactor. Nonetheless, because of certain expressions used—the "lierre vigoureux," the "immortelles," and the "mousse séchée(s)"—the text, as if taken over by the image-making of the subconscious, bears witness beyond simple veneration, at a less superficial and certainly unconscious level, to the presence of a substratum of erotic desire. Be that as it may, the elevation of the father into an object of worship by another woman reinforces and justifies the acts Angéline performs in his memory: the acquisition of the house where he dies and, later, her nocturnal hour of adoration before the portrait of her father: "Et qui donc à ma place ne l'eut pas ardemment et profondément aimé? Tous les soirs, après les prières, je m'agenouille devant son portrait, comme j'aimais à le faire devant lui, et bien souvent, je pleure...."[9]

The attitude of these three women toward Charles de Montbrun reinforces Angéline's worship of her father both during his life and after his death. Other women, the text seems to say, have loved him to the point of adulation: is not his own daughter, therefore, fully justified in her love? Adored by all women, Montbrun loved in return only one. Apart from his love for his daughter, he is emotionally self-sufficient: for she is no more than his reflection: "Je voulais qu'elle fût la fille de mon âme comme de mon sang ... et d'Angéline à moi il y a parfait retour...."[10]

Sprung from his flesh, molded by him, Angéline casts his own reflection back to Charles de Montbrun. The other is reabsorbed in the same: the ultimate narcissistic configuration. Absorbed in the contemplation of his own image, Montbrun shows himself impervious to seductions from the world: and the charming Madame S.'s theory that he wears a magic armor is confirmed by Mina. This armor is a metaphor for the complete immunity which envelops Montbrun and of which the gloves he wears for working are the concrete manifestation. In the same letter, Mina "lui met sur les lèvres" the words of Augustus to Cinna: "Je suis maître de moi." And this mastery of himself extends to every area of life, including the sexual: for, the chaste and candid Angéline astonishingly affirms: "Pour lui, *l'ensorcellement de la bagatelle* n'existait pas."[11] In his article "Un, autre, neutre: Valeurs narcissiques du même," André Green presents the following portrait:

Portrait of Narcissus: a unique being, all powerful in body and in spirit incarnated in his speech, independent and autonomous when he so wishes, but on whom others depend without, however, any feelings of desire towards them on his part. Sojourning amongst his own, his family, his clan, his race, he bears noticeable marks of those touched by the Divine, resembles God. He is their leader, Master of the Universe, of Time and of Death, completely engrossed in his dialogue, far from witnesses, with God who showers him with his favors—including the fall by which he is the elected object of sacrifice—interceding between God and people, bathing in the splendid solitude of his own light. This shadow of God is a figure of the Same, the immutable, the intangible, the immortal and the immaterial.[12]

It is not without a certain astonishment that one first reads this passage (where the recollections of the figure of Christ are evident), for it seems that each trait presented, without exception, can also serve for a description of the character of Montbrun. That is to say that Montbrun is much more the incarnation of an imagined ideal than the realistic representation of a human type. But we should not be led by Montbrun's narcissism into forgetting that he incarnates, at another level of the imagination, an ideal whose characteristics correspond both to the clerical ideology of the period and to the medieval chivalric code. Furnished with all these qualities, Charles de Montbrun, at once saint and demigod, is the incarnation of man as he must have existed before the Fall.

To this sanctity of the father corresponds the innocence of his child, perfect innocence confirmed in the text by, on the one hand, the complete suppression of the body and, on the other, the continuing analogy developed, in the first part of the novel at least, between Angéline de Montbrun and the Holy Virgin.[13] From the time of her birth Montbrun dedicated his daughter to the Virgin Mary, as a result of which Angéline wore, until her father's death, only blue and white. As for Maurice, among all the floral metaphors by which he describes his beloved appears this one: Star of the Morning, an expression borrowed from the litany of the Virgin. Angéline's incorporeality, her representation by the dreary Maurice in terms of fresh, unravished flowers, the comparisons with the Virgin, all these elements—and her name as well—contribute to the creation around Angéline of an aura of purity and innocence.

In the first part of the novel, therefore, Angéline, incorporeal and faceless ("Oui, c'est bien la fée de la jeunesse," says Maurice), a pure and innocent virgin, constitutes, together with her father, perfect man and demigod, an exact replica of the first human couple before the divine condemnation. (Was not Eve too issued from Adam's flank?) It is not merely the name of the place (Valriant) and the type of life they live there that go to recreate the primitive Edenic myth. There is also a direct allusion in the text: "Crois-moi, ma petite soeur, on ne parlait pas dans le paradis terrestre. Non, au jour de l'innocence, de l'amour et du bonheur, l'homme ne parlait pas, il chantait."[14] That the text of the first part of the novel serves to recreate the mythical Eden, and the third part the exact opposite of this world, others have already observed;[15] but what seems to merit examination is the exact moment at which the utopia of the first part collapses and is transformed into its opposite.

In her first version of the novel, Laure Conan attributed Angéline's disfigurement to a malignant tumor which required surgery; but in the second version it results from a bad fall. According to Le Moine, this change was made because the first version might have suggested too clearly the existence of a causal psychosomatic link between Angéline's disfigurement and her father's death.[16] It seems possible to advance another reason for the change, a reason founded not on a hypothetical preoccupation of the author which seems altogether too Freudian, but on what one could describe as a necessity of internal coherence.

If it is true, as I have remarked above, following others, that the first part is a retelling of the Edenic myth, then I think one can reasonably argue that the change from the earlier version reflects the author's desire to conform more rigorously to her model. In this case Angéline's fall would correspond to that of Adam and Eve. As their fall marked the couple's passage from Paradise to terrestrial life, so Angéline's fall, together with her father's death, determines her passage from innocent happiness to a life of suffering and anguish.

In this parallelism the reader will certainly have noticed that one element is lacking: Original Sin. For if in the Edenic myth the couple's fall is a direct consequence of the sin committed, one does not clearly see any correspondence in the narrative of Laure Conan. In fact, the text makes no direct mention of any fault committed. There is, nonetheless, at least one clear allusion:

Oublier qu'on a porté en soi-même l'éclatante blancheur de son baptême, et la divine beauté de la parfaite innocence.
Oublier la honte insupportable de la première souillure, la salutaire amertume des premiers remords.[17]

This reflective passage given by the author to her heroine establishes in the pattern of the novel the existence of a fault; and the consequences of this fault for the "soul" of the heroine are certainly dramatic, for they lead to a transition from the "éclatante blancheur du baptême," from the "divine beauté de la parfaite innocence" to the "honte insupportable de la première souillure."[18] At what moment, now, one asks oneself, did this transition take place? If we can answer this question, we shall perceive the exact nature of the fault to which the passage alludes.

If one restricts oneself within the temporal limits of the novel, it is certain that the transformation did not take place within the time represented by the first part (the epistolary narrative). Every letter attests Angéline's purity and innocence. Every reference to her reaffirms precisely these two qualities. That is to say that Angéline's transformation, which is due to a fault not specified in the text, must take place *after* the first part, that is, in either the second or the third. The brief narrative of the second part reveals not a trace of it. When the third part begins, nonetheless, the change is accomplished: the transformation is complete. But the temporal construction of the third part, we must remember, is complex. This part contains a number of flashbacks. One in particular seems significant in the question under discussion. It is the scene which takes place the evening before the death of Charles de Montbrun. Temporally, this scene belongs to the narrative of the second section: Montbrun died on 20 September; this scene therefore takes place on the evening of the nineteenth:

Mais ce soir-là, quelque chose de solennel m'oppressait. Je me sentais émue sans savoir pourquoi. Tout ce que je lui devais me revenait à l'esprit. Il me semblait que je n'avais jamais apprécié son admirable tendresse. J'éprouvais un immense besoin de le remercier, de le chérir. Minuit sonna. Jamais glas ne m'avait paru si lugubre, ne m'avait fait une si funèbre impression. Une crainte vague et terrible entra en moi. Cette chambre si jolie, si riante me fit soudain l'effet d'un tombeau.

Je me levai pour cacher mon trouble et m'approchai de la fenêtre. La mer s'était retirée au large, mais le faible bruit des flots m'arrivait par intervalles. J'essayais résolument de raffermir mon coeur, car je ne voulais pas attrister mon père. Lui commença dans l'appartement un de ces va-et-vient qui étaient dans ses habitudes. La fille du Tintoret se trouvait en pleine lumière. En passant, son regard tombe sur ce tableau qu'il aimait, et une ombre douloureuse couvrit son visage. Après quelques tours, il s'arrêta devant et resta sombre et rêveur, à le considérer. Je l'observais sans oser suivre ma pensée. Nos yeux se rencontrèrent et ses larmes jaillirent. Il me tendit le bras et sanglota: "O mon bien suprême! O ma Tintorella!"

Je fondis en larmes. Cette soudaine et extraordinaire émotion, réponda à ma secrète angoisse, m'épouvantait, et je m'écriai: "Mon Dieu! mon Dieu! que va-t-il donc arriver?"

Il se remit à l'instant, et essaya de me rassurer, mais je sentais les violents battements de mon coeur, pendant qu'il répétait de sa voix la plus calme: "Ce n'est rien, ce n'est rien, c'est la sympathie pour le pauvre Jacques Robusti."

Et comme je pleurais toujours et frissonnais entre ses bras, il me porta sur la causeuse au coin du feu; puis il alla fermer la fenêtre, et mis ensuite quelques morceaux de bois sur les tisons.

La flamme s'éleva bientôt vive et brillante. Alors revenant à moi, il me demanda pourquoi j'étais si bouleversée. Je lui avouai mes terreurs.

"Bah!" dit-il légèrement, "des nerfs." Et comme j'insistais, en disant que lui aussi avait senti l'approche du malheur, il me dit:

"J'ai eu un moment d'émotion, mais tu le sais, Mina assure que j'ai une nature d'artiste."

Il me badinait, me raisonnait, me câlinait, et comme je restais toute troublée, il m'attira à lui et me demanda gravement: "Mon enfant, si, moi ton père, j'avais l'entière disposition de ton avenir, serais-tu bien terrifiée?"

Alors, partant de là, il m'entretint avec une adorable tendresse de la folie, de l'absurdité de la défiance envers Dieu.

Sa foi entrait en moi comme une vigueur. La vague, l'horrible crainte disparut. Jamais, non jamais je m'étais sentie si profondément aimée. Pourtant je comprenais—et avec quelle lumineuse clarté—que rien dans les tendresses humaines ne peut faire soupçonner ce qu'est l'amour de Dieu pour ses créatures.[19]

The emotion of father and daughter, the daughter's tears, the repeated embraces, all convey the couple's disarray. And this disarray is the more profound because at its root is desire: bodily desire. Surprised by this desire, overcome after a fashion by this driving force, the bodies of Angéline and Charles embark on a sort of preparatory dance where the insistence of desire threatens to transform itself into a sort of fatalism before which reason falters. And, in effect, in the amorous ritual which unfolds, the only thing lacking for the fulfillment of its course is the actual act of love itself, the act towards which the whole scene tends. The ellipsis of this act on the surface of the text does not, however, prevent it from manifesting itself in the narrative. It is as if, censored on the conscious level, it nonetheless found a way of expressing itself by deceiving the censorious self of the author. Everything takes place as if the author's creative imagination, submitting to the censorship of her mind and incapable, therefore, of representing overtly the supreme transgression of the incestuous act, expresses it irrepressibly nonetheless, but covertly, or, more precisely, under guise of another order. For the scene ends with the spiritualization, or, if you will, the sublimation, of desire in both of the protagonists. The daughter, led by her father, returns to the ethereal realms of divine love.

In the immediate context, however, certain gestures as well as certain expressions, because of their ambiguity, carry suggestions of a different scene, of a scene proposed, one might say, by the creative imagination of the author, but repressed, held in check, and obscured by the primary scene, immediately apprehensible and conforming in every way to the stereotypes of the period. Three actions, to begin with, seem particularly significant: Charles takes Angéline in his arms; he carries her over and places her on the love seat; then he shuts the window and throws wood on the fire. These actions, described in a single sentence, create a passage the significance of which calls for exploration. Inserted in the scheme of the narrative at the moment when the disarray of the protagonists, provoked by the strength of their desire, is at its height, these actions shift the balance of the scene. Overcoming his agitation, Charles takes the initiative and keeps it throughout, while Angéline moves from frightened passivity to unapprehensive abandon. One cannot but notice that, in its development of the couple's relationship, this scene follows the archetypal pattern of the love scene: two bodies, suddenly face to face, surprised and overcome by their desire, pass through a stage of confusion most often expressed, as here, by incoherence in speech and act; then, once they have recognized the reciprocity of their desires, take certain specific actions, either actions which create a breakthrough withdrawal (in which case desire remains at the embryonic stage) or actions which prepare the way for the satisfaction of desire. Now, Montbrun's actions belong to this second category. The significance of his taking Angéline in his arms to place her on the love seat is so explicit as to need no comment. The closing of the window and stirring up of the fire, far from shattering the mood of entrancing desire, tend to strengthen it with their suggestion of increased intimacy. The closed window represents the complete exclusion of the outer world, while the fire, quite apart from its strong sensual/sexual connotations, assumes almost a solar function radiantly illuminating this henceforward enclosed world in which the lovers would normally give themselves completely over to their desire. Here we know, for the text says so plainly, that their increased intimacy, through the sublimation of their feelings, is outpoured into divine love. That fact admitted, they remain in the text, nonetheless, imprints of eros.

Charles, confounding through his easy discourse his paternity with that of God and so winning Angéline's trust, succeeds at last in reasoning away her fear. Her trust assured, her fright assuaged, the text continues: "Sa foi entrait en moi comme une vigueur." Completely sublimated and even spiritualized, this "penetration" of Charles, as it is expressed, carries, nonetheless, the clear suggestion of quite another kind of penetration, in the same way that what follows bears traces of the lovemaking. For the sexual experience evoked in the text assumes at once both the unique character and the intensity of the ultimate sexual act: "Jamais, non jamais je ne m'étais sentie si profondément aimée." Moreover, as a result of her enrapturement, by a sort of spiritual intuition, Angéline grasps in one luminous moment the whole vastness of divine love. Admittedly, the text does not explicitly portray the act of love; nonetheless the nature of the experience and the expressions used permit one to situate here, at this precise point, but subvertly, as a sort of inhibition in the text, the incestuous act of love between Charles de Montbrun and his daughter, Angéline.[20]

The arrangement of the material in the text supports this interpretation. Whereas the account of this scene is dated 7 July, the following page, the very brief entry dated 8 July, presents the following piece of information: "Quand je vivrais encore longtemps, jamais je ne laisserai ma robe noire, jamais je ne laisserai mon deuil."[21] This is the vow not of an orphan, but of a widow. And the narrator is constrained to recall that it was at the time of her father's death that she put on her black dress and set aside her blue and white clothing, clothing which she should not have put aside, the text continues, until her marriage, that is, until the moment of losing her virginity. Without a doubt this passage is intended to emphasize the movement from one consecration to another: consecrated originally to the Virgin, Angéline reconsecrates herself to the memory of her father. Nonetheless, the insistence on the change of clothing at this precise point in the narrative is highly significant as far as the "subconscious" content of the text is concerned. The establishment of a direct correspondence between, on the one hand, the blue and white clothing and, on the other, the virginity of the young woman permits one to infer that, at the subconscious level of the text, the disappearance of these two colors signifies a correlative loss of virginity on the part of the heroine.

Censored, repressed, the account of the fault, rising nonetheless to the surface of the text, ought not after all to astonish us: for it is worked into the main narrative of the twin love story which innervates the totality of the text and which confers on the novel its deep ambiguity. But one wonders at last whether the interest and value of this novel do indeed lie in the ambiguity of the narrative. For my part, even though this aspect of the story is by no means lacking in interest, I think that the novel deserves to endure for another reason.

For, quite apart from its narrative structure, the novel, particularly in its third part, presents the spectacle of an incommensurable solitude. Trapped in the somber depths of loneliness, Angéline de Montbrun gives utterance unflaggingly, in vehement tones, to her suffering. And because she knows that there is no hope of ever emerging from those depths, she looks for relief in resignation. And in vain! This relief so coveted remains inaccessible; for Angéline knows that it will be granted her only at the price of the body's death: "Autrefois, gâtée par le bonheur, je ne comprenais pas la vie religieuse, je ne m'expliquais pas qu'on pût vivre ainsi, l'âme au ciel et le corps dans la tombe. Maintenant, je crois la vocation de religieuse un grand bonheur."[22]

In light of this ultimately horrible and doubtless rather unorthodox description of the cloistered life, we understand that it is Angéline's desirous body which is at the root of her restlessness. And the love of God in which she would like to obliterate herself remains inoperable, does not overcome the imperious desire for the Other who is lost forever. Inescapably immured in her solitude, the heroine, nailed to the cross of her desire, sinks into such a total disarray of being that she assumes a certain, not untragic, grandeur. The prisoner of her loneliness, knowing moreover that this loneliness will end only with her death, Angéline comes to see the course of her life as, in some way, fated. There, in a nutshell, is a standard or "literary" interpretation of the third part of this novel. One can, however, look at it from another point of view.

This state of loneliness into which Angéline has sunk, not without some self-indulgence, corresponds in every way to what analysts describe as a "libidinal retreat," or, on another level, "narcissistic withdrawal," this latter term referring to those "defensive states in which the subject is on his guard and withdraws from an outer world which has become insupportable."[23] In other words, "self-withdrawal is the ultimate defense. Run to earth, the Self has no option but prompt withdrawal, a reaction which goes hand in hand with psychic—and perhaps even with actual—death."[24] In many cases, and this is certainly true in the case of Angéline, the world becomes insupportable because the trusted object, the "Ideal Self," for various reasons in each case, ceases to function as such. This "Ideal Self" is the form taken, according to Rosolato, by "the requirement for power and perfection"; this "grandiose Self" is the product of a kind of preconscious idealization of a libidinal object.[25]

Another analyst, Masud R. Khan, prefers the term "idolization" to "idealization." He defines idolization as "overinvestment in a real, exterior object, where the object is treated as a sacred fetish."[26] According to this definition, it seems clear that in Laure Conan's novel, Charles de Montbrun is presented as the object of an overwhelming idolization on the part of Angéline. Is this not the actual sense of the astonishing admission made by Angéline in a letter to Mina: "Chère Mina, j'aimerais mieux être sa servante que la fille de l'homme le plus en vue du pays."[27] The ancillary relationship which Angéline claims to prefer attests, on the one hand, to her elevation of her father to the status of a sacred being and, on the other, to her complete alienation from her Self. This short sentence expresses the desire to obliterate the Self in favor of the Other, in other words, that only the glorious "Myself" of the father should remain. "Narcissism," says André Green, "is the *Desire for the One.*" Angéline lived with her father in a relationship of assimilation which assured her of his permanent protection. When this was lost, she suffered what Rosolato calls "narcissistic rupture."[28] And it is after this rupture that she retired to Valriant to plunge into a life of solitude.

At a certain level of abstraction, *Angéline de Montbrun* can be seen as a reenactment of the myth of Narcissus. Whereas in the first part Narcissus exults, triumphant, in the third, incapable of raising himself to the longed-for and expected ecstasy, having lost his mirror, desolate, inconsolable and unconsoled, he is swallowed up in the dark contemplation of his forsakeness: Narcissus effects the crossing from Eros to Thanatos. From the happy untroubled narcissism of the first part the novel passes to deathly narcissism of the third. And, at a superficial first glance, this narcissistic transformation can be imputed quite naturally to the death of Montbrun. But before we embark on this aspect, two concepts call for elucidation: exultation and ecstacy.

Of the two forms of narcissistic employment, exultation, which is an out-flowing, an invasion of the object and the world, aims at completeness. It is obtained through the intervention of the projective idealization/idolization of an object which serves as support. As Rosolato explains:

This support . . . is *the object of Narcissistic projection*, chosen by the subject because of a certain resemblance which enables it to function more easily as a double. The *idealized* Father in particular and parents in general are at the center of these primary Narcissistic relationships and identifications. In the same manner, the *idealized child* enables one to retrace these images.[29]

Simplifying this a little, one can postulate that Guy Rosolato's description of the idealized Father and the idealized child corresponds to what we find in the first part of the novel. The reader is faced with a double narcissistic relationship, the daughter idolizing the father and vice versa.

After the narcissistic exultation of the first section, there follows, in the third, the ecstatic endeavor, the purpose of which Guy Rosolato defines as: "[T]he ideal concerned in *ecstasy* is to be able to attain pleasure through the most radical withdrawal from the object in the world."[30] The private diary, presented as loose pages in the third part of the novel, allows the reader to peruse the account of the failure of this desperate attempt. For it to have succeeded, a second object would have to have effectively replaced the paternal object, this second object seen as superior by nature, and in the contemplation of which Angéline might have attained the serenity she so longed for. But obsessed by memory, her body bound powerfully to the earth, Angéline is reduced to admitting the extent of her defeat: "Ah! Je voudrais penser au ciel. Mais je ne puis. Je suis comme cette femme malade dont parle l'Évangile qui était toute courbée et ne pouvait regarder en haut."[31]

In the closing text, in a letter addressed to Maurice, Angéline refuses one last time the invitation her fiancé presented to her. For, she says, quoting the words of Charles upon his deathbed when he commended her to God: "Amour Sauveur, je vous la donne, O Seigneur Jésus, prenez-la, O Seigneur Jésus, consolez-la, fortifiez-la."[32] The commendation of the dying man fixed the future of Angéline, however, in a sort of destiny. Determined, preordained, the unfolding of her life cannot henceforward be questioned, for it unfolds in obedience to another will and is, consequently, beyond her control: "Maurice, c'est lui qui a tout conduit, c'est sa volonté qui nous sépare."[33] At first glance, therefore, according to the text, it seems to be the last wishes expressed by the father which prevent Angéline from yielding to the entreaty of Maurice. A few lines farther on, nonetheless, one short sentence offers, obviously in a very incomplete way, a second explanation which the narrative repressed to a subtextual level: "Mais il en est qui n'arrivent au ciel qu'ensanglantés, et ceux-là n'ont pas droit de se plaindre."[34]

The term "ensanglantés" implies wounds, inflicted, one might think on first reading, on individuals whom life, quite simply, has treated roughly; but the continuation of the sentence obliges us, reading back, to postulate for this word a moral content. The word "ensanglantés" then, even while continuing to suggest wounds and combat, takes on a moral significance. However, if the context is taken into account, it quickly becomes evident that, in the subtext, the passage bears the marks of a deflowering, for only this type of "wound," uniting the physical and the moral, could produce such a result. This observation brings us back to the scene which took place on the evening before Montbrun's death.

That Charles de Montbrun died accidentally one cannot for a moment doubt. Nonetheless, in the light of what we have learned at the sub-textual level, his death takes on another dimension. Narcissus, as I have said, reigns triumphant in the first part of the novel, while in the third we watch his destruction. Between these two narcissistic sides of the narrative is placed this principal scene of the novel in which Narcissus both represses and draws attention to the incestuous act of Charles and Angéline. It is in a way the unspoken focus of the novel. At this level Narcissus, in love with his own image perceived in the Other, longs to embrace it, to possess it more completely, to possess it, in other words, perfectly; and in embracing it, transgressing the interdiction, he destroys it. The loss of his mirror was the punishment with which Narcissus saw himself afflicted. Charles de Montbrun dies, and Angéline is condemned immediately to know only the pangs of solitude, and this until the end of her days.

And where is Oedipus in all this? Has he not been lost from view, supplanted by Narcissus? Not at all. For, as Olivier Flournoy has observed: "Narcissism surrounds Oedipus. It is the space in which Oedipus can live, it is its time, its cradle, its grave."[35]

NOTES

1. Laure Conan, *Angéline de Montbrun*, Bibliothèque canadienne-française (1884; rpt. Montréal: Fides, 1976), p. 160. All quotations refer to this edition.

It is a wild wind that blows. The sea is white with foam. I like to see it disturbed to its bottomless depths. And why may I ask? Is it because the ocean is the most beautiful of all God's works? Is it not because it is so like the human heart? One and the other's depths are formidable and both have the terrible power of the thunderstorm and so disturbed may they be....

What does the storm tear away from the depths of the sea? What does passion reveal of the heart?

The sea protects its riches and the heart keeps its treasures. It does not know how to say the words of life: it does not know how to use the language of love and all the efforts of passion are similar to those of the storm which wrenches from the depths but useless fragments, strands of seaweed that one can see strewn on the sands and on the rocks, mixed with a bit of foam.

An English translation has been published: Laure Conan, *Angéline de Montbrun*, trans. and introd. Yves Brunelle (Toronto: University of Toronto Press, 1974).

2. Roger Le Moine, Introd., *Angéline de Montbrun*, in Vol. I of *Oeuvres romanesques* by Laure Conan (Montréal: Fides, 1974), p. 80.

3. Conan, p. 138.

If once more I could hear him, it seems to me it would give me sufficient strength to endure everything. His voice exerted such a delicious and marvellous power over me, it alone was able to pull me out from the deathlike despondency I knew after my father's death.

As long as I was able to behold his dear face, I was upheld by a mysterious force. His hand, his beloved hand with which he blessed me, rested in my own until the last moment.

4. Conan, p. 89.

Undoubtedly, when one suffers, nothing hurts more than indifference. But Maurice, how is one to live without seeing him, hearing him, ever, ever! Oh, what a depressing thought! It is night. It is cold. It is death.

5. Conan, pp. 66, 106, 144, 117, 69, 121, 124, 60, 151.

6. Conan, p. 126.

These children are so charming, dressed as on the day of their First Communion. Marie especially is rather striking in her pretty white dress and her pretty blue rosary she is wearing as a necklace. The first time Paul saw her he was dazzled by her beauty. However, he is now becoming used to it. The day of their First Communion, I invited them to dinner. I left them alone for a moment and when I returned, I found them gazing at each other in profound adoration.

This pair of infants does not fail to remind us of Bernardin de Saint-Pierre's pair, Paul and Virginie.

7. Conan, p. 121.

He began to pace to and fro. He had a habit of doing this. *Tintoret's Daughter* was in full light. Once, as he was walking, his eye fell on the painting he loved so much and his face darkened with pain. After a few more rounds he stopped in front of it and somber and reflective, considered it closely. I watched him not daring to follow his thoughts. Our eyes met and tears swelled from his eyes. He opened his arms to me and tearfully cried, "Oh, my most precious treasure! Oh, my Tintorella!"

8. Conan, p. 104.

The charming statue of the Holy Virgin that my father gave her when she lost her mother occupies the place of honor. A sturdy branch of ivy gracefully adorns it.

It is a balm for the soul and a balm for the heart and I was deeply touched when I saw my father's portrait surrounded by dried moss and forget-me-nots in this young girl's room.

9. Conan, p. 102.

And who else in my place would not have ardently and profoundly loved him? Every night after prayers, I kneel in front of his portrait the way I used to kneel in front of him and very often, I cry. . . .

See also p. 94.

10. Conan, p. 39.

I wanted her to be the daughter of my soul as well as of my blood . . . and as for Angéline, towards me there is total response. . . .

11. Conan, p. 159. Italics used in original text.

For him, the *enticement of sex* did not exist.

See also p. 75.

12. In *Narcisses*, special issue of the *Nouvelle Revue de Psychanalyse*, No. 93 (Spring 1976), p. 54.

13. I divide the novel into three distinct parts, although the author divides it into only two. The first part corresponds to the epistolary narrative (pp. 15-85), the second part to the third person narrative (pp. 85-88), and the third to the personal diary of Angéline (feuilles détachées—pp. 89-187).

14. Conan, pp. 29, 17. Italics used in original text.

Believe me, my little sister, no one spoke in the Garden of Eden. No, in the days of innocence, love and happiness, man spoke not, *he sang*.

15. See Le Moine, p. 84.

16. Le Moine, pp. 81-82.

17. Conan, p. 119.

Forget that one sheltered in one's heart the pure whiteness of one's baptism and the divine beauty of perfect innocence.
Forget the unbearable shame of the first blemish, the salutory bite of the first pangs.

18. Observe, incidentally, the conformity to the Edenic myth.

19. Conan, pp. 121-22.

But that evening, something solemn weighed upon me. I felt moved but without reason. All I owed him passed through my mind. It seemed to me I had never appreciated fully his wonderful tenderness. I felt a strong urge to thank him and to love him. The clock struck midnight. Never before had a death knell sounded so mournful, left me with such a dismal feeling. A vague and terrible fear clutched at my throat. This room so beautiful and so gay, suddenly took on the atmosphere of a tomb.

To hide my feelings, I stood up and went to the window. The sea had ebbed, but I could hear from time to time faint noises made by the waves. I tried determinedly to settle my feelings because I did not want my father to worry. He began to pace to and fro in the room. He had a habit of doing this. *Tintoret's Daughter* was in full light. Once, as he passed in front of it, his eye suddenly fell on the painting which he loved so much and his face darkened with pain. After a few more rounds, he stopped in front of it and somber and reflective, considered it closely. I watched him not daring to follow his thoughts. Our eyes met and tears swelled from his eyes. He opened his arms towards me and tearfully cried, "Oh, my most precious treasure! Oh, my Tintorella!"

I burst into tears. This sudden and powerful emotion, a response to my secret anguish terrified me, and I cried out, "My God! My God! What will become of us?"

He instantly took hold of himself and tried to reassure me but I felt his heart beating violently in his chest while he repeated ever so calmly, "It's nothing, it's nothing, it's only your feelings for poor Jacques Robusti."

And as I continued to cry and shivered in his arms, he carried me to the sofa by the fire; then he closed the window and threw a few pieces of wood on the coals.

The flames rose suddenly bright and vivid. Then, coming back to me, he asked me what it was that had upset me so. I told him about my deep fears.

"Bah!" he said lightly, "nerves." And as I insisted on saying that he also had felt the breath of tragedy, he said to me,

"I was moved for a moment but you know Mina tells me I have the makeup of an artist."

He teased me, tried to reason with me, fussed over me and when he saw I was still upset, he pulled me towards him and in a grave tone of voice asked me, "My child, if I, your father, had total control of your destiny, would you be terrified?"

Then, continuing, he spoke to me with loving tenderness of the folly, the absurdity of defying the will of God.

His faith swept over me and entered me like new-found vigor. The vague and horrible fear disappeared. Never, no never in my entire life had I felt so deeply loved. However, I understood— Oh, with such pure clarity!—that nothing in human tenderness could even give an inkling of the love of God for creatures.

20. Conan, p. 122.

21. Conan, p. 123.

Were I to live a long time, I will never discard my black dress. Never will I come out of mourning.

22. Conan, p. 146.

Formerly, spoiled by happiness, I did not understand religious life, I could not fathom how one could live in such a manner, the soul in heaven and the body in the grave. Now, I believe the religious vocation to be a great blessing.

23. Guy Rosolato, "Le Narcissisme," *Nouvelle Revue de Psychanalyse: Narcisses*, No. 93 (Spring 1976), p. 12.

24. Green, p. 61.

25. Rosolato, p. 22.

26. Masud R. Khan, "Entre l'idole et l'idéal," *Nouvelle Revue de Psychanalyse: Narcisses*, No. 93 (Spring 1976), p. 260.

27. Conan, p. 47.

Dear Mina, I would rather be his servant than the daughter of the most prominent man of the land.

28. Green, p. 49. Italics used in original text. Rosolato, p. 15.

29. Rosolato, p. 17. Italics used in original text.

30. Rosolato, p. 15. Italics used in original text.

31. Conan, p. 170.

Oh! I would like to think of Heaven. But I cannot. I am like that sick woman in the Gospel who was so bent over, she was unable to look up.

32. Conan, pp. 185-86.

God of love, I bequeath her to you, Oh, Lord Jesus, take her, Oh Lord Jesus, comfort her, fortify her.

33. Conan, pp. 185-86.

Maurice, it is he who has ordained everything, it is his will that separates us.

34. Conan, pp. 185-86.

But there are some who arrive in Heaven bloodied; those have no right to complain.

35. "Entre Narcisse et Oedipe, une image-écran ou un souvenir-écran," *Nouvelle Revue de Psychanalyse: Narcisses*, No. 93 (Spring 1976), p. 290.

2

Feminism and Traditionalism in the Early Short Stories of Gabrielle Roy

Paula Gilbert Lewis ───────────────

From 1938 to 1945 Gabrielle Roy worked as a journalist, predominantly for the Montreal-based newspaper, *Le Bulletin des Agriculteurs*. As of 1939 and until 1948, she began publishing short stories, mainly in *La Revue Moderne* and in *Le Bulletin des Agriculteurs*. The author's own opinion of this early fiction, in contrast to the admitted importance of her journalistic writings, was very low: she would have liked someone to collect and to burn them. She did concede the fact, however, that some of these early stories do contain future literary concerns and themes and can be seen, therefore, as precursors to her major fiction.[1]

As a Montreal journalist, born and raised in Manitoba and having moved to this Quebec city after a lengthy stay in Europe, Gabrielle Roy became fascinated with the urban metropolis and made it the setting for several journalistic articles and, of course, for her first novel, *Bonheur d'occasion*, in 1945. As for her early short stories, "Le Joli Miracle" in 1940 depicts the problems of poverty in Montreal, while the 1941 "La Sonate à l'Aurore" concerns the love and marriage that can be destroyed by war. Both short stories clearly prefigure *Bonheur d'occasion*. Three other early short stories, "Feuilles mortes," "La Justice en Danaca et ailleurs," and "Sécurité," also offer an additional response to the conclusion of *Bonheur d'occasion*: that it is useless to go to war, for world conflicts only feed upon exploitation, alienation, and absurdity.[2]

These same three stories, published in 1946 and 1948, later than most of Roy's others, should also be placed in a separate category as the most direct precursors of her major fiction, essentially because of their depiction of a pathetic male character. The two 1948 tales, in fact, can be seen as preliminary studies for the 1954 *Alexandre Chenevert*, with its atmosphere of imprisonment and absurdity. Adrien of "La Justice en Danaca et ailleurs" is an insignificant man who works too much. At one point in his life, he works overtime, does not declare the extra income, is audited, and insults the auditor. After his ten-minute revolt, he calmly returns to his role as another *fourmi* of the country. Constantin Simoneau of "Feuilles mortes" is the closest ancestor of Alexandre. He is a solitary, timid man who, without harboring any revolt within him, works too hard, fears losing his job, and accumulates debts. Like Chenevert, he lives with a constant sense of guilt and paranoia, the feeling that he is being judged. An insignificant man, Constantin is pathetically and poignantly portrayed.[3]

Other early short stories can be interpreted in a similar manner. In "Le Joli Miracle" the musician, Loubka, understands the duty of a writer to create, while she jealously views this profession alone as offering independence. One immediately thinks of Roy's "La Voix des étangs" of the 1955 *Rue Deschambault*. Similarly, the difficulty of writing and the agony of the writer before a creative void are expressed in the 1946 "La Source au désert," as they will be later, in 1961, in *La Montagne secrète*. This same short story also prefigures the 1972 *Cet eté qui chantait*, with an early emphasis on nature and the portrayal of the 1946 heroine, Anne, as sensitively communing with the natural world. Gabrielle Roy's increasing interest in the world of children did culminate in the 1977 *Ces enfants de ma vie*, but had originated in the 1940 "Gérard le pirate." And finally, if Bédette of "La Grande Voyageuse" in 1942 is a precursor of Roy's later obsessive nomads, the hero of the 1940 "Un Noël en route" is the brother of Gustave of the 1975 "Un Vagabond frappe à notre porte" in *Un Jardin au bout du monde*.[4]

It is predominantly the area of female characterization, however, that offers the most fertile ground for a study of Gabrielle Roy's early short stories. Many critics have seen Roy primarily as a feminine writer, that is, excelling in the creation of women characters, continuously underscoring the important role of the mother, concerning herself with the problems facing her literary women, and, finally, viewing all of her characters and their world "with the loving and protective concern of a mother."[5] The author obviously felt that her strength as a writer lay in this domain: "Moreover, one speaks well only of what one knows the best. It has always seemed to me that among writers, men, in general, speak better about men, and women about women, rather than the contrary."[6] Whether or not Roy and her literary creations are obsessed with the image of the mother, as believe Phyllis Grosskurth and Gérard Bessette, or whether or not that image is merely a literary theme among others, as states François Ricard, it must be agreed that the predominance of the Royan female character closely resembles the *québécois* myth of the powerful and protective maternal figure.[7]

Throughout her novels, Gabrielle Roy expresses a deep sense of both pride and pity toward her female creations. They are all traditional mother figures, the embodiment of the *québécoise* female, and the author's sensitive humanism toward them is clearly felt. But these women, especially Rose-Anna Lacasse of the 1945 *Bonheur d'occasion* and Elsa Kumachuk of the 1971 *La Rivière sans repos*, also represent an attack against this maternal myth. Roy's raised feminist consciousness underscores in the lives of her characters both the struggles, hardships, and pain that they are destined to endure, caught in an enclosed circle of their biological and social fate, and the dangers that are inherent in an obsessive maternal instinct. Despite their common desire for a new beginning, these Royan women are, in addition, forced to suffer alone, in the virtual absence of men who are usually on scene solely to impregnate the females. It is true that Gabrielle Roy adored children and considered them to be the culmination of a woman's life, but after reading her novels, one wonders if such a maternal life is worthwhile when so much suffering and solitude seem to be the inevitable results.

The female characters of the typical Royan short story are mothers, school-teachers, and future writers, or, like Christine of the 1955 *Rue Deschambault* and the 1966 *La Route d'Altamont*, young girls envisioning such roles for themselves. They are overtly content with their lives and traditionally resigned to the maternal destiny of women. Like Maman-Eveline of these same two works, they silence any desires for greater freedom and independence and suffer intensely when they are left alone without their children. Increasingly, like Martha Yaramko of the 1975 *Un Jardin au bout du monde*, they take solace and refuge in nature. These women, however, would never relinquish their maternal and familial roles, for they can at least displace upon their children, and especially upon their daughters, all of their thwarted dreams. As with her attitude toward her novelistic creations, Roy extends both her pride and her pity toward these fictional women.

Given these literary portraits of anguished and frustrated, but still traditional, women in her major fiction, it is not surprising that Roy has usually been treated as a feminine writer and viewed as a traditionalist rather than as a feminist. When one becomes familiar with all of her fiction, however, from her early short stories to her most recently published novels and collections of short stories, one sees an interesting development in her creation of female characters. Although neither feminist nor liberated in the 1970s and 1980s sense of these terms, Gabrielle Roy seemed to have been more concerned with independent, "revolutionary" female characters in her 1939–1948 short stories than in subsequent works. From 1939 until 1983, she clearly lost neither her deep preoccupation with female characters nor her sensitivity to their problems. But while feminist literature in Quebec, as elsewhere, has relatively recently become concerned with the creation of independent, liberated, and self-assertive women, as well as with its authors' involvement in feminine and feminist writing, Roy's early feminist awareness and, therefore, her initial depiction of women dissatisfied with their lot or determined to be more independent seemed to have developed into more of a general humanism, a deep sensitivity for women, men, children, and all of nature. Gabrielle Roy evolved from being a feminist to what one can call a feminine humanist.

Since this early fiction is particularly characterized by independent, even liberated female characters, it is, first of all, not surprising that males are painted either in a relatively negative light or, at least, as firmly tied to women. Of course there are a few male characters in these stories who are portrayed with good, positive traits; interestingly enough, these five such men were all created in 1940 or early 1941. In addition, only one male is presented as being cruel: Nick, of "La Lune des moissons," who, always drunk, beats his wife and daughter. Often the men in these early works appear simply as ridiculous, and Roy clearly treats them with amusing irony. In "La Justice en Danaca et ailleurs," for example, they think that they alone are competent, but in reality they are impractical; they cannot even perform "women's tasks" and are always forced to turn to the female.[8]

Almost all of Roy's early fiction, in fact, revolves around some aspect of a woman's life. In two of her short stories, the households consist entirely of women. In a third novella, one meets a mother and her ten daughters, while in two additional tales, all but one of the characters are female.[9] Throughout these and other early short stories, Roy treats every stage in a woman's life, from late adolescence or young adulthood to old age. Influenced by the society of the 1940s, her younger characters, despite a certain level of independence, are often traditionally concerned with finding a husband. Even the honest and natural Sophie of "Cendrillon '40" refocuses her attention toward a man when she realizes that he is attracted to her rather than to her more superficial, "made-up" modern sisters. It is, in addition, Henderson, the eligible bachelor–vacuum cleaner salesman, who first voices an exaggerated, chauvinistic attitude that is ironically depicted by the author: "'Nous avons à coeur de lui [any woman] épargner tout ouvrage fatiguant et malpropre. Nous voulons qu'elle ait de nombreux loisirs à consacrer à sa beauté et à sa tenue qui doit être toujours élégante si elle veut conserver le coeur de celui qu'elle aime.'"[10] Stressing both feminism and traditionalism, however, Roy soon thereafter creates Lucile, of "Avantage pour," who likewise professes that she will pursue a career rather than marriage, that men prefer independent women, and that she will never run after a man, but she quickly uses the ruse of tears to her advantage in order to gain the affection of Jean-Paul.[11]

This depiction of traditional women and of what can be called a marriage mania continues in other early short stories. The all-female household of "Le Roi de coeur," for example, is seen as a world of total disorder, in need of a man to straighten out this dizziness. The four women, anxious to marry well, are initially seen as being grateful to Ted for having dominated them and having put a sense of order into their lives. Eventually, however, it is Ted who succumbs to the confusion of these women and, in this sense, becomes dominated by their female life style. The world of women here prevails.[12]

Similarly, the importance of marriage is ironically treated in "Bonne à marier," as the younger women, almost ridiculously traditional, refuse to marry an older, wealthy widower who eventually is forced to choose their mother. The widower, Jean-Baptiste, is seen as an egocentric male who believes that any woman will want to marry him because of his wealthy, eligible status. He is treated as a man who, typically, cannot live alone and is therefore ironically reduced to marrying the mother of these young women. Roy seems to be directing her cynicism both toward women who are obsessed with getting married and toward men who, in their attempt to dominate these women, are soon overpowered by them. Other men in these early stories are similarly obsessive, confused, and easily dominated.[13]

Once a woman does marry, in this early Royan fictional world, her life can be extremely harsh and difficult, as for "La Grande Berthe" and for the Mennonite women so greatly admired by Roy. The life of a housewife can also be boring. Sally, of "La Fuite de Sally," cannot occupy her days alone at home and flees, for one day only, in order to rediscover herself as she was prior to her marriage. Lizzie, the heroine of Roy's first short story, "La Conversion des O'Connor," is a faithful wife and mother but decides that she needs to leave: "'J'en ai assez des O'Connor, de toute la bande. A moi la liberté!'"[14] As a 1939 *québécoise* woman, however, she adds that there is sufficient food left in the kitchen, and she soon returns from her little escapade to her traditional role in a family that still does not respect her but needs her. Roy, once again, portrays ironically both the woman and her family.

She is totally serious, however, when she describes the embarrassment of "La Grande Berthe" at being pregnant and her subsequent terrified stoicism during childbirth. Roy similarly treats with poignant gravity the situation of Juliette of "Sécurité" who desperately loves children, desires to adopt a child, but finally resigns herself to her husband's wishes to remain financially secure and, thus, childless. One must remember that, for Gabrielle Roy, a child was the justification of a couple in love.[15]

Precisely because of her almost reverential attitude toward children, Roy treats in a totally negative light Nathalie of "La Source au désert." When this woman becomes pregnant, she experiences "cette peur de souffrir, d'enlaidir, cette peur atroce...."[16] With an "accidental" fall down the stairs, everything is conveniently arranged, and Nathalie loses the baby. To the husband of this, in effect, self-abortionist, "en tout ceci, n'avait-elle été guidée que par le souci odieux de sa beauté?"[17] One has the distinct impression that Gabrielle Roy was seconding these words, for throughout this two-part short story, Nathalie is portrayed as a perverted, evil, and maliciously voluptuous female in the eyes of her husband, Dr. Vincent Raymond. She is constantly compared to Anne, her husband's true love, who represents purity, joy, and spring-like youth. But Anne is also Roy's first female martyr, since she refuses to rebel against her tragic destiny without Raymond and is not convinced of her ability to begin anew. It is in this particular short story, in fact, that Roy first clearly expressed this need, especially on the part of women, for *le recommencement*. It is the doctor who recognizes this essential difference between men and women: "En vérité, elles [women in general] étaient capables d'une chose que les hommes réussissent rarement: recommencer leur vie.... Refaire leur vie! L'instinct de durer, de se terrer. Une plus abjecte soumission à la vie que celle même de l'homme."[18]

Throughout Roy's early short stories, prefiguring her major fiction, there is a common element linking the strong female characters: precisely that of a determination to live and, if necessary, to begin a new life. Ironically, Anne, the symbol of pure love, is the one woman in these novellas who refuses this possibility, prefers to die slowly rather than to compromise her desired life with Raymond, and, thus, ultimately becomes the symbol of his sorrow and death. Roy certainly did not advocate a life such as that of Nathalie in this story, but she also did not, nor did she ever, recommend female martyrdom.

The most completely developed male character in Roy's early short stories and, in addition, one of the weakest and most pitiful is, in fact, Dr. Raymond of this 1946 two-part novella. Filled with hatred for Nathalie and obsessively in love with Anne who refuses to flee with him, Raymond has become a stranger even to himself, a self-hating man addicted to morphine. He honestly believes that he is typical: in contrast to women who will always attempt the typically Royan *recommencement*, a man "lorsqu'il est devant le désespoir, se tue d'un seul coup, ou bien, le fait à petit feu, se livrant à l'alcoolisme et encore comme lui à cette mort graduelle, inévitable par la drogue."[19] Raymond lives solely for Anne, and when he realizes that he can no longer be with her, he literally departs toward his solitary death, toward a cabin in the extreme North, without provisions, and already in a feverish and hallucinatory state. If the power of true love is exalted but seldom achieved by the female characters in Gabrielle Roy's major fiction, it is equally essential but, at times, poignantly destructive to women and mortally destructive to men in her early short stories.

Several of these early Royan female characters, however, are quite the opposite of Anne and present the image of the independent, working woman. Mariette of "Le Monde à l'envers" in 1939 not only works but is the boss; Bobinette of "A Okko" also works and lives alone; and Loubka of "Le Joli Miracle" used to work but has left her job because of sexual advances made toward her by her boss. Loubka also does not particularly like men, despite the fact that, ironically, her name means love.[20]

She is the literary sister of Judith, the militant, feminist, man hater of the 1940 "Les Petits Pas de Caroline." This heroine considers herself to be a true feminist: thirty-years old, unmarried, with no need for men. She meets Alain, an obnoxious chauvinist whom she treats with sarcasm and disdain:

> Ses narines [of Judith] se dilatèrent dans l'anticipation du combat.
> "Ecoutez, jeune homme. On a trop longtemps répandu dans ce monde la légende qu'une femme ne peut ouvrir une porte, allumer sa cigarette ou nouer ses lacets de souliers. Moi je suis venue ici [to the Gaspé Peninsula] pour prouver le contraire, et vous pensez que vous allez contrecarrer mes projets de réforme sociale...."[21]

Alain cannot understand Judith, for he has learned about the "weaker sex" from the sentimental, romantic trash written by a traditional female author, Caroline. Portrayed with an evident tone of sarcasm on the part of the author, this condescending, cynical male character is usually half-serious and half-mocking whenever he speaks of women in front of the feminist: "'Ah, voilà comment j'aime les femmes; douces, confiantes, pas trop encombrantes....'"[22] He will even quote from Caroline's novels essentially to irritate Judith: "'Caroline dit justement à ce sujet . . . attendez que je trouve le paragraphe. . . . Ah voici: "La femme éprouve le besoin d'être dominée. Elle n'aura d'admiration que pour quiconque la réduira par force, et d'un mauvais traitement elle conservera souvent un souvenir attendri."''[23] In spite of his chauvinistic ways, however, Alain falls in love with Judith, desires to "conquer" her, and intelligently wins her esteem and affection. He promises to allow her to burn the fictional garbage that has so warped his mind. But Judith cannot do this, for she is, in fact, Caroline. She is the feminist with a penchant for what she calls "ces fantômes de l'imagination,"[24] romantic and chivalrous lovers who no longer exist but continue to enthrall adolescents who still believe in love. Judith will eventually destroy Caroline, will no longer write such novels, but one does have the general impression that she will remain with Alain. Once again, Gabrielle Roy has ironically placed in her heroine both feminist and traditional characteristics, although here they are clearly developed to an exaggerated degree. Both extremes will be modified but not silenced within Judith. It does appear that traditionalism triumphs in the name of love, but the story purposefully remains open at its conclusion, inviting the reader to speculate about the future of this modern heroine.

This same strain of female independence does continue into middle age, as witnessed by Mlle Lajeunesse, the humorously depicted, self-sufficient heroine of both "Six Pilules par jour" and "Embobeliné." This woman, as her name comically indicates, truly believes in *le recommencement*, for she is, in 1941, the modern nutritionist, exerciser, health food and vitamin pill maniac. She may be humorous, but she is, in effect, youthful and happy. Much of this humor and irony is abandoned, however, when Roy creates women in their older age. "La Grande Berthe," for example, becomes resigned to the onset of menopause, and the pitiful old woman of "La Pension de vieillesse" dreams of her pension, receives it, and then dies. But although total independence is lost for these older women, Berthe does also ultimately triumph: she inherits her husband's money and keeps the family together with herself at the helm. And Bédette, "La Grande Voyageuse," although dependent upon the hospitality of her sisters, does learn to enjoy her, at times, humorously depicted nomadic life, traveling from one home to another. In the end, she also cleverly convinces the railroad company to pay her an indemnity in her old age.[25] Most of Roy's early female characters do valiantly succeed.

It is evident that throughout these early short stories, a constant, and frequently ironic, duality is present in almost all of Roy's female creations: they are both feminists and traditionalists. It must also be noted that the latter quality, more reflective of the 1940s, does usually appear to dominate. The fact, however, both that the independent nature of these fictionalized women—frequently dominating weaker men—often makes itself known and that the author was apparently deeply preoccupied with the concerns of women does indicate Roy's early feminist consciousness, hitherto minimized.

NOTES

1. Personal interview with Gabrielle Roy, 29 June 1980. Gabrielle Roy died on 13 July 1983 at the age of seventy-four.

2. Gabrielle Roy, "Le Joli Miracle," *Le Bulletin des Agriculteurs*, 26, No. 12 (décembre 1940), 8, 29-30; "La Sonate à l'Aurore," *La Revue Moderne*, 22, No. 11 (mars 1941), 9, 10, 35-37; "Feuilles mortes," *La Revue de Paris*, 56ᵉ année, No. 1 (janvier 1948), pp. 46-55; "La Justice en Danaca et ailleurs," in *Les Oeuvres Libres* (Paris: Librairie Arthène Fayard, N.S., No. 23, 1948), pp. 163-80; "Sécurité," *La Revue Moderne*, 29, No. 11 (mars 1948), 12, 13, 66, 69. "Sécurité" was first published in English as "Security," *Maclean's*, 15 September 1947, pp. 20-21, 36, 39.

3. Roy, "La Justice en Danaca et ailleurs," pp. 168-71, 174, 178–80; "Feuilles mortes," pp. 46-55.

4. Roy, "Le Joli Miracle," p. 30; "La Source au désert," *Le Bulletin des Agriculteurs*, 42, No. 10 (octobre 1946), 42, 32, 35, 36; "Gérard le pirate," *La Revue Moderne*, 22, No. 1 (mai 1940), 5, 37-39; "La Grande Voyageuse," *La Revue Moderne*, 24, No. 1 (mai 1942), 12, 13, 27-30; "Un Noël en route," *La Revue Moderne*, 22, No. 8 (décembre 1940), 8, 32-34. "Un Vagabond frappe à notre porte," published in 1975 as part of *Un Jardin au bout du monde*, originally appeared in *Amérique Française* (janvier 1946), pp. 29-51.

5. It is Phyllis Grosskurth who speaks of this "mother's-eye view" of the world. See *Gabrielle Roy*, Canadian Writers and Their Works (Toronto: Forum House, 1972), p. 57.

6. Gilles Dorion et Maurice Emond, "Dossier Gabrielle Roy: Questionnaire," *Québec Français*, No. 36 (décembre 1979), p. 35.

7. Phyllis Grosskurth, "Gabrielle Roy and The Silken Noose," *Canadian Literature*, 42 (1969), 7-13; Gérard Bessette, *Une Littérature en ébullition* (Montréal: Editions du Jour, 1968), pp. 224-27; Gérard Bessette, *Trois Romanciers québécois* (Montréal: Editions du Jour, 1973), pp. 182, 207, 208; François Ricard, *Gabrielle Roy*, Ecrivains canadiens d'aujourd'hui, No. 11 (Montréal: Editions Fides, 1975), pp. 31-32.

8. Gabrielle Roy, "Une Histoire d'amour," *La Revue Moderne*, 21, No. 11 (mars 1940), 8, 9, 36-38; "La Dernière Pêche," *La Revue Moderne*, 22, No. 7 (novembre 1940), 8, 9, 38; "Le Joli Miracle," pp. 8, 29–30; "La Sonate à l'Aurore," pp. 9, 10, 35-37; "A Okko," *La Revue Moderne*, 22, No. 12 (avril 1941), 8, 9, 41, 42; "La Lune des moissons," *La Revue Moderne*, 29, No. 5 (septembre 1947), 12, 13, 76-80.

9. Gabrielle Roy, "Cendrillon '40," *La Revue Moderne*, 21, No. 10 (février 1940), 8, 9, 41, 42; "Le Roi de coeur," *La Revue Moderne*, 21, No. 12 (avril 1940), 6, 7, 33-39; "La Grande Voyageuse," pp. 12, 13, 27-30; "Six Pilules par jour," *La Revue Moderne*, 23, No. 3 (juillet 1941), 17, 18, 32-34; "Embobeliné," *La Revue Moderne*, 23, No. 6 (octobre 1941), 7, 8, 28, 30, 33, 34.

10. Roy, "Cendrillon '40," p. 40.

"We have our heart set on sparing her [any woman] from any tiring and dirty task. We want her to have enough leisure time to devote to her beauty and to her style of dress which must always be elegant if she desires to keep the heart of the one she loves."

11. Gabrielle Roy, "Avantage pour," *La Revue Moderne*, 20, No. 6 (octobre 1940), 5, 6, 26.

12. Roy, "Le Roi de coeur," pp. 6, 7, 33, 35, 36, 38, 39.

13. Gabrielle Roy, "Bonne à marier," *La Revue Moderne*, 20, No. 2 (juin 1940), 13,

41, 42. The importance of marrying one's daughters, as well as the shame of not having a husband, is also treated in "La Grande Berthe," *Le Bulletin des Agriculteurs*, 39, No. 6 (juin 1943), 5, 9.

14. Gabrielle Roy, "La Conversion des O'Connor," *La Revue Moderne*, 21, No. 5 (septembre 1939), 4.

"I've had enough of the O'Connor's—of the whole bunch. I want my freedom!"

See also Roy, "La Grande Berthe," pp. 7, 8; "Femmes de dur labeur," *Le Bulletin des Agriculteurs*, 39, No. 1 (janvier 1943), 10, 25; "La Fuite de Sally," *Le Bulletin des Agriculteurs*, 27, No. 1 (janvier 1941), 9, 39.

15. Roy, "La Grande Berthe," pp. 7, 39-40; "Sécurité," pp. 13, 68; Alice Parizeau, "Gabrielle Roy, grande romancière canadienne," *Châtelaine*, 7, No. 4 (avril 1966), 120.

16. Roy, "La Source au désert" (octobre 1946), p. 34.

That fear of suffering, of becoming ugly—that horrible fear. . . .

17. Roy, "La Source au désert" (octobre 1946), p. 34.

In all of this, had she not been driven solely by that hateful concern for her beauty?

18. Roy, "La Source au désert" (octobre 1946), p. 10.

In truth, they [women in general] were capable of something at which men rarely succeed: to begin their lives once again. . . . To remake their lives! An instinct to endure, to entrench themselves in life. A more wretched submission to life than that of man.

See also "La Source au désert," *Le Bulletin des Agriculteurs*, 42, No. 11 (novembre 1946), 46; personal interview with Gabrielle Roy, 29 June 1980; Marc Gagné, *Visages de Gabrielle Roy* (Montréal: Librairie Beauchemin Limitée, 1973), pp. 143-44.

19. Roy, "La Source au désert" (octobre 1946), p. 10.

When he is faced with despair, kills himself at once or, rather, does it slowly, abandoning himself to alcoholism and, again like him [Dr. Raymond], to this gradual, inevitable death by drugs.

20. Gabrielle Roy, "Le Monde à l'envers," *La Revue Moderne*, 21, No. 6 (octobre 1939), 6, 34; "A Okko," pp. 8, 9, 41, 42; "Le Joli Miracle," pp. 8, 29-30.

21. Gabrielle Roy, "Les Petits Pas de Caroline," *Le Bulletin des Agriculteurs*, 26, No. 10 (octobre 1940), 45.

Her [Judith's] nostrils dilated in anticipation of a fight.
"Listen, young man. For too long one has spread throughout the world the myth that a woman is not capable of opening a door, lighting her own cigarette, or tying her own shoelaces. As for me, I have come here [to the Gaspé Peninsula] precisely in order to prove the opposite, and you actually think that you are going to thwart my plans for social reform. . . ."

22. Roy, "Les Petits Pas de Caroline," p. 47.

"Ah, that's how I like women; sweet, trusting, not too bothersome. . . ."

23. Roy, "Les Petits Pas de Caroline," p. 48.

"Caroline speaks precisely about this subject . . . wait until I find the paragraph. . . . Oh, here it is: 'A woman needs to be dominated. She will admire only the person who will subjugate her by force, and she will often tenderly remember when she was mistreated.'"

24. Roy, "Les Petits Pas de Caroline," p. 49.

These phantoms of the imagination.

25. Roy, "Six Pilules par jour," pp. 17, 18, 32-34; "Embobeliné," p. 8; "La Grande Berthe," pp. 41, 49; "La Pension de vieillesse," *Le Bulletin des Agriculteurs*, 39, No. 11 (novembre 1943), 8, 32, 33, 36; "La Grande Voyageuse," pp. 29, 30.

3

Le Survenant as Ideological Messenger: A Study of Germaine Guèvremont's Radio Serial

James J. Herlan

Germaine Guèvremont's widely read novel *Le Survenant*, first published in 1945, elicited a positive and enthusiastic response from Quebec reviewers. The book quickly established the reputation of Guèvremont, whom contemporary scholars generally rank with the other so-called "classic" novelists of Quebec: Ringuet, Gabrielle Roy, and Roger Lemelin.

The robust hero of *Le Survenant*, a nomadic type akin to the *coureurs de bois* who explored New France, has since become a legendary figure in Quebec fiction. As a protagonist, the Survenant has, in fact, led three separate but related lives: first in the original novel, later in the radio serial of the same name, and finally in the television adaptation. In this study, I will examine the ideological elements of the radio version, a text that represents an important component of Guèvremont's total literary production.

In the past, traditional critics tended to neglect this aspect of Guèvremont's writing, an omission that probably reflected their unconscious elitism. Unfortunately, this critical occultation fostered a certain cultural alienation by excluding from consideration a work that contributed immensely to Quebec's collective self-image.[1] In the light of current scholarly trends that recognize the importance of popular culture, however, researchers have begun to view the paraliterature of radio and television as a useful source for studying the evolution of Quebec.

It seems especially appropriate to consider the radio script, since it was this form of popular drama that for the first time provided the francophone population of Quebec with a clear reflection of its own society. According to Pierre Pagé, a Quebec media specialist, radio serials like *Le Survenant* helped to create meaningful cultural links between the dramatic works and the listening audience.[2] Presumably the links grew stronger to the extent that the public was able to identify with the characters who were portrayed on the air. In this connection,

Pagé adds that the portrayals offered by radio drama nourished the imagination of an eager audience, previously isolated, and initiated a Quebec-centered oral art.[3] Today, as Quebec continues its process of self-definition, the cultural relevance of radio drama, which helped to stimulate the first glimmerings of self-awareness, seems indisputable.

Moreover, the myth of the Survenant can be seen, in part, as a product of the media adaptations created by Guèvremont. Without minimizing the importance of the published work, one can recognize the influence of the radio hero, who popularized the fictional universe first introduced in the novel. Among other things, the radio serial clearly allowed the author to reach a much wider audience than she did through her book.

The radio version of *Le Survenant*, which is incomplete and unpublished, contains over three thousand pages of typewritten text. Before analyzing the script itself, it may be useful to establish the chronology of the radio adaptation so that its content can be accurately related to the historical context. The original radio version of *Le Survenant* began on 31 August 1953, and continued until 6 May 1955.[4] There were five broadcasts a week, Monday through Friday, with each episode lasting fifteen minutes. The popularity of the program can be assumed, since the original series was rebroadcast from the autumn of 1962 to the spring of 1965.[5] For the purpose of this analysis, however, the earlier period is more significant, because it was then that Guèvremont actually wrote the scripts. In this regard, it is worth noting that the era of Maurice Duplessis lasted until the end of the 1950s, a historical detail that will become more pertinent as the ideological themes emerge from the radio text. Indeed, even though the drama is set in the first decade of this century, it seems clear that *Le Survenant* can also be seen as a reflection of Quebec society in the mid-fifties.

The portrayal of the family unit, for example, provides useful clues about prevailing cultural norms during this period. In studying the principal families in the serial, the Beauchemins and their neighbors, one is struck by the absence of the mother from several family groups. The Beauchemin family, with whom the Survenant lives, is composed of the father (Didace), the son (Amable), the daughter-in-law (Phonsine),[6] and the married daughter (Marie-Amanda), who appears only rarely. The nearest neighbors, the Desmarais family, form a minimal unit: a father (David) and his daughter (Angélina). The family of the mayor, Pierre-Côme Provençal, is made up of the father, mother, and their children, but in fact the mother never actually appears in the radio drama. The DeFroi family, the poorest in the parish, has only a brother and sister. The only family that seems ''complete'' according to traditional expectations is the Salvails, a unit composed of the mother, father, daughter, and son.

At one level, the absence of maternal figures seems both surprising and puzzling. There is, of course, no ready explanation for the missing mothers, although one might speculate that the omissions allow the author to portray paternal domination without recourse to husband-wife dialogues that would further demean the female characters. In addition, the references to several deceased mothers might be seen as an attempt to convey an implicit message about the excessively heavy burdens that often weighed down the traditional Quebec mother. In any case, it is clear that Guèvremont's fictional family is characterized throughout the radio adaptation by the domination of the father figure, who often exercises a tyrannical authority over other family members and particularly over female characters. In the Beauchemin household, for example, this dominance is revealed by the authoritarian manner of Didace, who gives orders to his family much like an officer commanding his troops. Amable and Phonsine lack the courage to rebel against this domestic tyranny, a weakness that helps to underline the strength of the Survenant, who functions as a kind of surrogate son in the family.

In the Provençal household, Pierre-Côme also plays the role of a despotic father; insensitive and often brutal, he maintains a roughshod rule over his family. Even his eldest son, Odilon, who becomes the village bully when he is outside the confines of the home, does not dare to oppose the mayor's paternal authority. Pierre-Côme's arbitrary exercise of power, depicted as blatantly unjust, is a recurrent theme in many episodes.

In attempting to interpret the domineering behavior of what might be termed the peasant-father,[7] it is important to recall that, in fact, this type of paternal control was already on the wane in Quebec when the radio serial was being broadcast. Accordingly, it is not surprising that in response to changing social values the dominant ideology of the period attempted to prop up the *myth* of the traditional society in which the father figure ruled supreme. The utility of the myth is clear enough, since the concept of paternal domination of the home can easily be applied to society in general, especially when Church and State are perceived simply as extensions of the family structure. In *Le Survenant*, these connections are suggested symbolically by Provençal's dual role as head of his family and mayor of the village. The Provençal character helps in this way to perpetuate the myth of a monolithic male hierarchy.

This ideological perspective is entirely consistent with the political views of Maurice Duplessis, who as provincial prime minister advocated stability and order.[8] In this light, it is possible to detect a certain parallelism between the fictional mayor, who does not tolerate reproaches from his family or his neighbors, and the real prime minister, who would brook no criticism from his political adversaries. In both situations, the father figure exercises absolute authority which remains superficially unquestioned. At another level, however, the portrayal of a stable society guided by masculine leaders serves to mask the disturbing reality of a Quebec that was already beginning to experience economic and social instability in many areas.

Before continuing this analysis of ideological factors, it is essential to maintain the proper perspective by recalling that the radio version of *Le Survenant* was written, after all, as a serialized drama intended to attract listeners rather than as a propaganda piece aimed at altering public attitudes; that is, the ideological elements in the text are presumably unconscious manifestations of Guèvremont's inner value system but do not reflect her desire to propagandize the audience. Indeed, a close examination of the implicit messages in the radio dialogues reveals that they are often ambiguous and sometimes contradictory, conveying a kind of ideological ambivalence that would be inappropriate in the works of a true polemicist. With this clarification in mind, let us consider another institution that affected the social climate when Guèvremont was writing the radio scripts.

During the Duplessis years, the Church still stood as a bastion of social order, firm in its opposition to any changes that might upset its hegemony in the province. Like the Duplessis government, the Church was also organized as a male-dominated hierarchy where the exercise of authority was seldom troubled by notions of democracy. Interestingly, the importance of ecclesiastical figures emerges much more clearly in the radio version of *Le Survenant* than it did in the novel, where the parish priest, Father Lebrun, played a relatively minor role. In the radio serial, Father Lebrun, appearing frequently, becomes a community leader, as much in the civil domain as in the religious. Normally when any of the parishioners quarrel and cannot resolve their problem, they go to Father Lebrun, who is expected to find an equitable solution. It is evident as well that the priest is depicted as the ultimate local authority, since the public proclamations of Mayor Provençal are often treated as a joke.[9] Moreover, the mayor is usually obliged to defer to Father Lebrun's judgment if the two men are not in agreement, thus establishing the priest as the real arbiter in the village. This portrayal of the priest, seen as "father" of his parish "family," serves both to underline the presumed superiority of the father figure and to reinforce the myth that society is simply an extension of the family.

It is obvious that the corollary of presumed masculine superiority is female inferiority, and in the radio adaptation the female characters are usually presented as subordinate to the various males (fathers, husbands, brothers). In this connection, the vocabulary used by male characters is itself a significant factor in the drama. When they refer to women, for example, the men in the parish frequently use the word "créature," a term that is often demeaning even as a compliment (as in *une belle créature*). When the mayor, Pierre-Côme Provençal, employs the term, its pejorative sense becomes eminently clear: "Je vous dis que les créatures, elles nous en donnent du tinton. Quand c'est pas une . . . c'est l'autre."[10] Provençal's sexist viewpoint is typical, and in this sense the mayor often seems to embody the masculine value system that reigns in the Chenal du Moine. In the course of a festive occasion at the Provençal home, the Survenant asks Pierre-Côme two questions, to which the answers are most revealing:

SUR: Mais . . . les dames, elles . . . quand mangent-elles?

P-C: Après les hommes, quoi!

SUR: (RIRE DU SURVENANT AUQUEL P-C NE COMPREND RIEN) Et la galanterie?

P-C: C'est une fête pour les hommes. Pas pour les créatures![11]

It is interesting to observe that the hero, with his broader perspectives, introduces the concept of gallantry,[12] a notion so foreign to the traditional mentality of the mayor that he dismisses it automatically, without pausing to reflect on the issue. In a sense, the reaction of Pierre-Côme is typical of the rural parish, where the implicit inferiority of women is unconsciously accepted from generation to generation.

As I previously observed, women in Guèvremont's radio drama often play the role of a subordinate. Phonsine Beauchemin provides a striking illustration of the sort of female subjugation depicted in *Le Survenant*. Although her husband, Amable, is a weak male whose lack of virility is ridiculed by other men in the village, he is portrayed as domineering in relation to Phonsine, who functions as maid, cook, gardener, or even as nurse (when her spouse has a lame back). Although she docilely performs a never-ending round of daily chores, Phonsine is accorded few rights of her own. For example, when she asks Amable whether she can return to teaching school on a temporary basis, he refuses categorically to permit her to leave the house. Their dialogue is informative:

PH: Ça me reposerait d'l'ouvrage de maison. . . .

AM: De quoi c'est l'ouvrage de maison? C'est rien. Rien en tout.

PH: Rien pour toi, oui. S'il y a un ouvrage qui est ingrat, c'est ben ça. C'est *toujours* à recommencer . . . toujours . . . toujours quand on dit toujours la même tourlotte.

AM: J'ai pas marié une femme pour qu'elle s'en aille travailler ailleurs. J't'ai mariée, Phonsine, pour que tu restes à la maison.[13]

This traditionally masculine response appears to reflect, on a reduced scale, the extreme paternalism that characterized the Duplessis era in Quebec. At the same time, however, it is worth noting that Phonsine's protests convey a kind of embryonic feminism that may be significant. In this regard, it seems logical to presume that Germaine Guèvremont, as a talented and intelligent writer, offered some resistance to the most blatantly anti-feminist aspects of the dominant ideology, and that this resistance was manifested in a certain ambivalence that surfaced in various episodes of the serial.

The Beauchemins' nearest neighbor, Angélina Desmarais, furnishes another example of female servitude in the radio adaptation. Angélina is obliged to cook, keep house, cultivate the garden, pick the vegetables, and then take them to market in Sorel; in addition, she is expected to take care of her sick, widowed father and generally to sacrifice her needs in order to watch over him. Not surprisingly, the local parishioners admire Angélina's filial behavior, and no one questions the system that requires such total self-surrender. Angélina herself accepts her subordinate role without protest. Only the eventual death of her father lifts the parental yoke from Angélina, whose saintly character allows her to accept both subjugation and grief with equanimity. She is the one woman in the serial who can logically be called a martyr.

Although Phonsine and Angélina provide interesting illustrations of dutiful women trying to please the men in their lives, they do not measure up to the ultimate criterion, motherhood, which is the most acceptable role for women characters. Married women in the serial who produce many children are presented in a favorable light, while wives who have no children are portrayed as weaker and somehow less competent. Nowhere is this contrast more striking than in the Beauchemin family, in which the married daughter, Marie-Amanda, has babies every year, whereas the daughter-in-law, Phonsine, is unable to conceive. The remarkable fecundity of Marie-Amanda is, of course, enormously pleasing to Didace, the patriarch of the family.

Marie-Amanda, who is manifestly aware of her maternal role, does not hesitate to assert the importance of her progeny. For example, as the family prepares to eat its Christmas dinner, she seats her daughter at the place formerly occupied by her late mother, a decision that is questioned by Didace:

DID: De quoi c'est que tu fais là, Marie-Amanda? Tu l'assis pas à la place de ta mère?

M-A: Oui, mon père, vous m'avez toujours appris que quand une feuille tombe de l'arbre, une autre feuille la remplace. Reste là, Mathilde.[14]

The affirmation, even in the face of paternal reluctance, underlines the value placed on the generative function in the family structure. In order to realize her potential, a Quebec woman was expected to become a mother, and the radio serial clearly favors the prolific mother (like Marie-Amanda) who assures future generations. It is obvious that this encouragement of maternity accurately reflected the objectives of the dominant ideology, which stressed the growth of Quebec's francophone population.

In spite of the author's generally favorable portrayal of motherhood, a careful reading of the radio script suggests that she may also have had reservations about the validity of the role assigned to Quebec women. As I observed earlier, for example, Guèvremont's references to deceased wives create a certain ambiguity by implying that these traditional mothers may have died relatively young because of the exhausting pressures, both physical and psychological, that society placed on them. Let us note, however, that this ambivalence is expressed by implication only in the course of the drama.

Just as fertility is praised in this fictional model, sterility is degraded throughout the series. In the radio adaptation, Phonsine (unlike her counterpart in the novel, who eventually becomes pregnant) seems to exemplify the sterile wife and is frequently compared to Marie-Amanda, whose homemaking talents are always shown to be superior to those of her sister-in-law; in addition, Phonsine lacks energy and appears generally weaker than Marie-Amanda. The impression that the listener will receive is inescapable: maternity mysteriously makes a married woman better in every way. It is as if all other conjugal roles in the drama derive somehow from the maternal function, so that the fecund daughter is represented as happy and successful in her marital relationship, while the infertile daughter-in-law is seen as inept and less happy in her marriage.

It should be noted in passing that Didace Beauchemin makes occasional remarks critical of Phonsine's apparent inability to produce children, but that he never considers the possibility that his son Amable may be either impotent or sterile. This one-side paternal attitude accentuates, once again, the male chauvinism that characterizes the radio adaptation.

It is equally important to observe that, in spite of the high value placed on maternity, motherhood does not guarantee an improved status for women. In other words, if the husband allows his wife to participate in family management only as mother of their children, then motherhood becomes simply another form of feminine subjugation, since the interests and concerns of the woman are viewed not individually but always in relation to those of her spouse and children. For example, within the male-dominated value system portrayed by Guèvremont, Marie-Amanda appears to be an ideal wife, but she and Phonsine (a non-mother) are equally subjugated to their husbands' authority. Accordingly, the system remains unbalanced against women, who are encouraged to become mothers, only to discover later that parenthood confers no special privileges within the marriage.

On the one hand, the message that seems to emerge from this situation implies that married women should produce offspring (to increase the population of French Canada) while remaining submissive to their spouses (in order to assure the stability of the male hierarchy). On the other hand, it is equally apparent that the striking injustice of the system as depicted by Guèvremont conveys a subliminal message suggesting that submissive women are, in fact, victimized by the dominant ideology. Indeed, to the extent that her portrayal of female characters shows how often they are treated unfairly, the author's underlying message can be considered somewhat subversive. This is not surprising in the context of the ideological ambivalence that has previously been observed.

The dependent position of women in the Quebec family was also assured by the fact that they did not normally work outside the home, a tradition that is stressed in the radio version of Le Survenant. The only exceptions to this general rule concern the religious vocation and schoolteaching. The first function does not figure in Guèvremont's drama, but the second has a certain importance, as the village teacher plays an ongoing role in the broadcasts. This character, called Rose-de-Lima Bibeau, not only teaches elementary classes but is also engaged to Joinville Provençal, the mayor's second son. It becomes apparent in the course of the series that local norms allow her to continue teaching precisely because she is not yet married. As previously indicated, married women are not accorded the same privilege, so that when Phonsine wants to substitute for the absent Miss Bibeau, her husband categorically refuses to permit her to teach.

Even when female characters do work outside the home, they are not motivated by a desire for financial independence nor do they seek any real self-fulfillment in their occupations. It seems clear that the primary value of feminine work is compensatory, allowing the woman to pass time more or less productively while she waits to be discovered by the future husband who will legitimize her existence. The case of Bedette Salvail illustrates this point quite effectively: Bedette, the daughter of Jacob Salvail, causes a local scandal by leaving the Chenal du Moine in order to work in a restaurant in the nearby town of Sorel,[15] but the motivation for her departure is the hope that she will have the opportunity to meet more young men in town than she can at home. Prior to leaving, she faces a double dilemma: she is in love with the Survenant, who finds her too frivolous, while at the same time she is repulsed by the insensitive Odilon Provençal, who loves her and wants to marry her. To avoid this unpleasant situation, Bedette decides to become a waitress in Sorel, where, in addition, she hopes to escape the boredom of the village. It is evident, however, that she has no interest in pursuing a career as such. The long-range goal remains unchanged: Bedette wishes simply to find the right man to marry.

Similarly, Rose-de-Lima Bibeau may be vaguely interested in education, but it is obvious that teaching to her is mainly an activity that helps to fill a temporary void, as she awaits her wedding day. In an interesting dramatic twist, her fiancé, Joinville Provençal, falls under the influence of the Survenant, who rejects permanent attachments. As a result, Joinville becomes reluctant to set a date for their marriage, and Rose considers this hesitation a cruel rejection.[16] Feeling abused and unloved, she eventually suffers a sort of nervous breakdown, a condition that worsens to the point that she is unable to speak.[17] Her pitiful state serves to convey a powerful message about the total dependency of women in rural Quebec, women whose only real fulfillment was to be found in marriage. Accordingly, as Rose senses that she is no longer able to attract her fiancé, her entire being starts to disintegrate in a number of moving scenes. Her tormented condition accentuates, of course, yet another aspect of female subjugation as it emerges in Le Survenant. Like most of the portrayals of women in the series, this one frequently mirrors the dominant ideology of the 1950s, when the ideal woman in Quebec was a prolific mother whose principal contribution to society was her offspring.

Interestingly, however, Guèvremont does on a few occasions let her female characters rebel openly against male oppression. One of these moments occurs when, as previously noted, Bedette Salvail announces that she intends to leave home in order to work in the restaurant in Sorel,[18] a decision that provokes a strong negative reaction from the two characters who represent the local "establishment": Pierre-Côme Provençal, the mayor of the village, and Father Lebrun, the parish priest. Provençal goes so far as to ask Bedette's mother whether her daughter is leaving "obligée,"[19] suggesting that Bedette might be pregnant. Madame Salvail demands and receives an apology, but the mayor's speculation appears to be a typical response to a situation where an adolescent suddenly and inexplicably leaves the family nest. Bedette's independent behavior is thus depicted as so unusual that it becomes incomprehensible to her family and friends.

For his part, Father Lebrun also tries to intervene, paradoxically by asking the Survenant to convince Bedette to return to her family. Explaining his own motives to Didace Beauchemin, the Survenant says that if he asks Bedette to come back, "c'est uniquement pour faire plaisir à monsieur le curé qui espère toujours voir la brebis égarée revenir au Chenail du Moine."[20] The analogy between the biblical lost sheep and a woman who works outside the home provides a striking illustration of the value system defined by the Church and promoted by the clergy.

In spite of intense social pressures, however, Bedette manages to defend herself and affirm her own rights, as she effectively opposes the traditional values that the community tries to impose on her. After returning briefly to the Chenal du Moine, Bedette leaves again when "the Greek" (as the restaurant owner is called) pleads with her to resume work in Sorel. In a revealing monologue, she explains her motivation for accepting the Greek's offer:

Quand on pense que le Grec s'est rendu icite pour m'apprendre qu'il allait augmenter mes gages. Je veux p'us rester au Chenail du Moine. J'veux p'us. Pas de pianola ... pas de téléphone ... rien. Il passe un chat sur la grand'route à tous les deux jours. J'veux p'us y rester.[21]

Later, during a conversation with Amable Beauchemin, Bedette makes an even stronger declaration of self-affirmation:

BED: Demandez-vous pas après c'temps-cite pourquoi c'est faire que je m'en vas travailler à Sorel. Puis, que j'en voye don un chercher à me retenir.

AM: Compte pas sur moi pour te retenir, Bedette.

BED: Ni sur toi, ni sur personne. Au moins, à Sorel, y a du plaisir à y avoir. Icitte, c'est ennuyant comme la mort. Bye, le Chenail du Moine.[22]

It is apparent that Bedette's statements implicitly defend the rights of women and that her assertiveness reveals a feminist tendency, however rudimentary, that is in opposition to the masculine orthodoxy of the period.

Bedette's actions and declarations also serve to bring out the basic clash between the values associated with traditional societies and those associated with industrialized nations. Rejecting the peaceful, rural life of the Chenal du Moine, Bedette opts for modernity, symbolized by the player piano and the telephone in the Sorel restaurant. In this sense, the adolescent persona created by Guèvremont appears to embody some of the traits that characterized Quebec society as it passed through a transitional phase in the 1950s. There are, for example, several scenes where the interlocutors recognize that Bedette's departure is linked to the social evolution that is beginning to alter life in Quebec. In one such dialogue, between the local doctor and the Survenant, the latter defends Bedette:

DOC: Quel dommage que cette jeune fille ait quitté le Chenal du Moine! Pour servir dans
   un restaurant.

SUR: Le monde change, docteur. (STOP) Faut-il s'en plaindre?[23]

In another episode, Mayor Provençal also comments on the changes in the village:

[C]'est un nouveau règne qui commence! Ça commence par UNE automobile que Paquet-
Paul Hus s'est acheté. Ça commence par une fille du Chenail, comme Bedette, qui est
bien prime pour aller travailler à Sorel.[24]

On the ideological level, it is reasonable to link the arrival of the automobile to
the departure of Bedette, for the two events both contribute to the disintegration
of homogeneity in the village, especially to the extent that they both demonstrate
the importance of outside economic influences, one from the United States, the
other from Sorel. Although this kind of economic pressure is indirect, it nonetheless tends to erode traditional values, as illustrated in the radio drama by
Bedette's personal rebellion against the local establishment.

   Similarly, Catherine Provençal, the mayor's daughter, rebels against the injustices that prevail in her male-dominated family.[25] Her position is especially
difficult since she constantly faces the demands of three remarkably insensitive
males: her father and her two brothers, Odilon and Joinville. At one point,
Catherine expresses her frustration as she protests against the treatment she
habitually receives:

Oui, moi qu'avant longtemps tout l'monde appelera la vieille fille d'la maison. Moi
toujours icite, comme une veilleuse, à tenir le manger chaud *pour les garçons* ... moi
à éravauder le butin *pour les garçons.* . . .[26]

Catherine's response contains at least two latent messages, one of which conveys
her fear of being labeled an "old maid" by her neighbors; this concern is, of
course, related to the social value system already discussed in connection with
Bedette, Rose, and other female characters. The angry protest by Catherine also
communicates her outrage at the unjust family hierarchy that demeans female
members by defining them as servants.

   Catherine's opposition to her father's domination is all the more interesting
if one considers his political function in the community; thus, to the degree that
the mayor is viewed as a symbol of the established order, his daughter's resistance
acquires a broader social significance. In any case, the tentative revolt of Catherine, like the defiance of Bedette, seems to represent an incipient feminism that
runs counter to the traditional ideology favored by Duplessis and the elite in the
1950s.

   With the exception of Angélina Desmarais, who can in fact be described as
a martyr, the women in Guèvremont's radio adaptation offer at least token

resistance when they are confronted by the dominant male hierarchy in their family or in the parish. Usually their opposition is minimal and their protests are in vain, but the very fact that female characters resist at all appears relevant during the period in question. Indeed, Guèvremont's decision to portray women as even mildly self-assertive indicates her unwillingness to perpetuate blindly the myth of the ideal Quebec woman, maternal and all-forgiving, like Maria Chapdelaine's mother and similar figures who appear in the traditional *romans de la terre*. Rejecting the idealized characterizations that typified earlier works of fiction, Guèvremont chooses to create figures (both female and male) who reflect more realistically life in rural Quebec. Accordingly, her women are depicted as dependent characters subjugated by insensitive men, a situation that derives at least in part from social realities; at the same time, however, these women often rebel, if only tentatively, against the system. It seems reasonable to suggest that their mini-revolts are also more realistic to the extent that they communicate women's reactions more accurately and honestly than did the incredible patience displayed by saintly characters like Donalda Poudrier or Madame Chapdelaine, both created, incidentally, by male authors.[27] In fact, when compared to previous fictional models, Guèvremont's female personages appear at least moderately subversive, as they oppose certain traditional perceptions and practices.

Bedette Salvail is, of course, the most remarkable example of feminine assertiveness, but it is important to note that she is supported in her efforts by the Survenant himself. It is he who defends Bedette's right to work in Sorel and who informs the local doctor that social values are changing, implying as well that the changes are for the better. It is also the Survenant who suggests sarcastically that Mayor Provençal might consider treating the women of the parish with some degree of politeness and respect. These views expressed by the hero are far from typical and certainly do not conform to the beliefs endorsed by the traditional elite. The stand taken by the Survenant, however, is entirely consistent with his own convictions, which are often in opposition to those of his sedentary neighbors in the Chenal du Moine.

Indeed, as some critics of Guèvremont's novel have observed, the Survenant is himself a subversive character who frequently rejects the nineteenth-century value system perpetuated by elitist leaders, both intellectual and political. Most significant, perhaps, is the total rejection by the Survenant of the small farmer's fundamental belief in the importance of the land itself, a belief that also constituted an essential element in the survival ideology which evolved after the abortive rebellions of 1837–1838. According to the popular view, a man who owned no land possessed nothing, but when Didace Beauchemin tries to convince the Survenant of this point, the hero challenges his friend: "Non, j'ai rien, c'est vrai. Mais vous vous trompez quand vous dites que vous avez de la terre qui vous appartient. C'est vous autres qui appartenez à la terre."[28] As his statement indicates, the Survenant believes that the local *habitant* is held in bondage by

his farmland, which because of its constant need for attention becomes a possession that ultimately possesses its owner. For this reason, the hero refuses all
attachments to the land, in spite of pleas by Didace to ''put his roots down.''

From an ideological perspective, this rejection of such a cherished belief is
certainly subversive, but no more so than the Survenant's refusal to accept another
form of attachment that is equally prized: attachment to the family unit. As the
preceding analysis of women's roles has revealed, the dominant ideology implied
that it is only within the context of the family that happiness can be achieved.
This conviction is not shared by the Survenant, however, who refuses all family
ties; indeed, the very fact that the hero has no name further emphasizes his
rootlessness. He arrives on foot from *la route* and will presumably return to it
one day. Moreover, throughout the series, he is associated with the port in Sorel
and with the river itself, associations that suggest the movement of water as
opposed to the immobility of the farmland bordering the channel.

Although the Survenant is sometimes tempted, if only briefly, to settle down,
he can never quite bring himself to propose marriage to Angélina Desmarais,
who loves him and for whom he cares deeply. Such a family tie would make
him more nearly normal in the eyes of the community and would, at the same
time, give him access to Angélina's land. Their union would thus create a double
attachment for the hero, both to a local family and to the land itself. But the
marriage proposal is never formulated because the Survenant values his personal
freedom above the kind of security that is afforded by marriage and the ownership
of property. Like the early explorers and *coureurs de bois* who ranged through
New France, the Survenant finds little appeal in the sedentary, agricultural way
of life that characterizes the Chenal du Moine.

His dissident attitude separates him from his friend and benefactor, Didace
Beauchemin, as well as from other personages in the parish who are convinced
that ultimate happiness can be attained only in a family group firmly rooted in
its own soil. By consciously and deliberately refusing such ties, the Survenant
becomes a symbol of rebellion, a figure who implicitly provides an alternative
to the traditional lifestyle advocated by those in power. In this light, the Survenant
can be seen as a truly subversive character, for he openly confronts an ideological
belief that was seldom subject to direct criticism during the Duplessis years. It
is also important to note that the opinions of the Survenant are all the more
significant because he is, after all, the protagonist and the only genuinely heroic
character in the drama. Since much of the action centers on him, his dissidence
becomes a recurring theme, a kind of leitmotiv that serves to emphasize the
opposition between the hero and the traditionalists who predominate in the village.

Considered in this perspective, the Survenant's influence upon these rural
women and his defense of their rights are entirely compatible with his pattern
of behavior throughout the radio adaptation, in which his non-conformism serves
to counterbalance the blind compliance and the smugness of the other male
characters. Indeed, it is not unreasonable to suggest that the Survenant constitutes
an ideological menace as he continues to question the values which are so highly

prized by the community in general. In this sense, the disaffection of the hero seems to foreshadow the breakdown of old values, which began to crumble toward the end of the Duplessis era.

Symbolically, the Survenant's rebellious nature can be interpreted as an anti-thetical element in the social dialectic, as Quebec began to enter a period of transition that would accelerate rapidly during the following decade. In effect, society was already changing in the mid-fifties, and the resultant instability led many to cling to older values associated with the rural past, while others preferred to seek newer solutions. In this ideological conflict, characters like the Survenant and Bedette Salvail seem to embody the fresh values that distinguished the modern approach. Similarly, the radio adaptation of *Le Survenant*, analyzed as a dramatic work, reflects the gradual disintegration of the nineteenth-century ideology of survival. Moreover, the legendary hero of the serial becomes a fictional expression of the instability that occurred as Quebec edged slowly and sometimes painfully toward the Quiet Revolution.

NOTES

1. See Pierre Pagé's analysis of this issue in *Répertoire des oeuvres de la littérature radiophonique québécoise 1930-1970* (Montréal: Fides, 1975), pp. 39-41.

2. Pagé, p. 45.

3. Pagé, p. 39.

4. Pagé, p. 329.

5. Pagé, p. 329.

6. Alphonsine Beauchemin and Bernadette Salvail, as they were called in the original novel, are always referred to as ''Phonsine'' and ''Bedette'' in the radio adaptation.

7. See the explanation of Jean-Marie Piemme, *La Propagande inavouée*, Collection 10/18 (Paris: Union Générale d'Editions, 1975), p. 284.

8. See Denis Monière, *Le Développement des idéologies au Québec des origines à nos jours* (Montréal: Editions Québec-Amérique, 1977), p. 298.

9. This sort of negative reaction to public officials may also be also viewed as part of a dramatic convention established by Claude-Henri Grignon (Guèvremont's cousin) in his long-running serial, ''Les Belles Histoires des pays d'en haut,'' an adaptation of *Un Homme et son péché*.

10. *Le Survenant* (radiophonique), writ. Germaine Guèvremont, episode No. 379, 29 Dec. 1964 (hereafter cited as SR).

I tell you the women-folk make a lot of racket for us. When it's not one of 'em ... it's the other.

The original script from the 1950s was apparently lost. The typewritten text of the 1960s rebroadcasts is presumably identical with the original. The ellipses in the script that are quoted in this study do not indicate textual omissions, but rather pauses for speakers. All quotations are cited from the microfilm produced by Pierre Pagé and Renée Legris for the ''Archives de la littérature radiophonique,'' now held at the Bibliothèque Nationale du Québec in Montreal.

11. Guèvremont, SR, No. 447, 5 April 1965.

SUR: But ... the women-folk ... when do they eat?

P-C: After the men, naturally!

SUR: (SURVENANT'S LAUGH, WHICH P-C FAILS TO UNDERSTAND) And gallantry?

P-C: It's a party for the men. Not for the women-folk.

12. In today's society, the concept of gallantry could itself be considered condescending or paternalistic, but in the more traditional society of rural Quebec in the 1950s, *galanterie* would represent a relatively enlightened attitude.

13. Guèvremont, SR, No. 397, 25 Jan. 1965.

PH: That would give me a rest from the housework.

AM: What's housework? It's nothing. Nothing at all.

PH: Nothing for you, no. If there's one job that's thankless, it's housework. It's *always* there ... always ... always the same.

AM: I didn't marry a woman so she could go work elsewhere. I married you, Phonsine, so you'd stay at home.

14. Guèvremont, SR, No. 67, 26 Dec. 1962.

DID: What are you doing, Marie-Amanda? You seated her in your mother's place?

M-A: Yes, father, you always taught me that when a leaf falls from the tree another leaf replaces it. Stay there, Mathilde.

15. This incident, like many others in the radio adaptation, did not occur in the novel. In part, the additions are necessitated by the very structure of the radio serial, which was broadcast five days a week and which required new material and many digressions in order to keep the listening audience involved. The new content may also reflect changing social attitudes in the 1950s.

16. Not in the novel; see note 15.

17. Guèvremont, SR, No. 458, 21 April 1965.

18. Not in the novel; see note 15.

19. Guèvremont, SR, No. 170, 22 May 1963.

20. Guèvremont, SR, No. 248, 16 Jan. 1964.

It's only to please Father [Lebrun] who hopes to see the lost sheep come back to the Chenal du Moine.

21. Guèvremont, SR, No. 260, 3 Feb. 1964.

To think that the Greek came here himself to let me know he was going to raise my wages. I don't want to stay in the Chenal du Moine no more. No more. No player-piano... no telephone ... nothing. Every other day a cat might go by on the main road. I don't want to stay here no more.

22. Guèvremont, SR, No. 393, 19 Jan. 1965.

BED: After this don't ask why it is that I'm going to work in Sorel. And don't let me see anyone try to keep me here.

AM: Don't count on me to keep you here, Bedette.

BED: Not on you nor anyone else. At least in Sorel there's fun to be had. Here it's deadly boring. Bye, Chenal du Moine.

23. Guèvremont, SR, No. 226, 12 Dec. 1963.

DOC: What a pity that this girl left the Chenal du Moine! To wait on tables in a restaurant.

SUR: The world is changing, doctor. (STOP) Should we complain about it?

24. Guèvremont, SR, No. 304, 6 April 1964.

It's a new era that's beginning! It starts with ONE automobile that Paquet-Paul Hus bought himself. It starts with one girl from the Chenal, like Bedette, who's eager to go work in Sorel.

25. Not in the novel; see note 15.

26. Guèvremont, SR, No. 61, 17 Dec. 1962.

Yes, before long I'm the one everybody will call the old maid of the house. I'm always here, like a pilot light, to keep the food warm *for the boys* ... or I'm mending clothes *for the boys*....

27. Donalda, victimized wife of Séraphin Poudrier in Claude-Henri Grignon's novel, *Un Homme et son péché*, first published in 1933; Madame Chapdelaine, long-suffering mother of Maria in Louis Hémon's novel, *Maria Chapdelaine*, originally published in 1914.

28. Guèvremont, SR, No. 317, 23 April 1964.

No, I have nothing, it's true. But you're mistaken when you say that you have land that belongs to you. It's you people who belong to the land.

4

The Pursuit of the Real in Rina Lasnier's "Présence de l'absence"

James P. Gilroy ———————————————————

In the "Avant-dire" written by Rina Lasnier for the Fides edition of her collected poems, the poet defines her mission as an effort to come into contact with and approximate in words ultimate reality. She speaks of "la lointaine approximation de la Présence," that is to say, of the substance or being which gives life and meaning to all that exists.[1] Like the French Symbolists before her, Lasnier believes that there is in the universe an underlying spirituality which calls out to us and which makes itself manifest in miraculous moments of revelation when the opaqueness of people and objects gives way before epiphanous transparency.[2] The poems of "Présence de l'absence," representative in this regard of their author's constant poetic searchings, trace her pursuit of true being as it reveals itself in the beauty of nature and the ineffable communion of human love.

Paradoxically, the poet must somehow be detached from the world in order to possess it in its fullness. The essential presence at the heart of visible reality cannot be attained without a preliminary absence from the external appearances which both point to and yet mask the invisible essence. One discerns in this philosophy an echo of the Mallarméan ideal of virtuality according to which complete fulfillment can only be attained in non-realization. This ideal governs Lasnier's approach to life, love, and nature. It is clear, for example, that for her the person who truly lives is the one who is ever mindful of the eventual coming of death. Moreover, though in a slightly different context, she suggests at the end of her "Avant-dire" that the most sublime love derives its perfection from an absence of consummation on the physical level and is one which remains an entirely spiritual exchange.[3] When she goes from the moral realm to the aesthetic, the poet reveals a comparable viewpoint in her belief that essential reality cannot be wholly captured in words, can in fact be only suggested. In poetry as in love, silence is more expressive than language.[4]

What is unique to Lasnier's vision is the way she combines her search for plenitude through detachment from the concrete with a highly sensuous appreciation of the physical embodiments of the real. Love is no less delightful or at some moments agonizing for being sublimated. External nature is the richest source of the metaphors employed by the poet to make one aware of the metaphysical forces which transcend it. The truth of which she is in pursuit is of universal import, but her poetic expression of it is rooted in her life-experience as a woman of Quebec. She draws inspiration from her total being-in-the-world: "L'inspiration . . . c'est la chair, le sang, l'âme du poète portés à la rencontre de la beauté."[5] The landscape of her country becomes in her poems the objective correlative of her inner universe.

"Présence de l'absence" as a whole is divided into three parts, the middle segment constituting a kind of interlude with its eight "Chansons" inspired from traditional songs of Quebec. The opening title poem sounds the keynote to and brings into the clearest focus the ideological and metaphorical themes that will be elaborated in the briefer poems which follow. Like Paul Claudel, Lasnier takes her metaphors from the elemental forces of nature, and in the title poem, as in the entire volume, water, fire, light, and the heavens are the privileged incarnations of being in the visible world. This poem, as is often the case with Lasnier, is addressed to the beloved. The souls of the latter and of the female poetic voice strive toward a unity achieved by means of an osmotic interpenetration of their spirits. Moreover, there is not only a mutual openness between the two persons but also one between them and nature. Their love is a participation in the perpetual life-giving forces of the universe, a constant giving birth to the one by the other: "Tu nais sans cesse de moi comme les mille bras des vagues courant sur la mer toujours étrangère."[6]

It becomes increasingly apparent in the course of the poem, however, that their love goes beyond the physical world. It is a sentiment which invades the heavens and demonstrates its power even in the realm of the dead. It becomes a source of life for the whole universe: "C'est moi qui fais lever ce bleu de ton regard et tu couvres les plaies du monde."[7]

This love is able to attain such cosmic dimensions only because of a mutual elusiveness on the part of the lovers. It is because they do not totally possess each other in this world that they can enjoy such a fullness of self-giving in the transcendent: "C'est moi l'amour sans la longue, la triste paix possessive...."[8] Their absence from each other empowers their love to become a source of mystical vision, bringing them into contact with the unknown: "De ma fuite sont tes ailes, de ma fuite la puissance de ton planement."[9] Moreover, they are best able to express the depths of their sentiments for each other by not saying anything. Silence makes possible a more meaningful communication. They are able to inspire each other through a mutual distance at the center of their relationship. As the poet states, she is, figuratively, the yeast of his bread, he the magnetic force from which she does not deviate. Finally, their souls are able to take flight since they are not weighted down by physical presence. This spiritual lightness allows them to be consumed by a love which partakes of the fire of divine love: "Je suis l'embrasement amoureux de l'absence sans la poix de la glutineuse présence."[10] "Poix" here is, of course, homonymous with "poids."

It is in this opening poem of the *recueil* that the transparency of the poet's vision triumphs most forcefully over the opaqueness of external phenomena, and her confident assertion of her identity as woman and poet proves stronger than the discouraging doubts, sorrows, and failures of communication that will at later moments assail her. Throughout the remainder of the collection, poems expressive of these negative sentiments alternate with others in which the initial revelation emerges with greater or lesser fullness. Some of the shorter poems in the collection are, in fact, joined together in a relation of bipolarity, like panels of a diptych. For example, the lack of communication and openness tormenting the poet in "Perdu en montagne . . ." is remedied by the rediscovery of vision in ". . . Retrouvé par les eaux." On the other hand, the image of pristine purity evoked in "Lune blanche et . . ." is shattered by the awareness of evil unleashed upon the world in ". . . Lune rousse."[11]

A number of poems represent moments of grace when the presence of the transcendent in the immanent is revealed without any obstacles, when the poet recognizes the hidden significance in some humble object or in a momentary glance exchanged with the beloved. "Plénitude," for example, occurring near the beginning of the volume, presents a picture of universal serenity and abundance reminiscent of Victor Hugo's "Booz endormi." The poet captures an instant when humanity is at peace with God, the world, and itself. The opening line bathes the entire scene in light, while the final line evokes the flight of birds, a recurring symbol throughout "Présence de l'absence" for reaching up to heaven through love.[12] This passing mention of the birds' movement, like the laughter alluded to in the fifth line, serves only to point up the prevailing silence and motionlessness. Within the latter, however, pulsate the promise of life ("La femme sait que son sein est un boisseau") and its fruition ("Et la sève se repose sur ses cendres").[13]

The rustic setting and idyllic atmosphere of "Plénitude" recall the works of earlier poets of Quebec like Nérée Beauchemin and Blanche Lamontagne-Beauregard.[14] The title of the poem and its implicit message indicate, however, a transcendence of merely regionalist concerns. Though the setting may indeed be rural Quebec, it has in Lasnier's poem, as we have seen, a cosmic significance.

In "La Mouette," the poem which precedes "Plénitude," there is a similar celebration of vibrant immobility. Here supreme communion is achieved through an apparent absence of participation. Contrary to Charles Baudelaire's albatross or Stéphane Mallarmé's swan, the gull's immobilization has in Lasnier's poem a positive value and represents a stance freely and even joyfully assumed by this emblem of the female poet. The bird refuses to fly, refuses to see (the words "Pour ne plus voir . . ." being repeated with obsessive intensity)[15] on one plane of activity, the physical, so that its spirit may soar as did those of the couple in the title poem, so that it may possess mystically the beings to which it closes its eyes. One is reminded of a childhood reminiscence in the author's *Miroirs*, a collection of texts in prose published in 1960. In one passage, little Messadée climbs an old willow tree on her family's farm and closes her eyes so that she can imaginatively take in the beauty of the setting in all its fullness.[16]

Instead of merely observing the beauty and life surrounding it, the gull will transmute their essence into itself. In the end, the bird becomes the living expression of the water and light that give life to the scene. In the gull, nature becomes aware of itself. Like the poet, the bird is a distiller of quintessences. Moreover, like a poem, it becomes a vessel of communication simply by sitting in its resplendently expressive isolation.

In "Le Coteau," the union of the female poetic voice and the beloved attains an apogee of intensity that was initiated in the title poem. As in the latter, their love is here a communion with the totality of natural phenomena in addition to being an exchange between two persons. The man's silent, loving gaze becomes for her the very center of the universe, the epitome of celestial light and the fire of love. This association of love's exultation with the life of nature carries over into the following two poems, paired here again in diptych fashion. In "Le Pommier d'Asie" and "Le Catalpa" are contrasted the ineffably delicate inter-relationship of the engaged couple and the more intense mutual possession of husband and wife.[17]

These privileged moments of vision do not alter the fact that in some poems there is discernible a realization of the obstacles which the world and individuals place in the path of revelation and communication. In "Angoisse," for example, death seems to be the ultimate refuge for suffering humanity, a haven of absence from life and the only meaningful reality. In "Mensonge" the emptiness of the verbal exchange of the lovers seems to obscure the clarity of their mutual glance into each other's soul. Human time and eternity are opposed in "Le Temps."[18] It is made clear that the divine order is different in kind from the worldly order of things and that human life would be unbearable without the Spirit's infusion of the infinite into the finite.

The poet's frustration before those forces which impede vision reaches its culmination in the final poem of the first part, "Jungle de feuilles." Here the very life of the forest is stifled by the overabundance of its material growth. This overwhelming presence of the physical renders impossible any openness to the transcendent, any soaring of the spirit ("Labyrinthe des léthargies sans fuite de rêve...''). The forest is completely closed in upon itself in solipsistic isolation and impenetrable to the life-giving forces of the universe. Like people who are totally immersed in materialistic preoccupations, it is unable to participate in nature's symphony. Its dank humidity makes it unable to catch fire with the spark of divine love which would make it live and give witness. A victim of its own tepidity, the forest is in the biblical sense neither hot nor cold, but empty and unresponsive ("jungle tiède où manque la gloire amoureuse d'un corps incendié").[19]

It is something of a paradox that the word "Absence," which begins this poem, is given a pejorative connotation. Not the spiritually vital detachment from the mundane that it signifies in other poems, absence in "Jungle de feuilles" reassumes its usual negative meaning and designates an unappreciative turning away from life, light, and love, an attitude which is a complete contradiction of the poet's ideal. A similar redefinition of the idea of absence will take place in "Le Roi de jade," the collection's penultimate poem, where the onetime king's inhuman cruelty and refusal to love have cut him off from life's source and isolated him from his fellow beings. In the concluding passages of that same poem, however, the negative valorization of absence will be transformed into the positive absence which is art. The unexpected dénouement of "Le Roi de jade" is thus in keeping with the general inspiration of the whole collection, in which the positive significance of absence constantly triumphs over the negative. In the end, the royal figure carved on the poet's jade ring is given a new meaning as the sign making possible spiritual possession of the deceased beloved: "Car il m'aura choisie pour capture d'ombre / je l'aurai choisi pour roi-fantôme."[20]

As we have pointed out, a key element in Lasnier's poetic outlook is her discovery of the universal in the particular, of the transcendent in the immanent. While in the first and third sections of "Présence de l'absence," the peculiarly *québécois* aspects of her work consist mainly in her use of her nation's landscape and of her personal experience as metaphors for expressing her female poetic vision, the songs which constitute the central segment of the collection draw more directly upon national folkloric motifs. These songs, however, are as much the vehicle for communicating truths of universal scope as are the other poems. Her song sequence is, in fact, a microcosm of the themes haunting the entire *recueil*, namely, love, absence, suffering, good and evil, the unity of creation, and the presence of the divine in earthly life. Like Saint-Denys Garneau and Alain Grandbois, Lasnier has succeeded in transcending the old dichotomy of regionalist and cosmopolitan subjects which had been characteristic of earlier Quebec poetry. Her proud proclamation of Quebec as "MA TERRE" is completely sincere, but her use of national raw materials for her works does not detract from the relevance of her poetic quest for all peoples. Quebec is for her "le haut-lieu de l'incarnation" because it is the place where she has pursued this quest, where she has experienced intimations of the divine.[21] The essential realities which she finds incarnated in the life of her nation, however, go beyond national frontiers.

This theme of incarnation, of the embodiment of divine life in people and nature, is most explicitly announced in the hymns celebrating Christ's birth and His triumphal entry into Jerusalem ("Le Noël des animaux," "Les Palmes," "L'Anesse et l'ânon des rameaux"), for the mystery of the Incarnation of the Word of God in the person of Jesus is the clearest indication that earthly beings embody realities which transcend the earthly.[22] As we have seen, however, love between man and woman is also for Lasnier a manifestation of the divine in the human. This idea is at the heart of "Claire fontaine" and "Il pleut . . . ," where the images of fire and water are again used as symbols of eternal life. The fountain of absence in the first poem is the fountain of memory enabling the woman to contemplate the image of the now absent beloved. She can lose herself in the memory of him, possess him more fully because of his absence in the concrete: "Fontaine sans fond de la longue souvenance, / Mon coeur mire en larmes le rire de son visage, / Naïve amante perdue au fond de son image."[23] In the second poem, her tears of sorrow give way before the power of love as surely as the rainy landscape will be transformed by the sun's emerging rays. The lambs, replete with biblical overtones like the "buisson" of the fourth line, will be warmed by the sun and, figuratively, fired by that power of universal love of which the poet sings.[24]

The dialectic of openness to the transcendent and of the inner and outer obstacles to vision continues in the collection's third and final part. Lasnier again emphasizes the value of absence from superficial reality as the necessary method for coming into contact with its underlying essence. The themes of silence, death, and blindness are emblematic of this ideal of absence and are therefore accorded a positive valorization in this poetic universe. Some of the author's most moving poems about love and nature appear in this concluding segment of "Présence de l'absence." Moreover, several of them are in a relation of direct contrast with certain earlier poems and provide an affirmative response to the negative state of affairs which on occasion intrudes upon the atmosphere of confidence prevailing in the first part. "L'Arbre en feu," for example, is just such an answer to the already mentioned "Jungle de feuilles." The unloving opaqueness of the forest in "Jungle" is in marked contrast with the all-consuming love which enflames the tree in "L'Arbre." The tree of the later poem has unreservedly opened itself to divine love. In yet another contrasting pair, the serene assumption of human sorrows made possible by identifying them with those of Mary ("Noël de la mère vieille") represents a sublimation of the more desperate anguish voiced in the earlier "Angoisse."[25]

There is to be found, as well, in a number of the later poems the sense of all-embracing peace, harmony, and love which had already set the initial tone for the collection. Such is the case in "Présence de l'eau vierge," where water and light, images of transparent being permeating the entire volume, come together in a landscape expressive of cosmic plenitude. Poems like "C'est toi," "Le Lac," "Les Cheveux," and "Mirement" (the last title alone of which suggests limpidity and openness to another dimension of perception) continue the theme, announced in the title poem and in "Le Coteau," of the couple's communion with nature through love. Once more, the man and woman merge their love with nature's elements and make of this union the point of departure for a leap of the heart into the unknown.[26]

The more intimate union of the female poetic voice and her beloved by means of an absence from each other and the world is again a theme in "Les Voix" and "Le Reflet." In the former, as in "Claire fontaine," communication with the loved person is heightened by the presence in absence of memory. It is, moreover, a communication made more meaningful for being a silent one, an idea expressed in Lasnier's Mallarméan image of "ces purs oiseaux du silence.''[27] It is thereby pure of the imperfections and inadequacies of words, which can at best merely suggest the real and often render relationships more obscure than clear, as in "Mensonge" of the first part of the collection. In "Le Reflet," where the reconciliation following a lovers' quarrel becomes the source of a rich network of metaphors (sea, snow, light, eyes, birds) expressive of the beyond and of our vision of it, the beloved's eyes become blind to the surface beauties of the landscape in order to contemplate the true light of the spiritual realm: "Le bleu vient de plus haut que la lumière, / Il voit plus loin que l'écume de la mer.''[28]

A recurring motif in these final moments of the poet's meditation is that of death as the ultimate fulfillment, as the source of the most complete union with the transcendent. Such a valorization of death anticipates the idea which inspired Lasnier's later collection "Les Gisants" (1963).[29] One is again reminded of Mallarmé's celebration of the attainment in death of one's essential reality, although Lasnier's thought has none of her male predecessor's nihilism. Hers is the Christian's confidence in the loving divinity awaiting the soul in the hereafter. There is nonetheless a further reminiscence of Mallarmé in her description of an ancient elm tree as a Buddha seated in the nirvana of the sky ("L'Orme vieux"). The elm tree absents itself from the world of superficial reality, makes an introspective withdrawal into its own inner serenity. The physical world surrounding it is but a shadow of the unseen universal oneness in which the elm seeks to lose its individual being. It makes a leap into deathlike nothingness in order to arrive at true ontological wholeness.[30]

"L'Orme vieux," taking as it does a phenomenon of nature as an emblem of the poet in a moment of supreme tranquillity of spirit, recalls the earlier "La Mouette." The peace and ecstatic absence from concrete life which Lasnier associates with death are here even more vividly captured through symbolic implication than by the more literal expression of the same sentiments in "Mort et cendre." As in "La Mouette" and "Plénitude," the atmosphere surrounding the old tree is one of quiet immobility and dreamy contemplation. Here again, the author has taken a humble object from the *québécois* countryside and has transmuted it into a symbol of universal experience.[31]

Death cannot destroy the values of the spirit-like love and art. The theme of art's triumph over the forces that oppose it is manifested with increasing intensity as the collection moves to its close. The world and the person attain the supreme degree of absence in the word. Yet the same words which announce the absence of that to which they refer are the vehicles employed by the poet to communicate a fleeting awareness of the absolute reality which cannot be totally possessed in life or totally captured in artistic form. The dimension of true being is as elusive as the dance of the fish described in "Présence de l'eau vierge" as "une parole intérieure.''[32] The poet's triumph can therefore be at best a partial one, her vision a series of but momentary flashes of revelation.

Moreover, the poet's effort to suggest the ineffable presence of transcendent being seems, on one level, to be an entirely useless and gratuitous action, as she points out in "Inutilité." Like the seagull, however, the source of her greatness lies precisely, on another level, in her apparent inactivity. She absents herself from the pragmatic world of daily business in order to devote her attention instead to the potentially cosmic implications of what seem to be the most trivial happenings in nature and human life. Her "regard oisif," despite the modesty of the adjective, will become a source of life and revelation in her world.[33]

The poem's three concluding lines continue to suggest the idea of emptiness and sterility, and the childless poet wonders whether she herself is not "le vase retourné sur le vide."[34] Once more, however, as in the whole collection, fullness is found in an apparent emptiness, necessity in the gratuitous, presence in absence.[35] Though the poet's existence seems a void and her inspiration something vague and futile, the destiny of all creatures is dependent upon them. Her contribution, as a woman writer, consists in her eternal watchfulness; she renounces a superficial participation in human affairs in order to communicate, to give birth, on a higher plane through her poetry. She opens her being to and makes transparent in her works every manifestation of the ubiquitous but invisible divinity which permeates all beings. As she assures us in another poem: "Mais la terre tourne sur l'axe du poème, / Le vent seul emporte le mot de passe, / L'oiseleur tourne dans l'ubiquité de l'amour."[36]

NOTES

1. Rina Lasnier, *Poèmes*, 2 vols. (Montréal: Fides, 1972), I, 13.

The remote approximation of Presence.

2. Roger Duhamel wrote of Lasnier's poetry that she has the gift of second-sight and is able to perceive and express for our enchantment the dazzling light hidden in ordinary things. *La Patrie*, 29 janvier 1961, as quoted in Jean Marcel, *Rina Lasnier* (Montréal and Paris: Fides, 1964), p. 93.

3. Lasnier, pp. 16-18.

4. As Eva Kushner puts it: "In love, as in poetry, absence is a more real presence." Eva Kushner, *Rina Lasnier* (Paris: Seghers, 1969), p. 19.

5. Rina Lasnier, "Discours de présentation de Simone Routier à l'Académie canadienne-française," 1947, as quoted in Marcel, p. 24.

Inspiration ... is the flesh and blood and the soul of the poet brought to the encounter with beauty.

6. Lasnier, "Présence de l'absence," *Poèmes*, I, 259.

You are ceaselessly born of me like the thousand arms of the waves flowing upon the ever foreign sea.

7. Lasnier, "Présence de l'absence," *Poèmes*, I, 260.

It is I who uplift that blue of your gaze and you dress the wounds of the world.

8. Lasnier, "Présence de l'absence," *Poèmes*, I, 259.

I am love without long, sad possessive peace....

9. Lasnier, "Présence de l'absence," *Poèmes*, I, 260.

From my flight are your wings, from my flight the power of your soaring.

10. Lasnier, "Présence de l'absence," *Poèmes*, I, 260.

I am the loving conflagration of absence without the glutinous pitch of presence.

11. Lasnier, "Perdu en montagne . . .," ". . . Retrouvé par les eaux," "Lune blanche et . . .," ". . . Lune rousse," *Poèmes*, I, 265, 291.

12. Birds as a symbol of the flight of the spirit also appear in "Coeur-volant," "Mirement," and "L'Oiseau mort." See Lasnier, *Poèmes*, I, 286, 297, 301.

13. Lasnier, "Plénitude," *Poèmes*, I, 263.

The woman knows that her breast is a bushel-basket.

And the sap rests on its ashes.

14. Nérée Beauchemin (1850-1931), best known for his poetic collection, *Patrie intime* (1928), and Blanche Lamontagne-Beauregard (1889-1958), the author of several collections, including *Ma Gaspésie* (1928), wrote idyllic poems in the *terroir*, or regionalist, tradition about life in rural Quebec.

15. Lasnier, "La Mouette," *Poèmes*, I, 262.

So as to see no longer.

16. See Rina Lasnier, *Miroirs* (Montréal: Les Editions de l'Atelier, 1960), pp. 7-11, as reprinted in Marcel, pp. 28-32.

17. Lasnier, "Le Coteau," "Le Pommier d'Asie," "Le Catalpa," *Poèmes*, I, 266-68.

18. Lasnier, "Angoisse," "Mensonge," "Le Temps," *Poèmes*, I, 270-71, 264, 272.

19. Lasnier, "Jungle de feuilles," *Poèmes*, I, 273-74.

A labyrinth of lethargies without the flight of dream.

A tepid jungle lacking in the loving glory of a kindled body.

20. Lasnier, "Le Roi de jade," *Poèmes*, I, 310-13.

For he will have chosen me as the prize of shadow / I shall have chosen him as phantom-king.

21. Lasnier, "Avant-dire," *Poèmes*, I, 11-12.

The high place of incarnation.

22. Lasnier, "Le Noël des animaux," "Les Palmes," "L'Anesse et l'ânon des rameaux," *Poèmes*, I, 281-85.

23. Lasnier, "Claire fontaine," *Poèmes*, I, 278.

Bottomless fountain of long remembrance, / My heart gazes in tears at the laugh of his face, / Naive lover lost in the depths of his image.

24. Lasnier, "Il pleut . . .," *Poèmes*, I, 279.

25. Lasnier, "L'Arbre en feu," "Jungle de feuilles," "Noël de la mère vieille," "Angoisse," *Poèmes*, I, 288, 273-74, 305-07, 270-71.

26. Lasnier, "Présence de l'eau vierge," "C'est toi," "Le Lac," "Les Cheveux," "Mirement," *Poèmes*, I, 294, 287, 292, 308, 297.

27. Lasnier, "Les Voix," *Poèmes*, I, 289.

Those pure birds of silence.

28. Lasnier, "Le Reflet," *Poèmes*, I, 304.

The blue comes from higher up than the light, / He sees beyond the foam of the sea.

29. Reprinted in Lasnier, *Poèmes*, II, 121-213.

30. Lasnier, "L'Orme vieux," *Poèmes*, I, 300.

31. Lasnier, "L'Orme vieux," "Mort et cendre," "La Mouette," "Plénitude," *Poèmes*, I, 300, 298, 262-63.

32. Lasnier, "Présence de l'eau vierge," *Poèmes*, I, 294.

An interior word.

33. Lasnier, "Inutilité," *Poèmes*, I, 299.

Idle gaze.

34. Lasnier, "Inutilité," *Poèmes*, I, 299.

The vessel overturned upon nothingness.

35. In an earlier work on Rina Lasnier, Kushner studies at length "Inutilité" and its theme of the gratuitousness of beauty and artistic creation as the source of their value. Eva Kushner, *Rina Lasnier* (Montréal and Paris: Fides, 1964), pp. 35-36.

36. Lasnier, "Zerzontle," *Poèmes*, I, 309.

But the earth turns upon the axis of the poem, / The wind alone carries along the password, / The fowler turns about in the ubiquity of love.

5

Counter-Traditions: The Marginal Poetics of Anne Hébert

Susan L. Rosenstreich ⸻⸻⸻⸻⸻⸻

It is discomfiting to read the poetry of Anne Hébert. Though the reading of poetry is not guaranteed to be a reassuring experience, it is nonetheless difficult to set oneself the task of reading the poems of a *québécois* writer who dismantles the plausible myths making natural storms, man-made wars, loving procreation, and humiliating genocide understandable to us. Yet, estrangement from the kinds of experiences we have come to accept as common brings certain rewards. Hébert may destroy traditional notions of order, but, in exchange, her poetry expands the range of experience over which we are to impose a greater order.

The assertion that Hébert is concerned with reforming our vision contradicts common critical wisdom, which has weighed Hébert's commitment to the real world and found it inadequate. When *Le Tombeau des rois* was published in 1953, Roger Duhamel wrote that this second volume of Hébert's poetry employed a language of "arid peaks,"[1] exquisite, but remote. Sensitive to the same transcendent quality of language in the collection, André Rousseaux referred to Hébert's poetry as "music."[2]

The verbal distance between the poet and her readers has been interpreted by later critics as a withdrawal from the outside world into a private, defensive one. In his exhaustive study of the relationship between oneirism and Hébert's poetic themes, Guy Robert observed that the poet "being first and foremost a poet, her works cannot be dissociated from her most secret, most real personality."[3] This seclusion is seen as an escape from real problems in the analysis of Jean Ethier-Blais, who called Hébert's work "waiting literature . . . a literature which adheres to the reality of a people hesitant to define themselves as a nation."[4]

The assumption behind these assessments of Hébert's poetry—that literature has to do with reality only when it deals with contemporary situations—translates Hébert's use of prehistoric myths, events in the past, or traditions transplanted in Quebec from metropolitan France, into expressions of nostalgia, fear of reality, and a reluctance to face the future. Hébert is forced into a position much like the one in which Sartre placed Etienne Léro in his essay "Orphée noir," which serves as an introduction to Léopold Sédar Senghor's *Anthologie de la nouvelle poésie nègre et malgache de langue française*. Léro's abstract realism does little service to black culture, argues Sartre. Black culture exists only insofar as it rebels against white culture. Citing Aimé Césaire's impassioned poetry of Negritude as an example of this rebellion, Sartre observes: "What Césaire destroys is not all culture, but white culture; what he lays bare is not the desire for everything, but the revolutionary aspirations of the oppressed Black's specially concrete and determined form of humanity."[5] In Sartre's view, Negritude poetry is useful in that it is political, and can censor and determine the conditions of black culture.

Contrary to Sartre's theory that political power is the source of cultural strength, Michel Benamou's theory of ethnopoetics holds that cultural strength promotes political health. Ethnopoetics, as Benamou defines it, is an "attempt to abolish the divisive thinking about literature that casts it into the categories of central or marginal according to its power base."[6]

The contradiction between the two theories of culture is an important factor in the accurate reading of poets who, like Hébert, emerge from politically volatile cultures. Theories like Negritude and ethnopoetics force us to make a clear distinction between minority writers, who are participants in a political struggle between old and new powers, and marginal writers, who are engaged in a literary struggle between old and new perceptions. Benamou's definition of ethnopoetics favors marginalism precisely because it elevates the struggle for political power to the level of a debate over humanism, over changing perceptions of the human experience. The challenge for the marginal poet is not to prove the existence of differences, for which the evidence is all too ample, but to create resemblances. We can therefore expect marginal poets to transcend the limits of representational art, and to exploit the ability of language to transform our limited, quotidian view of the present into an expanded, extraordinary vision of the future.

Hébert's achievements in facilitating this transformation are not unlike those of Léon-Gontran Damas. One of the first Negritude poets, Damas proceeded in the precise direction Sartre contraindicates for Negritude poets. Damas thus provides an example of francophone marginalism from which to launch a discussion of Hébert's poetry.

In "Nuit blanche," Damas demonstrates how the marginal poet expands the reader's vision beyond political struggles in a culture. From the title's pun, at once a suggestion of a waking dream and a reference to the myth of Caucasian racial superiority, to the comic absurdity of the toothless Aryan at the end of the poem, Damas disarms the reader with his sense of humor and playfulness. Mocking the notion of racial superiority, the poet observes the blue Danube pass through a range of colors from pink to white, and finally, to the "Danube bleu blanc rouge vert rose / au choix," as he whirls in a dizzy nocturnal waltz with Gobineau, the French racist, and Hitler, Gobineau's disciple. Racial superiority is reduced to the senile ruminations of some "bon aryen / qui mâchonne sa vieillesse sur quelque banc de square."[7] Instead of arousing the reader to anger, the poet elicits compassion for that poor, misled "bon aryen." Bigotry, as Damas depicts it, is weakness and helplessness. Dividing groups into blacks and whites, Aryans and non-Aryans, right and wrong, is not a mark of political strength so much as it is a symptom of moral lassitude and blindness to reality which is not composed of convenient dualisms.

If Hébert's poetry lacks the humor and irony characteristic of Damas's work, her language imposes itself on us just as aggressively. True, the lyric tone of her first anthology, *Les Songes en équilibre*, seems to counter this statement. Published in 1942, this collection is remarkable for its tone of desolate lyricism and invites comparison between Hébert and Verlaine. Yet there is more to this early poetry than tone.

In "Eve," the poet alludes to Genesis, the theory of evolution, bucolic tradition, and modern technology, layering the poem with meanings addressing our reason as well as our senses. The poem opens on a note of reference to biblical mythology: "Commencement du monde."[8] Fragments from myths concerning the emergence of the planet, the first signs of life, and the origin of individual consciousness weave Darwin and Genesis into an exuberant textual background, against which we see dramatized a conflict between an Acadian-like past and modern technology. Hébert's Eve faces a choice between the pure life of the past and the corrupt life of modern times, recalling Longfellow's Evangeline, loyal to an ideal but plunged into the self-indulgent morality of cities in the New World. The conflict for Hébert's Eve, unlike Evangeline, is more complicated, its history originating with life itself. Torn between meeting expectations of selfless devotion and satisfying more selfish urges, Eve (as a triple female poetic voice) bears in her "coeur éternel" a conflict poorly disguised by the apparent order of the modern city, "rangé / Et rectiligne."[9]

"Eve" attributes the malaise of modern times to the inability of contemporary urban order to mask a conflict surviving from our collective moral past. Hébert's exploration of the roots of that malaise reveals a complex relationship between the present and the past, a relationship the significance of which cannot be simplified despite modern techniques of regimentation and reduction. Hébert has even suggested that attempting to suppress memories of the past increases the susceptibility of contemporary civilization to moral decay and passivity. Two novels by Hébert, *Kamouraska*[10] and *Héloïse*,[11] both with their female protagonists, adopt this theme, but a more analytical examination of the relationship between the past and the present appears in Hébert's second volume of poetry, *Le Tombeau des rois*, published in 1953. Two temporal frames are superimposed in this collection to produce a complicated vision of modern life. Written in language which interprets the female poet's personal experience as a universal experience, *Le Tombeau des rois* reveals and challenges the subtle control the past exercises over the destinies of cultures.

The title poem of the collection conforms poorly to the pattern of "a one-day oneiric cycle from birth to death,'' which Pierre Pagé ascribes to the volume as a whole.[12] ''Le Tombeau des rois'' projects an aura of dreaminess, it is true, and in that sense, seeming remote from the everyday world, the poem possesses an oneiric quality. But on close reading, the estrangement from quotidian experience in the poem is a reflection of the poem's elaborated reality. The poem, surging toward surrealism in the first line, ''J'ai mon coeur au poing comme un faucon aveugle,''[13] is immediately brought down to a realistic scale by the use of the simile. Rather than creating an oneiric state of unreality, the initial image alerts us, excites our tension and anxiety, and imbues the text with poignant realism.

The female narrator implies that a clue has lured her into the royal vault: ''Quel fil d'Ariane me mène / Au long des dédales sourds?'' (lines 10-11).[14] Yet another voice, speaking of the female narrator in the third person, disclaims her freedom to reason. Lines 13-15 (''En quel songe / Cette enfant fut-elle liée par la cheville / Pareille à une esclave fascinée?'')[15] tell us that the female narrator was drawn into the poem, if not involuntarily, at least instinctively. In contrast, the entombed pharaohs, though dead, display aggressive willpower, exercising imperious control over the narrator, luring her towards self-immolation in the hope of revitalizing themselves. But they find nothing when they reach for the narrator's heart ''pour le rompre'' (line 58).[16] Having broken herself into fragments before she entered the tomb, the narrator has protected her heart from the kings of the past, and resists their attempts to dominate her. The pharaohs are no longer a threat; the female narrator's fear of them is exorcised.

Yet the dead kings have a certain value for the female narrator/poetic voice. Their chestplates, decorated with ''quelques tragédies patiemment travaillées'' (line 29),[17] are offered ''sans larmes ni regrets'' (line 33)[18] for the narrator's dispassionate consideration, reminding her that the deeds of the past were governed by the conditions of the past. They require the narrator's understanding, but not her adulation. Her complicity with the dead would emprison her in the tightly circumscribed limits of rituals and gestures inherited from the past. But the female narrator/poetic voice prepared herself to explore unfamiliar territory before she entered the tomb, and successfully resisted the power of the past to determine the present.

Having broken the incapacitating spell of the past over those living in the present, the female narrator opens the tomb to let in dawn and the future, the ''reflet d'aube'' (line 62)[19] and ''le matin'' (line 65).[20] The past, with its pharaohs in fancy raiment, loses its awesome mystery, and the future, instead, becomes a source of the mysterious unknown as the poem ends with a question: ''D'où vient donc que cet oiseau frémit / Et tourne vers le matin / Ses prunelles crevées?'' (lines 64-66).[21] The female narrator/poetic voice has demystified the past and leads us to a new mystery, taking us from the known to the unknown, moving against the constraints of tradition into ever widening circles of knowledge. To be among the living in ''Le Tombeau des rois'' is to be counter-traditional.

Countering tradition is central to Hébert's conception of poetry as she describes it in "Mystère de la parole," a collection in the 1960 anthology of her *Poèmes*. In her foreword to the collection, Hébert writes that the poet struggles with "la terre muette et il apprend la résistance de son propre coeur tranquille et muet, n'ayant de cesse qu'il n'ait trouvé une voix juste et belle pour chanter les noces de l'homme avec la terre."[22] Rather than abjectly accept received ideas, the female poet actively seeks and makes audible a voice from the earth we consider mute. The mystery of words is the transformation of the known and familiar into the unknown and new.

Hébert reviews this process of transformation in the title poem of the collection. Our world at first seems naked and silent to us: "Dans un pays tranquille nous avons reçu la passion / du monde épée nue sur nos deux mains posée...."[23] That silence is broken and the world is filled with life when we train our senses upon it:

Des flèches d'odeur nous atteignirent, nous liant à la
terre comme des blessures en des noces excessives.

O saisons, rivière, aulnes et fougères, feuilles, fleurs,
bois mouillé, herbes bleues, tout notre avoir saigne
son parfum, bête odorante à notre flanc (lines 14-18).[24]

But naming the objects of our world is not sufficient to make them familiar to us. Word and world are still alienated from each other, and objects confuse us: "Les couleurs et les sons nous visitèrent en masse et par / petits groupes foudroyants, tandis que le songe doublait notre enchantement..." (lines 15-17).[25] When we accept the world as contingent to us, when our sense of it becomes that of a "jeune accouchée" (line 19),[26] and the world becomes "le printemps délivré" (line 19),[27] then word and world do merge in our minds. We see a proliferation of objects as a whole, nonsense becomes sense, and "... la parole se fonde, / soulève notre coeur, saisit le monde en un seul geste / d'orage, nous colle à son aurore comme l'écorce à / son fruit" (lines 28-30).[28] Hébert's words are not names; they are the significance of objects.

In Hébert's poetic mystery, naming each object simultaneously attaches it to all other objects, assigns it a place in relationship to, and in context with, all other objects. The poet addresses her poem to the many listeners she hopes to unify, "frères les plus noirs, toutes fêtes gravées en / secret ..." (lines 38-39),[29] all those who present themselves "Fronts bouclés où croupit le silence en toisons mus- / quées, toutes grimaces, vieilles têtes, joues d'enfant, / amours, rides, joies, deuils, créatures, créatures..." (lines 34-36).[30] The poet's function is to extract from these superficial differences a profound harmony: "Que celui qui a reçu fonction de la parole vous prenne / en charge comme un coeur ténébreux de surcroît, et / n'ait de cesse que soient justifiés les vivants et les morts / en un seul chant parmi l'aube et les herbes" (lines 41-44).[31]

As represented in the three poems we have discussed, Hébert's version of objective reality consists of an apparent mode and a concealed mode. There is the turbulence of inner conflicts beneath the impassive exterior of urban life in "Eve"; alongside the present in "Le Tombeau des rois" lies the powerful past; and within the silence and calm of the world in "Mystère de la parole," objects pulse with vitality. The revelation of this hidden world with its powerful forces is initially alarming to the reader. But the woman poet familiarizes us with this new level of reality, and relates it to our well-known surroundings so that we accept the coexistence of the two levels.

The poet's purpose is not merely one of revelation. She aligns the forces of the two realities to erase the conflicts which dull our perception of the common world. Hébert wants us to reject the world as we have been taught to see it, identifying objects and segregating them into familiar and alien camps. Poetry should reconcile us with that which is alien; otherwise, we remain prisoners of the past, afraid to explore reality beyond the distinctions separating objects. When we overcome our fear of reality, when we reject ideas received from the past, we use that past to enhance our perception of reality.

The use of the past in the interest of the best possible future is the basis for Hébert's counter-traditions. But if her counter-traditions serve a protective and conservative function, they also perform the task of revolution. Hébert's mystery of words is a theory of deep change, for words operate like traditions, constantly expanding their significance, broadening our apprehension and experience of objective reality. Hébert's words change our world.

The female poet who exerts pressure on words to alter their significance and our perception advances on the outer limits of meaning, on the signifying edge of words. This edge separates sense from nonsense, that which is already known from that which is yet to be understood. This is the margin on which Hébert writes. But her acute awareness of reality and her drive to see beyond superficial distinctions do not permit her to err on the side of universalism, where those distinctions are denied. Hébert does not assume that objects share some universal, essential bond. She creates that bond through her poetry.

NOTES

1. Roger Duhamel, "Poésie des cimes arides," *L'Action Universitaire*, No. 2 (January 1954), pp. 88-89.

2. André Rousseaux, *Le Figaro Littéraire* (8 mai 1954), p. 2, as cited in Pierre Pagé, *Anne Hébert*, Ecrivains d'aujourd'hui, No. 3 (Ottawa: Fides, 1965), p. 95.

3. Guy Robert, *La Poétique du songe: Essai thématique sur la poésie d'Anne Hébert* (Montréal: Cahiers de l'Association Générale des Etudiants à l'Université de Montréal, 1962), p. 13.

4. Jean Ethier-Blais, "Destin et devenir de la littérature québécoise, in *Littératures ultramarines de langue française: Genèse et jeunesse: Actes du colloque de l'Université de Vermont, Burlington*, eds. Thomas H. Geno and Roy Ireland (Sherbrooke, Québec: Naaman, 1974), p. 90.

5. Jean-Paul Sartre, "Orphée noir," Introd., *Anthologie de la nouvelle poésie nègre*

et malgache de langue française, ed. Léopold Sédar Senghor (Paris: Presses Universitaires de France, 1948), p. xxvii.

6. Michel Benamou, "The Concept of Marginality in Ethnopoetics," in *Minority Language and Literature*, ed. Dexter Fisher (New York: Modern Language Association of America, 1977), pp. 152-54.

7. Léon-G. Damas, "Nuit blanche," in *Anthologie*, ed. Senghor, pp. 17-18.

> Blue white red green pink Danube / take your pick.
> Goodly aryan / gumming his old age on some park bench.

8. Anne Hébert, "Eve," in Pagé, p. 141.

Beginning of the world.

Hébert's original text, *Les Songes en équilibre* (Montréal: Les Editions de l'Arbre, 1942), is out of print and unavailable.

9. Hébert, "Eve," in Pagé, pp. 142-43.

Ordered / And rectilinear.

See Patricia Smart, "La Poésie d'Anne Hébert: Une Perspective féminine," *Revue de l'Université d'Ottawa*, 50, No. 1 (janvier-mars 1980), pp. 62-68.

10. Anne Hébert, *Kamouraska* (Paris: Editions du Seuil, 1970).

11. Anne Hébert, *Héloïse* (Paris: Editions du Seuil, 1980).

12. Pagé, p. 95.

13. Anne Hébert, "Le Tombeau des rois," *Poèmes* (Paris: Editions du Seuil, 1960), p. 59.

I hold my heart as I would a blind falcon atop my clenched fist.

The original publication of *Le Tombeau des rois*," Pref. Pierre Emmanuel (Québec: Institut littéraire du Québec, 1953) has been reprinted as "Le Tombeau des rois" in Hébert, *Poèmes*, pp. 7-61, and the title poem appears on pp. 59-61. Future references will be to the 1960 edition of *Poèmes*.

14. Hébert, "Le Tombeau des rois," *Poèmes*, p. 59.

What Ariadne's thread leads me / Through the soundless maze?

15. Hébert, "Le Tombeau des rois," *Poèmes*, p. 59.

In what dream / Was this child chained at her ankle / Like a hypnotized slave?

16. Hébert, "Le Tombeau des rois," *Poèmes*, p. 61.

To break it.

17. Hébert, "Le Tombeau des rois," *Poèmes*, p. 60.

A few tragedies patiently crafted.

18. Hébert, "Le Tombeau des rois," *Poèmes*, p. 60.

Without tears or regrets.

19. Hébert, "Le Tombeau des rois," *Poèmes*, p. 61.

Dawn's light.

20. Hébert, "Le Tombeau des rois," *Poèmes*, p. 61.

Morning.

21. Hébert, "Le Tombeau des rois," *Poèmes*, p. 61.

For what reason, then, does this bird tremble / And turn toward morning / Its pierced eyes?

22. Hébert, "Poésie, solitude rompue," in *Poèmes*, p. 67.

The mute earth and one realizes the resistance of one's own serene and mute heart, not resting until finding a good and true voice to sing the union of humans with the earth.

23. Hébert, "Le Mystère de la parole," *Poèmes*, p. 73.

In an untroubled land we received the passion / of the world bare sword lain upon our hands.

The entire collection, "Le Mystère de la parole," appears in Hébert, *Poèmes*, pp. 63-105.

24. Hébert, "Le Mystère de la parole," *Poèmes*, pp. 73-74.

Arrows of odor pierced us, binding us to the
earth like wounds from excessive pleasure

Oh seasons, river, alders and ferns, leaves, flowers,
damp woods, blue grass, all that we have bleeds
its perfume, an odorous beast by our side.

25. Hébert, "Le Mystère de la parole," *Poèmes*, p. 74.

Colors and sounds came to us in masses and in / small, darting groups, while dreaming doubled our enchantment....

26. Hébert, "Le Mystère de la parole," *Poèmes*, p. 74.

A young female just delivered of child.

27. Hébert, "Le Mystère de la parole," *Poèmes*, p. 74.

Newborn spring.

28. Hébert, "Le Mystère de la parole," *Poèmes*, p. 74.

The word is established / lifts our hearts, seizes the world in one flash / of a storm cleaves us to its dawn as the peel / to its fruit.

29. Hébert, "Le Mystère de la parole," *Poèmes*, p. 75.

Blackest brothers, all celebrations carved in / secret....

30. Hébert, "Le Mystère de la parole," *Poèmes*, p. 75.

Kinked brows where silence crouches in musk- / scented hair, all distortions of faces, heads of old people, cheeks of children, / loves, wrinkles, joys, sorrows, creatures, creatures....

31. Hébert, "Le Mystère de la parole," *Poèmes*, p. 75.

May the one who has received function of the word take you / in charge like a heart dark with burdens, and / not rest until the living and the dead are justified / in a single song between dawn and the grasses.

6

Female Spirals and Male Cages: The Urban Sphere in the Novels of Gabrielle Roy

Paula Gilbert Lewis ─────────────────────────

In 1967 Gabrielle Roy published an introduction to a photographic album dedicated to the Montreal World's Fair, *Terre des Hommes/Man and His World*.
In this essay, she refers to the earth as "ce petit point dans l'ensemble de
l'univers, notre pays, notre chez-nous."[1] Five years later in her prose poem to
nature, *Cet été qui chantait*, she refers to her readers as "les enfants de la
Terre,"[2] as "enfants de toutes saisons à qui je souhaite de ne jamais se lasser
d'entendre raconter leur planète Terre."[3] Many of her characters had already
been listening to what she had called, in 1961, "des ententes secrètes" between
humanity and certain aspects of the universe,[4] for Roy had always believed that
one must remain open to an understanding of both human nature and the surrounding world.

There exists, in fact, a profound influence of environment—defined as one's
physical and, at times, social milieu—upon all Royan characters, on both their
actions and their thoughts. Whatever that surrounding location may be, there is
a close rapport and even a communion between the individual and exterior space,
to the extent that outside nature can be personified and become a character in
its own right. In analyzing this important aspect of Roy's fiction, Paul Socken
has indicated that since Royan characters, and in particular her urban characters,
are fundamentally alone, alienated in an incomprehensible, modern world, and
since they have become strangers to themselves and to nature, they have a deep
need to adapt themselves to the natural world, to rediscover their surroundings
so as to understand better both themselves and others. When one is sensitive to
and aware of one's milieu, and when one perfects one's own explanation or
description of the world, one possesses that world, makes it one's own, for the
elements of nature, in Roy's fiction, reflect distinctive human emotions. Without
his distinguishing between female and male protagonists, Socken believes that
for Gabrielle Roy, there exists in the universe a basic harmony and unity to

which all humanity belongs. An ideal, therefore, is to be found in a mutual reconciliation between the world of people and, predominantly, the natural world.[5]

In order to convince her readers that such a reconciliation is possible, Roy must powerfully and realistically depict both her female and male characters and their world. The individuals who people these works are both distinct beings and archetypal figures. As for her talent in describing exterior environment in her works, Roy has been seen as a social realist and as a quasi-photographic writer. She herself has spoken of the importance that her early journalistic writings had on her formation as an author, since these articles had afforded her the opportunity to travel, research, and minutely observe everything around her both in Quebec and in Canada. She believed that, influenced by the nineteenth-century French novelists of the movement of Realism, she was merely a realistic observer who wrote about what she saw and then added her own personal, creative sense of imagination.[6]

One can, however, pursue this influence even further. It is true that, like Honoré de Balzac, Gabrielle Roy depicts her exterior and interior, that is, psychological, spaces as being mutually reflective, but more specifically, that exterior space, the physical and social milieu into which her characters have been placed, greatly determines the lives of her literary creations. Given the power of that outside influence, along with the inevitable presence of heredity within a particular family, one can state that there exists in Roy's literary universe a determinism or fatality that is not unlike that of Emile Zola and his quasi-scientific theory of Naturalism in literature. Her urban characters suffer because, living in an artificial milieu, they lack any contact with the natural world of the country, while her rural creatures also endure their own form of isolation but possess daily opportunities to relate to their natural surroundings.[7]

Throughout Roy's fiction there exists an oscillation between the city and the country, with the sensation of loneliness and yet solidarity in the former locale and with freedom and yet solitude in the latter. The author has stated that most everything in her life and in her works could be traced back to the fact that she was born on the little rue Deschambault where, at one end, was a stop for the tram that could take her to Winnipeg and, within fifteen minutes, to humanity. At the opposite end of the street was a small group of trees and the beginning of wild nature to which she could go whenever she needed solitude and contact with the natural world. As a child, she spent much time walking back and forth along that street, drawn toward nature, and then, when tired of it, able to frequent the world of people. Considering her deep need for both locations, therefore, she found it unjust that she had always been accused of hating the city, of depicting it in an entirely negative light in her creative works. She maintained, to the contrary, that cities, especially with their cross section of ethnic groups, were fascinating and exciting. What Roy disliked about large metropolises was modern urban planning that preferred apartment buildings and cement to parks. To put a stop to the hell that modern people were creating for themselves, one must not abolish cities but, in Roy's opinion, countrify them.[8]

These mixed feelings toward the city are evident in Roy's four 1941 journalistic articles describing the city of Montreal and serving as a source of information to the future novelist for her 1945 *Bonheur d'occasion*. As she later stated in an article treating her early years in Montreal, Gabrielle Roy discovered this urban metropolis alone and on foot, during numerous walking tours of the entire city. Unaware of any aspect of Montreal, she was interested in everything that she saw: "En pèlerin, émue, éreintée, je l'ai traversée en entier, je l'ai connue dans son plus laid, dans son plus tragique, dans son plus altier du haut de la montagne, dans son meilleur, dans son pire et, quand je m'y attendais le moins, dans sa gaieté irrésistible."[9] Her 1941 articles are, in fact, thus described, as though her readers themselves were walking alongside the journalist. She writes of all quarters of the city and, most interestingly, of the rue Sainte-Catherine, depicted as though it were a person. She speaks of the poverty in Montreal, of "la plainte du peuple,"[10] as later, in retrospect, of hearing "soupirer le peuple."[11] In "Du port aux banques," she portrays the constant hurrying of people who work as termites, enslaved by their new addiction to material comfort. Life in a large city is frenetic: "Il ne faut pas que le bruit cesse. Il ne faut pas que l'agitation tombe. Il ne faut pas s'arrêter. Il ne faut pas penser."[12] "Après trois cents ans," Roy's fourth article on Montreal, presents a history of the city, underscoring its formation by two nations and suggesting, as explicitly stated in her more recent remembrances, that both cultures can benefit from a willing exchange:

Il [Montréal] est français dans son exubérance et sa confusion politique, anglais dans les affaires, cosmopolite au port, américain dans la rue Sainte-Catherine, provincial dans l'est, puritain à Westmount, snob à Outremont, nationaliste au Parc Lafontaine, canadien-français le 24 juin, saxon à Noël ... bilingue quand il le faut et profondément hybride dans l'âme. Nul doute que cette ville étonnante ne soit l'oeuvre de deux nations.[13]

Despite the obvious fact that, during her initial years in Montreal, Roy learned to love the city, even with its distasteful facets, it is essentially the negative that she stresses in her major fiction, and specifically in three of her novels. *Bonheur d'occasion* is the tragic story of rural women and men, represented by the Lacasse family, who have left the country with the naive hope of bettering themselves in the large, increasingly industrialized city of Montreal. Never becoming fully adapted to the rapid progress and to the frenetic, costly lifestyle surrounding them, they stagnate, remaining neither rural nor urban. With large families that are increasingly difficult to raise and that are slowly disintegrating, these individuals find themselves caught in Saint-Henri, a section of the city that teems with poverty and misery. They are trapped in the odors of filth and poverty that pervade their homes and, pathetically, their intimate sexual lives. Even the clouds of Saint-Henri are formed by a continual "tourbillon de suie,"[14] emanating from the surrounding chimneys and symbolizing the enclosed circle that engulfs both women and men in their wretched misery. Ashamed and yet often resigned to their fate, the inhabitants of Saint-Henri, and especially the young, bitterly condemn society for allowing such conditions to exist. They specifically attack the fact that, with the widespread unemployment in these early 1940s, there is something innately wrong with a social order that allows such a waste of human energy. With no work and, therefore, little money, these people tend to lack any sense of dignity or self-esteem and, like Azarius and his younger friends, Pitou, Boisvert, and Alphonse, spend much of their time sitting in bars, complaining about their pre-determined social and economic status, or dreaming of possible escapes.

Contributing to this pathetic urban situation is the fact that the inhabitants of Saint-Henri are daily faced with the sight of Westmount and are painfully tempted by the rue Sainte-Catherine. Using the technique of placing in opposition specific geographic locations, Roy often contrasts Saint-Henri and Westmount, as she opposes the French- and English-speaking Montrealers:

Mais au-delà, dans une large échancrure du faubourg, apparaît la ville de Westmount échelonnée jusqu'au faîte de la montagne dans son rigide confort anglais. Il se trouve ainsi que c'est aux voyages infinis de l'âme qu'elle invite. Ici, le luxe et la pauvreté se regardent inlassablement, depuis qu'il y a Westmount, depuis qu'en bas, à ses pieds, il y a Saint-Henri.[15]

Within Montreal these two sections remain in conflict, for the people who live in Saint-Henri are jealously drawn toward the mountain—image, for Jean Lévesque and Emmanuel Létourneau in particular, of success and escape. Even Emmanuel, who is far wealthier than his peers in Saint-Henri but who shoulders the burdens of his neighbors' poverty, cannot penetrate the calm and order of this section of the city and senses a profound uneasiness as he walks through its streets. Similarly, the material luxuries in the windows of the stores on the rue Sainte-Catherine continuously tempt and even mock the poor inhabitants of the city, especially Florentine. Advertisements tell them to buy, to become a part of a society of consumers, but if the city of Montreal is forever in movement and if the temptations and expensive distractions of this city continuously try to seduce them, these people remain inert within their own section of town and within their poverty.

The structure of the city of Montreal, therefore—and in particular of Saint-Henri within that city, both as depicted in *Bonheur d'occasion*—is that of a prison or cage, even a concentration camp, in which all individuals are forced by outside circumstances and by heredity to live. In this claustrophobic atmosphere, people can barely breathe, as they are pushed into a concentrated space, as well as—given the passage of little more than three months within the novel and the feeling of urgency to make a decision about one's future in the face of war or pregnancy—into a sense of restricted time. Described by André Brochu as a series of concentric circles or spheres of existence, both individual and collective, the city of *Bonheur d'occasion* and the urban lives intertwined within it represent a hell from which the characters yearn to escape.[16]

The form of escape from or identification with this urban world of poverty depends upon the individuals who are attempting to leave: whether they are families, men, or women. The families of Saint-Henri, in their hope of departure, participate in a phenomenon effectively described by Roy. Every spring they move from one apartment to another for, as Jean observes, with the arrival of spring in Montreal comes the season of pitiful illusions, of foolish hopes for *recommencement*. Roy herself, in retrospect, affirmed that "la grande masse semblait partir de son plein gré, comme pour se donner l'illusion de la liberté. Ils en étaient malades...."[17] But this annual *déménagement* is truly an illusion of freedom, for these poor families, in their horizontal moves from one sector or cage to another within the same sphere, remain locked inside their misery.

The French feminist theorist Claudine Herrmann describes man's space as one of domination, conquest, and fullness. Accordingly, in an attempt to determine their own lives, many of the male characters in this novel do escape from the city, rather than trying to dominate it. It is evident from the beginning that Jean, in particular, will succeed, will effect a vertical form of liberation, since he is consistently identified with wind, boats, and trains that pass through Saint-Henri without stopping to worry about poverty. But Jean is the only person in the novel to negate or to conquer his destiny and to leave Montreal, and he does so by relinquishing his sense of humanism and by profiting from that which destroys many of his peers. The other men of Saint-Henri, who are able to escape from their misery, do so only to go to war. In their only form of salvation, they are the partially willing pawns of a dominant male society/state that has kept them within the circle of urban misery and now sends them away toward their death. In a false conquest of their own sense of space and as part victim and part volunteer, most of them will not return to Saint-Henri.[18]

Woman's space, in Herrmann's view, is one of separation, exclusion, frustration, and a void, while the female body, imprisoned by that space, often becomes integrated into the city—a space usually dominated and defined by man. In *Bonheur d'occasion* female bodies and destinies do ultimately—and involuntarily—become identified with the city itself. If Montreal can be seen as an enclosed circle, specifically as "l'inquiet tourbillon de Saint-Henri,"[19] then the fictional lives of these Montreal women, and especially of Florentine, are similarly described either as being engulfed within that spiral or as whirlwinds themselves: "A force de regarder danser la neige sous ses yeux, il lui [Jean] semblait qu'elle avait pris une forme humaine, celle même de Florentine, et qu'épuisée mais ne pouvant s'empêcher de tourner, de se dépenser, elle dansait là, dans la nuit, et restait prisonnière de ses évolutions."[20] Although Florentine will eventually raise her economic and social status by her marriage to Emmanuel, she will remain tied to her mother, Rose-Anna, and to the other women of Saint-Henri. Caught in the round, female structures of motherhood, crowds, and hereditary misery, therefore—created by men—these female protagonists will be forced to remain, as well, within the ironically female urban sphere of Montreal.

This same city of Montreal, as depicted in Gabrielle Roy's second novel,

Alexandre Chenevert, is not that of the horrid poverty in her first novel. It is, rather, that of a modern urban metropolis in which middle class, white-collar workers, in particular, are continuously bombarded with dire national and international news on the radio and in the press and equally inundated with the impersonal and commercial slogans of advertisements. When Chenevert returns to Montreal from a brief vacation, for example, and is faced once again with the disasters of the world, he raises his eyes to the sky, as if to seek help in the horizon or in God. He reads instead: "BUVEZ PEPSI COLA."[21] Everywhere, in fact, religion is being sold, even marketed in the impersonal Christmas greetings from businesses. Poor, modern, urban dwellers have become slaves to these banal formulas and, like the bank teller, soon discover that they themselves can write only "dans le ton des messages publicitaires."[22]

Life in Montreal is also noisy. Chenevert hates these sounds that appear to be allied against him so as to disturb his sleep. He also dislikes the idea of so many people living in such close proximity, to the extent that, knowing one's neighbors by their particular noises, one cannot even argue in peace. The urban world of *Alexandre Chenevert* is, in addition, that of crowds, fighting, pushing, hurrying, and, especially, standing in long lines. Himself standing in a line at the North Western Lunch cafeteria, Chenevert closes his eyes:

Et alors l'imagination folle d'Alexandre lui présenta l'entassement de la vallée de Josaphat [at the Last Judgement]; toutes les files de la terre, les patientes files de tous les temps s'allongeaient les unes aux autres. . . . Aucun bruit, aucun discours, aucun son dans la Vallée; seulement cette marche silencieuse, au pas, ce docile mouvement de la foule qui d'elle-même obéissait encore à l'alignement.[23]

Whether jostling one another or quietly standing in interminably long lines, however, the inhabitant of the modern city is miserable: commuting in a tram, "dans une curieuse pose de supplicié,"[24] distant from primitive carefreeness, and seeing families disintegrate, as people become mechanical, impersonal beings. In this sense, Chenevert is accurate in his assessment of human misery, for he is a part of it.

Urban space in *Alexandre Chenevert* is essentially similar to that described in *Bonheur d'occasion*, only in this instance the character who is caught within and identified with this enclosed, claustrophobic, and circular structure is male. Most of the bank teller's urban settings, in fact, have been identified as interior and engulfing: his bathroom, apartment, tram, teller's cage, and cafeteria. Instead of depicting one major island of poverty within the larger city of Montreal, however, Roy has chosen in this novel to portray her hero, like other urbanites, as passing from one geographical concentric circle or cage to another, somewhat like the annual moves of the families of Saint-Henri, but remaining within the large urban sphere. In order to be able to breathe, therefore, Chenevert, like Roy's earlier male and female urban characters, dreams of escape from his life in Montreal and finally decides to leave the city for the open nature of the nearby countryside, immediately symbolized by a river (often characterized as female—like personages ironically still caught in the city): "A gauche de la route, il y avait le pénitencier. Mais Alexandre se trouvait regarder du côté de la rivière. Et lui, qui ne connaissait pour ainsi dire rien d'autre au monde que la ville, ses poteaux, ses numéros, il la quittait, étonné, troublé, comme s'il sortait de prison. Que d'espace, de lumière, de liberté!"[25]

Alexandre Chenevert is not, however, a rural individual but a true urban dweller. Unlike Azarius and Rose-Anna, unlike many of the older couples of Saint-Henri, he is not attached to the country and, in effect, feels *dépaysé* in this linear displacement at Lac Vert. After a few days of total isolation, he realizes that he needs the city, needs to communicate with others, and needs to return to what he now sees as anonymity, as the comforting solitude of urban life, that is, the knowledge that thousands of others are similarly alone in Montreal. He even goes as far as becoming nostalgic about humanity: "Il rêva aussi de journaux, de magazines en grosses piles sur le trottoir, apportant les nouvelles du monde. Là était la vie, l'échange perpétuel, émouvant, fraternel."[26] Without ever truly relating, the inhabitants of the city represent human solidarity.

The Montrealer returns, of course, to the grotesque artificiality of urban life, symbolized by an electric figure of Christ (male; the patriarchal Church) on the side of the highway. As Chenevert's bus approaches Montreal, there is increasing traffic, confusion, and stagnant air. When he finally arrives in the bus station, he realizes that he is experiencing something even worse than solitude. He is feeling the absurd misunderstanding of being one among many unknown others in the city—a sentiment often attributed to the woman, caught in a sphere dominated by men: "Il eut la curieuse sensation qu'il ne pourrait pas être plus à l'étranger à Moscou, à Paris. . . . 'Voyons,' pensa Alexandre: 'j'ai vécu toute ma vie à Montréal; je suis né ici, j'y mourrai probablement.' Il éprouva la terrible ingratitude de la ville à son endroit."[27] He decides, therefore, that one should never leave the city, never take a vacation in the country, for one's determined home and urban existence appear too monstrous when one does return. For Alexandre Chenevert, in particular, this return, or rather this need to return to the city, will bring him to his final escape into the enclosed structured, urban, and here male circle of death.

If Chenevert voluntarily returns to Montreal in order to die, then Pierre Cadorai of *La Montagne secrète* is likewise sent to Paris, never to leave. A fiercely independent, solitary, rural being, Cadorai will meet, for the first time in his life, other artists with whom he can communicate, but who are seen by him as prisoners of the city and, therefore, according to his friend Stanislas, as not well equipped for life. Encountering the modern annoyances of traffic, noise, and neon signs, this Canadian adventurer and painter will experience in the urban metropolis a new, more frightening sensation of isolation, "la si mystérieuse solitude des rues emplies de monde, de pas et de lumières!"[28] Like Chenevert, Cadorai will need to leave the city, will take one glorious vacation in the countryside, and will return to the city to dream of the open, wild nature of his beloved Canadian mountain but to remain in his small, enclosed apartment in order to die. Once again, the structured, male urban circle will close.

It is noteworthy that Gabrielle Roy's two major male characters both return from traditionally maternal, protective, and yet open nature to the traditionally male-dominated city and to their death, while her two heroines, Rose-Anna and Florentine, involuntarily associated with the confines of urban structure, remain there not necessarily in order to die, but rather to continue the endless struggle to find happiness. This unusual combination of male and female circular imagery for the city, both of which are enticing but destructive, is especially interesting in the works of an author who, seen as a humanist rather than as a feminist, increasingly preferred to place all her characters in the open surroundings of nature. In *Cet été qui chantait*, an ode to that nature, the elderly Martine is seen as having been exiled for fifty years in a city apartment "sans air ni horizon."[29] She returns to the country, to her dear river, and then, like the male characters, goes back to the city before dying: "Martine à peine de retour dans l'étroit logis sans horizon et sans lumière, s'en alla vers les espaces ouverts que toute sa vie elle avait désirés.[30] It seems as though many of Roy's protagonists—both female and male— need to return to the country prior to death and then back to the city in order to die in an enclosed space, before eternally returning into open nature.

NOTES

1. Gabrielle Roy, "*Terre des Hommes*: Le Thème raconté," *Fragiles Lumières de la terre: Ecrits divers 1942-1970*, Collection Prose Entière (Montréal: Quinze, 1978), p. 203.

That little dot in the entire universe, our country, our home.

Roy's introduction was originally published as "Introduction: Le Thème raconté/The Theme Unfolded," in *Terre des Hommes/Man and His World* (Montréal and Toronto: La Compagnie canadienne de l'Exposition universelle de 1967/Canadian Corporation for the 1967 World Exhibition, 1967), pp. 21-60.

2. Gabrielle Roy, *Cet été qui chantait* (Québec; Montréal: Les Editions Françaises, 1972), p. vii.

Children of the Earth.

3. Roy, *Cet été qui chantait*, p. 76.

Children of all seasons who, I hope, will never tire of listening to the tales told by their planet, Earth.

4. Gabrielle Roy, *La Montagne secrète* (1961; rpt. Montréal: Librairie Beauchemin, 1974), p. 145.

Secret understandings.

5. Paul Socken, "L'Harmonie dans l'oeuvre de Gabrielle Roy," *Travaux de Linguistique et de Littérature* (l'Université de Strasbourg), 15, No. 2 (1977), 275-92; "The Influence of Physical and Social Environment on Character in the Novels of Gabrielle Roy," *DAI*, 38 (December 1977), 3489A-90A (University of Toronto); " 'Le Pays de

l'amour' in the Works of Gabrielle Roy," *Revue de l'Université d'Ottawa*, 46, No. 3 (juillet-septembre 1976), 317.

6. Personal interview with Gabrielle Roy, 29 June 1980.

7. André Brochu, "Thèmes et structures de *Bonheur d'occasion*," in *L'Instance critique* (Montréal: Leméac, 1974), pp. 220-23; Paula Gilbert Lewis, "Gabrielle Roy and Emile Zola: French Naturalism in Quebec," *Modern Language Studies*, 11, No. 3 (Fall 1981), 44-50; Jacques Blais, "L'Unité organique de *Bonheur d'occasion*," *Etudes Françaises*, 6, No. 1 (février 1970), 28-31; Georges-André Vachon, "L'Espace politique et social dans le roman québécois," *Recherches Sociographiques*, 7, No. 3 (septembre-décembre 1966), 261-73.

8. Personal interview with Gabrielle Roy, 29 June 1980.

9. Gabrielle Roy, "Le Pays de *Bonheur d'occasion*," in *Morceaux*, ed. Robert Guy Scully (Montréal: Les Editions du Noroît, 1978), p. 114.

As a pilgrim, moved, worn out, I walked around all of it [Montreal]; I have known it [the city of Montreal] at its ugliest, at its most tragic, at its loftiest from the top of the mountain, at its best, at its worst, and when I least expected it, in its irresistible gaiety.

10. Gabrielle Roy, "Les Deux Saint-Laurent," *Le Bulletin des Agriculteurs*, 37, No. 6 (juin 1941), 40.

The moan of the people.

11. Roy, "Le Pays de *Bonheur d'occasion*," p. 117.

The people sigh.

12. Gabrielle Roy, "Du port aux banques," *Le Bulletin des Agriculteurs*, 37, No. 8 (août 1941), 11.

The noise must not cease. The commotion must not subside. One must not stop. One must not think.

13. Gabrielle Roy, "Après trois cents ans," *Le Bulletin des Agriculteurs*, 37, No. 9 (septembre 1941), 39.

It [Montreal] is French in its exuberance and political confusion, English in business affairs, cosmopolitan at the port, American on Saint Catherine Street, provincial in East Montreal, Puritan in Westmount, snobbish in Outremont, nationalistic in Lafontaine Park, French-Canadian on 24 June, Anglo-Saxon at Christmas ... bilingual whenever it is necessary, and deeply hybrid in its soul. There is no doubt that this surprising city is the work of two nations.

14. Gabrielle Roy, *Bonheur d'occasion* (1945; rpt. Montréal: Librairie Beauchemin, 1973), pp. 32, 221.

Whirlwind of soot.

This novel was made into a film and received its world premiere in Moscow, soon after Roy's death in July 1983. Since then the film has received mixed critical reviews.

15. Roy, *Bonheur d'occasion*, p. 33.

But over there, in a large notch in the suburb, appears the town of Westmount, spread out all the way up to the ridge of the mountain in its rigid English comfort. It is thus there as an invitation to the infinite voyages of the mind. Here luxury and poverty stare tirelessly at one another, since as long as there is Westmount, there lies below, at its feet, Saint-Henri.

16. Roy, *Bonheur d'occasion*, pp. 26-27, 53, 101-03, 150-51, 208; André Brochu, "La Structure sémantique de *Bonheur d'occasion*," *Revue des Sciences Humaines*, 45, No. 173 (janvier-mars 1979), 37-47.

17. Roy, "Le Pays de *Bonheur d'occasion*," p. 121.

The masses seemed to depart voluntarily, as if to give themselves the illusion of freedom. They were sick of it....

See Brochu, "La Structure sémantique," pp. 37-47.

18. Claudine Herrmann, *Les Voleurs de langue* (Paris: Editions des Femmes, 1976), pp. 138-39; Roy, *Bonheur d'occasion*, pp. 12, 26-29, 32-34, 44, 53, 75, 101-02, 186, 204-05, 208, 221-23, 227, 252, 286, 291, 334-40, 344-45; Brochu, "Thèmes et structures," pp. 229-33; Brochu, "La Structure sémantique," pp. 37-47.

19. Roy, *Bonheur d'occasion*, p. 12.

The restless whirlwind of Saint-Henri.

See also Herrmann, pp. 139, 149, 150, 152.

20. Roy, *Bonheur d'occasion*, pp. 26-27.

While looking at the snow dancing before his eyes, it seemed to him [Jean] that it had assumed a human form, even that of Florentine, and that exhausted but not able to stop from turning and overly exerting itself [or herself], it [or she] danced there, in the night, and remained a prisoner of its [or her] own evolutions.

See Brochu, "Thèmes et structures," pp. 220, 224, 225, 228-39. Analyses of both male and female characters can also be made in reference to their identification with *la droite* or *le cercle* and therefore with direct or circular roads. Circularity can, however, be creative for women in different geographic spheres. See Nicole Bourbonnais, "La Symbolique de l'espace dans les récits de Gabrielle Roy," *Voix et Images*, 7, No. 2 (hiver 1982), 367-84.

21. Gabrielle Roy, *Alexandre Chenevert* (1954; rpt. Montréal: Librairie Beauchemin, 1973), p. 270.

DRINK PEPSI COLA

22. Roy, *Alexandre Chenevert*, p. 252.

In the same tone as commercial messages.

23. Roy, *Alexandre Chenevert*, p. 58.

And then Alexandre's crazy imagination conjured up the image of the crowds, piling up in the Valley of Josaphat [at the Last Judgement]; all the earthly lines, the pateint waiting lines of all ages stretched out one after the other.... No noise, no talk, no sound in the Valley; only this silent march, in step, this docile movement of the crowd that on its own, followed the straight line.

24. Roy, *Alexandre Chenevert*, p. 167.

In a curious pose as if an executed prisoner.

25. Roy, *Alexandre Chenevert*, p. 191.

On the left side of the road was the penitentiary. But Alexandre found himself looking on the side of the road with the river. And he who knew nothing in the world other than the city, its lampposts, its street numbers, he was leaving it, surprised, disturbed, as if he were getting out of prison. Oh what sense of space, what light, what freedom!

See Agnes Whitfield, "*Alexandre Chenevert*: Cercle vicieux et évasions manquées," *Voix et Images du Pays*, 8 (1974), 107-20, 125.

26. Roy, *Alexandre Chenevert*, p. 259.

He also dreamed of newspapers, of magazines in huge piles on the sidewalk, bringing news of the world. It was there that one found life, a constant, moving, fraternal interchange.

27. Roy, *Alexandre Chenevert*, p. 268.

He had the odd feeling that he could not be more of a stranger in Moscow or in Paris.... "Come on," thought Alexandre: "I have lived my entire life in Montreal; I was born here, and I shall probably die here." He deeply felt the city's terrible ingratitude toward him.

It is interesting to note that Roy, a woman writer, identified more with this male character than with any other character. This may help to explain her atypical use of the cage or circle as masculine in this novel. Personal interview with Gabrielle Roy, 29 June 1980.

28. Roy, *La Montagne secrète*, p. 140.

The mysterious solitude of streets filled with people, footsteps, and lights!

29. Roy, *Cet été qui chantait*, p. 146.

Without either air or a view.

30. Roy, *Cet été qui chantait*, p. 160.

Scarcely back in her cramped lodgings without a view and without light, Martine departed for the open spaces that she had desired her entire life.

7

From Feminism to Nationalism: The Theater of Françoise Loranger, 1965-1970

Carrol F. Coates

Françoise Loranger's theater focuses on the process of liberation and affirmation of life, from the first to the last of her five full-length plays.[1] In the first two plays, *Une Maison, un jour* and *Encore cinq minutes*, she depicts the bourgeois family structure as it had developed in Quebec through the late fifties. Wife and children were supposed to subordinate personal desires to the views of the husband/father in order to preserve the family in the midst of a group of anglo-phones whose expectation was for the "French-Canadians" simply to disappear. In both plays, a household which had formerly enjoyed the services of a domestic staff no longer has servants, and the wife/mother is seen by other members of the family as being self-indulgent and disorderly. The household no longer reflects the elegance and propriety of the ideal bourgeois order.

Dominique (*Une Maison...*) has been reluctant to press upon her father, a retired judge, the realization that his fortune is gone and that the family house has been sold to pay his debts. Dominique's brother, Vincent, is furious that their father still has illusions about being able to arrange matters so they could remain in the house. Moving day has arrived, but nothing has been packed. Dominique's younger daughter, Nathalie, enters in her pyjamas to have breakfast. Michel, Dominique's out-of-work husband, does likewise.

Catherine, Dominique's older daughter, is as severe a critic as Uncle Vincent. Dominique has always had a winning personality which attracted everyone who came into the house. Secretly jealous, Catherine cannot reconcile her mother's charm with the disorder of the household: "S'ils avaient su quel désordre cachait cet accueil chaleureux! . . . Quel laisser aller! Cette maison où tout se perdait, se gaspillait, se détériorait! Que j'ai détesté vivre ici! Qu'il me tardait de me marier pour te prouver à quel point il était facile de réussir là où tu échouais si lamentablement."[2] Ironically, Catherine has made her own household so efficient and orderly that she has failed to realize that her husband, Daniel, was attracted by the less disciplined charm of her mother and younger sister. By the end of the play, moral disorder will have been added to physical chaos: Daniel and Nathalie will have made the discovery that their love for each other is mutual. If Daniel maintains his marriage, it will be only for the protection of the children.

Dominique's strength is that, in the midst of difficult circumstances, she retains a sense of self and a sensitiveness to the well-being and suffering of others. She appreciates her ambitionless husband's poetic compliments. She comforts Catherine for the pain which she feels and will continue to endure. Dominique has served her invalid father without complaint for years. After an unsuccessful attempt to keep Daniel and Nathalie apart, Dominique finally counsels Nathalie to follow her own heart: "Bonne ou mauvaise, il faut la [voie] suivre. C'est par là qu'il faut commencer, j'imagine, pour savoir qui tu es, et pour le devenir. . . . Comment faire autrement si l'on veut un jour comprendre quelque chose à quelque chose?"[3]

According to Catherine and Uncle Vincent, Dominique is to blame for the disorder and lack of discipline in the household. Her failure to adhere to the rigid values of Quebec's bourgeois society is not mere weakness, however. Dominique may not be an active agent of change, but her intelligence and openness have led her to respect and to accept the revolt of her husband and younger daughter.

Gertrude, the wife/mother of *Encore cinq minutes*, is an extreme example of the psychological paralysis to which the bourgeois order can reduce a woman. Her inability to décide on the decor she prefers for the vacant room of her daughter is a concrete manifestation of the intense conflict within Gertrude. The criticisms and demands of her husband and two children have exacerbated the moral paralysis produced by a repressed sense of guilt for an abortion which she underwent before marriage.

Henri, Gertrude's husband, can be seen as a representative bourgeois of the period of the Duplessis regime. He is resentful that his wife and children do not appreciate the standard of living which he has provided. He is unrepentant when Gertrude reveals her knowledge of his current love affair. He is defensive at his son's accusation that his success is due to compromise with the English masters. He accuses Gertrude of having almost made a homosexual of their son: for this reason, he sent Renaud to study in France. In Henri's view, the present disarray of the house is Gertrude's fault.

To Henri's criticisms of Gertrude will be added those of both Renaud and Geneviève. Renaud reproaches his mother for her "petites préoccupations personnelles et bourgeoises"[4] and with refusing to offer his sister's vacant room to a girlfriend through sheer "égoïsme."[5] Geneviève, who left home with a lover just to get away from her parents' quarrels, is shocked to find her old room being redecorated by her mother, when Renaud's room had been kept untouched, like a shrine. Geneviève finds her parents tormenting each other as they always had and concludes that she could never return to live at home. Closely following upon the sadistic interrogation in which Henri discovers Gertrude's secret abortion, Renaud shocks his mother with the revelation that he has remained at home for his own egotistical purposes: "Je ne renonce pas à l'idée de te changer."[6] Gertrude flies into a rage, overturning furniture, throwing objects on the floor, refusing the anxious solicitations of both children: "Ne me commande pas! Ne te mêle plus jamais de me dire quoi faire! Jamais plus personne ne me dira ce que j'ai à faire!"[7]

In a final confrontation with her husband and children, Gertrude demonstrates that her indecisiveness and inability to carry on a coherent conversation have vaporized. Without knowing exactly where she is going, she has determined to test her capacity to survive by herself and to control her own fate. Her resolution wins new respect from her children and even the grudging acquiescence of her husband, as she is walking out with suitcase in hand.

Although all of the full-length plays are broken into two acts, it is worth noting the structural inscription of social disorder in *Encore cinq minutes*. In Act I, there is a quasi-symmetry in the return of certain configurations of characters:

⎡   ⎡   ⎤   ⎤
〈Gert alone〉 〈Gert + Renaud〉 〈Gert + Henri〉 〈Gert + Renaud〉 〈Gert alone〉

Gertrude's first and last confrontation with another character, in this act, will be with the son towards whom she has experienced ambivalent affection—that of a mother and of a woman. Her conflict with Henri is strategically placed as a long dialogue in the middle of the act, punctuated by Henri's brief exits. This symmetrical structure is disturbed only by Renaud's remaining on stage for a short time after his father's first entry.

Act II, on the other hand, develops in a linear sequence of confrontations between characters, with no symmetry visible. The three shocks (the memory of her abortion, Geneviève's confirmation that the family situation is unbearable, and Renaud's revelation of his paternalistic attitude towards his mother) compound to provoke Gertrude's reaction in defense of her own ego. The unshakeable bourgeois order (symmetry) has been disrupted.

With *Double Jeu* (first performed on 18 January 1969 at the Comédie Canadienne but written before *Le Chemin du Roy*), Françoise Loranger takes a critical step away from the techniques of traditional theater: the dialogue is no longer the dominant element and the distinction between spectator and actor is broken down.[8] The characters are designated by number rather than by name. During performances, the actors eventually name themselves to the spectators in order to elicit a reciprocal identification and sense of participation. Stage directions are printed on the left-hand page in the published text, and they are, at moments, more extensive than the dialogue. The actors mingle with the spectators during the intermission, and the second act begins with improvisations by members of the audience who have been inspired by the pre-organized but variable "improvisations" carried out by actors during the first act.

There is the germ of a drama in the relationships between the numbered characters, who are taking an evening course in behavioral psychology or sociology at a CEGEP (Collège d'Enseignement Général et Professionnel). On this particular evening, the students have been asked by the professor to engage in a test requiring them to assume roles in a psychodrama. The students are apprehensive about opening themselves up to ridicule by their peers and doubtful about the professor's intentions.

In its uninterrupted form, the narrative of the psychodrama is less than one page long. A young woman (*jeune fille*) sees a young man across a river and falls in love with him. In her search for a means of crossing the flooding river, she first encounters a hermit in the forest. Although annoyed at being accosted, the hermit eventually takes pity and tells the young woman where she can find a ferryman. The latter agrees to embark on the dangerous crossing if the woman will undress and let him view her naked. Having paid this price, the woman discovers a new obstacle on the other bank: an immense swamp must be crossed in order to reach the spot where the young man was. A surveyor is willing to guide her through the swamp if she will make love with him. Having accepted, the woman at last reaches the man of her desires and naively recounts her adventures. Instead of appreciating the strength of her love, the young man reacts with moral rigidity, condemning the woman for having yielded to the immoral demands of the ferryman and the surveyor. He refuses to descend to her level or to allow her to climb up to the height where he stands.

The thematic aspect of this play is to be examined on two levels: that of the individuals involved in self-discovery and that of the society, in which self-discovery figures that of communal (or national) identification.

"1" and "2," both schoolteachers, are engaged to be married. In introducing himself, "2" says that he is attending night school because he wants to go beyond the elementary level of teaching. He reveals the degree to which he has assimilated the sexist values of bourgeois society when he speaks for his fiancée: "D'ailleurs ma fiancée pense comme moi."[9] "1" shows, although with initial timidity, a tendency to separate herself from her fiancé's reasoning: "C'est-à-dire . . . je suis moins ambitieuse mais. . . . Il a raison de penser à son avenir."[10] In playing out the psychodrama, these signs of difference become much more explicit: "2" has set opinions and is totally uninterested in change or in self-discovery. In a continual effort to control his fiancée's behavior, "2" threatens her when she considers playing the role of the young woman in the psychodrama, criticizes her for putting too much passion into her role-playing, sulks when she tries to consult him, and, finally, disparages her character to the group: ". . . elle est avant tout en quête de sensations."[11] "1," on the contrary, is full of life and curiosity. Of all the students in the class, she is the one who enters most fully into the psychodrama and makes fundamental discoveries about herself and her fiancé. Among other effects, she inspires her fellow students with her enthusiasm, sense of wonder, and courage. She gains the strength to accept the rejection of her fiancé at the end of the play, to realize that life with him would have been possible only at the price of complete submission to his domination.

A certain number of traits in "1" and Nathalie set them apart, as the younger generation, from the wife/mother figures, Dominique and Gertrude. Although there is an age difference of about ten years between the two younger women ("1" is thirty-two years old), neither is yet totally involved, or trapped in the bourgeois society. By breaking their engagements in the course of the respective plays, the young women avoid the closed cycle of domination and submission. Each asserts her right to explore her own way, to elect values differing from those professed by the older generations (and some of their peers). The element of revolt in Nathalie's behavior, however, is mitigated by her apparent submission to a self-sacrificing role in her new relationship with her brother-in-law. The burden of an "illicit" love in the face of family and society may be too much for both Nathalie and Daniel. "1," in *Double Jeu*, seems to be without family ties and her options are more open. In addition, she is taking advantage of education for learning about herself as well as for whatever possibilities it may offer for advancement. Her participation in the psychological test has enhanced her sense of her own individuality, of her ability to love, and has given her courage to strike out on her own without male/social approval.

The role of the surveyor is played by "3," a municipal employee, who is attracted to "1." He brings to the role more than a traditional man's interest in an attractive young woman, however. He suggests to "1" the social dimension of her personal evolution: "Assumer ce pays est aussi difficile que de s'assumer soi-même";[12] "Ce pays, c'est toi, qu'est-ce que tu attends pour t'en apercevoir?"[13] It seems manifest that, in a text composed before De Gaulle's visit to Quebec, Loranger was already surpassing the theme of subjugated woman's self-discovery and was heading towards the expression of a theme of national identification, a theme which was to become dominant in the two following plays.

Le Chemin du Roy was an entertainment of sorts, depicting the anger and hostility of Anglo-Canadians and the jubilant sense of renewal and self-affirmation of the *Québécois* on the occasion of General De Gaulle's truncated visit to Quebec and Canada, in July 1967. The setting for this play is a parodic hockey game whose players are well-known politicians of Quebec City and Ottawa. In Act I, the game is fought with vigor, with Quebec scoring all the points (Quebec City—4, Ottawa—0). In scene [x],[14] De Gaulle's progress along the "Chemin du Roy," from Quebec City towards Montreal, is broadcast, ending with the playing of the "Marseillaise," which brings emotions to a fever pitch. The final scene is the climax of the first act: as the players cluster around the gigantic feet of an unseen statue of the General, excerpts of De Gaulle's actual speech from the balcony of City Hall (24 July) are heard, ending with the (in)famous "Vive le Québec libre!"

In the second act, the game is disrupted by Quebec's withdrawal. The players and majorettes assume various identities and give the reactions of segments of the Canadian and Quebec populace to De Gaulle's speech: reactions of politicians, of people in the streets of Montreal, of the media, of the bourgeois, and of demonstrators. In each of the first eight scenes there is a mixture of anglophone and francophone comments. In the last two scenes we hear, first, a sampling of angry anglophone reactions ("I never talked French in Montreal and I never will!")[15] and, finally, the expression of the *Québécois*'s renewed sense of community ("Le Québec est à faire, nous le faisons").[16]

Like the other plays, *Le Chemin du Roy* merits a far more complex analysis. Françoise Loranger testifies that, following De Gaulle's visit, nine months were spent in research: "neuf mois de travail acharné à relire les journaux, à extraire l'essentiel des tonnes d'information qu'ils contiennent...."[17] I have not had the opportunity to make the time-consuming search through the media in search of actual reports in order to compare them with the text, but I take Loranger's statement as literally true. Without making this claim of a comprehensive search for textual sources, two highly significant examples of selective quotation, both recognizable to any reader or spectator, can be examined in connection with the conclusions which have already been drawn about the use of feminist themes in *Double Jeu* to symbolize the emergence of the nation.

The first of these two quotations is, of course, De Gaulle's speech. About one-half of the actual speech is quoted in the published text of *Le Chemin du Roy*. Most of the first paragraph is included, with only minor changes and one important deletion at the end of the paragraph (a clause in which De Gaulle took partial credit for France's role in Montreal's accomplishments). A substantial second paragraph, in which De Gaulle evoked France's reawakening interest and confidence in the French of Canada, is entirely suppressed. Several phrases from the concluding lines of De Gaulle's actual speech are then added in the text, including only part of his concluding series of vivats. De Gaulle's actual conclusion was as follows: "Vive Montréal! Vive le Québec! Vive le Québec libre! Vive le Canada français et vive la France!"[18] Loranger and Levac suppress the final references to French Canada and France. This important deletion places the emphasis squarely on the motto of the *Rassemblement pour l'Indépendance Nationale*, "Vive le Québec libre!"[19]

This modified version of De Gaulle's speech is both literally and figuratively the central element of the play, by its placement at the end of the first act and by the sustained discussion, in the second act, of the furor and enthusiasm which it provoked. The speech was the culminating point of De Gaulle's actual trip, since it led to Ottawa's decision not to receive him formally and to his abrupt departure on 26 July.

The second quotation is excerpted from the well-known song by the Beatles, "She's Leaving Home." At the end of Act II, Scene i, François Aquin and Réne Lévesque announce their intention to quit the game in order to dissociate themselves from the statement which will be issued criticizing De Gaulle's breach of protocol. The next scene, in which Lester B. Pearson (Prime Minister of Canada at the time of De Gaulle's visit) is alone on stage, is signalled by excerpts from the song. Pearson, center stage, holds a goalie's mask denoting the absent Quebec players and professes regret for Quebec's resignation: "What sort of an answer should I make him? A rude one? ... 'Out you go!' ... Dief and his likes would be very pleased of course! But then they don't care for Quebec. And I do. . . .''[20] According to Pearson, Quebec is "provocative, arrogant, snobbing us, jeering at 'God Save the Queen,' boohing her own national anthymn and not the least considerate of the brand new flag I gave her!''[21]

In response to this, we hear the end of the second stanza of the Beatles' song in which they wonder how she could have acted so thoughtlessly; how she could have done this. Like the unnamed girl in the song, Quebec has fallen in love with a stranger: "Think of it!" says Pearson. "He just had to come and smile at her and there she was, beaming with delight in his arms!" The voices of the Beatles reply that they don't know what they did wrong and that they didn't even know that they had done something wrong. Pearson wonders whether Quebec can "still be recaptured": "Could money do it? More money? But, baby, you don't know how to spend the money I give you! Still, I'll give you more if that's what you want!" The Beatles answer (the end of the last stanza) that money cannot buy fun, since there was always something inside that was denied. Pearson pleads, "Don't go! Just tell me what you want.''[22] The various politicians reply in succession: "Un Statut particulier," "Les Etats Associés," "Le Fédéralisme," "Association souveraineté," "L'Indépendance!''[23] Abandoning his pleading tones, Pearson lets his impatience show through: "Whatever name she gives it, it's always heading toward a divorce!" The final fragment of the Beatles' refrain that she is leaving home provokes a cry of rage from Pearson: "We're not through yet, Baby!''[24]

In *Double Jeu* it was simply suggested, by the surveyor, that the young woman's experience of self-discovery could also represent that of the country. In *Le Chemin du Roy*, the thematic ground of a national identity to be assumed becomes the figure upon which the play is focused. The analogy between play and song is not quite exact—the girl in the song is leaving her parents' house, while Quebec is seen abandoning a husband (Canada). The song is cleverly used, by Loranger and Levac, to make the malaise of the song's parents set a tonality for an analogous yearning for the lost unity between Canada and Quebec. Neither the parents nor Pearson are capable of seeing their own role in provoking the rupture.

Médium saignant was first produced on 16 January 1970, at Montreal's Comédie Canadienne, just nine months before the kidnappings of Robert Laporte and James Cross by the Front de Libération du Québec. The setting for the play is the "Centre Culturel" of a suburban community of Montreal. The members of the Municipal Council, arriving at the Center for a special meeting, interrupt the preparations of a group of young actors and musicians for a Mardi Gras festival the following day. Although the town clerk forgot to notify the *animateurs*, the Council asserts its prerogative to hold the meeting. Hearing that the language issue will be raised at the meeting, the *animateurs* decide to stay to witness the discussion. The language issue turns out to arouse all the fearful

undercurrents of domination and hostility: between *Québécois*, English Canadians, and neo-Canadians; between older and younger generations; between the
more conservatively and the more radically oriented citizens.

As in the two previous plays, there is little plot, in the traditional sense of
the word. The first act leads from the initial confrontation between the *animateurs*
and the members of the Council on whether the Council has the right and possibly
even the duty to declare French the language for all business of the Council,
rather than switching to English for the benefit of an English minority which
refuses to learn the language of the majority. In the second act, the Council is
tending towards passage of a resolution calling for the exclusive use of French
in its meetings. The vote is not taken, however, after Olivier's confession that
even he (the youngest and most radical member of the Council) is afraid of the
consequences. Olivier suggests that they are all victims not only of fear, but
also of suppressed hatred.

The members of the Council begin to deny that they harbor any such shameful
sentiments, but a courageous citizen rises and confesses: "Ben moi, je les z'haïs,
les anglais! Je les z'haïs, du verbe z'haïr. Un verbe inventé exprès pour eux
autres."[25] This is the trigger for a series of confessions: the anglophone Canadians
(both English and immigrants) hate the francophones; the younger and older
generations look askance at one another; women and men distrust each other.
The vicar is the last to open up. Protesting, at first, that he hates no one, he
suddenly shifts: "Personne! Personne à part moi! c'est moi que j'haïs, c'est
moi!"[26] He continues: "Je m'haïs d'être ce que je suis: un être humain."[27] This
process of self-criticism ends with an attempt to exorcise the demon of fear in
order to get on with the business of living. The play ends with a litany whose
essence is: "Démons, démons de toutes nos peurs. Démons, démons hors de
moi. . . ."[28]

After reading *Double Jeu* and *Médium saignant* in close sequence, it becomes
apparent that a common theme informs both plays: that the individual *Québécois*
or *Québécoise*, like the community as a whole, tends to let life slip by because
of various fears. They let themselves be dominated and subjected to the worst
standard of living and the worst humiliations through fear of not being able to
stand up to hostile forces, actual or anticipated.

"2" (*Double Jeu*) would fit right in as a member of the Municipal Council
(*Médium saignant*). His fiancée characterized him as "un homme qui a peur de
la vie."[29] *Médium saignant* brings this basic theme home to an absolutely contemporary issue, at the moment of the play's revival in the fall of 1976, as well
as in early 1970 for the original production. Behind the ethnic fears of *Québécois*,
Anglo-Canadians, and neo-Canadians lie the fears of individuals and smaller
groups, fears which lead towards the passive acceptance of the institutionalization
of domination and repression. It is my impression that the feminist themes of
Loranger's earlier plays gave way to the initial enthusiasm of self-affirmation
of the *Québécois* during and after De Gaulle's visit and, then, to the mounting
tension of national self-determination in the face of increasing apprehension and

hostility on the part of non-francophone Canadians. This does not imply, of course, that Françoise Loranger, any more than other *Québécoises*, thought that the problems of women in a patriarchal society had been solved.

It can be suggested, in conclusion, that *Médium saignant* represents the culmination and the most comprehensive expression of the functioning of fear beneath apparently unrelated psychological, social, and political issues. Françoise Loranger worked from the feminist perceptions of her so-called "bourgeois theater" (*Une Maison* ... and *Encore cinq minutes*, along with several shorter plays and television dramas) towards the broader statements of later, more experimental plays which were closer to contemporary issues at the moment of production.

Le Chemin du Roy was written and produced in the atmosphere of (*québécois*) enthusiasm and (Anglo-Canadian) furor over De Gaulle's public articulation of the *indépendantiste* slogan, "Vive le Québec libre!" *Médium saignant* premiered only two years later, when the *prise de conscience* of the *Québécois* had been focused by the demonstrations in Saint-Léonard over the language issue. If the feminist themes of the earlier plays are mostly absent from the two last plays (although it is the *wife* of the absent Italian councilor who articulates a mother's concerns for her family during the meeting of the Municipal Council in *Médium saignant*), it is not proven that Loranger no longer believed in the feminist issues which informed her earlier works. It is, rather, most certainly a sign that other political issues were foremost in the political discussions of the final years of the *Révolution tranquille*, from 1967 through 1970. Françoise Loranger's experiments with theatrical technique sought to provoke spectator awareness and participation: she succeeded to a considerable extent in 1968, 1969, 1970, and once more on the eve of René Lévesque's election in 1976.

The women of the first three plays (*Une Maison* ... , *Encore cinq minutes*, and *Double Jeu*) are first seen caught in the web of social relations which require that they publicly accept the "superiority" of husband or fiancé and quietly make up for his failings, particularly in the education of children and the maintenance of order in the home. The younger women are shown breaking the pattern of paternalistic domination more easily than the women of an older generation. This younger generation leaves home, accepts love without marriage, breaks marriage engagements, educates itself, and seeks self-awareness before social status.

Le Chemin du Roy stands apart from the other four plays in the sense that there are no substantial fictional characters: the hockey players are all known political figures and their dialogues are adapted from actual reports of their speeches or pronouncements following De Gaulle's electrifying visit to Quebec. The expressions of fear of the politicians in this play correspond closely to those of the Municipal Councilors in *Médium saignant*.

On the basis of this reading of Françoise Loranger's plays, we can conclude that, while men and women share some of the same fears, the *Québécoises* have been doubly colonized, by patriarchal society as well as by the English Canadians.

Loranger's women are thus more often able to recognize and to cope with their own fears, and, as a consequence, they act more quickly than the men to break the vicious cycle of domination to which they find themselves subjected. Women are less in evidence in *Le Chemin du Roy* and *Médium saignant* simply as a result of the actual political situations evoked. The primary characters portrayed are male politicians at the provincial and federal levels, the only woman being Judy Lamarsh, a Liberal minister appointed by Pearson (*Le Chemin* . . .) and male members of the Municipal Council (*Médium* . . .). At a secondary level, we could engage in a further analysis, by pointing out the various political attitudes of the women who are among the citizens attending the meeting of the Municipal Council: Anna Sabrini, the wife of the Italian member of the Council, defends her husband and their choice of English as the language of instruction for their children; Pascale, a younger woman engaged in theater, demonstrates a sense of personal independence and of social awareness akin to that of "1" at the end of *Double Jeu*. It is the men, therefore, including some of the younger generation, who show themselves to be more consistently fearful and incapable of even attempting to redirect their lives, throughout the plays examined.

Whatever the circumstances which have led Françoise Loranger to drop out of the forefront of theatrical creation in Quebec since *Médium saignant*, she deserves recognition for the accelerated pace with which she turned from radio and television drama to the production of increasingly timely and effective theater, which brought issues of intense concern to the stage of Quebec during the critical last five years of the Quiet Revolution.

NOTES

1. In order to avoid the over-simplification and difficulties of comparing scripts written for different purposes (radio, television, legitimate theater), discussion is limited to the published, full-length plays: *Une Maison, un jour, Encore cinq minutes, Double Jeu, Le Chemin du Roy*, and *Médium saignant*.

2. Françoise Loranger, *Une Maison, un jour*, Poche Canadien, No. 16 (1965; rpt. Montréal: Le Cercle du Livre de France, 1968), p. 55.

If they had known what disorder this warm welcome hid! . . . What slovenliness! This house where everything got lost, wasted, broken! How I hated living here! How eager I was to get married so I could prove how easy it was to succeed where you had failed so miserably.

This play premiered at Montreal's Théâtre du Rideau Vert on 15 February 1965.

3. Loranger, p. 152.

Good or bad, you have to follow your own [way]. That's where you have to begin, I suppose, in order to know who you are, and to become that. . . . How can you do anything else if, some day, you want to understand anything about anything?

4. Françoise Loranger, *Théâtre 2: Encore cinq minutes* (Montréal: Le Cercle du Livre de France, 1967), p. 12.

Petty, personal bourgeois preoccupations. . . .

5. Loranger, *Encore cinq minutes*, p. 50.

Egotism.

6. Loranger, *Encore cinq minutes*, p. 72.

I won't give up the idea of changing you.

7. Loranger, *Encore cinq minutes*, p. 74.

Don't give me orders! Don't try to tell me ever what to do again! Nobody will ever tell me again what I should do.

8. Françoise Loranger, "Au lecteur," in *Double Jeu*, Collection Théâtre Canadien, No. 11 (Montréal: Leméac, 1969), pp. 206-07.

This is only a first and somewhat hesitant step towards new forms of theater born from the experimentation of different groups throughout the world, especially of the Living Theater in New York.

9. Loranger, *Double Jeu*, p. 17.

Besides, my fiancée thinks like me.

10. Loranger, *Double Jeu*, p. 17.

That is ... I'm less ambitious, but.... He's right to think about his future.

11. Loranger, *Double Jeu*, p. 103.

More than anything she's looking for sensation.

12. Loranger, *Double Jeu*, p. 165.

Taking responsibility for this country is as difficult as taking responsibility for oneself. ...

13. Loranger, *Double Jeu*, p. 167.

This country is you—what are you waiting for to see that?

14. The tenth scene of Act I is not noted in the text. Laurent Mailhot believes that it is the broadcast report of De Gaulle's progress along the "Chemin du Roy," on pp. 89-90 of Françoise Loranger and Claude Levac, *Le Chemin du Roy*, Collection Théâtre Canadien, No. 13 (Montréal: Leméac, 1969). See Jean-Cléo Godin and Laurent Mailhot, *Théâtre québécois II: Nouveaux Auteurs, autres spectacles* (Montréal: Hurtubise HMH, 1980), p. 74, n. 23. *Le Chemin* ... premiered at Montreal's Théâtre du Gésu on 29 April 1968.

15. Loranger, *Le Chemin du Roy*, p. 125.
16. Loranger, *Le Chemin du Roy*, p. 127.

Quebec remains to be made, we are making it.

17. Loranger, *Le Chemin du Roy*, p. 7.

Nine months of arduous work rereading newspapers, extracting the essential part of the tons of information they contain....

18. Charles De Gaulle, *Vers le terme: Janvier 1966-avril 1969*, Vol. V of *Discours et messages* (Paris: Plon, 1970), p. 192.

Long live Montreal! Long live Quebec! Long live free Quebec! Long live French Canada and long live France!

The entire speech is reproduced on pp. 191-92 of the volume cited.

19. Loranger, *Le Chemin du Roy*, p. 91.

Long live free Quebec!

20. Loranger, *Le Chemin du Roy*, p. 106.
21. Loranger, *Le Chemin du Roy*, p. 107.

22. Loranger, *Le Chemin du Roy*, p. 107.

23. Loranger, *Le Chemin du Roy*, p. 109.

A particular status, Associated States, Federalism, Sovereignty-Association, Independence!

24. Loranger, *Le Chemin du Roy*, p. 109.

25. Françoise Loranger, *Médium saignant*, Collection Théâtre Canadien, No. 18 (Montréal: Leméac, 1970), p. 117.

Well, as for me, I hate the English! I hate them, with the verb to hate.

The speaker understands the z sound of an improperly made liaison (the French verb, *haïr*, begins with an aspirate h) to be the first consonant of the word, *z'haïr*. Françoise Loranger may well have sought to provoke laughter with the comic mispronunciation in an absolutely serious statement at a moment of high tension on an explosive issue.

26. Loranger, *Médium saignant*, p. 124.

Nobody! Nobody, except me! I'm the one I hate, it's me!

27. Loranger, *Médium saignant*, p. 125.

I hate myself for being what I am: a human being.

28. Loranger, *Médium saignant*, pp. 131-32.

Demons, demons of all our fears. Demons, demons, get out of me. . . .

29. Loranger, *Double Jeu*, p. 201.

A man who is afraid of life.

8

Louise Maheux-Forcier and the Poetics of Sensuality

Maurice Cagnon ⎯⎯⎯⎯⎯⎯⎯⎯⎯⎯⎯⎯⎯⎯⎯⎯⎯

"Le chant que je devais chanter n'a pas été chanté jusqu'à ce jour." This quotation in exergue to Louise Maheux-Forcier's first novel, *Amadou*,[1] signals the initiatory voyage that comprises all of the author's works, and specifically the early trilogy, *Amadou, L'Ile joyeuse*, and *Une Forêt pour Zoé*. Though the words are the poet Tagore's, Sappho's call is also clearly heard, as Nathalie, the protagonist, evokes in multiple experiences the omnipresence of the young Anne with whom she had come to know her first love. In the long nocturnal flashback which architects the book, the narrator filters her entire life through that initial, sacral moment, exploded at the work's outset in cosmic, mythical terms. Within *Amadou*'s novelistic world, Anne may or may not have actually existed; she might, in fact, be a necessary figment of Nathalie's fertile imagination, the keystone to creating a personal mythology that would repel her restrictive moral and religious upbringing.

Maheux-Forcier unfolds her novel as a parable equating Anne with Nathalie's beloved maple tree, planted on the day of her birth: "C'était au commencement du monde et j'étais amoureuse d'un arbre ... jeune et beau";[2] "après cet arbre j'ai aimé une fille ... Anne! ... [m]erveilleuse [qui] m'attendait du fond des âges."[3] Both are conceived (in the denotative and connotative senses of the word) as universal, immemorial phenomena transcending any specificity of time and space, as sources and incarnations of Truth and Beauty, as bearers of a morality of Love to counterbalance conventional social and spiritual norms. The text makes it clear, however, that the compensation which they offer for those norms may be no more than illusory, for as the work closes, Sylvia, the surrogate Anne figure, writes to Nathalie that their renascent dawn will be "*comme si c'était le commencement du monde.*"[4] It is, in fact, precisely at the dawn of the protagonist's anguish-ridden night that she kills her husband, the representative of prevailing mores, and sets her house afire, destroying herself and Sylvia's letters. The rebirth into love is not meant to be, for Sylvia has but usurped Anne in an effort to eradicate what was and must remain the unique, irrevocable moment of Nathalie's existence: an idyllic and idealized love-as-friendship which can be preserved intact and unsullied only in death: "Peut-être alors je retrouverai une paix ineffable jusqu'à la fin des temps dans l'éclaboussant bonheur de mes quinze ans retrouvés."[5]

Throughout *Amadou*, the sensual experience is invoked in grand imagistic contexts of cloudless millennia, wondrous apparitions, gardens of unknown flowers, of ageless castles and cathedrals, avalanches of fire and time.[6] Nathalie, in her imagination, mobilizes all her fairy-tale powers to create a terrestrial paradise of the good and the beautiful, of happiness and plenitude which she then peoples with Anne the flawless: "Anne était vivante.... Je l'avais créée: elle était moi-même; elle était mon amour."[7] This oneiric will informs much of the novel as Nathalie speaks of seeing as in a dream, of prolonging a dream. Shaped by dream into an invented princess, she is destined for a sole, irreplaceable encounter with a perfect image of Love and Truth beyond the confines of this world: "image irréelle et fantastique de cette enfant belle et douloureuse."[8] Although Nathalie remains open to new sexual relationships, heterosexual and homosexual, inevitably the hallucinatory golden visage of Anne dictates a refusal of them as dishonest and thus invalid. Avowing that she is neither a man nor a woman, that is, seemingly accepting her bisexuality, Nathalie nevertheless reverts to an ethos adumbrated by Anne and lived in the homosexual love which they shared: "[Un] être est bon et beau; il fait ce qui lui plaît sans jamais mentir, sans jamais nuire à personne et c'est le bonheur."[9] Nathalie is impelled to destroy her husband Julien, for he considers Nathalie's fabled liaison with Anne and her real one with Sylvia as moral blemishes to be extirpated: he shames her one evening into a lesbian café (a particularly sordid experience in Nathalie's eyes); he later spies on her and confiscates precious letters from Sylvia.

Time and again, Maheux-Forcier underscores the notion of an adolescent love that is very much a matter of serenity and joy, and not passion, a love which must be eternal, indifferent to sex, age, reason, and law, a love which is less sexuality than a sensuality haloed with purity and childlike innocence. Adult love appears rather as possession and submission, as a caricature of that sense of the marvelous which instinct bears with it: "une simplicité de coeur et une spontanéité de gestes libératrices."[10] The delirious freedom Nathalie seeks bespeaks a Lawrentian tonality: she refutes the narrow egotism and fierce solitude that her father inculcated and that forbade all contact and friendship as opiate myth. What she yearns for, and what Anne brings to her, is a relationship that is at once a total sharing of personalities and a preservation of the individual self: "Je n'étais plus seule: j'étais seule avec Anne!"[11] For Nathalie, Anne is both a friend and a lover in experiencing a sensuality often described in moral terms of tenderness and admiration, in aesthetic terms of beauty and perfection. Theirs is a union of souls which can be known only in the plenitude of the instant as an ephemeral, but unforgettably permanent work of art, a gratuitous and awesome chimera: "[Tu] sentiras l'oeuvre d'art quand, à la seule pensée de retrancher ou d'ajouter quelque chose, tu frémiras de détruire l'équilibre, de tout saboter."[12]

Nathalie admits that she is incapable of understanding the reality which surrounds her, but she is intensely adept at inventing and imagining what she calls fugitive visions. Indeed the novel often gives the impression of a fable cast under a spell: "[Tout] cela tient du prodige, de la magie, de la sorcellerie, d'une main invisible posée sur nos existences."[13] The narrator presents herself and her double, Anne, as fairy-like creatures in "un merveilleux triptyque,"[14] living out a child's dream of a cavern full of wonders in which Nathalie reigns as fay. She dwells in a romanesque chapel, symbol of the self, in which she (re)creates enchanted atmospheres and privileged worlds all revolving about the theme of chaste love and the resplendent but invisible presence of Anne. Nathalie refers to this Norman chapel as the heart of her story, that is, the essence of her being. It is in this passage that the author develops some of the most highly charged and poetically beautiful images of *Amadou*. Dream and reality intertwine in an atemporal setting, the religiosity of which establishes Anne and Sylvia as rival goddesses vying for the narrator's fidelity. In this charmed decor which begets astonishment and discovery, the theme and image of the luminous canticle reach their apogee. Throughout the novel, Anne's radiantly blond hair had become for Nathalie a talisman made of precious metal. Nathalie now metamorphoses the chapel's yellow hangings into walls of sunlight, transforms empty echoes into the somber and mournful rhapsodic beauty which transcribes her painful and failed efforts at realizing the perfect fusion of soul and body: "[J]'étais à jamais . . . des reflets luisants, joyeuse au soleil, illuminée . . . mais en réalité . . . je portais la mort en moi."[15] The image of Anne's flowing mane singing "comme une traînée de poudre lumineuse au soleil"[16] is immediately associated with Nathalie's tree, "mon premier amour [qui] chantait . . . de toutes ses feuilles."[17] The image also applies to Sylvia, become a divinity accomplishing ritual gestures with a magical chalice: "[L]a cascade . . . de ses cheveux dénoués . . . scintille."[18] Near the book's close the images recur as Sylvia attempts to free Nathalie from the memory of the dead Anne: "[J]e serai la lumière . . . et mes cheveux couleront . . . pour effacer le Botticelli de ton parc ensorcelé."[19]

In the final analysis, *Amadou*'s poeticized sensuality is perhaps accounted for by its protagonist's repressive Catholic background: "[L]es fleurs d'une enfance catholique sont vivaces et on ne guérit pas facilement."[20] The mother's constant admonitions to Nathalie of divine wrath bring about deep-seated feelings of guilt. Upon learning of the death of Gaspard, the pet dog, Nathalie, not insignificantly, rushes forth to protest her innocence; Anne's death by drowning remains ambiguous and Nathalie's reaction to it ambivalent. It is only when she discovers a total absence of feelings of culpability in Sylvia that Nathalie can accept her penchant for fabulation. Compensating for the pernicious influence of religion's notions of good and evil and desirous of justifying homosexual love, *Amadou*'s heroine makes of sexuality a poetically moral sensuality. She fashions herself from and her life into poetry, "une fée irréelle au fond d'un château."[21] Anne becomes a fantastic and fragile bird able to impart song to nocturnal trees, and Sylvia, a bird whose ashen wings forebode separation and death. But whatever face it may take, there is but one truth: "[L]a seule chose ... c'est ... un miracle poétique."[22]

Like the protagonist in *Amadou*, Isabelle in *L'Ile joyeuse* is an adult looking back upon a pivotal experience in the ritualistic passage from childhood through adolescence to adulthood.[23] At the ages of fifteen and sixteen, Nathalie and Isabelle rebel against the yoke of social conventions and moral tenets imposed upon them by fanatically religious mother figures whose aggressive piety, directly centered on obsessions of the flesh, takes on for both characters a clearly sexual connotation. In *Amadou* Nathalie attempts to counteract the religious enigma and unhealthy curiosity it provokes by molding a Truth and an Aesthetics "en dehors de la vie,"[24] "complètement hors du monde."[25] For Isabelle, early adolescence proves to be the most tormented and erotic period of her life, for which she seeks a palliative by imagining a phantasmagoric universe where she can evolve alone and free of all strictures. The elaboration, destruction, and ultimate restoration of this personal mythology structures *L'Ile joyeuse*.

Maheux-Forcier's female protagonist, like those of the two other works of the trilogy, must deal with and try to accept her homosexuality, a painful fact that is moralized in musical terms and poetic imagery. Her love for Julie is a composition in a major chord, while Julie herself is a luminescent creature of mane, all fire and flame, "une ... cantate en noir et blanc avec des récitatifs en perles grises à la place des yeux et la couleur de la bouche volée à toutes les oranges de la terre."[26] Sensuality and shared love are lived in a different tonality, which annihilates dissonance and brings with it a miraculous quietude, an intimacy of friendship, and tender communion. Images of radiant light blend with the musical, as when Julie's words illuminate a particular concrete reality, and by a sort of incandescent sortilege they compose the source of an exultant rebirth to life: "[L]'amour ... cela rayonne et cela se partage. L'amour vrai, c'est joyeux."[27] Isabelle invents what she calls luminous reason that will metamorphose pitiable reality into the marvelous. As an unimaginable being of moon and clouds, "quelque chose entre la lune et la biche ... l'éther et l'eau de source,"[28] she forges her world of wondrous legends, the quintessence of which dates to her childhood: "Trésor lointain de mon enfance ... la poésie des choses ... la poésie des mots."[29] If certain of these legends concocted by a credulous sixteen-year-old come to be demythified during Isabelle's heterosexual affair with Stéphane, a mature Isabelle's visionary powers will reimprint on her life the lost magic of childhood. Where earlier she escapes the banal routine of daily existence to enter into her legendary creations, she later sheds the immense weight of boredom by means of nomadic mirages: "[J]e suis un oiseau de braise et j'émigre vers un pays rutilant où je pourrai fondre mes plumes avec le soleil."[30]

The joyous island of the book's title is the central image around which Maheux-Forcier articulates the entire novel. A sacred temple reaching beyond even the reach of memory, beyond time and space, it is another landscape, another planet spoken of in terms of a cosmic union of human and natural forces.[31] On a golden, naked isle the protagonist penetrates the burning womb of nature: "[R]etrouvant l'innocence d'antiques peuplades, je délivrais mon corps ... pour le donner au soleil dans sa nudité première."[32] The phantom island is a portable and liberating myth which enables Isabelle to transform other realities in the quest for her true reason for existing. Stéphane's sexuality will thus be considered the false light of her childhood, while the sensual love experience with Julie represents its candid luminosity, the inexorable duty of self-recognition which in turn allows the strength to assume not only an inalienable freedom but also the absurdity of life and the certitude of death: "On peut enfin vivre sur une île ... l'amour ... [l]a vérité, c'est l'île!"[33] For Maheux-Forcier, this notion of love and truth associated with Isabelle and Julie's physical relationship is diametrically opposed to the tyrannical and the possessive; it stresses rather that physical possession is little or nothing compared to generous giving and receiving which refute sacrifices and concessions. The author, imagist above all, presents the theme by way of a solemn processional with Isabelle the priestess holding high the ostensorium containing the sacred host, the awesome secret of the entire ceremony: a peaceful yet intensely shared tenderness. As in *Amadou*, Maheux-Forcier underlines the key notion that sensuality is a purificatory morality: "[Q]uand Julie ... rejetait sa chevelure en arrière ... il me semblait que j'étais lavée de quelque souillure ... dans l'eau pure de ses yeux gris";[34] or again: "Julie paraissant devant moi, c'est le premier jour de la terre, et je reste habitée, complète, intacte ... une voix harmonieuse dans l'orchestre du monde ... un oiseau sur la neige."[35]

The golden island and its translucid birches serve as means for Isabelle to poeticize her vision of the world, to protect herself from deception and pain by creating a world apart, for herself and in itself: "[J]e bâtis des poèmes."[36] Indeed, Isabelle and Julie's dark paltry room becomes "un grand tournesol qui frisait ses pétales";[37] its shabby blue rug forms a river round the bed, and a straw mat is Isabelle's sandy isle. The episode is significant for it reveals both the fragility of such poetic reconstructions and Isabelle's tenacity to transcend the routine and banal into her fabulous geography. As tender glows of gold and blue irradiate the room, she becomes aware that her poem is merely a child's tale, punctured by memories of solitude, suffering, and humiliation. Hence she quickly weaves larger tapestries from childhood images: "Julie ... j'achèterai des îles.... Nous irons planter des bouleaux sur la lune, nous grignoterons des étoiles et nous créerons des musiques."[38] Through invented words and prodigious phantasms, Maheux-Forcier's heroine obstinately realizes her will to happiness that aspires to immortality and eternity.

The book's adult figures, even Julie, come to incarnate the loss of the dream of childhood, "le deuil de la fille éblouie qui sort de l'enfance";[39] they possess the desire to destroy in Isabelle what has been destroyed in themselves. Violence, cruelty, madness, submission comprise so many appurtenances of this destructive force, of adult sexuality, against which the protagonist reacts by making of herself a cartographer of illuminated chimerical countries, "restituant mon île joyeuse,"[40] countries of creative solitude, mythical countries of fire and magic, and above all, tender landscapes of childhood, "[nimbés] de mystère et de fantasme."[41] Isabelle accepts the impossibility of total, intact, shared love and happiness, the evanescence of human communication, but she also accepts the signal importance of the play betwen guise and honesty in relations with others and her own responsibility in living out what might have been truth but was in fact lie:

> Tout avait été faux autour de moi, un amoncellement d'erreurs et de travestis: Julie aurait dû être une soeur que je n'ai pas eue, ma mère, une voisine charmante que je n'ai pas connue, Jeannot, la petite fille que je n'aurai jamais enfantée.... Stéphane aurait pu être ... l'aventure indéchiffrable ... et merveilleuse....
>
> Mais il aurait fallu d'abord que moi non plus je n'aie pas été déguisée. Il aurait fallu que j'aie été vraie.[42]

In *L'Ile joyeuse*'s short final chapter, Isabelle has, after a number of years, come upon Julie and Stéphane in a tawdry nightclub where Julie, once a budding concert pianist, now plays with a mediocre pick-up band. Maheux-Forcier's expanded imagery transcribes Isabelle's shattered reality: "[I]l est né une tempête épouvantable, quelque chose entre la musique et la fin du monde."[43] Julie is no longer "terriblement rousse et terriblement belle"[44] but "horriblement maquillée, horriblement rouge."[45] In the midst of this demonic setting, a girl-child suddenly bursts one of the club's blue balloons, likened to a moon, an action which triggers an illuminating upheaval in Isabelle: "La fille au bord de l'enfance ... est venue du fond des abîmes, terre et cendre animées pour cet instant glorieux.... Je suis heureuse."[46] The incident reawakens Isabelle's personal quest for her ideal truth and beauty, enabling her to shed years of accumulated boredom and void during this "dernière nuit du monde"[47] before the aureate dawn of deliverance. Having lived lives other than her own, having expected solutions to absurdity and uselessness from the outside, she now is capable of reaching deep within herself: "[L]e miracle s'est produit.... Du fond de mon enfance, mon île était revenue [imprégnée] de vérités ressuscitées: mes rêves, mes vérités!"[48] Freeing herself from chaos, she recreates her vision of the cosmos made of the tender sensuality of her joyous island and its innocent happiness: "[J]e découvrais le premier chant du monde, le chant pur de l'oiseau.... [J]e débouchais, une fois encore, sur l'infini par la porte miraculeuse des poèmes."[49]

Thérèse, the central character and writing conscience of *Une Forêt pour Zoé*, is in many respects an avatar of Nathalie and Isabelle.[50] Maheux-Forcier keeps certain recurrent imagery intact throughout the triptych, so that here again, for example, the flowing mass of luminous hair forms the blazon for each of Thérèse's loves: Zoé, Marie, Mia, and Isis. The tree, strong maple or fragile birch, serves as referent for life or death, security or vulnerability, support or betrayal, courage or cowardice, wisdom or folly. The author's protagonists glide about in an enchanted land of artifice and magic, filled with evil spells, benevolent charms, disturbing premonitions. Unlike Maheux-Forcier's treatment of earlier incarnations of her protagonists, however, considerable emphasis is placed on Thérèse's own incandescent power of astonishment before the world and of the sexual attraction she exerts on others. Her powers of imagination are no less demanding: "Il me fallut tout inventer. . . . Il me fallut épeler le monde."[51] The image and theme of flight are reechoed as a primordial need to live a fragmented, contradictory plurality of the self, a need that is also perceived as a danger. Like Nathalie and Isabelle before her, Thérèse adopts false selves by her submission to please and emulate others whom she loves. In a movement characteristic of Maheux-Forcier's protagonists, Thérèse doubles into and virtually becomes Zoé, Marie, Mia, and Isis: "Je pénétrais dans l'image . . . le miracle."[52] Having achieved her new identities, she steps towards another, and secret, existence: "[U]n oiseau déployé . . . me transporte sur une planète où les pierres précieuses sont la monnaie courante."[53]

In her conceptualization of the love relationship, Thérèse invents scenarios, the aim and essence of which compose, this time, not only a quest for childhood but also a desire to shed the past. Far more than Nathalie and Isabelle, Thérèse is torn between adult sexuality and adolescent sensuality, represented respectively by Isis and Zoé. The truth of Zoé is a rejuvenescence in the eternal; "libre, heureuse, fantasque,"[54] she exemplifies independence from binding ties that compromise the individual self: "une liberté matérielle, tangible et totale . . . concédée au désir de son coeur et de sa chair."[55] Refusing imposed social and moral norms, she wills to become "une vraie femme, imperméable à toute notion apprise, à toute volonté extérieure à la sienne. . . ."[56] Zoé, that is, childhood, imparts to Thérèse the immediate awareness of the plenitude of the moment, the feeling of having deserved being herself in a privileged corner of the universe, of accepting without guilt the intense satiety offered by "le partage immédiat d'exaltantes minutes."[57] Zoé is happiness; Zoé wards off her solitude and boredom; Zoé contains the inexplicable and consenting joy of being alive, of knowing the world through a sense of wonder, surprise, and discovery. Zoé pulls Thérèse out of the present, but in doing so draws her back into a past which Maheux-Forcier now views as possibly a sort of corpse, stark and stiff in death. Obsessed by Zoé-childhood, Thérèse might also be possessed by it, experiencing her adult sexual relationships under the spell of an unsympathetic magic that enslaves her to a long-ago idyllic vision: "J'ai . . . tant voulu vivre l'avenir au lieu du passé. . . . [I]ls sont innombrables . . . mes pareils, à n'avoir pas non plus guéri de l'enfance."[58] Indeed, for much of the book Zoé will prevail as the center of time and space, her presence firmly ensconced in a temple dedicated to the cult of total honesty, the refusal of all fallacious pretexts.

As in the earlier novels, the overwhelming need to preserve the awe and wonder of childhood-adolescence is in good measure connected to the guilt-inducing tenets of the book's mother figure, whose millennial religious prejudices lead her to the belief that "la chair est triste et . . . l'enfer est rouge."[59] Happiness is an indecency experienced by natural enemies, the passage from adolescence to adulthood occurs according to sinister principles "qui font de l'enfant un adulte et de l'adulte, un être déchu de son enfance."[60] Hence the larger importance that Maheux-Forcier here lends to the fear of aging, the refusal of the ugly and decrepit in things and beings as unimaginably monstrous, to the theme of suicide: "[L]a réalité est [une maladie] dont il faut guérir!"[61] Hence too, more forcefully and forthrightly stated than in *Amadou* or *L'Ile joyeuse* are the notions of sensuality as a morality, of a poeticized sexuality that would counterbalance and be devoid of guilt and sin. In this respect, Isis assumes a pivotal role in the novel, as she is deemed the only adult character fit to know Zoé-the-child. In "une vieille société mal faite et tout au fond de l'âme,"[62] Isis stands as an appeal against useless reminiscences, despair, and the temptation to suicide. There where Zoé represented an immobile perfection in sensuality, a happiness permanently locked in upon itself, Isis connotes a pleasure beyond time and consecration, "dans l'immédiate perfection d'une seconde qui ... branchera aux plus hauts sommets de l'univers."[63] Maheux-Forcier pits her characters in an arena bounded by union and separation, the eternal and the perishable; and as opposed to her earlier protagonists, Thérèse is able to accept both terms of the dialectics. That perfect happiness does not exist and that the erotic does not eradicate the chaste are, in *Une Forêt pour Zoé*, taken not as moments of resolution but as points of departure.

"Recommencer est toujours un droit";[64] "[il faut] chercher à nous ... donner une seconde [vie] pour réparer la première";[65] "réinventer la joie d'être vivante":[66] if Maheux-Forcier thinks of her characters as prisoners, she considers them innocent prisoners whose fortunate lot it is to live in a world not fixed by a static past but in a state of constant becoming. Like Anne for Nathalie, Zoé is omnipresent in Thérèse's life; the latter bears her childhood anew, and as a child-adult confronts the laws of society, its contempt, religious obstacles, and moral conventions, far from quotidian order and routine: "[L]a vie [est] comme un fleuve à partir de la source au miroir de la mer, sans les inventions humaines, sans barrages, ni ponts, ni phares dont nous n'avons pas besoin."[67] As Zoé did, so Thérèse inextricably links love and friendship: "[E]n cette terre malade / l'amour ... on lui [donne] nom d'amitié";[68] "[on fait] l'éloge de l'amitié."[69] The wisdom of Isis-Zoé further enables Thérèse to rid herself of the guilt of her lesbianism and openly admit the pleasure of homosexual love against the prevailing notion of life as divided into two sexes, organized in families and justified by the beyond. Maheux-Forcier posits heterosexuality and homosexuality, sensuality and homosexuality as innumerable and reconcilable greys between extremes of white and black. Thérèse conquers the right to her authenticity as the sole truth: "[E]tre moi-même à la face du monde ... conquérir le droit d'asile au soleil pour toutes les amours étiolées";[70] Isis-Zoé thereby gives her the courage to refuse a self-betrayal and to accept a truth which, out of a sense of shame for the sexual, appears to adult society as abnormal and sacrilegious. Betrayal consists, furthermore, in possessing rather than offering; and for the author the sensual experience is the gift of conjugating the real and the fantastic, of sharing "ce que nous portons en nous de plus fragile, de plus capricieux et de plus impératif":[71] that enigmatic tenderness and grace of voluptuousness which give a meaning to life.

Maheux-Forcier elaborates in *Amadou, L'Ile joyeuse*, and *Une Forêt pour Zoé* a poetics and a morality of sensuality that are for her a prayer uttered from a verdant palace garden, a magic communion of souls held in a distant land of fire. Her composite female protagonist is a legendary personage within the invariable cycle of life and death, and the trilogy closes as Thérèse relegates Zoé to the fullness of a timeless past and envisions Isis as the whimsical enticement or perhaps the real possibility of a future happiness. The reader is, appropriately, left in an atmosphere best described by an image which epitomizes the ethics and aesthetics of Maheux-Forcier's novelistic universe: "la lumière tendre des demi-saisons."[72]

NOTES

1. Louise Maheux-Forcier, *Amadou* (Montréal: Le Cercle du Livre de France, 1963).

The song that I had to sing has not been sung before this day.

2. Maheux-Forcier, *Amadou*, p. 2.

It was at the creation of the world and I was in love with a young and beautiful tree.

3. Maheux-Forcier, *Amadou*, pp. 12-13.

After this tree I loved a girl . . . [w]onderful Anne [who] was waiting for me from the beginning of time.

4. Maheux-Forcier, *Amadou*, p. 150. Italics added.

As if it were the beginning of the world.

5. Maheux-Forcier, *Amadou*, p. 157.

Perhaps then I will find, in rediscovering the burst of happiness I knew at the age of fifteen, an ineffable peace that will last until the end of time.

6. See Maheux-Forcier, *Amadou*, p. 141, 139, 47, 43, 13.

7. Maheux-Forcier, *Amadou*, p. 13.

Anne lived. . . . I had created her: she was myself; she was my love.

8. Maheux-Forcier, *Amadou*, p. 64.

Unreal and fantastic image of this beautiful and sorrowful child.

9. Maheux-Forcier, *Amadou*, p. 54.

[A] human being is good and beautiful; he does what pleases him without ever lying, without ever hurting anyone, and that is happiness.

10. Maheux-Forcier, *Amadou*, p. 130.

A simplicity of heart and a spontaneity of liberating gestures.

11. Maheux-Forcier, *Amadou*, p. 50.

I was no longer alone: I was alone with Anne!

12. Maheux-Forcier, *Amadou*, p. 73.

[You] will sense a work of art when, at the very thought of taking away or adding something, you will shudder at destroying its balance and ruining everything.

13. Maheux-Forcier, *Amadou*, p. 72.

[All] that suggests wonder, magic, sorcery, an invisible hand resting upon our lives.

14. Maheux-Forcier, *Amadou*, pp. 32-33.

A wondrous triptych.

15. Maheux-Forcier, *Amadou*, p. 33.

I was forever ... glistening reflections, happy in the sunlight, and radiant ... but in reality ... I carried death within me.

16. Maheux-Forcier, *Amadou*, p. 14.

Like a trail of luminous powder in the sunlight.

17. Maheux-Forcier, *Amadou*, p. 14.

My first love [which] sang ... with all its leaves.

18. Maheux-Forcier, *Amadou*, p. 98.

Her loose-flowing hair ... sparkles.

19. Maheux-Forcier, *Amadou*, p. 149.

I will be light ... and my hair will flow ... and blot out the Botticelli from your bewitched park.

20. Maheux-Forcier, *Amadou*, p. 131.

The flowers of a Catholic childhood are long-lived, and one does not heal easily.

21. Maheux-Forcier, *Amadou*, p. 108.

An unreal fairy deep inside a castle.

22. Maheux-Forcier, *Amadou*, p. 113.

The only thing ... is ... a poetic miracle.

23. Louise Maheux-Forcier, *L'Ile joyeuse* (Montréal: Le Cercle du Livre de France, 1964).

24. Maheux-Forcier, *Amadou*, p. 65.

Outside of life.

25. Maheux-Forcier, *Amadou*, p. 73.

Completely outside the world.

26. Maheux-Forcier, *L'Ile joyeuse*, p. 154.

A ... cantata in black and white with recitatives of grey pearls in place of eyes and the color of her mouth stolen from all the oranges of the earth.

27. Maheux-Forcier, *L'Ile joyeuse*, p. 133.

Love ... radiates and is shared. True love is joyous.

28. Maheux-Forcier, *L'Ile joyeuse*, p. 61.

Something between the moon and the doe ... ether and spring water.

29. Maheux-Forcier, *L'Ile joyeuse*, p. 14.

Faraway treasure of my childhood ... the poetry of things ... the poetry of words.

30. Maheux-Forcier, *L'Ile joyeuse*, p. 166.

I am a bird of embers, migrating to a glowing red land where I can melt my feathers with the sun.

31. Maheux-Forcier, *L'Ile joyeuse*, pp. 20, 54.

32. Maheux-Forcier, *L'Ile joyeuse*, p. 20.

Rediscovering the innocence of ancient tribes, I offered the sun my body in its original nakedness.

33. Maheux-Forcier, *L'Ile joyeuse*, p. 153.

We can at last live on an island ... love and truth are the island!

34. Maheux-Forcier, *L'Ile joyeuse*, p. 140.

When Julie ... flung back her hair ... it seemed as though I were cleansed of some impurity ... in the pure water of her grey eyes.

35. Maheux-Forcier, *L'Ile joyeuse*, pp. 146-47.

When Julie appears before me, it is the first day of creation, and I remain alive, complete, intact ... a melodious voice in the orchestra of the world ... a bird on the snow.

36. Maheux-Forcier, *L'Ile joyeuse*, p. 30.

I construct poems.

37. Maheux-Forcier, *L'Ile joyeuse*, p. 81.

A huge sunflower curling its petals.

38. Maheux-Forcier, *L'Ile joyeuse*, p. 129.

Julie, I will buy islands.... We will plant birches on the moon, we will nibble at stars and create harmonious melodies.

39. Maheux-Forcier, *L'Ile joyeuse*, p. 51.

The affliction of the dazzled young girl who leaves childhood behind.

40. Maheux-Forcier, *L'Ile joyeuse*, p. 96.

Reconstructing my joyous island.

41. Maheux-Forcier, *L'Ile joyeuse*, p. 95.

[Tinged] with mystery and phantasm.

42. Maheux-Forcier, *L'Ile joyeuse*, pp. 156-57.

Everything around me had been false, an accumulation of mistakes and travesties: Julie should have been a sister whom I did not have, my mother, a charming neighbor whom I did not come to know, Jeannot, the little girl to whom I will never have given birth.... Stéphane could have been ... the obscure and wondrous adventure....

But it would first have been necessary that I myself not be a travesty. It would have been necessary that I be genuine.

43. Maheux-Forcier, *L'Ile joyeuse*, p. 161.

A frightening tempest arose, something between music and the end of the world.

44. Maheux-Forcier, *L'Ile joyeuse*, pp. 76-77.

Terribly red-haired and terribly beautiful.

45. Maheux-Forcier, *L'Ile joyeuse*, p. 161.

Horribly made-up, horribly red.

46. Maheux-Forcier, *L'Ile joyeuse*, p. 163.

The young girl at the threshold of childhood ... has come from unfathomable depths, bringing life to earth and ashes for this glorious instant.... I am happy.

47. Maheux-Forcier, *L'Ile joyeuse*, p. 167.

Final night of the world.

48. Maheux-Forcier, *L'Ile joyeuse*, pp. 169-70.

The miracle occurred. ... From the heart of my childhood, my island had returned, [imbued] with truths come to life again: my dreams, my truths!

49. Maheux-Forcier, *L'Ile joyeuse*, pp. 170-71.

I was discovering the first song of the universe, the bird's pure song.... I emerged, yet again, into the infinite through poetry's miraculous door.

50. Louise Maheux-Forcier, *Une Forêt pour Zoé* (Montréal: Le Cercle du Livre de France, 1969).

51. Maheux-Forcier, *Une Forêt pour Zoé*, p. 65.

I had to invent everything. ... I had to spell the world.

52. Maheux-Forcier, *Une Forêt pour Zoé*, p. 117.

I entered the image ... the miracle.

53. Maheux-Forcier, *Une Forêt pour Zoé*, p. 152.

A bird, its wings spread wide, carries me to a planet where precious stones are the everyday currency.

54. Maheux-Forcier, *Une Forêt pour Zoé*, p. 27.

Free, happy, whimsical.

55. Maheux-Forcier, *Une Forêt pour Zoé*, p. 118.

A sensual, tangible and total freedom ... granted to the desires of her heart and flesh.

56. Maheux-Forcier, *Une Forêt pour Zoé*, p. 26.

A real woman, impervious to any acquired notion, to any will other than her own.

57. Maheux-Forcier, *Une Forêt pour Zoé*, p. 91.

The immediate sharing of rapturous moments.

58. Maheux-Forcier, *Une Forêt pour Zoé*, pp. 14-15.

I ... wanted so much to live the future instead of the past.... [T]here are countless ... people like me who also have not been able to recover from childhood.

59. Maheux-Forcier, *Une Forêt pour Zoé*, p. 52.

The flesh is a sorry affair and ... hell glows red.

60. Maheux-Forcier, *Une Forêt pour Zoé*, p. 51.

Who make of the child an adult, and of the adult a being fallen from its childhood.

61. Maheux-Forcier, *Une Forêt pour Zoé*, p. 41.

Reality is [an illness] from which one must be cured.

62. Maheux-Forcier, *Une Forêt pour Zoé*, p. 45.

An old and ill-conceived society that has penetrated into the depths of the soul.

63. Maheux-Forcier, *Une Forêt pour Zoé*, pp. 132-33.

In the immediate perfection of a second which ... will join the highest summits of the universe.

64. Maheux-Forcier, *Une Forêt pour Zoé*, p. 36.

To start over again is still and always a right.

65. Maheux-Forcier, *Une Forêt pour Zoé*, p. 36.

[One must] attempt to give oneself a second [life] to make good the first.

66. Maheux-Forcier, *Une Forêt pour Zoé*, p. 71.

Reinvent the joy of being alive.

67. Maheux-Forcier, *Une Forêt pour Zoé*, pp. 164-65.

Life [is] like a river flowing from its source to the mirror of the sea, without human inventions, without barriers, or bridges, or lighthouses for which we have no need.

68. Maheux-Forcier, *Une Forêt pour Zoé*, p. 75.

On this sickly earth / love [is called] friendship.

69. Maheux-Forcier, *Une Forêt pour Zoé*, p. 173.

[One sings] the praises of friendship.

70. Maheux-Forcier, *Une Forêt pour Zoé*, p. 185.

To be myself before the world ... to gain the right of sanctuary in the sun for all inhibited loves.

71. Maheux-Forcier, *Une Forêt pour Zoé*, p. 132.

What we bear in us that is most fragile, most whimsical, most imperative.

72. Maheux-Forcier, *Une Forêt pour Zoé*, p. 170.

The delicate light 'tween seasons.

9

Love on the Rocks: Anne Hébert's *Kamouraska*

Murray Sachs ————————————————————

Anne Hébert's haunting and powerful novel *Kamouraska*, which is surely destined to endure as a masterpiece of *le roman québécois*, brilliantly reconstructs a notorious real-life scandal which had shocked the inhabitants of Quebec in 1839. In a bold prefatory note which served the novel as epigraph, the author firmly staked out her own position on the issue of the relationship between fact and fiction which she knew would be raised by her work:

Quoique ce roman soit basé sur un fait réel qui s'est produit au Canada, il y a très longtemps, il n'en demeure pas moins une oeuvre d'imagination. Les personnages véritables de ce drame n'ont fait que prêter à mon histoire leurs gestes les plus extérieurs, les plus officiels, en quelque sorte. Pour le reste, ils sont devenus mes créatures imaginaires, au cours d'un lent cheminement intérieur.[1]

In the most carefully precise language, Anne Hébert's epigraph asserts that her reconstruction of the nineteenth-century story owes little to the known facts and everything of real consequence to her own creative imagination. The justification for so sweeping a claim lies in the text of *Kamouraska* itself, which indeed gives scant narrative space to the scandalous raw material of the real-life source: adultery, the brutal murder of the husband by the lover, and the lover's subsequent flight from justice, leaving the widow to stand trial alone for complicity in the murder. The raw material sketches a lurid adventure of lust and crime in which Anne Hébert obviously had little interest, since *Kamouraska* is not at all that kind of novel. Her interest was rather in character, in motivation, in feelings, and in the apparent link between Quebec's rugged landscape and the human passions bred there. As the concluding sentence of the epigraph seems to imply, the real-life actors in the Kamouraska drama had long occupied her imagination, not as a matter of prurient interest, but because she saw in their story an actual example of the way the Quebec environment can affect individuals; and in the course of the "lent cheminement intérieur" of which she speaks, those actors had gradually become assimilated in her imagination to other creatures of her own invention by means of whom she had sought, throughout her career and in various literary forms, to articulate the same themes. The ultimate implication of the epigraph, indeed, appears to be that, however different from her previous compositions *Kamouraska* may, on the surface, appear to be—and she was mindful of the fact that she had never before used a historical happening as a source of inspiration, nor told a story so explicitly rooted in time and place—it was nevertheless not a new thematic departure for her, but simply a continuation, by other means, of her pursuit of the artistic objectives she had always had. *Kamouraska*, in short, had its real origins not in a newspaper *fait divers*, but in the first halting steps of her own literary career.

Born into a prominent Quebec family of writers and intellectuals, Anne Hébert came to her literary vocation naturally and at a suitably early age. She began her career, in the customary manner, with poetry. During that first decade of her writing career, however, she also tried her hand at the short story, and she published a small group of her experiments in that form in 1950, when she was thirty-four. The volume, called *Le Torrent*, contained one story dated 1939, the year she first began to publish her poems, but most bear dates in the mid-1940s, including the title story, which is clearly the finest piece of work in the collection, as well as the one most clearly related, in its themes and techniques, to the concerns that would later animate *Kamouraska*. "Le Torrent" is, to begin with, a first-person narrative, a sort of autobiographical meditation in poetic prose by a young narrator named François, who has been brought up in an isolated house in the woods by his sternly tyrannical mother. When he rebels, at the age of seventeen, against her wish that he become a priest, she strikes him angrily across the ears with her heavy keys, rendering him deaf and leaving him with a constant roaring noise in his ears: the roar of the wild mountain stream near their house. Subsequently, his mother is killed when she is thrown from a rebellious horse, and François pays a man money to obtain the man's daughter for a companion, to assuage his loneliness.

The relationship proves unsatisfactory for both, and the girl leaves him, whereupon he regains his hearing and is free of the roaring noise. This release is hardly liberating, however, for François must now face the truth that he has nothing left in his life but his own bitter past to relive over and over. The story's ending abruptly illuminates for the reader the haunting sentence with which it opens: "J'étais un enfant dépossédé du monde."[2]

Even so rapid a summary demonstrates that the story is determinedly unrealistic, having the tone and manner of a fantasy, and that the details of the plot form a network of symbols. While the story's intended meaning remains elusively wrapped in suggestion rather than statement, it is impossible to mistake its central theme, which is the pain of growing up in an authoritarian society and in a wild physical setting unsubdued by the arts of civilization. The vague and fantastic world of "Le Torrent" is recognizably the same as the real and highly specific world of *Kamouraska*. Among the remaining stories of *Le Torrent*, "Le Printemps de Catherine" seems especially worth mentioning because of its poignant demonstration that love can, in the right circumstances, lead logically to murder; and "La Maison de l'Esplanade" offers a chilling vignette of the tenacity with which class barriers are maintained in the city of Quebec, permanently separating the gentry of *la haute ville* from the common folk of *la basse ville*. Interestingly enough, the same theme of rigid and dehumanizing class distinctions in old Quebec was evoked again, some twenty years later, in a technically more sophisticated story called "Un Grand Mariage," which Anne Hébert included in a revised edition of *Le Torrent*, containing new material and published in Paris by Editions du Seuil in 1963. The similarity of theme and setting in "La Maison de l'Esplanade" and "Un Grand Mariage," which appear together in the 1963 edition of *Le Torrent*, affords a unique opportunity for comparison, and permits the reader to measure Anne Hébert's personal growth in the craft of fiction between the respective dates of composition, 1942 and 1962. The superior craft in "Un Grand Mariage," especially the plotting and characterization, already display the skills that would be needed to write *Kamouraska*.[3]

Following the experiments of the 1940s in the lyric poem and the short story, Anne Hébert next turned to the writing of drama, in her restless search for an appropriate literary identity. During the early 1950s she worked on radio, television, and film scripts, in the employ of the Canadian Broadcasting Corporation and the National Film Board—both agencies of the federal government of Canada. From this new apprenticeship there eventually emerged a small volume of theatrical writing published in Montreal in 1967, and consisting of a dramatic poem for radio called *Les Invités au procès*, produced on the CBC in 1952; a play for television, *La Mercière assassinée*, performed on the CBC in 1959; and a play for the stage, titled *Le Temps sauvage*, which the famous Théâtre du Nouveau Monde mounted in 1966. All three plays afford intimations that the themes and character types of *Kamouraska* were already in the process of development in Anne Hébert's creative imagination, during this entire fifteen-year period. *Les Invités au procès*, for example, depicts a gentle man who proves capable of murder when his wife becomes unfaithful, while *La Mercière assassinée* depicts a gentle woman who proves capable of multiple murders, patiently planned over a long lifetime, as revenge for humiliation visited upon her, in her youth, by her social betters. The violence of murder is absent from *Le Temps sauvage*, but not the violence of revolt, which shatters the unity of a family chafing too long under the rigid control of a domineering matriarch, who has confined them in an isolated house in the wilderness. The catalyst of the family revolt is a young female relative, recently orphaned, whose free spirit inspires rebellion not only in the children but, surprisingly, in the meek father of the family who seemed long since to have abdicated his manhood to his cold shrew of a wife. But what brings *Le Temps sauvage* closest in theme to *Kamouraska* is its emphasis on the effects of a wilderness environment on human behavior.

It is the matriarch, Agnès Joncas, who has insisted on bringing up her children in an isolated house on a mountainside, north of Montreal. The growing years should be "le temps sauvage" for a family, she maintains, so the children can be kept "à l'abri du monde entier, dans une longue enfance sauvage et pure."[4] But she herself later admits the high human cost exacted by the preservation of this primitive innocence when she remarks to her son: "Mon pauvre petit! tu ne seras sans doute jamais un homme. Qui est jamais tout à fait un homme ou une femme dans ce pays d'avant la création du monde?"[5]

The play *Le Temps sauvage* is the work of Anne Hébert which immediately precedes *Kamouraska* in the writing, having been composed in the middle 1960s. Its thematic resemblances to *Kamouraska* are therefore perhaps to be expected. Yet there is one work, more remote in time of composition, which resembles *Kamouraska* even more, in themes, plot, characters, and literary techniques. Indeed, in retrospect it appears to the informed reader to be almost a first draft of *Kamouraska*: Anne Hébert's first novel, *Les Chambres de bois*. This work was undertaken after Anne Hébert made the decision, in the mid-1950s, to spend part of each year in Paris—perhaps to escape the sense of being artistically and personally stifled which she seemed to feel in the puritanical ambiance of Quebec— a feeling she had expressed, earlier, in veiled terms, in her published poems and stories. *Les Chambres de bois* was probably written in Paris and was the first of her works to be published there, by Editions du Seuil, in 1958.[6] The same publishing house would, soon thereafter, issue revised editions of her collected poems and her short stories, each volume with new material added, and would become the publishers of *Kamouraska* (1970) and of her most recent novels, *Les Enfants du sabbat* (1975), *Héloïse* (1980), and *Les Fous de Bassan* (1982). It was this Paris publishing firm which undertook to make Anne Hébert's work known outside of Quebec.

Les Chambres de bois clearly marks a new phase in the development of Anne Hébert's career, following her flirtation with the drama, both because it is associated with her move to Paris and because it was her first attempt at a longer work of fiction. It was perhaps also a symptom of the author's new personal sense of liberation that *Les Chambres de bois* was the first narrative she ever wrote which is told exclusively from the point of view of a female protagonist. The protagonist, named Catherine, is in her late teens as the story begins and finds herself burdened with the care of her younger sisters because she is the oldest child, and their mother has died. The father, a passive figure, is given to long silences, and an aunt of Catherine's has taken on the role of authority figure in the family, as substitute for the mother. The aunt and the father together decide that it is time for Catherine to marry, when her hand in marriage is requested by a strange and inarticulate young man named Michel who lives in the *château* and is therefore considered a "catch," being both noble and wealthy. Catherine obediently—perhaps even hopefully—accepts the arranged marriage, but it proves to be painfully unhappy for both, because Michel is emotionally immature and cannot give Catherine the love she desires. For a long time, he refuses even to consummate the marriage, having been brought up to regard sex as sin and women as agents of Satan. Moreover, his life is completely dominated and controlled by his iron-willed and haughty older sister whom he worships and detests by turns. Michel takes Catherine to live, not in a mansion but in a bare two-room apartment with wood-paneled walls—the *chambres de bois* of the title, which gradually take on the confining atmosphere of twin coffins. Eventually Catherine finds the great courage needed to revolt against her predicament and leaves Michel. Living alone by the seaside, Catherine attracts the attention of another strange and silent young man named Bruno. But because Bruno, unlike Michel, seems capable of tenderness and is gently affectionate with her, Catherine agrees to become his wife, thus again embracing marriage as her inevitable destiny and only hope of happiness. This rueful resignation to a risky fate is symbolized in the book's closing scene, in which Catherine pays a farewell visit to Michel, to return to him the ring he had once given her as the token of their dream of happiness together in marriage.

The story is told in gently rhythmic prose, and the people and places of the plot all have a dreamlike quality, detached from reality, only vaguely identified. It is impossible to know in what country or at what time the story takes place, since Catherine, whose point of view controls the narrative, seems oblivious to the sense of time and place in her exclusive concern for emotions. This deliberate air of detached unreality tends to suggest to the reader that everything done or said in the book has significant symbolic value. There is certainly no conventional attempt made to maintain a coherent, sequential narrative. Instead the work proceeds fitfully, by means of a series of brief, unnumbered scenes or episodes, with blank spaces on the page to indicate the passage of time or a change of setting—a technique that seems almost cinematographic, and that would be used again, but with more controlled and subtle effect, in *Kamouraska*.

More intriguing still is the fact that *Les Chambres de bois* sets up substantially the same plot situation and employs the same character types as does *Kamouraska*, though without following the situation through to any kind of resolution. Thus Catherine, like the heroine of *Kamouraska*, is first presented as a vibrant young teenager, trapped in, and oppressively controlled by, her female-centered family. She makes the conventional bid for happiness by marrying the scion of an aristocratic, château-dwelling family. When she finds that her husband is hopelessly immature, and his style of life anything but aristocratic, she leaves him but soon turns for solace to another young man who is not an idle aristocrat but a competent professional man earning his own living as an engineer. In all essential respects, therefore, the story of Catherine, Michel, and Bruno parallels the story of Elisabeth d'Aulnières, Antoine Tassy, and George Nelson in *Kamouraska*, though in *Les Chambres de bois* the story of the relationship between Catherine and Bruno is not told, or even explored in any depth, since the novel concludes just as that relationship begins to take shape. Nothing in the concluding sequence of the novel permits the reader to know whether Catherine's acceptance of marriage with Bruno, at the end, is intended to constitute a happy ending for her love quest, or the ultimate defeat of her revolt against the tyranny of social convention. The ending can be read either way. That inconclusiveness is the principal artistic weakness of *Les Chambres de bois*: it gives the entire novel a tentative and unfinished air, as though it were the first draft of a story whose meaning and shape had not yet fully matured in the author's own mind. One might speculate that the fault is a natural one for a first novel. What seems incontestable, however, is that in Anne Hébert's artistic development, *Les Chambres de bois* was a kind of preliminary sketch, or rehearsal, for the eventual composition of her most fully realized masterpiece, *Kamouraska*.

Kamouraska is at least twice as long as *Les Chambres de bois* and many times more complex in its structure. The complexity results from an ingenious technical invention of the author by which two intertwined stories are told, having two different time frames and two separate casts of characters and yielding multiple levels of meaning for the reader. That invention, which has the purpose of rendering the first-person technique more natural, consists of superimposing on the historical drama of Kamouraska a fictional but entirely plausible crisis in the subsequent life of the female protagonist. As the novel opens, the scandal of Kamouraska is more than twenty years in the past, and its central figure has, for eighteen years, been the respectable wife of a notary in Quebec City, by whom she has had eight children. Madame Rolland is suddenly confronted with a crisis because her husband, gravely ill for some weeks, is now expected to die at any moment. As she performs the wifely duty of the death watch, her thoughts are involuntarily invaded by the insistent memory of an earlier death watch, involving her first husband. And thus the double narrative is launched: both the account of the crisis in the Rolland household, which will last about twenty-four hours, and the simultaneous reliving of the earlier drama, in the waking thoughts and in the dreams of Madame Rolland during that same period. Instead of having to provide a frame for the narrative, which would account for the fact that the protagonist retells her own story, in her own words, Anne Hébert is thus able to present the narrative, with complete naturalness, as a transcription of what is going through the mind of her female protagonist as she keeps the vigil beside her husband's sickbed. The artistic difficulty, of course—managed with remarkable skill by the author—is to present the confused and turbulent thoughts of the protagonist, weaving erratically back and forth between the present and the past, and between her identity as the matronly Madame Rolland and as the young Elisabeth d'Aulnières-Tassy, without losing the coherence of the narrative thread or discouraging the reader's attention.

The introduction of the first-person narrative voice is accomplished expeditiously and unobtrusively. The opening paragraph consists of terse, matter-of-fact statements in the *passé simple* by an anonymous narrator, to set the scene: "L'été passa en entier. Mme Rolland, contre son habitude, ne quitta pas sa maison de la rue du Parloir. Il fit très beau et très chaud. Mais ni Mme Rolland, ni les enfants n'allèrent à la campagne, cet été-là."[7] The second paragraph, still in the third person, modulates in tone to a more descriptive and analytical imperfect tense, informing the reader of what Madame Rolland is thinking: "Son mari allait mourir et elle éprouvait un grand paix.... Mme Rolland attendait, soumise et irréprochable."[8] A few sentences later, in the same paragraph, the style shifts again, to *style indirect libre*, imperceptibly moving the reader into the rhythm and pattern of Mme Rolland's thought processes: "Tout semblait vouloir se passer comme si le sens même de son attente réelle allait lui être bientôt révélé. Au-delà de la mort de l'homme qui était son mari depuis bientôt dix-huit ans."[9] Finally, the third paragraph introduces the first-person pronoun, and the anonymous narrator disappears: "Il aurait fallu quitter Québec.... Il n'y plus personne que je connaisse en ville."[10] The narrative remains in the first person for the rest of the book, until the very last page when the anonymous narrator quietly returns to record the novel's last moments, thus restoring distance between reader and characters, and enabling the reader to take gentle leave of Mme Rolland's tragic universe.[11]

The technical virtuosity of the opening has the prime purpose of firmly fixing the novel's focus, assuring that all events, past and present, will be exclusively filtered through the consciousness of the female protagonist. There were both advantages and necessities in the adoption of so restricted a point of view. It was certainly the only means by which the complex double vision and double time frame could have been managed without resort to constant explanatory interruptions and shifting of gears in the narrative. It was the ideal means of ensuring that the reader could make the necessary imaginative leap and enter sympathetically into the events of another age, as though experiencing them in person. For those readers who came to the novel with some prior knowledge of the real-life events depicted, moreover, the device effectively undercut preconceptions by assuring a perspective on the events no official account would have duplicated. There were also, of course, the usual gains and losses that attach to the use of any first-person narrative format: heightened vividness in the characterization of the narrator-protagonist, but a corresponding loss of vividness in the portrayal of other characters; reduction of aesthetic distance, yielding the greatest possible sensation of reader involvement with characters and events; and the ability to avoid the awkward artificialities of formal narrative by adopting the directness and natural flow of the spoken word. But the predominant motivation for the particular choice of point of view was surely that Anne Hébert wished her readers to recognize in the Kamouraska material what she herself had come to see in it: an instance of the victimization of women by certain facets of patriarchal Quebec society. That is why the story had to be told in terms of the private, innermost feelings of the woman most intimately involved in the affair, the woman who stood publicly accused of being guilty of murder. Seeing the events through her eyes, the reader would better be able to grasp the limits of her guilt and understand why she could properly see herself as more sinned against than sinning. It is worth recalling, in this connection, that Anne Hébert declared, in a radio interview in 1974, that one of the themes of *Kamouraska* is "la déculpabilisation de la femme"—freeing woman of guilt.[12]

A mark of the novel's skillful construction is that all of the main themes are evoked in the very first chapter, beginning with the theme of waiting for death. Mme Rolland has ambiguous feelings about this theme, which will be present from one end of the novel to the other: although she knows herself to be irreproachable in her conduct towards her dying husband, she senses, in a touch of paranoia, that she is looked upon with suspicion in the household and in the city outside: "On m'observe. On m'épie. On me suit. On me serra de près."[13] And she herself feels disturbed and uneasy in this state of waiting, because it recalls the time, twenty years earlier, when she was waiting for word from her lover that her first husband was dead. She admits to herself that now, as then, the death would signify, for her, not grief but freedom: "Bientôt je serai libre à nouveau. Redevenir veuve.... Partir, à la recherche de l'unique douceur de mon coeur."[14] But she recalls that on the earlier occasion she had suffered a bitter disappointment after the death: "C'était à Sorel. Après le malheur de Kamouraska. Au retour de mon amour de Kamouraska. Je n'avais jamais été aussi proche du bonheur. Et lui, l'homme unique, il a fui, les mains pleines de sang."[15] Thus the theme of the death watch evokes, for Elisabeth, a set of opposite reactions: anxiety and guilt, on the one hand, and thoughts of freedom and happiness on the other. Even the thoughts of freedom and happiness, which Elisabeth tends to equate, are in fact also contradictory, since the freedom is only valued as the route to happiness, which Elisabeth can only define as love, obtainable only at the sacrifice of freedom. Elisabeth's whole view of the world thus involves a network of inherently contradictory aspirations which cannot be happily resolved. An uneasy awareness that her life's ideal is a tissue of contradictions, and therefore impossible of attainment, is movingly expressed by Elisabeth in a painfully ambivalent incantation which closes the book's first chapter: "L'amour meurtrier. L'amour infâme. L'amour funeste. Amour. Amour. Unique vie de ce monde. La folie de l'amour."[16] From those words one might properly conclude that the fundamental themes of *Kamouraska* are to be the legendary and inseparable pair, love and death; and that, for the protagonist, each of these two fundamental themes will invoke, in turn, subsidiary pairings of opposites: hope and fear, serenity and guilt, freedom and bondage, happiness and disaster. Both this fundamental pair of themes, and all the subsidiary echoes, do indeed haunt the novel at every turn, and in a variety of forms, setting the novel's tone and spirit and underlining its ultimate meaning.

These themes are invoked mainly, but not exclusively, with reference to the life experiences of the narrator-protagonist. For example, early in her troubled evocation of her own past, Elisabeth goes so far as to imagine that she must first have shown her longing for freedom when she was still a fetus in her mother's womb:

Ma mère en grand deuil me porte dans son ventre, comme un fruit son noyau. Cette petite a poussé dans un cocon de crêpe. Peut-être pourrais-je voir des images du monde d'alors par les yeux, rougis de larmes, de la jeune veuve qui est ma mère? Le cercueil

de mon jeune père quitte la maison. Ma mère s'évanouit. Et moi, bien enfermée à double
tour, je lui donne des coups de pied dans la foie. Pour la réveiller. Je me démène comme
un cabri. Nous pourrions en mourir toutes les deux, ma mère et moi, d'un évanouissement
aussi terrible et prolongé.
—Quelle petite fille malfaisante!
Est-ce là la première voix du monde qui parvient à mes oreilles?[17]

This passage is particularly rich in the suggestive associations that accompany
such a theme as freedom in this novel: we note that freedom is also the love of
life and the struggle against death, for Elisabeth, while for her just-widowed
mother, love and death have become so inseparable that freedom and life have
lost their meaning. As for society—"la première voix du monde"—it will view
Elisabeth's struggle for life and freedom as "malfaisante," a form of evil, of
which it will constantly accuse her, inducing feelings of guilt.

In a profound sense, this fetus fantasy summarizes the meaning Elisabeth finds
in the course her entire life has taken and the central meaning the whole novel
is meant to convey as well. An echo of that fantasy returns, on the last page of
the novel, constituting Elisabeth's final image of her tragic personal fate:

Dans un champ aride, sous les pierres, on a déterré une femme noire, vivante, datant
d'une époque reculée et sauvage. Etrangement conservée. On l'a lâchée dans la petite
ville. Puis on s'est barricadé, chacun chez soi. Tant la peur qu'on a de cette femme est
grande et profonde. Chacun se dit que la faim de vivre de cette femme, enterrée vive,
il y a si longtemps, doit être si féroce et entière, accumulée sous la terre, depuis des
siècles! On n'en a sans doute jamais connu de semblable. Lorsque la femme se présente
dans la ville, courant et implorant, le tocsin se met à sonner. Elle ne trouve que des
portes fermées et le désert de terre battue dont sont faites les rues. Il ne lui reste sans
doute plus qu'à mourir de faim et de solitude.
   Malfaisante Elisabeth! Femme maudite.[18]

The image Elisabeth has of herself at the end is therefore that of the permanent
pariah, a person of such passionate attachment to life, freedom, happiness, and,
above all, love that society, feeling itself threatened, closes its doors and condemns her as evil.

This closing image simply encapsulates the range of reactions she has encountered at every turn of her life. Growing up under the stern disciplinary
tutelage of her widowed mother and her three maiden aunts, she feels she was
treated as though she were "une bête sauvage qu'on a enfermée et qui guette
dans l'ombre pour vous sauter dessus."[19] Her arranged marriage with Antoine
Tassy—desirable, she was told, because he is the young lord of Kamouraska—
feels more like death than love to her: "Je vais me marier.... Est-ce l'amour?...
Je crois que je vais me noyer."[20] Antoine Tassy, indeed, fears her vitality once
they are married, beats her, rejects her, threatens her with a joint suicide, equating
marriage not with love but with death: "'Viens| donc avec moi. Cette corde est
assez grande pour deux, Elisabeth, ma femme. Les liens du mariage, c'est ça.

Une grosse corde bien attachée pour s'étouffer ensemble.'''[21] She believes she has freedom, happiness, and love within her grasp, at last, in her relationship with the young American doctor, George Nelson, but he too eventually repudiates her as an evil influence. "*'It is that damned woman that has ruined me*,'" he says in English to the medical student who has been studying with him, just as he prepares to flee to Vermont.[22]

The pattern of fear and rejection which Elisabeth seems to inspire, sooner or later, in everyone—and which smacks of the medieval in its superstitious attribution of the power of witchcraft to a woman—reaches its climax in the book with the moment when her sick husband asks that the nurse be sent for, to give him his medicine. In her paranoia, she is sure that her husband of eighteen years is thus rejecting her out of fear that she will kill him as she was accused of having done to her first husband. She imagines what he is thinking: "Il ne faut pas que je boive une seule gorgée quand elle est là. Non. Rien quand elle est là. Elle me tuera. Surtout qu'elle ne me prépare pas mes gouttes elle-même!"[23] The book's final nightmare image of Elisabeth as pariah expresses her despairing inner reaction as she takes in the truth that her husband has apparently survived this crisis and will not die. The bitterness that wells up in her at that moment of realization that her husband is alive is grimly identical to the despairing reaction she had experienced at the end of the death watch for Antoine Tassy, in her *folle jeunesse*: she is not to be free, after all, to pursue the happiness in love she has ceaselessly craved in life! The moment reduces her to tears, and in the book's final, ferocious irony, the tears are misinterpreted: '"—Voyez donc comme Madame aime Monsieur! Voyez comme elle pleure...."[24]

The ending makes clear the significance of the simultaneous double narrative which structures the book. Almost at the very moment Elisabeth finishes reliving in her imagination that youthful nightmare of love and death with Antoine Tassy and George Nelson and awakens from her dream, she is summoned to Jérôme Rolland's bedside to see that he has survived the crisis. The story of the sick-bed vigil for her second husband thus turns out to be no more than an ironic reprise of the vigil for her first husband. The second nightmare of love and death merely confirms the first: for Elisabeth d'Aulnières-Tassy-Rolland and her ilk, there can *never* be, in this world, the life of freedom and love she longs for. That is her tragic and irreversible destiny.

The central truth on which Anne Hébert chose to focus, in exploring the raw material of the Kamouraska scandal, and which she represented so poignantly as the tragic destiny of Elisabeth d'Aulnières, should not be thought to exhaust the meanings which she managed to weave into her richly textured and intricate novel. *Kamouraska* is also, in significant degree, a political novel about English-French relationships and the colonial mentality in nineteenth-century Quebec, a social novel about class, sex, and economic differences, and a philosophical novel about the proper role of tradition, morality, and the Church in the life of the individual. Moreover, the central tragedy of love forever unattainable is not presented as solely Elisabeth's destiny, nor even as exclusively a woman's destiny. The subjectivity of the first-person technique of course requires that the spotlight focus primarily on the central figure. Since, in this case, the central figure is a woman, the novel is presented from a woman's perspective. It is, moreover, quite probable that Anne Hébert deliberately chose to place a woman at the center of this novel's concern in order to emphasize the element in the real-life case which had generally been obscured and little understood. In that sense, *Kamouraska* is undeniably a novel in which a woman's fate is the central theme. Yet the author has been careful to extend and universalize that theme. Such secondary figures as the servant Aurélie and Elisabeth's mother are also shown to be, in quite different ways, victims of the same tragic destiny as Elisabeth. Anne Hébert is at particular pains to portray George Nelson, too, as something more than a coward and a moral weakling. He is, after all, an honorable and altruistic doctor, of strict religious principles and of a deeply compassionate nature, who is horrified at the speed and ease with which his principles disintegrate, giving way to lust and violence. He, too, is a victim of the environment and a tragic figure in the drama of blighted love in which he plays so great a part. There is even a hint of the tragic in the abject figure of Antoine Tassy, clearly made into a self-destructive boor by the coarse environment of the *bas du fleuve* where he grew up and the iron-willed domination exercised over him by a cold and unfeeling mother who forever distorted his view of women. Arch-villain though he is in the drama of *Kamouraska*, Antoine Tassy is also one of its victims. The tragedy that is central to *Kamouraska* is most often female in scope, but is ultimately portrayed as a human tragedy, visited upon individuals of both sexes, by social, cultural, and environmental forces as much as by innate characteristics.

The most conspicuous emblem of this concept is the title which Anne Hébert chose for her novel: *Kamouraska*. It is an old Indian name, given to a village between Quebec City and the Gaspé, on the rock-bound banks of the St. Lawrence River. Now it is a fact that too little of the action of the novel takes place in Kamouraska to make that place name the inevitable choice for the book's title. One must suppose, therefore, that Anne Hébert saw something essential to the novel's meaning in the name itself, to have insisted on its use as the title. She might, to begin with, have counted on the harsh and alien sounds of the name to evoke for her readers a wild and rugged landscape as setting for the drama of primitive passions she would recount. She might even have intended that the barbaric-sounding syllables of Kamouraska would convey the *québécois* character of her book, especially for readers in France who might be put in mind of the town of Péribonka, setting of Louis Hémon's famous novel *Maria Chapdelaine*. But it is the text of the novel itself which points to the most significant ideas the title was meant to call to the reader's attention.

Kamouraska first enters Elisabeth's consciousness when she meets Antoine Tassy, at a hunting party. The occasion is suggestive of something primordial in the character of both, no doubt. As the "seigneur de Kamouraska," Antoine is of the wealthy, landed aristocracy, but Elisabeth finds him coarse-mannered and crudely sensual: "Il vient du bas du fleuve. Je ne sais rien de lui. Mais c'est un voyou, j'en suis sûre. De bonne famille, mais un voyou quand même."[25] After the marriage, she journeys to Kamouraska with Antoine to live in the family manor house. The trip itself is uncomfortable, on rough roads; and the country inns they stop at, which enchant Antoine, horrify Elisabeth with their indigestible food and ugly furnishings. "Je crois que je m'encanaille dans cette auberge de campagne," notes Elisabeth.[26] The estate at Kamouraska is large but ungracious and devoid of refinement. Even the weather is unbearable: "Il y a trop de vent ici. . . . Le vent me fait mourir."[27] The rough and primitive conditions of life in this milieu seem to make the inhabitants rough and primitive as well, widening still further the gap between Elisabeth and her husband, who turns surly and petulant on home ground. A clear symbol of this irremediable discord between Elisabeth and the inhabitants of Kamouraska appears after the first child is born: "La belle-mère apporte un châle de laine du pays qu'elle vient de tricoter. La mère affirme que c'est trop rude pour son fils. La belle-mère, vexeé, frappe avec sa canne sur le plancher."[28] As Antoine's behavior grows more crude and violent, life becomes literally impossible in Kamouraska for Elisabeth, and she goes back to her home in Sorel, back to the more "civilized" end of the river. But the point has been amply made: it is not possible for a happy life and tender feelings to flourish in that wild and rocky environment. True, Antoine's character is part of the problem. He is immature, weak-willed, undisciplined, and guilt-ridden in the presence of his domineering mother. But he is also bestial and vicious in his manners and his impulses—a product of his physical environment as much as of his family environment.

Kamouraska will, naturally, be the site of George Nelson's climactic outburst of male violence in which the unsuspected beast in him emerges, and he angrily murders Antoine Tassy. The murder is the more shocking, both to himself and to the reader, because he is a doctor, committed by profession to healing. Significantly, Elisabeth tends to think of this event, somewhat antiseptically, as "le malheur de Kamouraska."[29] As she replays the event in her anguished dream and imagines George Nelson making his way through the snow along the river, she begins to repeat to herself the names of the towns he passes. Her emotions grow intense as she pictures him nearing Kamouraska: "Bientôt les sonorités rocailleuses et vertes de Kamouraska vont s'entrechoquer, les unes contre les autres. Ce vieux nom algonquin; il y a jonc au bord de l'eau. Kamouraska!"[30] For Elisabeth—and surely for the reader, too, by that time—the word alone conjures up the rocky, untamed terrain, the inhuman weather, and the roughness and violence born of such conditions. The village itself, representing the typical French settlement in the new world, stands in the novel for the primitive environment which gives rise to primitive passions. Is love possible in such a land? Elisabeth recalls how quickly her youthful marriage turned into hostility in the atmosphere of Kamouraska: "Nous passons au manoir de Kamouraska notre cruelle jeunesse, sans fin. . . . S'affrontant. Se blessant. S'insultant à coeur joie, sous l'oeil perçant de Madame mère Tassy."[31] Elisabeth's tragedy is not just that the rigid, matriarchal, and Catholic society of French-speaking Canada produces weak-willed males incapable of love. It is also that this rugged land and unrelenting climate make *everyone* who grows up therein somehow unsuited to the gentle needs of love. Elisabeth's tragedy is in part the consequence of her place of birth.

Did it perhaps occur to Anne Hébert that, buried inside the savage syllables of the Algonquin name Kamouraska, there lurks, almost unnoticed, the fragile French word *amour*? Whether or not the author consciously intended it so, the title surely expresses symbolically one of the controlling concepts in the novel, namely that in Kamouraska, love is swallowed whole, and thus denatured, rendering man's—and, even more, woman's—destiny there inevitably tragic.

NOTES

1. Anne Hébert, *Kamouraska* (Paris: Editions du Seuil, 1970), p. 6.

Although this novel is based on a real event which occurred in Canada, a very long time ago, it remains nevertheless a work of the imagination. The real-life actors in this drama have only lent to my story their most overt actions, those which are most offical, as it were. For the rest, they have become creatures of my imagination, in the course of a slow inward journey.

This novel has been made into a successful film. See Claude Jutra, dir., *Kamouraska*, with Geneviève Bujold.

2. Anne Hébert, "Le Torrent," in *Le Torrent* (Montréal: Editions Beauchemin, 1950; rpt. Paris: Editions du Seuil, 1963), p. 1.

I was a child dispossessed of the world.

3. This revised edition has also appeared in a Canadian edition as Anne Hébert, *Le Torrent*, Collection L'Arbre, No. 1 (Montréal: Editions Hurtubise HMH, 1974).

4. Anne Hébert, *Le Temps sauvage; La Mercière assassinée; Les Invités au procès*, Collection L'Arbre, No. G-2 (1967; rpt. Montréal: Editions Hurtubise HMH, 1967), p. 11.

Sheltered from the entire world, in a lengthy childhood that is natural and pure.

5. Hébert, *Le Temps sauvage*, p. 19.

My poor boy! you will no doubt never be a man. Who is ever completely a man or a woman in this country from before the world was created?

6. Anne Hébert, *Les Chambres de bois* (1958; rpt. Paris: Editions du Seuil, 1979).

7. Hébert, *Kamouraska*, p. 7.

The summer went by in its entirety. Counter to her custom, Mme Rolland did not leave her house in Parlour Street. The weather was very fine and very warm. But neither Mme Rolland nor the children went to the country, that summer.

8. Hébert, *Kamouraska*, p. 7.

Her husband was going to die and she was experiencing a great inner calm.... Mme Rolland was waiting, submissive and above reproach.

9. Hébert, *Kamouraska*, p. 7.

Everything seemed to want to happen as if the very significance of her actual wait was going to be revealed to her. Over and above the death of the man who had been her husband for nearly eighteen years

10. Hébert, *Kamouraska*, p. 7.

It would have been better to leave Québec.... There is no longer anyone I know in town.

11. See Robert Harvey's discussion of four narrative voices in *Kamouraska d'Anne Hébert: Une Ecriture de la passion*, Cahiers du Québec, No. 69 (Montréal: Editions Hurtubise HMH, 1982), pp. 19-36.

12. As cited by Philip Stratford, "*Kamouraska* and *The Diviners*," *Review of National Literatures*, 7 (1976), 122. Margaret Laurence is the author of *The Diviners*.

13. Hébert, *Kamouraska*, p. 7.

They're observing me. They're spying on me. They're following me. They're sticking close to me.

14. Hébert, *Kamouraska*, pp. 10-11.

Soon I'll be free again. Become a widow again.... Set off in search of the unique tenderness of my heart.

15. Hébert, *Kamouraska*, p. 10.

It was at Sorel. After the accident of Kamouraska. When my love got back from Kamouraska. I had never been so close to happiness. And he, that unique man, he fled, his hands full of blood.

16. Hébert, *Kamouraska*, p. 11.

Murderous love. Infamous love. Fatal love. Love. Love. The only life in this world. The folly of love.

17. Hébert, *Kamouraska*, p. 51.

In full mourning, my mother carries me in her womb, as a fruit carries its stone. This little girl has grown inside a cocoon of black crepe. Maybe I could see pictures of the world of that time through the tear-reddened eyes of the young widow who is my mother? The coffin of my youthful father leaves the house. My mother faints. And I, secure in my double-locked confinement, I keep kicking her in the liver. To wake her up. I fling myself about like a baby goat. We could both die of it, my mother and I, of a fainting spell so terrible and so protracted.
—What an evil little girl!
Could that be the first voice of society that is reaching my ears?

18. Hébert, *Kamouraska*, p. 250.

In an arid field, under the stones, they dug up a blackened woman, alive, belonging to a wild and distant era. Strangely preserved. They released her in the small town. Then they barricaded themselves, in their own houses. So great and deep is the fear they have of this woman. They say to themselves that the hunger for life of that woman, buried alive, so long ago, must be so fierce and total, having accumulated under the earth for centuries! Doubtless they have never known anything like it. When the woman appears in town, running and imploring, the alarm starts to sound. She finds only closed doors and the desert of compacted earth, of which the streets are made. There remains nothing more for her, no doubt, than to die of hunger and solitude.
Evil Elisabeth! Cursed woman!

19. Hébert, *Kamouraska*, p. 51.

A wild beast who has been locked up, and who is watching in the shadows for a chance to pounce upon you.

20. Hébert, *Kamouraska*, p. 69.

I am going to be married.... Is it love?... I think I am going to drown.

21. Hébert, *Kamouraska*, p. 87.

"Come on with me. This rope is big enough for two, Elisabeth, my bride. That's what the bonds of matrimony are. A heavy cord firmly attached so we can choke together."

22. Hébert, *Kamouraska*, p. 248.

23. Hébert, *Kamouraska*, p. 15.

I must not drink a single swallow when she is here. No. Nothing when she is here. She will kill me. Above all, don't let her prepare my drops herself!

24. Hébert, *Kamouraska*, p. 250.

"Just see how much Madame loves Monsieur! See how she weeps...."

25. Hébert, *Kamouraska*, p. 67.

He comes from the lower St. Lawrence. I don't know anything about him. But he's a ruffian, I'm sure of it. From a good family, but a ruffian just the same.

26. Hébert, *Kamouraska*, p. 73.

I think that I am degrading myself in this country inn.

27. Hébert, *Kamouraska*, p. 76.

There is too much wind here.... The wind makes me feel that I'm dying.

28. Hébert, *Kamouraska*, p. 85.

The mother-in-law brings a shawl, made of the local wool, which she has just knitted. The mother insists that the wool is too rough for her son. The mother-in-law, annoyed, strikes the floor with her cane.

29. Hébert, *Kamouraska*, p. 10.

The accident of Kamouraska.

30. Hébert, *Kamouraska*, p. 206.

Soon the rugged and green sounds of Kamouraska are going to clash against one another. That old Algonquin name; there are rushes along the edge of the water. Kamouraska!

31. Hébert, *Kamouraska*, p. 76.

In the manor house of Kamouraska we are spending our cruel youth, without end.... Confronting each other. Hurting each other. Insulting each other to our heart's content, under the piercing eye of his mother, Madame Tassy.

10

Redefining the Maternal: Women's Relationships in the Fiction of Marie-Claire Blais

Mary Jean Green ——————————————————

In the first published novel of Marie-Claire Blais, *La Belle Bête*, a daughter sets fire to her mother and throws herself under a train, leaving her own daughter to wander off alone. In sharp contrast to this image of female hostility, two of Blais's most recent novels, *Les Nuits de l'Underground* and *Le Sourd dans la ville*, end with a younger woman's effort to bring an older woman back to life. And her most recent work to date, *Visions d'Anna*, concludes on a note of reconciliation between mothers and daughters, a reconciliation which promises to bring salvation to both.

In her novels Blais has recorded the disintegration of an outdated vision of the family and of the mother-figure who was traditionally at its center. Moving beyond this critique of existing social structures, she has begun to work out a new model of human interaction based on the very relationships among women which she had earlier seemed to reject. In Blais's recent work, this model—based on the reciprocal caring of mothers, daughters, sisters, friends, and lovers—offers the only hope of human survival in the violent climate of the modern world.

La Belle Bête, published in 1959, is a story of the radical disruption of the mother-daughter relationship and, indeed, of all familial interaction. The characters are marionnettes placed against a vaguely sketched backdrop, but the drama they play out is not far removed from political or psychological reality. The widowed mother, Louise, lives through her relationship with her idiot son, Patrice, whose face reflects back her own empty beauty. Failing to find a similar reflection of herself in her intelligent but ugly daughter, Isabelle-Marie, Louise rejects her emotionally and relegates her to a Cinderella-like existence of menial work.[1] Rescued momentarily by a conveniently blind Prince Charming, Isabelle-Marie has a daughter of her own. Having failed to transcend her mother's values by creating a new self-image, Isabelle-Marie is unable to provide a happier life for her child. Instead, she finds herself reenacting her own relationship with her mother by rejecting her daughter, whom she can see only as a mirror of her own ugliness: "Mais c'est à Isabelle-Marie que l'enfant ressemblait. Dès sa naissance, Isabelle l'avait trouveé plus monstrueuse qu'elle-même et ce visage d'enfant, affligé de la même laideur, porteur de son sang et de ses traits labourés, la révoltait."[2]

Yet Isabelle-Marie is not therefore content to accept the injustice of her fate. Finally giving vent to her resentment, she disfigures her brother by plunging his face into boiling water and subsequently sets fire to the family house, thereby killing her mother. Although she rejects her mother's world, she is incapable of making a new life for herself: she finally throws herself under a train, leaving her daughter alone to face an uncertain future.

Lucien Goldmann has read *La Belle Bête* in political terms, as a transposition of Blais's vision of the state of *québécois* society. In his view, the hostility between mother and daughter in the novel reenacts the conflict between the traditional Quebec community, ignorant and mortally ill, and the intellectuals of the new generation, who, like Isabelle-Marie, are full of destructive rage but powerless to effect social change.[3] This, of course, was the social reality of the period immediately preceding the *Révolution tranquille*, the very period in which *La Belle Bête* was written and published—a moment when the old order of society had clearly outlived itself but when the forces of renewal had not yet proven their ability to move toward positive change.

But the problem in *La Belle Bête* is not only that of the Quebec intellectual, and the situation it describes is not merely a political one. The relationships on which the novel focuses are located within the family; it is, most importantly, a psychological novel, in which the central problem is that of hostility between generations of women.[4] As critics have noted, human relationships in *La Belle Bête* are characterized by mirroring:[5] each of the characters seeks essentially to find her/his own image in the eyes of another. But in the case of the mothers and children, the demand for mirroring is much stronger. Louise expects her children to conform to her image and to repeat her existence. When her daughter fails to resemble her completely, she can only condemn her as ugly. Isabelle-Marie does rebel against her mother's judgment, but she has also internalized it, and she persists in attempting to conform to her mother's image. Rather than rejecting her mother's ideal of beauty, she seeks out as a husband the one man who, because he is blind, will believe her false description of her own beauty. Unable to accept herself in her difference, she can hardly accept this difference in the face of her own daughter: not surprisingly, this child appears to be "monstrous." Since a relationship of reflection and repetition is the only one she sees as possible between mothers and daughters, Isabelle-Marie can only attempt, by the murder of her mother and her own suicide, to smash the maternal images. These acts might have the effect of leaving her daughter free to develop a self of her own, although Blais's conclusion to the novel suggests little reason for optimism.

The breakdown in familial relationships to which Blais gave such violent expression in *La Belle Bête* was itself not unrelated to the changes in Quebec society which were taking place at the time of its writing. The traditional nine-teenth-century social structure, whose values still officially dominated Quebec in the 1950s, had been built around the family, with its large numbers of offspring who represented, in a most concrete way, the means of survival for the Quebec francophone community. So essential a role was played by the family, centered around the life-giving mother, that the maternal figure was idealized in literature as the emblem of this traditional order. And when Quebec writers began to express their rejection of this order, their condemnation was, in many instances, directed against this mother-figure, now seen as a force of repression and a barrier to change.

This violence against the mother is found most notably in works by Quebec's great women writers—in Anne Hébert's early story "Le Torrent," in Françoise Loranger's *Mathieu*, as well as in Blais's *La Belle Bête*. The works of a slightly earlier generation of women writers, the generation of Gabrielle Roy and Ger-maine Guèvremont, lack the violence of their successors, but they, too, testify to a breakdown in mother-daughter relationships.[6] For women in post–World War II Quebec, who were experiencing the decadence of the traditional order in their own lives, the rupture with the mother-figure was more than symbolic. It must have reflected their own inability to identify with their mothers—not just their own biological mothers, of course, but an entire generation of *québécois* women whose lives had been committed to the preservation of traditional values.

Recent feminist historical research has suggested that the hostility which has often seemed to characterize the mother-daughter relationship in our own time (and which seemed, as well, to be a feature of all female relationships in the years immediately preceding the "second wave" of feminism) has not always existed in the same way. Carroll Smith-Rosenberg's work on female friendships in nineteenth-century America has revealed the presence of a level of intimacy among women, related and unrelated, which was encouraged by the society and which played an essential role in the social structure. Relationships between mothers and daughters seem to have been particularly close and supportive, a factor which Smith-Rosenberg attributes to the stability of female roles: "As long as the mother's domestic role remained relatively stable and few viable alternatives competed with it, daughters tended to accept their mother's world and to turn automatically to other women for support and intimacy."[7] Although research like Smith-Rosenberg's has not, to my knowledge, been undertaken for nineteenth-century Quebec, evidence of the nature of women's relationships in Quebec's traditional rural society can be seen in literature. For example, the classic Quebec novel *Maria Chapdelaine*, an idealization of the traditional rural family, shows exactly the type of mother-daughter relationship described by Smith-Rosenberg, a relationship in which daughters willingly identified with and repeated the lives of their mothers.[8]

The historical record of strong female relationships has led Adrienne Rich to speculate on their relative absence in today's world, a development she ultimately attributes to changes in women's role expectancies from generation to generation:

[T]he growth of nineteenth-century feminism, the false "liberation" (to smoke cigarettes and sleep around) of the twentieth-century flapper, the beginnings of new options for women as birth control gained in acceptance and use, may have had the initial effect of weakening the mother-daughter tie (and with it, the network of intense female friendships based on a common life-pattern and common expectancies).[9]

Rich is speaking, of course, of the experience of women in the United States. Similar developments were much longer in coming in Quebec, but when change came, it came with unusual rapidity. If social change can have disruptive effects on women's relationships, it is not surprising to find extreme examples of such ruptures in literature written by women in Quebec. Both the extensive urbanization of the province in the 1930s and 1940s and its abrupt secularization in the 1960s certainly had their effect in separating generations of women and throwing established patterns of social relationships into disarray.

Thus it is not unexpected that hostility between generations of women should appear in Blais's early novels, written in the era of the *Révolution tranquille*—a moment of extreme tension and accelerated change. In her major novel of the mid-1960s, *Une Saison dans la vie d'Emmanuel*, Blais specifically attacked the repressiveness of a mother-daughter relationship based on identity and repetition—a relationship much like the one shown in *Maria Chapdelaine*. In Blais's vision, the role assigned to women by traditional Quebec society reduces her to the status of a nameless, faceless animal, whose only function is to bear, feed, and often bury an unending series of babies. In her portrayal of the numerous daughters, Blais shows the horror of replicating such an anonymous void. The daughters, most of whom are referred to as "the big A's" and "the little a's," are themselves interchangeable; they are separated only according to size and identified by their common initials. Their virtual anonymity is indicative of their mutual destiny, the cow-like existence of their mother:

Les Roberta-Anna-Anita avancèrent comme un lent troupeau de vaches, chacune entourant de ses larges bras une espiègle petite fille aux cheveux tressés, qui, dans quelques années, leur ressemblerait, et qui, comme elles, soumise au labeur, rebelle à l'amour, aurait la beauté familière, la fierté obscure d'un bétail apprivoisé.[10]

The mother and her anonymous daughters are harshly caricatured, but Blais's more ambiguous portrayal of Grand-Mère Antoinette betrays some hints of a positive vision of female caring. She can be seen as an allegorical mother-figure, but her reality extends beyond such a characterization. On the positive side she is a strong nurturing force who fights to preserve the life and work of the tubercular poet-son, Jean Le Maigre. She upholds the children's need for education against the ignorant father and is a source of emotional sustenance for the infant, Emmanuel. She also tries to aid the one rebellious daughter, the sensitive Héloïse, but in this relationship the negative and repressive side of Grand-Mère Antoinette's nature comes to the fore. Having denied her own sexuality by shielding her body with mounds of clothing and having committed herself to the life-denying teachings of the Church, Grand-Mère Antoinette cannot show her granddaughter the way to the new life she is seeking. In order to give free expression to her sexuality, the aptly named Héloïse must break completely with the world of both grandmother and mother, thus providing another instance of intergenerational rupture. Héloïse eventually does find happiness in a brothel: in Blais's inversion of traditional values, a life of prostitution appears far less exploitive and debasing than the traditional role of wife and mother. While Héloïse is taken farther along the path to liberation than Isabelle-Marie's abandoned daughter, her solution is clearly a humorous one, not meant to be taken seriously. Héloïse clearly does not seem intended to provide a model for a new generation of women, although she does emphasize the need to effect a complete break in the repetitive cycle of feminine identity.

With the exception of the cruelly satirized mother and daughters of *Une Saison dans la vie d'Emmanuel*, the female characters of Blais's early fiction are cut off from relationships with other women. Those who, like Héloïse and Isabelle-Marie, have chosen to remove themselves from the traditional pattern of female continuity have not succeeded in laying the foundations for a new female identity or a new mode of connection to others.

In *Manuscrits de Pauline Archange*, the triptych-novel which dominates Blais's writing of the late 1960s, the task of overcoming her emotional isolation becomes, for the first time, a conscious goal of the protagonist. Pauline is still instinctively unwilling to enmesh herself in the cycle of repeated debasement which seems to condemn female lives. This is evident in her childhood friendships and, especially, in her relationship with her mother, who seems to embody the humiliation of women's existence, a fate in which Pauline herself has determined not to participate. The child is capable of perceiving and even pitying the mother's suffering from a debilitating illness, but she refuses to make the loving gesture which represents to her a confirmation of the bond of identity between mother and daughter: "[C]raignant, plus que tout, de rompre notre fragile lien de pudeur et de silence, par ce geste de consolation qu'elle attendait de moi, lui confirmait ainsi que nous n'appartenions pas à la même race meurtrie."[11]

Although she is unwilling to take her place among the humiliated victims of social oppression, Pauline is equally unwilling to abandon her compassion for them. In her relationships with the others in her life, she finds it hard to express this compassion while at the same time maintaining her independence. It is her writing which allows her to bring together these two needs. Her fellow victims— her mother, as well as her cousin Jacob, brutalized by a cruel father—propose themselves as the subjects of her creative effort: "Et ma mère, qui avait toujours eu si peu d'existence pour elle-même, ne vivant toujours que pour les autres, sortait de l'ombre comme un portrait inachevé et l'absence de ses traits effrayés semblait me dire: 'Achève cette brève image de moi.' ''[12] In her creative vision Pauline betrays an appreciation of the maternal role which had not been clearly present in Blais's earlier work.

The concept of the artist as a person who combines creativity and compassion is embodied in Pauline's image of Dürer's Angel, the alter ego she conjures up at the end of the triptych. A vigorous, creative figure, the angel nevertheless remains tied to the earth and devoted to the alleviation of human suffering:

[I]l voyait au loin ce que moi je ressentais dans ma misère, la cupidité, l'aveuglement des hommes, un horizon voilé de sang—un avenir dont la honte habitait toutes ses pensées, oui, n'était-ce donc que pour ce monde obscur, assassin de la beauté et saccageur de l'innocence, qu'il allait bientôt se mettre à l'oeuvre, lui qui ne désirait que le bonheur des hommes et leur contemplation sans haine?[13]

Pauline finds a real-life approximation of the model to which she aspires in the doctor, Germaine Léonard, who cares for her at the convent school. Germaine Léonard has already broken with the traditional pattern of female debasement in order to attain her financial and sexual independence. Yet she is able to retain what for Blais has always seemed to be a positive and essential part of the female role: concern and care for others. The nurturance provided by Grand-Mère Antoinette and by Pauline's own mother is continued in Germaine Léonard's devotion to her suffering patients, a devotion which, for the first time in Blais's work, does not go hand in hand with humiliation. She is an early exemplary figure in Blais's universe of women, and her role as healer and comforter of the sick and dying will reappear in later novels, in such figures as Lali Dorman of *Les Nuits de l'Underground* and Guislaine of *Visions d'Anna*. Yet her capacity to reach out to others is limited by her inability to penetrate beyond traditional social appearances: in Pauline's final encounter with her, Léonard can only comment contemptuously on the state of the girl's clothes, without responding to the material deprivation of which they are a symptom. Thus, although Germaine Léonard begins to approximate the ideal for which Pauline is searching, it is Pauline Archange herself who, as a writer, moves closest to attaining it. In her imaginative creation she can begin to understand even Germaine Léonard herself, moving beyond superficial appearances in a way the older woman has not been able to do in Pauline's case. In *Manuscrits de Pauline Archange* then, the female protagonist, like Blais's earlier women characters, remains somewhat isolated from the others in her life. By the end of the triptych, however, she has found a way of reaching out to them through her art.

The search for a new female identity and a new form of relationship moves definitively from art to life in *Les Nuits de l'Underground*. Set in the Montreal lesbian "underground" of homosexual bars and all-night parties, the novel provides Blais with the occasion for examining a large number of relationships among women. As in *Manuscrits de Pauline Archange*, Blais finds an archetype of the new type of relationship she is describing in art. Here, however, the model is not a single figure but a couple, Rodin's sculptural representation of a mother embracing her dying daughter. For Blais's protagonist, Geneviève, "ne figurait-elle pas . . . les diverses expressions d'une maternité morale qu'elle avait souvent eu l'occasion d'observer entre femmes?"[14] Geneviève can understand this type of relationship through the insight gained from her brief passion for Lali Dorman, a woman whose demeanor betrays signs of a mysterious sadness. More sensitive than Germaine Léonard, Geneviève feels the need to look beneath Lali's surface aloofness to seek her hidden sources of suffering: she discovers painful memories of a wartime childhood in Austria, a mother's madness, the terror of a world collapsing around her. As a result of her own suffering, Lali devotes her life to those whose pain is even greater—the dying cancer victims for whom she cares on her job and an emotionally unstable lesbian friend, whom she considers her "brother." Indeed, as she ministers to "René" with the tender gestures of an older sister, Lali seems to be recreating in her friend the family of younger brothers and sisters she has left behind in Austria.

Through Lali's example of devoted caring and the sensitivity to suffering which her own relationship with Lali has awakened in her, Geneviève attains a new understanding of the meaning of love, a lesson she can pass on in her turn to the older woman she meets in Paris. What Geneviève can offer Françoise is not only a new love but what amounts to a physical and spiritual resurrection. The younger woman's love opens to Françoise the possibility of understanding her real nature, which she has kept hidden even from her own family, and reawakens in her the will to live, giving her the courage to undertake medical treatment for the disease which has been undermining her health: "Geneviève, qui avait eu l'air de ne rien demander, lui demandait tout, car n'exigeait-elle pas dans son intransigeance, que Françoise revienne non seulement à la vie, mais qu'elle crée une vie nouvelle, auprès d'elle. . . ."[15] By the end of the novel, Françoise is recovering from a dangerous operation and is on the road back to life.

The novel's ending, however, focuses not on the new couple formed by Geneviève and Françoise but on the whole group of women whose lives Geneviève has been describing. Geneviève's relationships with Lali and Françoise are echoed in an entire network of women's relationships with each other, just as Françoise's return to health is repeated in the recovery of a sick friend who has been nursed by René. Thus, the image of a maternal or sisterly caring relationship which Blais finds in the Rodin sculpture is not limited to an isolated couple but informs a large number of relationships which echo and reflect one another.

This concept of a network of relationships is embedded in the narrative framework of Blais's next novel, *Le Sourd dans la ville*.[16] Here the narrative is no longer dominated by a single protagonist. Instead, the interior reality of a number of characters—that interior reality which Geneviève had devoted herself to uncovering in *Les Nuits de l'Underground*—is presented directly to the reader through the technique of a shifting point of view. In contrast to the device of separated monologues, which Blais had employed earlier in *L'Insoumise*, here the multiple perspectives of the characters are interwoven in their common struggle with suffering and approaching death.

The world of the novel seems at first to bear witness to the disintegration of traditional social structures: Judith Lange has become alienated from her bourgeois family; Florence has been abandoned by both husband and son; and most of Gloria's many children have gone their separate ways—as have their various fathers. It is a world of intergenerational hostility between women: Judith's mother, content with her life as an affluent housewife, cannot understand her daughter's preoccupation with the less fortunate. Gloria's daughter, too, has rejected her mother's cheerful acceptance of poverty and has turned her back on her family as she seeks upward mobility through a college education. The relationship of the characters to each other is, in most cases, purely a matter of chance: they are brought together primarily through their common frequentation of Gloria's Hôtel des Voyageurs, an almost symbolic haven for the isolated individuals who inhabit this thoroughly modern urban landscape.

Yet, even in this world of alienation, certain of the women characters are able to create and sustain meaningful human relationships. Two fundamental sets of relationships are at the center of the novel: Gloria's maternal devotion to her dying son, Mike, and a parallel relationship uniting Judith Lange and Florence, the latter of whom is bent on achieving her own death. The presence of Gloria and Judith Lange dominates the world of the novel—as might be suspected by their religiously inspired names.[17] Both women are different incarnations of the same female trait, a trait which has begun to assume more and more importance in Blais's fiction: care and concern for the suffering of others.

Gloria represents this type of concern in its most traditional and most physical form, while Judith Lange is a more spiritual variant.[18] Gloria, a classic example of the good-hearted whore, is also the first wholly positive portrait in Blais's work of an actual mother. Like her traditional *québécois* counterpart, she has borne many children, and she devotes herself to their care. Unlike her predecessors, however, she displays an open enjoyment of sexuality and supports her children and lovers by her dual occupation as strip-tease dancer and proprietor of a sleazy bar. A major share of her attention is claimed by her son, Mike, who is slowly dying of a brain tumor (Mike's real name, Michel Agneli, makes clear the extent to which he is an emblem of the suffering of the lamblike innocent victim). Gloria brings him comfort in his pain-inspired nightmares and provides him with nourishment for body and spirit, although she can offer only burned spaghetti and the impossible dream of a motorcycle trip through the American West. Beyond her care for Mike, Gloria is a life-giving center to which all the other characters are irresistibly attracted. She is so clearly a traditional mother-figure that Blais openly compares her with Munch's artistic rendition of a Madonna and gives her the traditional religious epithet, "Mère de la Douleur."[19] Although Gloria's free-wheeling sexuality would surely meet with disfavor from the Church, the ideal of maternal care she represents is not very different from that of the traditional Quebec mother-figure.

While Gloria tends to the physical needs of her children and clients, Judith Lange tries to minister to their minds and spirits. A professor of philosophy, she is overwhelmed by the problem of innocent suffering in every form, from the individual cases she encounters in her nocturnal visitations to the mass murders of the concentration camps, which she constantly evokes in her classes. It is she who has once before brought Florence back from the brink of suicide, and, after Florence succeeds in shooting herself in Gloria's hotel, the last words which penetrate her consciousness are Judith's plea: " 'Reviens, reviens avec moi sur la terre.' "[20] As suggested by her name, Judith is another and more fully developed incarnation of Dürer's Angel, which had provided the closing image in *Manuscrits de Pauline Archange*, an angel whose creative activity is tied to a preoccupation with human suffering. Through her, the traditional maternal activity represented by Gloria is given another and more contemporary incarnation.

With *Le Sourd dans la ville* Blais expands the vision of maternal caring beyond the lesbian context of *Les Nuits de l'Underground* to embrace a more complex reality of human relationships in a modern city. The city, like the modern world as a whole, is dominated by the brutal criminality of Gloria's lovers, the inhuman indifference of Florence's bourgeois husband, and the inevitable cruelty of disease and old age. Through the acute sensitivity of Judith Lange, this immediate and individual suffering is linked to the mass murders of recent history, and these multiple sources of human suffering and death are united in the image of "le sourd," a term which recurs in various contexts throughout the book. As these sources are deaf and indifferent to human feelings, Judith Lange opposes to them the value of consciousness, displayed in her own sensitivity to suffering and commitment to relieving it.

Gabrielle Poulin has seen *Le Sourd dans la ville* as merely repeating and reaffirming the overtly lesbian vision of *Les Nuits de l'Underground*:

The postulate, which was only suggested in *Les Nuits de l'Underground*, that the love of women who give themselves to each other, constitutes the hope of the earth . . . this postulate is set up as a certainty and is affirmed, at the end of *Le Sourd dans la ville*, with the full force of an irrefutable conclusion.[21]

In Poulin's interpretation, "le sourd" of the title is to be equated with *le mâle*. But in the novel Blais indicates that the capacity for caring which she values, while found primarily in women, could inform the lives of both sexes. This is made clear in her depiction of Mike, who ministers to his little sister and offers the despondent Florence the only comfort he knows how to give, in the form of a plate of spaghetti. It is true that the older men in the novel, like Gloria's string of criminal lovers, do seem to display a monstrous insensitivity—but so does Judith's mother. Blais seems to be condemning not men themselves, but a masculine stereotype, shaping the lives of individuals and society as a whole, which cuts men off from the maternal caring qualities displayed by women.

Blais's 1982 novel, *Visions d'Anna*,[22] continues to develop her concept of maternal caring as a force capable of opposing the destructive tendencies of the modern world. And here, for the first time in Blais's work, the strength of motherly, daughterly, sisterly, and lesbian relationships seems able to regenerate even the entity which had been the target of Blais's early satire—the family.

The novel opens on characters who seem as isolated from one another as those of *La Belle Bête*. The book is dominated by the drug-induced musings of Anna, who is experiencing a total alienation from a society she sees as bent on self-destruction. Like Judith Lange of *Le Sourd dans la ville*, Anna is haunted by thoughts of mass catastrophe, but her visions concern not the past, but a not-far-distant future of nuclear holocaust. In Anna's obsessed imagination, the black cloud which appears in a picture drawn by her little half-sister evokes a ghastly image of the silent destruction of the child herself and her whole stereotypical bourgeois family. Unlike Judith Lange, however, Anna is unable to overcome her own alienation in order to reach out to others. Hurt by her father's rejection of her hippie lifestyle, she is unable to respond to the plea for understanding made to her by her younger friend Michelle, another victim of teen-age drug addiction, or to respond to the sympathetic concern of her mother, Raymonde.

Because of the emotional distance of the fathers and the alienation of the daughters, Anna and Michelle, the two interconnected family groups who form the center of the novel are both in a process of disintegration. As Anna tells her mother, it is no longer possible to believe in the peaceful vision of nineteenth-century bourgeois existence, depicted in the painting by Boudin which Raymonde has hung in Anna's room. The painting and the rose-colored wall on which it is hung become a *leitmotiv* in the novel, recalling both the lost ideal of the traditional family and the countervailing reality of Raymonde's care for Anna.

A working-class parallel to the families of Anna and Michelle is provided by the story of a destitute family from Asbestos, encountered in the travels of Raymonde's former lover, Alexandre. Rita, a mother with two young sons, has been abandoned by her drunken and unemployed husband. As she struggles to support her children in a seaside resort town, she is taken in by a truck driver, who beats the older boy until he runs away. The mother spends hours searching for him, dragging her younger son with her as she wanders through a deep fog. When Rita's family is finally reunited, she vows to re-establish their life together on a new basis.

All three of the family groupings are clustered around a mother: Anna's father has rejected her mother and herself to pursue his successful career, and Michelle's father, although not totally unsympathetic, is incapable of establishing contact with his daughters. The adult male figures in the novel seem unwilling to involve themselves in lasting relationships. Even the sensitive Alexandre, who yearns to emulate Aliosha Karamazov, leaves Raymonde and Anna to go off on his own: "'[L]es hommes,' disait-il, 'ont toujours éprouvé ce besoin d'être libres de leurs liens, quand les femmes, elles, au contraire, sont sensibles à ce qui les rattache à la terre. . . . '"[23] Blais's characters thus display the differential attitudes toward human relationships which psychologists have observed in women and men: women in our society seem dependent on and embedded in relationships with others, while men develop a sense of independence and autonomy. As Nancy Chodorow states: "The basic feminine sense of self is connected to the world, the basic masculine sense of self is separate."[24] Similarly, in Blais's fiction, the emotional isolation of the male characters forms a sharp contrast to the involvement in relationships shown by her women.

Even more clearly than in *Le Sourd dans la ville*, Blais here identifies this masculine autonomy, expressed in indifference and even in violence, with the major problems of contemporary society: individual cases of cruelty toward children, as well as the global menace of nuclear destruction and impending ecological disaster. Thus, when Anna returns home after her flight to the Caribbean, she sees herself as coming back to the "terre des hommes." In her ironic reference to "terre des hommes," the theme of the Montreal World's Fair, Blais indicates her unwillingness to subscribe to its celebration of "man and his world":

[E]lle était revenue sur cette terre des hommes . . . elle était de retour dans cette histoire de l'humanité où les larmes ne cesseraient de couler, âpres et violentes, les bourreaux; les dénonciateurs étaient toujours là, sympathiques, souriants, affables, elle savait aussi que si elle était de retour parmi eux, c'était pour participer à leurs crimes.[25]

But while the individual men in her novel are shown abandoning their relational commitments and rejecting their children, Blais provides at least one image of another potential male identity in the little boy Anna observes on the plane, happily playing with his collection of dolls: "[C]e garçon conservait encore la qualité de son indépendance, il était créateur, son imagination serait délirante, si demain on lui laissait la vie, ces mêmes doigts pourraient dessiner, peindre, pensait Anna, sa mère respectait en lui la mission de cet art paisible. . . . "[26] As in the image which ends *Manuscrits de Pauline Archange*, this portrait of a child links the qualities of creativity and nurturance; Blais seems to be suggesting that human destructiveness could be kept to a minimum if all children, including little boys, were left free to explore their own innate capacities.

In *Visions d'Anna* it is particularly mothers—and here the maternal figures are all biological mothers—whose efforts oppose the violence of the surrounding world. Like the mother from Asbestos in her long search through the fog, they continue their nurturant activities even in the face of their children's rejection. Anna's mother, Raymonde, has devoted her whole life to such nurturance. Even her relationship with Anna's father had been largely a maternal one, as she took him into her life as an ill and penniless American draft resister and supported him and his child by stealing, when necessary. Peter's rejection of Raymonde and Anna is largely a rejection of his own potential for dependence and vulnerability, qualities he would like to deny in himself. The ideal of maternal care, however, is not limited to its role within the family: the mothers of both Anna and Michelle are professional women whose work consists of life-supporting activities. Raymonde works with a program for delinquent girls (it is she who manages to get Michelle out of jail), and Michelle's mother, Guislaine, is a doctor who cares for dying children.

Although they suffer from the profound alienation of their generation, both Anna and Michelle are ultimately responsive to their mothers' compassionate concern. While Anna is in the Caribbean, she dreams of her mother taking her hand and guiding her through the city, as she had when Anna was a child. It is this recurring dream which prompts Anna to reestablish the tenuous line of communication home through her intermittent postcards. Even in the voluntary isolation of her room, she is linked to Raymonde through the maternal gifts of the rose-colored wall and the Boudin painting, which form the background of her reveries. And at the end of the novel, when she finds the will to return to life, it is to her mother that she returns. But Anna's gesture of sympathy is reciprocated, since it coincides with Raymonde's refusal to continue her participation in a system of social control which Anna has seen as repressive.

Guislaine provides a similar source of support for Michelle, and at the end of the novel, they, too, are brought together in an evening of mutual understanding. As in the case of Raymonde and Anna, their feelings of caring and concern are mutual, proceeding not only from the mother but from the daughter as well. Michelle's response to her mother is based on her perception of Guislaine's own suffering on her account, and as they walk together after dinner, she is able for a moment to assume the nurturant role: "Michelle enveloppait de ses bras frêles les épaules de sa mère, elle disait dans un murmure, très vite, 'tu sais, cette ride, à ton front, je sais que j'en suis la cause.... '"[27] The mutuality of the relationship of these two mother-daughter couples is not, however, limited to mothers and daughters alone. Through Michelle's lesbian sister, Liliane, who makes a brief appearance at the end of the novel, this model of relationship is extended to include a similar type of mutual caring which can unite sister with sister and friend with friend. Firm in her belief in the power of women's relationships, Liliane retains the hope that one day her mother will be able to come to terms with her avowed lesbianism.

All these mutually-supportive relationships seem to exemplify what Adrienne Rich has sketched out as a new vision of relationships between women:

We are, none of us, "either" mothers or daughters; to our amazement, confusion, and greater complexity we are both. Women, mothers or not, who feel committed to other women, are increasingly giving each other a quality of caring filled with the diffuse kinds of identification that exist between actual mothers and daughters.... [I]t is a timidity of the imagination which urges that we can be "daughters"—therefore free spirits—rather than "mothers"—defined as eternal givers....

To accept and integrate and strengthen both the mother and the daughter in ourselves is no easy matter,... But any radical vision of sisterhood demands that we reintegrate them.[28]

In the novels where Blais recorded the breakdown of the traditional family and the tragic isolation of the individual, she showed herself to be conscious of the larger context of social reality within which these changes were occurring. Similarly, she sees the work of reconstructing relationships between individuals as essential to the reestablishment of a new form of social order, an order in which human concerns would once again provide a check to pervasive violence and destruction. Thus, in the relationships she describes in her recent fiction, Blais sets up a model of "feminine" caring, capable of combatting the "masculine" autonomy and violence which dominate the surrounding culture. In her emphasis on the connection between the personal and the social, and in her attempt to extend the relational capacities possessed by women to the society as a whole, Blais shares in a more general movement in contemporary feminist thought. Nancy Chodorow, for example, sees the restriction of mothering to women, and its consequent absence from the domain of masculine activity, as having negative consequences not just for women but for society as a whole.[29] And Dorothy Dinnerstein makes a direct connection between our society's gender arrangements, the rigid separation of nurturance from dominance, and the problems of the modern nuclear era:

[O]ur male-female arrangement helps us maintain *our ambivalence toward the existence of other separately sentient beings*.... [W]hat this arrangement lets us do is deny each other as fellow creatures (not wholly, of course; but in all the predatory, life-mutilating ways that keep what men call brotherhood a so far radically unrealized project)....[30]

It is somewhat ironic that, in her effort to define a new mode of human relationship, Blais has placed at the center of her vision the qualities of compassion and concern explicitly identified with the mother—the very mother she had rejected and even killed in her early novels. But Blais had long perceived in her maternal figures—even an ambiguous one like Grand-Mère Antoinette— a positive value which provided the hope of human continuity. Liberated from the repressive role which had been assigned her in the patriarchal system, the maternal figure, as Blais now sees her, has become free to exercise her essential capacity for caring—a capacity which may be shared by all women, mothers or not, and which is capable of animating an entire network of human relationships. As the life-giving mother had been the symbol of survival for her people in the world of nineteenth-century Quebec, it is the model of maternal nurturance and compassion which now, in Blais's twentieth-century vision, holds out the hope of survival for us all.

NOTES

1. Jennifer Waelti-Walters, *Fairy Tales and the Female Imagination* (Montreal: Eden Press, 1982), pp. 45-57.

2. Marie-Claire Blais, *La Belle Bête* (1959; rpt. Montreál: Le Cercle du Livre de France; Pierre Tisseyre, 1968), pp. 101-02.

But Isabelle-Marie was the one the child looked like. From the moment of her birth, Isabelle had found her more monstrous than herself, and this child's face, afflicted with the same ugliness, bearer of her blood and her furrowed features, revolted her.

3. Lucien Goldmann, "Note sur deux romans de Marie-Claire Blais," in *Structures mentales et création culturelle* (Paris: Editions Anthropos, 1970), pp. 353-64.

4. Joan Coldwell, "*Mad Shadows* as Psychological Fiction," *Journal of Canadian Fiction*, 2, No. 4 (1973), 65-67.

5. See, for example, Margot Northey, *The Haunted Wilderness* (Toronto: University of Toronto Press, 1976), p. 75, and Douglas H. Parker, "The Shattered Glass: Mirror and Illusion in *Mad Shadows*," *Journal of Canadian Fiction*, 2, No. 4 (1973), 68-70.

6. Mary Jean Green, "Gabrielle Roy and Germaine Guèvremont: Quebec's Daughters Face a Changing World," *International Journal of Women's Studies*, 1, No. 3 (Summer 1979), 243-57.

7. Carroll Smith-Rosenberg, "The Female World of Love and Ritual: Relations between Women in Nineteenth-Century America," *Signs*, 1, No. 1 (1975), 17.

8. Smith-Rosenberg, p. 16.

9. Adrienne Rich, *Of Women Born: Motherhood as Experience and Institution* (New York: Bantam, 1981), pp. 236-37.

10. Marie-Claire Blais, *Une Saison dans la vie d'Emmanuel* (Montreál: Editions du Jour, 1965), p. 45.

The Robertas-Annas-Anitas moved on like a slow herd of cows, each wrapping in her ample arms a mischievous little girl with braids who, in a few years, would look like them and who, like them, broken to labor, resistant to love, would have the familiar beauty, the obscure pride of tamed cattle.

11. Marie-Claire Blais, *Manuscrits de Pauline Archange* (Montréal: Editions du Jour, 1968), p. 25.

Afraid, more than anything else, of breaking our fragile bond of modesty and silence by this gesture of consolation that she awaited from me, thus confirmed that we did not belong to the same ravaged race.

12. Blais, *Manuscrits de Pauline Archange*, p. 96.

And my mother, who had always had so little existence for herself, always living only for others, emerged from the shadow as an unfinished portrait and the absence of her frightened features seemed to be telling me: "Finish this brief image of me."

13. Marie-Claire Blais, *Les Apparences* (Montréal: Editions du Jour, 1970), p. 146.

He saw in the distance what I myself felt in my misery, the cupidity, the blindness of people, a horizon veiled with blood—a future whose shame invaded all his thoughts, yes, was it only for this dark world, assassin of beauty and destroyer of innocence, that he was soon going to set to work, he who only wanted people to be happy and to be able to comtemplate them without hatred.

14. Marie-Claire Blais, *Les Nuits de l'Underground* (Montréal: Alain Stanké, 1978), pp. 45-46.

Did she not represent ... the various expressions of a moral maternity that she had often had occasion to observe among women?

15. Blais, *Les Nuits de l'Underground*, p. 265.

Geneviève, who had seemed to be asking nothing, was asking everything of her, for was she not demanding, in her intransigeance, not only that Françoise return to life but that she create a new life with her....

16. Marie-Claire Blais, *Le Sourd dans la ville* (Montréal: Alain Stanké, 1979).

17. Maroussia Ahmed, "La Technique de l'inversion dans les romans de Marie-Claire Blais," *Canadian Modern Language Review*, 31, No. 5 (May 1975), 380-86.

18. This sort of mind/body duality is not uncommon in Blais's work. See Karen Gould, "The Censored Word and the Body Politic: Reconsidering the Fiction of Marie-Claire Blais," *Journal of Popular Culture*, 15, No. 3 (1981), 14-27.

19. Blais, *Le Sourd dans la ville*, p. 22.

Mother of Sorrows.

20. Blais, *Le Sourd dans la ville*, pp. 210-11.

Come back, come back with me to earth.

21. *Lettres Québécoises*, No. 18 (été 1980), p. 21.

22. Marie-Claire Blais, *Visions d'Anna* (Montréal: Alain Stanké, 1982).

23. Blais, *Visions d'Anna*, p. 15.

"Men," he said, "have always felt this need to be free of their bonds, when women, on the contrary, are sensitive to what ties them to earth...."

24. Nancy Chodorow, *The Reproduction of Mothering: Psychoanalysis and The Sociology of Gender* (Berkeley: University of California Press, 1978), p. 169.

25. Blais, *Visions d'Anna*, p. 154.

She had returned to this world of men—she was back in this history of humanity where tears would never stop flowing, bitter and violent, the executioners, the informers were always there, friendly, smiling, affable, she also knew that since she was back among them, it was to participate in their crimes.

26. Blais, *Visions d'Anna*, pp. 150-51.

This boy still had the quality of his independence, he was creative, his imagination would run wild, if tomorrow they left him his life, these same figures could draw, paint, thought Anna, his mother respected in him the mission of this peaceful art.

27. Blais, *Visions d'Anna*, p. 158.

Michelle put her frail arms around her mother's shoulders, she said in a murmur, very rapidly, "you know, that wrinkle, on your forehead, I know it's there because of me...."

28. Rich, p. 257.

29. See Chodorow, pp. 218-19.

30. See Dorothy Dinnerstein, *The Mermaid and the Minotaur* (New York: Harper and Row, 1976), p. 247. Italics in the original text.

11

Antonine Maillet and the Epic Heroine

Majorie A. Fitzpatrick _____

Traditionalist, feminist, nationalist—how is one to classify the broad range of Antonine Maillet's important female characters? The answer has to be: partly each, yet not exclusively any of the above. At the risk of offending partisans of all three groups, I suggest that the wonderfully gifted Maillet—surely one of the best storytellers writing in French today—has simultaneously transcended the confining stereotypes of traditionalism, the humorlessness of some feminism, and the narrow vision of fanatic nationalism. At the same time, no author currently writing has created women who are at once more classically feminine, more liberated . . . and more Acadian.

How has Maillet achieved this remarkable synthesis? One thinks, of course, of her humor and her narrative genius, but in addition there is the striking use she makes of female protagonists. When one examines their characters, personalities, objectives, and actions, it is clear that many of these women have much in common with the typically male epic hero. Indeed, "heroine" seems almost too derivative a word to apply to these strong, memorable figures. They come closer to the powerful but unquestionably feminine women that Maya Angelou refers to as "she-roes."[1]

Although Maillet's best known character is doubtless la Sagouine, the kind of epic heroine (let us resign ourselves to the traditional word) alluded to above is better exemplified in her narrative works, of which three will be considered here: *Mariaagélas*, *Les Cordes-de-Bois*, and—obviously—*Pélagie-la-Char-rette*.[2] Two of these sparkling novels proclaim the centrality of their women protagonists right in their titles. The third, *Les Cordes-de-Bois*, in fact does so as well, since the title refers to the entire clan of extraordinary women known as the Mercenaires, whose most impressive (and central) figures are la Piroune and her daughter la Bessoune.

The strictures that threaten the freedom and self-fulfillment of these redoubtable Mercenaire women are reflected spatially in the setting of the novel: a stifling, hypocritical, "well-ordered" village called le Pont after its most prominent physical feature, standing cheek by jowl with the rakishly timber-covered butte called les Cordes-de-Bois, home of and synonym for the Mercenaires. The entire novel will revolve around the opposition between these two microcosmic universes and the principles they represent.

More specifically, however—in a major departure from much feminist literature—the struggle will pit la Piroune and la Bessoune against another woman, Ma-Tante-la-Veuve, a fire-breathing, witch-hunting virago who has become the self-appointed guardian of the morals of le Pont. In this novel, as in *Mariaagélas* and more subtly in *Pélagie*, we thus find both the forces for "good" (the struggle for freedom, the refusal to bow to convention, the determination to conquer obstacles) and the forces of "evil" (self-righteous hypocrisy, adherance to convention, the cult of personal power for its own sake) led by women. Maillet virtually suggests that only another woman would have the boldness, the shrewdness, the energy to serve as a worthy adversary for the likes of the world's Pirounes and Bessounes. The latter, seen as personal scourges by Ma-Tante-la-Veuve, give scandal precisely because they refuse to be bound by the traditional limits on their freedom to which the "respectable" village ladies docilely adhere. If the continuous dust-ups between the Mercenaires and Ma-Tante-la-Veuve owe more to the *héroï-comique* tradition of Boileau's *Lutrin* than to the epic heroism of Roland facing the Saracens, the fact remains that the two courageous Mercenaire women, relying only upon their own resources and wile, overcome numerous and often apparently insurmountable obstacles strewn in their path by an implacable foe.

The same pattern emerges in *Mariaagélas*. The young heroine, Maria, born into a family known for its rejection of the petit bourgeois norms of village society, has as chief antagonist the female incarnation of that society in all its hypocritical rectitude: la veuve à Calixte. In many ways the struggle between these two is even more sharply etched (though narrower in its feminist implications) than the conflict between the Mercenaires and Ma-Tante-la-Veuve, since Maria and la veuve à Calixte seem to take their greatest satisfaction from outsmarting each other. While the Mercenaires and Ma-Tante-la-Veuve symbolize irreconcilable mores that necessarily come into confrontation, the unending fight between the outlaw Maria and the ambitious veuve à Calixte has more the quality of a personal grudge match. In both cases, however, the author's—and therefore the reader's—sympathies clearly lie with the renegade women, who willingly forgo comfort, respectability, acceptance, and even legality in exchange for freedom and self-fulfillment.

Has Maillet set up these female antagonisms for the sake of symmetry, or are Ma-Tante-la-Veuve and la veuve à Calixte simply surrogates for men in what is essentially a male-ordered universe? Can we make a case for the latter by noting that both women are identified only by titles that define them in terms of their relationship to men? One might take such an argument one step further and

observe that both these dragons, while serving as champions of the most be-
nighted traditionalism, are freed from some of its more oppressive routine aspects
by their very widowhood.

As tempting as it is to pursue this line of thought, a better explanation may
in fact be the one suggested earlier. While the heroines and their antagonists
find themselves (the latter willingly, the former most involuntarily) in a world
whose parameters have been largely shaped by authoritative men, the fundamental struggle as they conceive it seems not to be between male and female,
but between institutional constraint and individual freedom. Women are lined
up against women, not in some mutual self-destructive loathing, but because
they make worthy and *interesting* adversaries. Indeed, as the narrator points out
in one sardonic passage in *Mariaagélas*, both heroine and villain are so accus-
tomed to coping mainly with men that they occasionally underestimate each
other:

La veuve à Calixte connaissait tout ça [that most rumrunners were eventually caught
and jailed by the authorities], et savait par conséquent qu'un jour ou l'autre le sort tomberait
sur Mariaagélas comme sur les autres contrabandiers. Mais la veuve à Calixte avait oublié
une chose: Mariaagélas n'était pas un contrabandier, mais une contrabandìere.

De son côté, Mariaagélas avait négligé de reconnaître les attributions de la veuve,
s'imaginant que sa fonction se limitait à de petits commérages de bénitier ou de bureau
de poste. Depuis belles années, pourtant, la veuve à Calixte débordait chaque saison son
rôle et étonnait tout le monde.[3]

Pélagie-la-Charrette, for all its good humor and savory Acadian epithets,
comes closer than either of the other novels to being a true epic. The struggles
played out in mischievous fun between the Mercenaires and Ma-Tante-la-Veuve,
between Maria the bootlegger and la veuve à Calixte, are repeated in deadly
earnest by Pélagie and her prime adversary, no less a figure than Death herself
(feminine in French). Pélagie's quest is not merely for personal freedom but for
the very life of Acadia, the Promised Land whence she was expelled during the
Great Dispersion and to which, against all the wiles of the Foe, she is determined
to lead her little remnant of survivors. Death takes many forms along Pélagie's
route, all of them female or identified by feminine nouns. At one particularly
desperate moment in the journey she is *la Faucheuse*, the Grim Reaper, whom
Pélagie bests only through exhausting and heroic efforts. Be it noted, however,
that Pélagie's triumph depends on her moral force rather than physical strength,
for which she unhesitatingly relies upon the men in the company. As *la Faucheuse*
lurks impatiently nearby, Pélagie's Cart, symbol of life and hope, is sinking
inexorably into the Salem swamp. While the men bend every ounce of their
strength to extricate the wagon, Pélagie wages her titanic struggle out of the
depths of her soul:

Les chroniqeurs du dernier siècle ont juré que Pélagie n'avait pas bougé durant toute
la scène, qu'elle se tenait droite comme un peuplier, la tête au vent. Elle n'aurait pas

crié, ni prié, ni montré le poing au ciel comme l'on a prétendu. Personne ne l'a vue se
jeter à genoux et se lamenter, ce n'est pas vrai. Personne ne l'a entendue hucher des
injures aux saints, ni les supplier pour l'amour de Dieu.

"Et alors, son cri?"

"Elle a dit un seul mot, un seul. . . ."

"Ma vie!" qu'on entendit monter des marais de Salem et rouler sur les roseaux jusqu'au
pont de bois.

La charrette a dû l'entendre, car elle a grincé de toutes ses pentures et de tous ses
essieux. Deux fois en un jour on s'en venait impudemment lui barrer la route? Qui osait?[4]

Another female manifestation of Death on Pélagie's path is the phantasmagoric
black cart, the *charrette noire*, which attaches itself to Pélagie's companion
Bélonie-le-Vieux and is visible only to him. While Pélagie imbues her own cart
with her vibrant sense of life, hope, purpose, and freedom, Bélonie's cart seems
instead to define him as it rumbles mockingly along with the pilgrims like a
malevolent shadow, sapping energy and provoking despair. As Pélagie is to her
Cart of Life (alive, active, generative of hope), so the Cart of Death is to Bélonie
(resigned, passive, prepared to be trundled to his death). Only with the discovery
of a living grandson, long thought dead, does Bélonie truly, totally, join in the
communion of Pélagie's joyous will to survive, to reach Acadia again. Robbed
of its essence, Bélonie's death cart then disappears, never to return. The epic
heroine, wielding as sole weapons her own vitality (maternal as well as personal)
and the wagon that embodies it, has faced down the greatest adversary of hu-
mankind, won the race against doom, and saved her less hardy friend. Though
the nature of her struggle and the mode of her triumph are, as we shall see,
defined by her womanhood, she thinks of them not as primarily a victory of
Woman over Man, but of Life over Death.

This is not to say that the gender of Maillet's protagonists is irrelevant to their
struggles—quite the contrary! In every case the fact that a struggle is necessary
at all is a consequence at least partly of their sex, and both the nature of the
obstacles they face and the weapons they use in overcoming them are tied to it
as well.

The linkages in *Mariaagélas* are multiple but quite clear. At eight years of
age the profit-minded preschooler Maria was out cornering the village market
in returnable bottles while she was thought to be safely at home, like a good
little girl, with her grandmother. At fourteen she was destined, like other girls
of similarly humble circumstances, to be shipped off by her father to work in
the shops, or to go into domestic service, but Maria was not about to accept
either option. With scornful disregard for her future employability in any "respectable" home, she settled a perceived insult by the schoolmistress to her
younger sister by storming into the schoolhouse one day, "avant que personne
n'eût pu prévoir le coup, et sous le regard ébarroui des petits de la petite
classe, . . . avait administré à M'zelle Mazerolle le plus formidable poing dans
l'oeil de mémoire scolaire."[5]

Moreover, Maria was not the first woman of her family to reject the traditional destiny: her Aunt Clara, much admired by the adolescent Maria, had become a prostitute and a vagabond in preference to remaining in the horrid conditions of a succession of sweat-shops. In her last such job Clara had even organized the other women in a short-lived mutiny, torched the shop, and spent time in prison. Despite the cost, Maria was deeply impressed by Clara's refusal to conform and looked to her as a model in her own budding life of outlawry. Nor did she aspire to the "respectable" women's roles as dependent wife, doting mother, pious parishioner, and loyal good citizen. No one—not her father, the priest, the schoolmarm, or tradition—was about to tell Mariaagélas what she must do or what she must become, or not become. Fortified by her natural taste for adventure and her business acumen, she therefore seemed to fall almost by fate into a highly profitable profession—bootlegging—that made her a moral, social and legal outlaw.

From then till the end of her days, Maria took mischievous pleasure not only in running the most successful bootlegging operation in her area during those dangerous Prohibition days, but in carrying out her feats under the very nose of the sanctimonious veuve à Calixte. In one supremely ironic ruse, Maria played upon two of the most deeply entrenched stereotypes of her society. Disguising herself as a nun, she had a bootlegging partner drive her and a full cargo of illegal liquor in her own Buick across the American border, counting accurately upon the gallantry of the *québécois* border guards towards her sex and the respect of the Irish-American guards for her habit to protect her from the usual close search. Her contempt for the limitations placed upon her free choice by tradition and prejudice inspired her to use them as weapons in the service of her own illegal ends.

The outlawry of la Piroune and la Bessoune in *Les Cordes-de-Bois* was more social than statutory, but as disruptive of local society as that of Mariaagélas. Like Maria, they were members of a renegade family whose women were known for flouting the conventions (in this case principally sexual) established by their "betters." Again the battle lines were drawn early, and again a small act of defiance signaled the charge. The bourgeois society of le Pont was centered, typically, around the parish church, whose Angelus bells called all right-thinking townspeople (notably innocent young girls) to pious meditation. The Mercenaires, however, worshipped at a shrine belonging to a very different myth. The nubile Piroune, in particular, was drawn to the quay instead of the church, and one fateful evening she jingled the little bells on the buoy at the very moment the Angelus was sounding. Though Ma-Tante-la-Veuve would not have believed it, the narrator claims that this was not a gesture of contempt, but one of affirmation:

[L]a Piroune, à cette époque de sa vie, ne cherchait dans les bateaux que des souvenirs, une sorte de mémoire-hommage à l'ancêtre. Elle se rendait au quai comme Marie-Rose et Jeanne-Mance [two of Ma-Tante-la-Veuve's many respectable nieces] à la niche de Marie-Immaculée: en pèlerinage. Cette orpheline de père et de mère semblait s'accrocher à son passé, faute d'avenir, à son lignage tout plein de mystère et de faits glorieux qu'elle revivait là sur sa bouée.[6]

Indeed, the first of the Mercenaires had surfaced generations before in some mysterious fashion from the sea,[7] had braved nature and the local owner to establish his brood permanently on top of the butte, and had passed down both his affinity for the sea and his rejection of conventions to his many descendants, now mostly women. As her male progenitor had emerged from the sea, la Piroune's own mother, Barbe-la-Jeune, had disappeared into it after saving the lives of some sailors stranded on ice floes by a sudden thaw.

The motif of the sea is all-pervasive in this novel (and prominent in the two others), but in contradictory ways. It gives birth and brings death. It promises hope (the vigil of la Piroune at the quay, where passing sailors come to meet her and often stay), and inflicts despair (la Bessoune's efforts to drown herself after her young priest/lover has apparently done just that). It beckons to far-off lands (the Irish sailor, "Tom Thumb," finds it an almost irresistible lure), and validates the regeneration of the entrenched Mercenaires (la Bessoune is born nine months after her mother, la Piroune, heroically saves a child snared in some ship's rigging and celebrates with the cheering assembled sailors). Neither exclusively male nor female in its symbolism, it is a self-complete, eternal, mystical life force, permeating all Acadian myth and legend. La Bessoune, twinless twin of an unknown father, is indeed a child of the sea, whose wildness and freedom she fully incarnates. Like the rest of her line, she will not be mastered by mere ordinary mortals and their silly laws, any more than they can dictate to the restless waves of the unending sea.

As a child la Bessoune puts up with the discipline of Church and school only as much and as long as she pleases, then abandons both. With adolescence she steps easily into the footsteps of her mother, selling contraband liquor and offering the bounty of her own sensuous nature to passing sailors. La Piroune and la Bessoune do not so much challenge the institutions of le Pont as ignore them, with an insouciance that often leaves Ma-Tante-la-Veuve in a state of spluttering frustration. The mere existence of the Mercenaires is an intolerable affront to the well-ordered universe of le Pont, whose futile efforts to control them result in constant, inevitable confrontation.

While the Mercenaire women thwart Ma-Tante-la-Veuve mainly by attracting most of her potential male allies to their side through sheer joyous sensuality, their ultimate ironic triumph comes on the widow's own supposed home ground: the domain of the spirit. Like everything else in le Pont, charity has been institutionalized. At a yearly "auction" held by the parish church, the destitute are assembled and farmed out to whatever families bid the lowest amount and promise to provide for them. One year, a truly pathetic case disturbs the smug rhythm of the auction: Henri à Vital, a once-popular local *raconteur* who had gone off for adventure to the States and was now back, a poor paralytic wreck, finds no takers. Ma-Tante-la-Veuve and the others are willing enough to do their

Christian duty for the elderly and sickly, who can be counted upon not to survive beyond a decent interval. But who, the sweating auctioneer suddenly realized, would take on the wheelchair-bound Henri à Vital, "pas un vieillard encore, ni tout à fait un déshérité, qui mangerait ses trois repas par jour et pouvait vivre encore des années?"[8]

Into the silence that follows steps la Piroune, prodded by la Bessoune, who offers to take Henri à Vital—for nothing. Ma-Tante-la-Veuve, nearly apoplectic, tries to sidetrack this scandalous turn of events, but the new young curate, overriding his stunned pastor, vigorously supports the right of the poor to go off with whomever they choose. Henri à Vital, predictably, heads right for the Cordes-de-Bois, as do a pair of orphans who have clung instinctively to la Piroune's welcoming skirtfolds.

The narrator describes the sweet taste of vengeance the whole affair leaves in the mouths of the Mercenaires as they savor the discomfiture of their archenemy:

Effectivement, le vicaire avait le pied sur celui de son curé, c'est la Bessoune qui l'a vu. Et elle sourit, la Bessoune. Un sourire qu'elle flanqua sous le nez de la Veuve en plein mitan de l'estrade de l'encan des pauvres. Tout était à l'envers, ce jour-là: les chenapans et les vieux renards qui faisaient leurs Pâques à la Trinité occupaient la tribune de l'église: les filles à matelots narguaient le Tiers-Ordre et les confréries; les pauvres achetaient les pauvres; et voilà que le vicaire marchait sur les pieds de son curé.

On a dit que la Bessoune avait été saisie alors d'un tel élan d'éblouissement et de reconnaissance, qu'elle aurait sauté au cou du jeune prêtre, là, à la face de toute la paroisse qui en aurait fait: aah![9]

This incident, with its climactic position near the end of the novel, underscores an interesting aspect of the question of womanhood in this particular Maillet universe. For Ma-Tante-la-Veuve the sexual behavior of the Mercenaires is a thing apart, a sin-in-itself, a violation of all the old guilt-inducing strictures of Church and polite society. For la Piroune and la Bessoune, however, sexual gratification is not an avenue into which they are reluctantly channeled for want of freedom, but a perfectly natural manifestation of the freedom they already joyously feel. As human beings, and specifically as women, they are whole beings of free-spirited openheartedness, no more self-conscious about the sharing of their bodies than they are about sharing family loyalty or the maternal warmth to which the poor and the abandoned are instinctively drawn. The struggle they are forced to wage is not within themselves, but against an embittered foe who cannot even understand, much less successfully prevent, the totality of their freedom, both defined by and expressed through their specific nature as women.

We see in Pélagie-la-Charrette the same harmony between a passion for freedom and strong womanly traits of the most traditional sort. Survivor (unlike her husband) of the sack of Grand-Pré at the time of the Great Acadian Dispersion, she has seen friends and relatives strewn all up and down the Atlantic coast and has spent fifteen years tied alongside black slaves to the plough of a Georgia planter. When she finally decides she has had enough, her revolt is inspired in equal measure by heroism of soul—strong, brave, decisive, bent on action—and by a vivid belief in her critical role as surviving mother of a whole race. The Cart of Life that she sets plunging northward on the path to liberty is also a warmly enveloping rolling home, full of the weak and defenseless, crammed with pots and pans, sheltering the pitiful remnants of a nearly exterminated generation. Hopelessness and suffocation are not, however, related to the dark interior of Pélagie's wagon, but to the monotonous closed circle traced by the Georgia planter's plough, the mud that nearly sucks the wagon under in Salem, and the frenetic, aimless charge of Bélonie's Cart of Death. Pélagie's womanhood is as traditional as a tigress fighting to save her cubs and as liberated as the warrior hero who saves a nation. It is the essential context of her being, the condition that gives form and meaning to her epic quest for life and freedom—not a contradiction but an affirmation.

The only power strong enough to distract Pélagie even momentarily from her relentless drive northward is the call of the nearby sea—here, as elsewhere in Maillet, a mysterious atavistic force of compelling power for all Acadians. Both progenitor and protective mother, master of nature and alluring mistress, proof of freedom and assurance of continuity, the sea links man and woman, past and future, life and eternity. Tempted as she sometimes is to divert her route towards its magical embrace, Pélagie sees it as above all a guaranteeing sign of her odyssey's ultimate success: "La mer restait leur plus sûr lien avec l'Acadie du Nord. On peut s'égarer dans la forêt, ou se cogner le front aux monts; mais la mer du nord ne saurait aboutir qu'aux pays."[10]

We have seen the strength of Maillet's assertive women, but what of the men in their worlds? In all three novels the important role of chief antagonist is given to another woman (though in Les Cordes-de-Bois and Mariaagélas these women may, through their widowhood, represent an institutionalized, bourgeois, male-dominated society). There are, however, several important male characters in these novels, and there are—perhaps surprisingly—very few instances of hostility in the relations between them and the epic heroines. A few of the men are subjects of mild scorn, like the simple-minded soldier Bidoche and the informer Ferdinand in Mariaagélas, or the strait-laced pastor in Les Cordes-de-Bois. Some are sympathetic but clearly secondary characters, such as Maria's bootlegging partner le Grand Vital and the stream of men captivated and lured to the butte by the Mercenaires.

Of greatest interest, however, are the examples of genuine respect and affection between the epic heroines and certain men around them. Hinted at in the family loyalty of Mariaagélas, which extends even to her rough-spoken father, this kind of warm relationship blossoms more clearly in Les Cordes-de-Bois. Two of la Bessoune's "conquests" are most unlikely partners: "Tom Thumb," the homesick Irish sailor always going back off to sea—except the last time—and the earnest young curate.

The latter, first drawn to the butte by the desire to convert the lawless Mercenaires, soon falls under their spell. They, and particularly la Bessoune, seem to possess already all the joy, selflessness, and freedom that he has come to preach. After long months of pleasure on the butte and scandal in the village, the priest is reported one night to have stepped off the bridge into the dark sea. As reported by Catoune, another Mercenaire and the only witness, his parting words are a confession of guilt to the village charge that for all his natural virtues he has not led a single soul to God: "C'est Ma-Tante-la-Veuve qu'avait raison ... qu'il a dit."[11] To this Catoune adds her own assessment: "Fallit qu'il mettit l'océan entre lui pis le monde ... fallit qu'il éteignit le feu ... le feu qui y brûlait les boyaux."[12] When the heartbroken Bessoune tries soon thereafter to join her lost lover at the bottom of the sea, she is saved by Tom Thumb, now a permanent inhabitant of the Cordes-de-Bois. His healing compassion, inspired by the Mercenaires' own rough-hewn love, thus completes the redemptive cycle. In a final, gentle benediction, a report later filters back that the curate did not drown after all but has been spotted on a ship bound for Rome.

Tom Thumb, as we have noted, comes to rest at the Cordes-de-Bois only after innumerable short stays followed by renewed sea voyages. The narrator's commentary on his ultimate decision to stay explains what the spirit of the Mercenaires, and the Acadia they symbolize for him, has come to mean in his life:

Vous aviez cru, vous, qu'il allait partir comme ça, le Tom Thumb? quitter un pays qui lui rendait son Irlande transposée et transfigurée, pour une Irlande réelle et misérable qui mourait de faim? Allez donc! C'est en Amérique que l'Irlande est belle. Et c'est en Acadie que Tom Thumb pourrait en rêver à son aise.

Il s'ébroua, le petit matelot, et offrit sa plus splendide grimace à la Bessoune.

"Moi pis le grand Brendan," qu'il dit, "on ira par terre et mer chercher les héros: les géants, les saints, les navigueux, les sorciers, les holy men ... et on juchera tous ces salauds sur le faît des Cordes-de-Bois. Pis ça sera là le centre du monde," qu'il fit.

La Bessoune ne répondit pas. Mais Charlie Boudreau jure qu'elle a mis sa main dans celle de Tom Thumb, et qu'ils sont partis tous les deux par les dunes vers les Cordes-de-Bois.[13]

The end of Tom Thumb's lifelong search for mythical Celtic heroes has come in the undemanding affection of the outcast Mercenaires, for whom love is sharing, not dependency. Like freedom and heroism, it is not to be found in some distant, inaccessible place, but within the soul.

No one could be less dependent than the determined Pélagie-la-Charrette, who takes her vocation as epic heroine very seriously. Others defer to her natural leadership without question, as when, on a day when she decides to give her flagging troup a pep talk, "l'Acadie entière lève des yeux bleus suppliants sur son chef qui déjà s'empare de la tribune."[14] When she has finished, "elle redescend de la tribune en se drapant dans sa cape comme un consul romain dans sa toge."[15] The narrator notes the stirring effect of her speech on the little band of travelers: "Ce jour-là, on l'aurait couronnée de lauriers, la Pélagie, si on avait été en saison."[16] Her admiring friend, Captain Broussard dit Beausoleil, characterizes her thus: "Quelle femme, cette Pélagie! capable à elle seule de ramener un peuple au pays. De le ramener à contre-courant."[17]

Yet the two most cherished friends of this Pélagie—heroine, leader, object of admiration—are men. Though her relationships with Bélonie-le-Vieux and with Captain Broussard dit Beausoleil are very different, each is rooted in love of a very special kind. Bélonie, noted *croniqueur* described as already old at the outset of the trek, brings out Pélagie's protective instincts: "maternal" would not be too strong a word. Her youth contrasts with his age, her strength and vigor with his feebleness, his black cart of despair—of resignation to death— with her Cart of Life. Pélagie, who must have strength enough for them both, refuses to leave Bélonie behind: "Pélagie n'aurait pas eu le coeur de laisser derrière le doyen des déportés, même s'il devait traîner avec lui jusqu'à la Grand' Prée [sic] sa charrette fantôme."[18]

Onwards she prods and encourages him, mile after mile, until at last along the coast of Massachusetts the miracle occurs. The *Grand'Goule* (formerly the deportation ship, *Pembroke*, seized from the English by the exiles themselves) intercepts Pélagie's wagon near Salem. Captain Beausoleil hails the straggling band and proudly presents one of his crew: young Bélonie, grandson of Bélonie and unsuspected survivor of the Great Dispersion. Pélagie's obstinate determination to keep the old man alive is now abruptly vindicated; the death wagon becomes a pointless relic, and Bélonie-le-Vieux joins the ranks of Life. Maillet, through her narrator, uses an astonishingly effective reversed sex-role image to convey the intensity of Bélonie's joy at that moment:

Le ciel lui-même a dû ce jour-là enregistrer le cri du capitaine Beausoleil-Broussard, puis le renvoyer rebondir à la tête de Bélonie-le-Vieux qui le reçut comme un coup de pied au ventre. Si jamais un homme depuis le début des temps, a éprouvé l'ombre d'une douleur de l'enfantement, c'est le Bélonie de la charrette. A cent ans, ou presque, il venait de mettre au monde sa lignée.[19]

Pélagie and the gallant Beausoleil have a very different sort of relationship. She often turns to him for the same sort of strength and moral support that Bélonie seeks from her. The first meeting of Pélagie and Beausoleil after the Dispersion, when the *Grand'Goule* comes into port as Pélagie's wagon is passing through Charlestown, shows the depth of their mutual affection:

Le front du capitaine se déride et ses joues éclatent dans un large rire à l'ancienne comme Pélagie n'en a point entendu depuis le temps. Alors les bras de cette femme éperdue se referment sur son coeur pour le garder au chaud et l'empêcher de bondir hors du coffre: ce rire vient du passé, mais point de l'Au-delà. Et de la poitrine de cette veuve d'Acadie qui traîne depuis tant d'années une plaie ouverte, s'arrache un cri que même les morts auront entendu:
"Il est en vie!"[20]

From then on Beausoleil is Pélagie's guiding star, paralleling at sea the route of her wagon on land. Their reunions at a succession of coastal points are so

many marks of progress along Pélagie's path to Acadia. Beausoleil helps save
her foundering cart in the Salem swamp and cheers her when her courage wavers.
At their last rendezvous before her final push through Maine, Pélagie measures
the extent of her debt to Beausoleil and the depths of her affection and gratitude:

Il était là, son capitaine, son chevalier, son héros, l'homme qui avait par trois fois
risqué sa vie pour elle, qui avait calé dans la vase mouvante pour la troisième fois qui
est toujours la dernière, pour elle, pour les siens, et à la fin pour sa charrette. C'est lui
à la fin qui l'avait sauvée, sa charrette, lui qui s'était agrippé aux ridelles, à la vie, à la
mort.
   Et elle se serra contre lui, se berça la tête au creux de ses épaules en murmurant des
gloussements et des mots qu'il n'entendait pas.... Il avait risqué sa vie pour elle qui en
échange avait offert la sienne. Leur double vie en otage l'un pour l'autre. Plus rien
n'effacerait ça dans le ciel. La charrette à jamais en serait le gage.[21]

   The bond suggested here is beyond the sexual, though it involves mutual self-
giving, profound union, and regeneration. The same is true of the love that links
Pélagie with Bélonie—clearly not sexual, yet bursting with the seed of rebirth,
of new life. Both Bélonie and Beausoleil disappear at the end—Bélonie into the
forest, Beausoleil out to sea—and thus quickly pass into the domain of legend.
Pélagie herself is the source and inspiration of that legend as she and her Cart
of Life at last go to their final rest in the soil of the new Acadia. Thus Acadia
itself becomes the heaven of the emerging myth, the medium of ultimate union
between Pélagie and the two men she loves. Pélagie is the brightest star in the
new constellation, neither diminishing Bélonie by offering him her strong protection nor herself diminished by accepting the same from Beausoleil. She is
the epic heroine whose quest for life and freedom has given significance to the
lives of the others, and it is her womanhood that shapes that quest. Her triumph
is in defining the roles of the others without limiting them.
   Pélagie herself asserts the primacy she attaches to womanhood by selecting
her daughter Madeleine rather than one of her sons to carry on after her death.
Near Pélagie's grave in the new Acadia, Madeleine takes up the challenge to
renew the race and "refaire l'Acadie":

C'est tout près, dans la vallée de Memramcook, qu'elle abattrait son premier arbre,
Madeleine LeBlanc, sous le regard ahuri de son homme et de ses frères qui n'en croient
point leurs yeux.... Allez, flancs mous, c'est icitte que je nous creusons une cave et
que je nous bâtissons un abri!... Madeleine, digne rejeton de la charrette par la voie
des femmes.[22]

   "La voie des femmes"—the royal road to the rebirth of Acadia! All the
heroines in these Maillet novels could in some sense be symbols of Acadia—a
small nation, weak in the eyes of a world that knows only physical force, but
strong in her desire to live and flourish despite all obstacles. Refusing the right
of others either to condemn her to death or to dictate the conditions of her life,

this Acadia triumphs over her foes by courage, boldness, humor, shrewdness, and nobility of spirit. There is heroism in her struggle, but also a saving mischievousness that excludes excessive solemnity. She is Maria the bootlegger, refusing the life of the shops, thumbing her nose at the fate others have reserved for her. She is la Piroune, using the buoy bells to broadcast the invitation of a generous heart across the open sea. She is above all Pélagie, hitching up her hem and setting off in a dilapidated wagon towards life and liberty. Her traditionalism does homage to a past born in the Celtic mists of the sea and tempered in the fire at Grand-Pré; her liberation creates a nation that determines its boundaries by the location of its soul; her nationalism is a reflection of the universal human quest for life and freedom. One may smile at her indulgently, but always with admiring affection, for Acadia is still living her epic—glorious, and, in its way, consummately female.

NOTES

1. Maya Angelou, untitled dramatic interpretation and poetry reading, Black Arts Festival, Dickinson College, Carlisle, Pennsylvania, 5 April 1978.

2. Antonine Maillet, *Mariaagélas*, Collection Roman acadien (Montréal: Leméac, 1973; rpt. Montréal: Editions Marabout, 1981); Antonine Maillet, *Les Cordes-de-Bois* (Montréal: Leméac, 1977); Antonine Maillet, *Pélagie-la-Charrette* (Montréal: Leméac, 1979; Paris: Grasset, 1979). All references are to the 1973 edition of *Mariaagélas* and to the Leméac edition of *Pélagie-la-Charrette*. Although they are not discussed here, readers will also want to be aware of the new English-U.S. translated edition, Antonine Maillet, *Pélagie*, trans. Philip Stratford (New York: Doubleday, 1982), and of the sequal to the original novel: Antonine Maillet, *Cent Ans dans les bois* (Montréal: Leméac, 1981), printed in France as *La Gribouille* (Paris: Gallimard, 1982).

3. Maillet, *Mariaagélas*, p. 73.

Calixte's widow knew all that and therefore knew that some day fate would catch up with Mariaagélas as it did with the other bootleggers. But Calixte's widow had forgotten one thing: Mariaagélas wasn't a bootlegger but a "bootleggeress."

For her part, Mariaagélas had failed to recognize the widow's talents, supposing that her function was limited to minor holy water font or post office gossip. Yet for many a year Calixte's widow had been overflowing the banks of her role every season and surprising everyone.

4. Maillet, *Pélagie-la-Charrette*, p. 292.

The chroniclers of the last century swore that Pélagie hadn't budged during the entire scene, that she stood straight as a poplar, her head to the wind. She reportedly didn't shout, nor pray, nor brandish her fist at heaven as some have claimed. No one saw her sink to her knees and wail, that wasn't so. No one heard her whistle insults at the saints, nor beg them for the love of God.

"So, her shout?"

"She said a single word, just one...."

"My life!" people heard rising from the Salem swamps and rolling over the reeds up to the wooden bridge.

The cart must have heard her, for all its hinges and axles grated. Twice in one day they were impudently trying to bar its way? Who had the nerve?

5. Maillet, *Mariaagélas*, p. 14.

Before anyone could have foreseen the blow, and under the stunned gaze of the little ones in the primary class ... had dealt M'zelle Mazerolle the most tremendous punch in the eye in school memory.

6. Maillet, *Les Cordes-de-Bois*, p. 68.

La Piroune, at that stage in her life, was searching the ships only for memories, a sort of memorial-homage to the ancestor. She would go to the quay like Marie-Rose and Jeanne-Mance to the grotto of Mary Immaculate: on a pilgrimage. That child, fatherless and motherless, seemed to cling to her past, for lack of a future, to her lineage full of mystery and of glorious feats that she used to relive there on her buoy.

7. It will be remembered that the Sagouine also belonged to a people that emerged mysteriously from the sea, the Pucqis, in the earlier novel, *Don l'Orignal*, by Antonine Maillet (Montréal: Leméac, 1972).

8. Maillet, *Les Cordes-de-Bois*, p. 300.

Not yet an old man, nor a completely destitute one, who would eat his three squares a day and could live for years yet.

9. Maillet, *Les Cordes-de-Bois*, pp. 304-05.

Sure enough, the curate was stepping on the pastor's foot, it was la Bessoune who saw it. And la Bessoune smiled. A smile that she thrust under the nose of the Widow smack in the middle of the poor-auction platform. Everything was wrongside-to that day: the scamps and the old foxes that made their Easter Duty on Trinity Sunday were occupying the church loft; the sailors' daughters were snapping their fingers at the Third-Order and the confraternities; the poor were buying the poor; and here was the curate stepping on his pastor's toes.

It's been said that la Bessoune had been seized with such a surge of dazzlement and gratitude that she reportedly fell upon the young priest's neck, there, right in front of the whole parish which supposedly said: ha!

10. Maillet, *Pélagie-la-Charrette*, p. 205.

The sea remained their surest link with the Acadia of the North. One may get lost in the forest, or bang one's head on the hills, but the northern sea can't end up anywhere but in the homeland.

I thank Professor Paula Gilbert Lewis for pointing out the continuing—indeed height-ened—importance of this link in the sequel novel (Maillet, *Cent Ans dans les bois*), in which Pélagie's descendant Babeé, representing the Land, marries Pierre, symbol of the Sea.

11. Maillet, *Les Cordes-de-Bois*, p. 337.

It's Ma-Tante-la-Veuve who was right ... he said.

12. Maillet, *Les Cordes-de-Bois*, p. 337.

He had to put the ocean between himself and everybody else ... he had to put out the fire ... the fire that was burning in his guts.

13. Maillet, *Les Cordes-de-Bois*, pp. 344-45.

You had thought he was going to leave just like that, Tom Thumb? leave a land that gave him back his Ireland transposed and transfigured, for a real, miserable Ireland dying of starvation? Come on! It's in America that Ireland is beautiful. And it's in Acadia that Tom Thumb could dream about it as much as he pleased.

The little sailor snorted and offered la Bessoune his most splendid grimace.

"Myself and the great Brendan," he said, "we'll go off over land and sea looking for heroes: giants, saints, navigators, sorcerers, holy men ... and we'll perch all these so-and-so's on the ridge-pole of the Cordes-de-Bois. Then that'll be the center of the world," he said.

La Bessoune didn't answer. But Charlie Boudreau swears she put her hand in Tom Thumb's, and that the two of them set off across the dunes towards the Cordes-de-Bois.

14. Maillet, *Pélagie-la-Charrette*, p. 269.

All Acadia raises its pleading blue eyes to its leader who is already seizing the rostrum.

15. Maillet, *Pélagie-la-Charrette*, p. 269.

She steps back down from the rostrum draping herself in her cape like a Roman consul in his toga.

16. Maillet, *Pélagie-la-Charrette*, p. 269.

That day they would have crowned Pélagie with laurel if it had been in season.

17. Maillet, *Pélagie-la-Charrette*, p. 113.

What a woman, that Pélagie! Capable of leading a people single-handed back to its homeland. Of leading it against the current.

18. Maillet, *Pélagie-la-Charrette*, p. 14.

Pélagie wouldn't have had the heart to leave behind the doyen of the deportees, even if he had to drag his phantom cart with him all the way to Grand' Prée.

19. Maillet, *Pélagie-la-Charrette*, p. 278.

Heaven itself must have recorded the cry of captain Beausoleil-Broussard that day, then sent it bouncing back upon the head of Bélonie-le-Vieux who received it like a kick in the belly. If ever a man since the beginning of time has felt the trace of a labor pain, it's the Bélonie of the cart. At age 100, or nearly, he had just given birth to his posterity.

"La charrette" in this remarkable passage can be interpreted in two senses: as the now superfluous phantom wagon that was one of the lexically feminine manifestations of Pélagie's mortal adversary, Death; or as the equally feminine Cart of Life, Pélagie's own wagon, in which old Bélonie becomes, with the discovery of his living grandson, a full-fledged spiritual, as well as physical, passenger at last. Given Bélonie's sudden experience of something resembling childbirth on the one hand, and the constant association through-out the novel of life and its continuation with Pélagie on the other, I find that one interpretation does not necessarily exclude the other.

20. Maillet, *Pélagie-la-Charrette*, pp. 88-89.

The captain's brow wrinkles, and his cheeks burst in a big laugh in the old style such as Pélagie hasn't heard in ages. Then this lost woman's arms close over her heart to keep it warm and prevent it from leaping out of her chest: this laugh is coming from the past, but not from the Beyond. And from the breast of this widow of Acadia who has been suffering from an open wound for so long there is torn a shout that even the dead must have heard:
"He's alive!"

21. Maillet, *Pélagie-la-Charrette*, p. 300.

He was there, her captain, her knight, her hero, the man who had thrice risked his life for her, who had lowered himself into the shifting mud for the third time that's always the last, for her, for her people, and in the end for her cart. It's he in the end who had saved it, her cart, he who had clung to its side-rails, to life, to death.

And she pressed against him, cradled her head in the hollow of his shoulders murmuring little clucks and words that he didn't understand.... He had risked his life for her, and she in exchange had offered her own. Their double life in hostage for each other. Nothing would ever surpass that in heaven. The cart would forever be the pledge of it.

22. Maillet, *Pélagie-la-Charrette*, p. 346.

It's right near by, in the valley of Memramcook, that she, Madeleine LeBlanc, would chop down her first tree, under the startled gaze of her man and of her brothers who don't believe their eyes.... Let's go, you softies, hereabouts is where I'm digging us a cave and building us a shelter!... Madeleine, worthy offspring of the cart by the female line.

12

Beyond the Myths and Fictions of Traditionalism and Nationalism: The Political in the Work of Nicole Brossard

Louise H. Forsyth ————————————————————

> Du poétique au politique, un seul et même engagement: cultiver la vie. S'identifier. Regarder le miroir jusqu'à ce qu'il renvoie une image *intégrale*, jusqu'à ce qu'il devienne fenêtre, ouverture sur l'espace du réel et de l' imaginaire. Aussi longtemps que la réalité.
> Du poétique au politique, un seul mobile: agrandir l'espace de plaisir jusqu'à s'en faire un hologramme, une histoire, un projet qui dépend de moi collective, d'elles, d'elle, où la jouissance appelle l'intelligence.[1]

Nicole Brossard is one of the leading writers of Quebec today. Her works and activities have served to redefine Quebec letters and culture so effectively that her voice and the voices of many other women speaking and writing autonomously out of woman-centered space are being heard and heeded. She is an original and innovative author whose writing practice in prose, poetry, and theory led the way through the seventies, for both female and male writers, to the emergence of a new modernity in literature. This modernity represents a significant challenge to all cultural traditions. It has been the most significant current of literary production in Quebec since 1970. Those who have been part of the movement recognize the active role of leadership Brossard has played in it: "Known, read, and respected by the writers who are working toward a renewal of social and literary patterns, Nicole Brossard continues to intervene in and to proclaim her breaks with social practice through the establishment of increasingly compelling bonds among the body, language and ways of life."[2]

Nicole Brossard is, then, at the center of a dynamic group of writers and cultural activists who are throwing out a serious challenge to the very foundation of the codes, symbols, and practices of dominant culture and its values. Her works make it impossible for the reader to take the representation systems of such a culture seriously any longer. She believes that these systems must be viewed in a fresh light, set aside, or exploded so that the ideological basis, on which those who monopolize power in our society necessarily depend and which they turn to their own advantage in so exclusive and violent a way, is broken irreparably, never to be replaced. Brossard's writing is a strong political statement, an absolute refusal of imposed values. At the same time her writing is a quest for inner sources of energy, an affirmation of personal and social freedom, a full appropriation of her rights as a woman in all spheres of social activity.

Since 1965 her focus has been on the power of language to liberate the individual and restructure social institutions. She has worked primarily on the word as signifier—an active agent carrying and seeking meaning—in her lucid exploration of woman's imaginary realm, her body, and her condition in society. In all her texts, Brossard considers writing to be a praxis, a means to intervene effectively on the forum of society while giving form to woman's vision of the universe. Since language is symbol, the body and its desire are transformed by writing so that they enter the symbolic dimension where they become political by being communicated and shared. Brossard writes for herself; she writes for other women who are also writing and reading. She writes so that the images and symbols arising out of women's experience can circulate dynamically and be exchanged in the many dimensions of human space—geographic, psychological, socio-cultural—which must open and unfold if women are to be able to situate themselves in their authentic place.

Nicole Brossard was born in Montreal in 1943. She has already produced a large and varied corpus, having written in all the genres usually defined by literature, criticism, and journalism: poetry, novels, drama, film, essay, analysis, and commentary. She has also participated in many conferences, the proceedings of which have been published and so offer an explicit statement of her position on a number of issues related to her writing and her feminism. As well as her full-length pieces, she has written a considerable number of short texts and articles. Several of these were published in *Les Têtes de Pioche*, a radical feminist newspaper which she co-founded in 1976. Among her many short texts, those published in *La Barre du Jour*, a literary journal which she co-founded in 1965, are of particular importance. While theoretical questions and imaginative creation are explicitly linked in all her full-length works, it is frequently in her short texts that the reader is able to seize most immediately her theoretical positions.

In all areas, Brossard's theoretical views arise out of her radical position regarding established social values and structures. She has held radical political views from the beginning of her writing career. In the early seventies she began to speak out as a radical feminist and to work closely with other women who held similar views. In Quebec's large feminist community, there have always been a significant number of radical women who are heterosexual. In Brossard's case, however, her radical feminist involvement was necessarily linked to her lesbianism, since her political and creative expression emerge out of her conscious awareness of a unique physical presence in the material world. Her perspectives on society have consistently reflected in an immediate and vital way her sensitivity and experience as a woman, knowing desire, loving women with her body, spirit, and imagination.

ANALYSIS, SOLIDARITY, AND WRITING: *LA BARRE DU JOUR*

In 1965, the same year that Nicole Brossard published her first collection of poetry, she was co-founder of the literary journal *La Barre du Jour*. She had just finished her studies at the Université de Montréal, a center of militant nationalist fervor. Many of the finest poets, novelists, and playwrights which Quebec produced during the Quiet Revolution—a period of major political and cultural renewal—were or had been students at the Université de Montréal. A group of former students of the university had founded in 1963 a journal which soon became the recognized organ of the nationalist movement: *Parti Pris*. The goal of *Parti Pris* was an independent, socialist Quebec, free of political influence from the Catholic Church. Nicole Brossard shared these goals and was touched by the nationalism and analyses of the writers of this group in a way which was to determine the nature of her feminist praxis: "En 1963, nous avons lu *Parti pris* et nous avons compris. Il n'y avait pas à discuter: les positions critiques de cette revue ajoutées à notre expérience quotidienne du Québec ... achevèrent de transformer notre impatience en un naturel contestataire."[3]

Brossard shared the immediate socio-political goals of the *Parti Pris* generation and was also in agreement with many of its views and priorities: nationalism must confront the problems of the present and make an absolute break with past traditions; analysis is essential to any effective form of political action; a people alienated from its language is without the means to envisage and affirm its freedom and autonomy; the real problem is interiorized fear and defeat. The *Parti Pris* group was made up of creative writers and activists, some of whom were poets and novelists, while others were theoreticians strongly influenced by a Marxist perspective. The combination of poetic creativity and revolutionary fervor was most effective during the Quiet Revolution in formulating political goals, while releasing creative energy and allowing a dynamic collective imag- ination to form a vision of a new society. The writers of the *Parti Pris* group proved by example that a dynamic text, incorporating a poetic and a theoretical dimension, is an effective weapon in the struggle for social change. The texts of these writers were aggressive and violent; the writers themselves were not.

Since the sixties Brossard has remained aware of the parallels between the goals and strategies of this group of militant nationalists at *Parti Pris* and her own feminist analysis and strategies. The differences, however, must not be overlooked. Even before she declared herself a feminist, she and others of the *Barre du Jour* group—both female and male—knew they did not simply wish to duplicate or continue in the same way what *Parti Pris* had done. They had to go beyond, and they chose to do so by deconstructing social codes and placing central emphasis on their body, their material presence in the world, and their practice of writing. The *Parti Pris* generation was influenced by Sartre, Memmi, Berque, and Fanon. The *Barre du Jour* group was inspired to a new radicalism by reading Bataille, Barthes, Lacan, Foucault, and Derrida, as well. This led them to transgress, through a variety of processes, the most firmly entrenched taboos of Quebec society—particularly moral and sexual—as when Nicole Brossard spoke out as a lesbian and radical feminist, naming and celebrating every part of her woman's body, its drives and its fluid ecstacies, in order to affirm her own full control and possession of them. The approach of the *Barre du Jour* writers was and still is to synthesize socio-political analysis and the creative process, a synthesis achieved by the lucidly examined desire of the writer's inhabited body—mind, body, and spirit working dynamically together. In coming to this approach, Nicole Brossard and the others have sought material wholeness of being, which necessarily brings with it liberation of each individual from within. This has remained the source of her radical position, as a writer, feminist, activist, and lesbian.

At the time of the October Crisis in 1970 and the proclamation of the War Measures Act, Nicole Brossard and her co-editor, Roger Soublière, organized a conference to protest the arrest of poet Gaston Miron and the more than four hundred others who were thrown into prison at the time but never officially charged. The conference and the subsequent publication of its proceedings were both a public gesture of solidarity with the nationalist writers and militants of the sixties and a statement of resolve to go much further than they did, using an aggressive, subversive literature as the weapon of attack:

Alors que sur le terrain poético-politique tout semblait avoir été dit—et nous n'avions pas envie de devenir des répétiteurs impuissants— . . . nous qui partagions l'angoisse et la révolte des Québécois avons choisi de faire porter notre travail sur le langage. Pendant que d'autres renchérissaient sur notre situation alarmante, nous cherchions à combattre à l'intérieur de ses frontières une sémantique qui . . . faisaient le jeu culturel de ceux contre lesquels les ''politiques'' se battaient. A travers ces expériences nous avons parlé de nous, de nos sexes si longtemps enfouis dans les neiges québécoises.[4]

The new writers, soon to create a significant corpus of *nouvelle écriture*, had found their vital focus.

La Barre du Jour has provided a necessary meeting place for Nicole Brossard, a place where ideas circulate and where she can carry out her reflection in solidarity with others who share her radical approach to writing and to feminism. It was with this group of writers, primarily, that she found the necessary understanding to go ever further in her exploration.

Brossard published her first explicitly feminist text, ''Vaseline,'' in 1973 in a special issue of *La Barre du Jour* on the theme of ''Transgression.''[5] Her identification of herself as a feminist, soon a radical feminist and lesbian, led her to modify, but not to depart drastically from, the approach she and other writers had developed in *La Barre du Jour*. New exciting feminist texts were produced as she followed lucidly and without any reservation the uncharted path of her woman's awareness. Of particular significance is "Le Cortex exubérant," which appeared in *La Barre du Jour* in 1974. The text is simultaneously an intellectual and poetic examination of the ramifications of lucidly inhabiting her body, heeding its desires, and writing out of its inhabited space. This is a difficult process of reintegration, one which causes the woman considerable anger, as she realizes all that is missing, how she has been fragmented by cultural practices, all that a patriarchal society has put in her way to suppress the expression of her experience. Brossard gives herself exuberantly to the task, despite the difficulty. Her body opens itself to the avalanche of the flow of its liquid pleasures and identifies itself with the text in the process of forming: "Une logique fabuleuse de lèvres errantes s'en suit."[6] The text is the symbolic reflection of full self-knowledge. Body and text become an animate and integral whole, as the play on words suggested in the title underlines (*corps + texte = cortex*). The text is the place where feminist subjectivity can establish itself at the structural center and write itself: "La cellule dispose d'un environnement. L'écrire à la lettre se fiant au mouvement de la langue."[7] Brossard is determined to take possession of that environment, to rid it of patriarchal discourse, to enlarge it, and to ensure that its energy circulates, without waiting for those who exercise ideological dominance to say that her goal is reasonable. The evidence of reason and what is received as reasonable has served to dominate women for too long: "CETTE ECRITURE ... ELARGIT LE CENTRE OUVRE LE CERCLE EXPULSE AU LARGE LE DISCOURS DECOUPE LES ENTENTES TACITES LES EVIDENCES ... DE LA RAISON (toute *raison* ayant en conseil exécutif, une *compagnie* précieuse à défendre, une *réserve* à protéger, un ongle blanc à nettoyer, nous trompons la raison *qu'on nous donne*)."[8] Brossard's text announces with irony and repeated violence that it will not pardon those who have dispossessed woman so completely that she does not even have the words to speak the evidence of her senses: "[T]out logos ne ferait qu'envenimer la chose du discours / le verbe du père finira bien un jour par s'épanouir ailleurs qu'en mon trou de cul."[9]

Brossard was aware that other women were exploring their woman's experience, facing problems similar to hers, knowing the same frustration and anger. In order that words might circulate and solidarity become a fact, she organized in 1975 the first special issue of *La Barre du Jour* centered uniquely on a feminist theme and to which only women were invited to contribute. The theme was "Femme et langage," the same theme as that of the "Rencontre québécoise internationale des écrivains," organized that year by the other important organ for writers in Quebec during the sixties, the literary journal, *Liberté*.[10] The question asked by Nicole Brossard for this first special feminist issue of *La Barre du Jour* on "Femme et langage" was: "Comment la femme qui utilise quotidiennement les mots (comédienne, journaliste, écrivain, professeur) peut-elle utiliser un langage qui, phallocratique, joue au départ contre elle?"[11] The texts produced in response to this question show that several women had already given serious thought to this question which is fundamental to all feminist reflection.

In her own text in this issue, *"E* muet mutant," Nicole Brossard assumes aggressively the mute "e" of her condition, the symbol in the linquistic code of her powerlessness and marginal position. She declares the silent, humble letter to be in mutation. According to Brossard, women must take possession of language and turn it to their own ends. The accepted representation systems of our socio-cultural reality have excluded women, except as objects of male desire, while at the same time they have satisfied even further that desire and have reinforced the sense of identity shared among the dominant male group. The words of men make up the code of power on the public forum, while the words of women are considered unimportant, ineffective, inconsequential—the babble accompanying the daily routine of the domestic sphere, to which no one need listen, since it is established in advance that such words convey no significant information. The dominant culture has decreed that when women give voice to their own passions and experience, they are seen to be speaking in madness, delusion, delirium, or evil, all of which must be suppressed and denied. Brossard affirms that women must speak out of the silence, absence, and void of their condition. Women must explore the fissures and cracks of the structures of dominant culture, enlarge the holes, cause short-circuits, and make the structures crack open. Women must establish contact with their own white radiant center and use the energy released to invent freely and boldly in their private and public activities. This process involves an affirmation of sexuality, with no taboos respected, for taboos restrict movement: "Sexe son sexe son écrit, elle n'écrit pas les jambes croisées. Elle prend son désir et ne s'écarte point de son sujet qui la ramasse."[12] Brossard sees radical feminist writing as similar to a woman's orgasm when the *haut-lieu* of the clitoris is caressed with love: the body and the text explode with radiant energy in all directions out of their ardent center. Such writing has sufficient energy to illumine itself and to destroy the will to power which has effectively suppressed and decentered it for so long: "L'écriture. . . . Lieu à redéfinir, à épuiser dans une pratique—ainsi que l'orgasme qui disperse toute cohérence linguistique. Qui rayonne par en-dedans le centre du pouvoir sur soi."[13]

The words women have spoken in private must be written and must circulate so that they enter the operative symbolic order of society. They must be taken out on the public forum where they will receive collective recognition. Women can affirm themselves as subject, and they can also choose the subjects to be discussed in discourse. They can thereby use discourse to structure reality in harmony with their perception. It is a matter of occupying space on women's own terms, taking control of language, and opening their eyes to see reality in a different light: "Peut-être s'agit-il surtout de prendre un espace et de l'occuper. D'avoir l'oeil ouvert sur ce qui se passe et qui souvent nous dépasse faute d'interrogations, faute d'informations. Intervenir dans les rouages phallocratiques, ceux du pouvoir à côté d'elles et qui les concerne."[14]

Brossard is fully cognizant of the fact that women have no recognized tradition of using language in written form to analyze their condition, to communicate their discoveries, to give form to their experience. The conceptual void out of which they speak of necessity makes it easy for those in the cultural mainstream, who have at their disposal the received discourse and the great codes of literature, art, philosophy, psychology, theology, sociology, and politics, simply to ridicule the expression of women's experience and to declare their aspirations not serious. For Brossard the situation is so urgent that women do not have the time to develop all the arguments necessary to convince the experts. Besides, to modify her practice in an attempt to develop such arguments would be to agree to play the game according to the rules already established by the dominant group in the patriarchal society. Brossard's writing is an immediate passage to action, structured according to the internal logic of her own perceptions. She will not wait to find all the convincing arguments nor will she wait for permission to act. Her political weapon of choice will be the active, aggressive, subversive writing practice she developed with the *Barre du Jour* group, but which she has had to modify to suit her own research.

There have been six special feminist issues of *La Barre du Jour*—or of *La Nouvelle Barre du Jour*, as it has been called since 1977—since the first issue on the theme of language in 1975. Each has been a further collective exploration, serving to reinforce dynamic solidarity and yielding exciting discoveries through texts which give form to yet another aspect of the untold facets of women's dreams, images, and experience. An interpretive community of women sharing a new world view has emerged. Nicole Brossard prepared three of these special issues: "Le Corps, les mots, l'imaginaire"; "Célébrations"; "La Femme et la ville." Other special issues of *La Nouvelle Barre du Jour*, prepared by other radical feminist writers, Jovette Marchessault and Germaine Beaulieu, were "La Mermour" and "La Femme et l'humour." The first text in the 1982 feminist issue of *La Nouvelle Barre du Jour*, "La Complicité," prepared by Louise Cotnoir, is by Nicole Brossard and is entitled "A la lumière des sens." In this text she affirms her ongoing solidarity with women. At the same time she sees complicity as possibly an even deeper bond, an ardent, dynamic bond, which can form between women who have had enough time to begin the exploration together, who have had the courage to take an open radical stand, and who can see that they have accomplished change. Together, in their complicity, such women have been able to "se radicaliser comme un imaginaire."[15] Women who share this magnificent, burning, luminous complicity, having known the ecstasy of being integral and whole, occupy space in their own way. They have found the source of wisdom and vision: "la magnificence la SENSATIONNELLE complice, ma continent de joie, ma science, ma *sapience*."[16] Brossard knows it is vital to celebrate and nurture both solidarity and the very precious instants of vital complicity, for, despite all that feminists have accomplished, every day brings its evidence that patriarchy is not undone:

Il est sans doute utile ici de rappeler que les notions d'obligation morale et de respon-sabilités que les femmes ont intériorisées sont, pour le moment (un bien long moment) mises au service des solidarités masculines libérales, traditionnelles, révolutionnaires (nationalisme, socialisme) ou encore évolutionnistes (écologies).[17]

It has been with the *Barre du Jour* group, as it evolved and unfolded over the past seventeen years, that Nicole Brossard has affirmed her solidarities and developed the weapons necessary to her praxis: *la nouvelle écriture* and *l'écriture au féminin*, both aggressively subversive of received ideology and affirmative of dynamic personal freedom. She moved with the original group beyond the political and social nationalism of the sixties and then moved still further beyond its analysis to a new solidarity and complicity as a radical feminist, exploring around the radiant center and on the surfaces of her lesbian sensitivity and awareness—on the spires of a still unknown trajectory.

FEMINISM: "LA VIE PRIVEE EST POLITIQUE": *LES TETES DE PIOCHE* AND *LA NEF DES SORCIERES*

After World War II the union movement began what was to become a rev-olutionary change in the status of working people of Quebec. There was con-siderable cooperation among unionists, socialists, and nationalists, particularly after the death of Quebec's premier, Maurice Duplessis, in 1959. These groups formed a militant left, which was numerous and well organized through the sixties and into the seventies. As the new wave of feminism made its first tentative beginnings among rural and urban middle-class women in the mid-sixties, younger women who were active in the militant left were becoming aware of the need to go beyond simple social reform and to bring about sweeping social change, both in their own movements and in society at large. By 1969 women were playing such a significant role among the militants that it was they who organized the first significant demonstration against the government's newly adopted anti-assembly law. Two hundred women were thrown into jail on that occasion. This dramatic demonstration marked the beginning of a new phase in the militant left and also inaugurated a revolutionary feminist movement in Quebec with the creation of the Front de Libération des Femmes du Québec, the FLF(Q), a name chosen because of its close resemblance to the most active militant movement of the sixties, the FLQ, the Front de Libération du Québec.[18]

As women reflected on their condition and organized to demand their rights, the conflict between feminist priorities on the one hand, socialist, nationalist priorities on the other grew increasingly bitter, often violent. The conflict has been particularly serious when it has served to divide the community of women working actively to bring about social change.

Nicole Brossard was well aware of these various political movements and the debates among them. Although sympathetic, however, she was not active in any of them. When she became a social activist and worked with groups of women in a variety of contexts, it was as a radical feminist, that is, in groups of women where the only goals were feminist. She agreed with the goals of both those involved in the class struggle and those working for an independent Quebec; nevertheless, she believed that the fundamental struggle for women must be against a patriarchal society. For this purpose, women must organize on their own, do their own analysis, adopt their own strategy, and establish their own goals. She believed that the very violent opposition of the militant left to the women's movement in Quebec, particularly against women forming their own organizations and developing their own theory, was a clear enough indication of the pervasive and fundamental sexism in groups of both the right and the left.

In 1975 Nicole Brossard and a group of five friends, a mixed group of lesbians and heterosexuals who shared common feminist views, began to meet weekly to exchange ideas and to establish the basis for the production of a radical feminist monthly newspaper. The first issue of the paper, *Les Têtes de Pioche*, appeared in March 1976. It was the first radical feminist publication in Quebec, and as such it introduced a new phase in the evolution of the movement. The collective explained the meaning of the title the group had chosen for the paper and so summarized its political/feminist position: in addition to assuming proudly and wearing as a badge of honor the denigrating insult that social discourse throws at strong women by calling them *têtes de pioche*, the title meant, in its various parts, *Les* for solidarity, *Têtes* because in this matter the heart alone is not enough, and *de Pioche* for determination. The paper was to be a place for meeting and exchange, an information tool, and was to provide concrete and useful information about what women were saying and doing. There was the hope that *Les Têtes de Pioche* would play the same vital role in the feminist movement that *Parti Pris* had played in the nationalist movement of the sixties.

As a radical feminist group, the collective sought to redefine the political and foster effective action among women. They knew without any doubt that in order to do this they had to begin from the position that for women the personal is political: "Langage politique, réalité politique du féminisme ayant comme point de départ: la vie. Nous disons que c'est politique de penser, de tenir compte de la vie.... C'est politique d'exiger le droit de n'être pas harcelées, battues, violées par l'homme maître."[19] In its editorial policy, the primary objective of the *Têtes de Pioche* collective was to create:

[U]n journal pour les femmes, ne traitant que des problèmes nous concernant. Un journal servant à découvrir, conscientiser, partager tout ce qui nous touche dans notre vie de tous les jours.... Nous croyons qu'il est grand temps pour toutes les femmes de parler, de dire et dénoncer les conditions de vie qui leur sont faites.[20]

Like radical feminist groups elsewhere, their goal was not to take power from the "masters" in order to exercise it themselves. In this, they are unlike every other kind of revolutionary group which has ever existed. They wished, instead, to destroy all social structures which allow power to be concentrated in one dominant group, with one ideological perspective, whatever the ideology might be. Nicole Brossard, along with the others of *Les Têtes de Pioche*, was fighting for, and has always fought for, multiplicity, diversity, freedom for each individual to develop and act according to her desire and her impulses. Because of her distrust of all claims to have found final answers, it is inconceivable to her that any single ideology could hold the promise of a just society, where all are free and autonomous. The exercise of power and authority, therefore, particularly when it seeks to draw its legitimacy from monolithic traditions or from one abstractly developed ideological position, is illegitimate:

Nous en tant que féministes, nous ne voulons pas "le pouvoir." Nous voulons en démasquer toutes les formes. Le traquer sans répit, l'acculer "au pied du mur" pour qu'enfin "il tombe, meure, se désintègre dans toutes ses contradictions!" Ce que nous voulons c'est le droit d'existence. Nous voulons de l'espace, de la place pour vivre, pour rire, et aimer. De l'espace pour bouger, danser, découvrir, créer, inventer un nouveau mode de vie qui ne soit plus, qui ne se conjugue plus seulement au masculin![21]

Les Têtes de Pioche appeared regularly for over three years until June 1979. It must be seen as a very positive initiative, both for those who were involved in its production and for Quebec feminists generally. It reported on events, raised and discussed effectively matters of common interest, opened its columns fully to wide participation, and served to give woman's perspective on social reality. It made a major contribution to feminist analysis and reflection at a time when the feminist movement was strongly aware of the need to articulate its reality.

At the same time, participation in *Les Têtes de Pioche* was difficult for all those involved. Disharmony emerged just a few months after the beginning and led thereafter to frequent changes in the constitution of the collective, although Nicole Brossard, Michèle Jean, and Eliette Roux remained throughout the life of the paper. Working in a collective, where one of the goals is to avoid the hierarchical structures of traditional organization, has been tried on several occasions by Quebec feminists. Such collective undertakings have frequently produced exciting and innovative results in many areas, but never without conflict and pain for those involved. As a possible source of conflict, the question of priorities regarding socio-political goals has already been discussed. At *Les Têtes de Pioche* the tension seems to have been heightened because of the non-resolution of internal contradictions and conflicts, a situation which underlines the difficulty of establishing and defining effective modes of political action which meet the needs of radical feminism in an adequate way. These unresolved contradictions and tensions arose out of each woman's experience in society and what, in her personal analysis, she perceived to be the origin of her oppression. The conflicts were of three kinds: sexual—can lesbian and heterosexual women work together as radical feminists?; socio-economic—can women of all classes agree on common problems and bring a common basis of analysis to their praxis?; and finally, political—how significant is the national question? While the third source of conflict was potentially explosive and gave rise to criticism from outside the paper, it was the socio-economic and sexual divergences which consistently disrupted the harmony of the group and finally brought about the end of the paper.

In 1975-1976 Nicole Brossard was also engaged in other creative projects arising out of her radical feminist activism. She made the film *Some American Feminists* with Luce Guilbeault, a film which took her beyond the borders of Quebec to the larger community of English-speaking radical feminists in the United States.[22] At that time American feminist analysis was ahead of that of both France and Quebec. Nicole Brossard has continued to seek bonds with women outside Quebec as she searches for a feminist cultural community and a basis for woman's common memory with: Ti-Grace Atkinson, Adrienne Rich, Mary Daly, Monique Wittig, Luce Irigaray, Michèle Causse. She has also affirmed her strong affinity with certain writers of earlier periods, such as Gertrude Stein, Djuna Barnes, and Virginia Woolf.

In the mid-seventies, Nicole Brossard was continuing her collaboration with women within the community of Quebec, as well, women who were in the process of effecting radical socio-cultural change. She and France Théoret, also an extremely exciting feminist writer and member of the original *Têtes de Pioche* group, organized the creation and production of a six-woman collective dramatic performance, *La Nef des sorcières*, which was presented in 1976 at Quebec's most established theatre, Le Théâtre du Nouveau Monde. In real as well as symbolic terms, this was a major occupation by women of one of patriarchy's central spaces.

In her own text for *La Nef des sorcières*, "L'Ecrivain," Nicole Brossard offers the monologue of a writer reflecting on the creative process, aiming to find the ardent center of her creative force. She sees the strength which comes from knowing that other women are exploring their inner space, and she expresses violent anger against all that continues to alienate, suppress, and divide women. She finds her energy and her strength in knowing that women are taking a clear and lucid look at their own private experience, and that they are touching themselves and each other in so doing. Such acts are radically political and promise to alter the course of the history of humanity drastically.[23]

"LA FICTION THEORIQUE"

Very little has been said in this essay about the major part of the Brossard corpus: the several books she has published. Of particular interest for the study of the political theme in her work are the five books of prose. They are exciting explorations of woman's space and the dynamic, explosive power of language. These books of prose successfully synthesize poetry, the genre in which she began her writing career, the novel, and theory in an active, imaginative process of creating the text, a process which remains open and unfinished. In them Brossard works out the various aspects of her writing which this essay has attempted to discuss. She has called the synthesis of poetry, novel, and theory "theoretical fiction" and has identified this approach as central to her work for the past several years. In these novel-length prose works, she refuses to use linear discourse to demonstrate theory directly or to represent reality; she refuses equally to fragment herself and her reader through an acceptance of the mind/body dichotomy. And so her books must be both understood and experienced; they must be read actively, imaginatively, and creatively. As an author she uses words for the purpose of creating her own autonomous universe, in whose organic, unfolding process she is lucidly and ardently involved. She makes a strong appeal to the freedom of the reader to join her in the creative process and so to share her revolutionary purpose. The space which takes form in her texts and in which she finds her being may be, singly or simultaneously, the streets of Montreal or another large city, the material realm of her woman's desire, the field of motherhood, the imaginary space of the writer/reader.[24]

Brossard believes that the structures of what our society takes to be reality, along with its interrelated representation systems, are nothing more than the projection of the fantasies and fictions of those who excercise power and enjoy the privilege of being in the dominant group: "Reality is constructed, reproduced, and transformed by a patriarchal mind, a one-track mind. Let's name some fictions: the military complex, the price of gold, the television news, pornography." The world as symbolized is, then, upside-down for women, with their realities considered to be but inconsequential fiction:

On the other hand, women's realities have been perceived as fictions. Let's name some realities: maternity, abortion, rape, prostitution, physical violence.... So if you are writing with a feminist consciousness you suddenly find yourself writing at the edge, at the very limits of fiction and reality. You can use delirium to travel from one to another, entering a spiral, spinning.[25]

Nicole Brossard's own works of fiction are lucidly produced and release the energy of woman's suppressed imagination in order to cause her awareness of reality to explode in dynamic form as an aggressive denunciation of the destructive fictions which control our world. Her writing shows how seriously she has taken her statement: "Ecrire: je suis une femme est plein de conséquences."[26] Her works are a strong affirmation of her own and every woman's rights as a citizen and as a woman, women who have explored and laid claim to their own space, both private and public. In her works and in her activities with other women, Brossard has made an extraordinary contribution to the emergence of a cultural community of women in touch with their woman's bodies, lucidly aware of and affirming their rights as whole, integral human beings: "Je veux mes rigoureuses que nous entreprenions la démarche, la coïncidence de nous voir politiquement propices à l'affirmation. Sentir que l'oeil entreprend de nourrir par le dedans de ce qu'il fixe, la forme vitale du féminin. A prolonger la fiction, *en réalité*, je regarde les choses en face."[27]

Each of Brossard's works is a further step in her strategy to give form to women's reality and to achieve political goals through her writing. Such a view of writing as the major weapon in her strategy is apparent in the title and contents of an anthology she recently edited of some works by many of the writers with whom she had shared the journey of the past decade: *Les Stratégies du réel/The Story So Far*.[28] She has already accomplished major change in the Quebec political and socio-cultural scene. With undiminished energy she continues to look into the future by exploring all dimensions and possibilities of the present. The aim of her activities as a writer and political activist is to establish her place, as a woman, at the center of society's cultural and political space, not on the fringes where she can be exploited and dominated as an object of male manipulation. Brossard's work is a radical break with tradition and with political militantism, with all forms of ideological orthodoxy. Her writing is a conscious transgression of the norms imposed on women, whatever the code might be to legitimate them.

NOTES

1. Nicole Brossard, "Notes et fragments d'urgence," in *Femmes et politique*, ed. Yolande Cohen, Collection Idéelles (Montréal: Le Jour, 1981), p. 19.

From the poetic to the political, one and the same commitment: to cultivate life. To self-identify. To look in the mirror until it sends back an *integral* image, until it becomes a window, an opening on the space of the real and the imaginary. As much time as reality.

From the poetic to the political, a single motive: to enlarge the space of pleasure until a hologram is made from it, a history, a project that depends on the collective I, on women together, on her, in the place where enjoyment is called and calls upon intelligence.

This text was first published as "Fragments d'urgence" in a special section, "L'Ecrivain et la politique," in *Le Devoir*, 19 avril 1980, p. 21.

2. Claude Beausoleil, "Le Centre blanc," *Le Devoir*, 16 décembre 1978, p. 26.

3. "De notre écriture en sa résistance," in "Document Miron," *La Barre du Jour*, No. 26 (octobre 1970), p. 3.

In 1963 we read *Parti pris* and we understood. There was no room for discussion: the critical positions of that journal, added to our daily experience of Quebec, completed the transformation of our impatience into a natural militantism.

4. Nicole Brossard et Roger Soublière, "Document Miron," *La Barre du Jour*, No. 26 (octobre 1970), p. 5.

While in the poetico-political field it seemed that everything had been said—and we had no wish to become powerless repeaters—we who shared the anguish and the rebellion of the people of Quebec chose to bring our work to bear on language. While others placed even greater emphasis upon our alarming situation, we sought to combat from within its confines a semantic field which, in the cultural game, served the interests of those against whom the "political" writers were fighting. Through these experiments we spoke about ourselves, about our sexual reality which had so long been concealed beneath the snows of Quebec.

5. Nicole Brossard, "Vaseline," in "Transgression," *La Barre du Jour*, Nos. 41-42 (automne 1973), pp. 11-17.

6. Nicole Brossard, "Le Cortex exubérant," *La Barre du Jour*, No. 44 (printemps 1974), p. 16.

A fabulous logic of wandering lips follows.

7. Brossard, "Le Cortex exubérant," p. 21.

The cell has an environment at its disposal. To write it letter for letter trusting in the movement of the tongue.

8. Brossard, "Le Cortex exubérant," p. 4. Capitalization and italics in original text.

THIS WRITING ENLARGES THE CENTER OPENS THE CIRCLE EXPELS OUT INTO OPEN SPACE THE DISCOURSE CUTS APART THE TACIT AGREEMENTS THE PIECES OF EVIDENCE OF REASON (all *reason* having in executive council, a precious *company* to defend, a *reserve* to protect, a white nail to clean, we deny the reason *that is given to us*).

9. Brossard, "Le Cortex exubérant," p. 17.

Any logos could do nothing but poison the thing of discourse itself/some day the Word of the father will finally broadcast itself in some place other than in my ass-hole.

10. *Liberté*, 18, Nos. 4-5, année 1976, Nos. 106-07 (juillet-octobre 1976).

11. Nicole Brossard, "Préliminaires," in "Femme et langage," *La Barre du Jour*, No. 50 (hiver 1975), pp. 8-9.

How can the woman who uses words daily (actress, journalist, writer, teacher, professor) use a language which, phallocratic, plays against her from the beginning?

12. Nicole Brossard, "*E* muet mutant," in "Femme et langage," *La Barre du Jour*, No. 50 (hiver 1975), p. 16.

Sex, her sex, her writing, she does not write with her legs crossed. She takes her desire and does not move away from the subject of it, from herself as subject. It brings it together for her.

13. Nicole Brossard, "*E* muet mutant," p. 22.

The act of writing. Place to redefine, to exhaust in a practice—just like the orgasm that disperses all linguistic coherence. That radiates from within the center of power over oneself.

14. Brossard, "*E* muet mutant," p. 23.

Perhaps it is above all a matter of taking a space and occupying it. Of having our eyes open on what is happening and which often escapes us for lack of interrogation, for lack of information. To intervene in the phallocratic wheels, those of the power structure which concern women.

15. Nicole Brossard, "A la lumière des sens," in "La Complicité," *La Nouvelle Barre du Jour*, No. 112 (mars 1982), p. 9.

To radicalize themselves as in the imaginary.

16. Nicole Brossard, "A la lumière des sens," p. 14.

Magnificence accomplice SENSATIONAL, my joyous woman's continent, my knowledge, my science, my *sapience*.

17. Nicole Brossard, "A la lumière des sens," p. 13.

No doubt it is useful here to recall that the notions of moral obligation and of responsibilities which women have interiorized are for the moment (a very long moment) placed in the service of masculine solidarities: liberal, traditional, revolutionary (nationalism, socialism) or then again evolutionist (ecology).

See also "Le Corps, les mots, l'imaginaire," *La Barre du Jour*, Nos. 56-57 (mai-août 1977); "Célébrations," *La Nouvelle Barre du Jour*, No. 75 (février 1979); "La Mermour," *La Nouvelle Barre du Jour*, No. 87 (février 1980); "La Femme et la ville," *La Nouvelle Barre du Jour*, No. 102 (avril 1981); "La Femme et l'humour," *La Nouvelle Barre du Jour*, No. 106 (octobre 1981).

18. See Marie Lavigne and Yolande Pinard, *Les Femmes dans la société québécoise* (Montréal: Boréal Express, 1977); Michèle Jean, *Québécoises du 20ᵉ siècle* (Montréal: Le Jour, 1974); Violette Brodeur, Suzanne Chartrand, Louise Corriveau et Béatrice Valay, *Le Mouvement des femmes au Québec: Etude des groupes montréalais et nationaux* (Montréal: Centre de la formation populaire, 1982); Le Collectif Clio, *L'Histoire des femmes au Québec depuis quatre siècles* (Montréal: Les Quinze, Editeur, 1982); *Québécoises deboutte!*. eds. Véronique O'Leary et Louise Toupin, I (Montréal: Editions du Remue-Ménage, 1982); *Québécoises deboutte!*, II (Montréal: Editions du Remue-Ménage, 1983).

19. "Editorial," *Les Têtes de Pioche*, 2, No. 1 (mars 1977), 1.

Political language, political reality of feminism having as its point of departure: life. We say that it is political to think, to take account of life. It is political to demand the right not to be harassed, battered, raped by man the master.

20. *Les Têtes de Pioche*, 1, No. 9 (février 1977), 2.

A magazine for women, dealing only with problems concerning us. A magazine serving to uncover, raise consciousness, share everything which touches us every day in our lives. We believe that it is high time for all women to talk, to speak of and denounce the conditions of life which are created for them.

21. "Editorial," *Les Têtes de Pioche*, p. 1.

We, as feminists, do not want "power." We want to unmask it in all its forms. To hunt it down tirelessly, to drive it back "to the foot of the wall" so that finally "it might fall, die, disintegrate in all its contradictions!" What we want is the right of existence. We want space, room to live, to laugh, to love. Space to move, to dance, to discover, to create, to invent a new way of life which is no longer, which is no longer conjugated solely in the masculine.

22. Luce Guilbeault, dir., and Nicole Brossard, prod., *Some American Feminists*, National Film Board of Canada, 1976.

23. Nicole Brossard, "L'Ecrivain," *La Nef des sorcières* (Montréal: Quinze, 1976), pp. 74-75. The other contributors to this play are France Théoret, Marthe Blackburn, Odette Gagnon, Marie-Claire Blais, and Pol Pelletier.

24. See the bibliography for a complete listing of Brossard's works of fiction. *Un Livre* has been translated as *A Book*, trans. Larry Shouldice (Toronto: Coach House, 1976); *Sold-out* has been translated as *Turn of a Pang*, trans. Patricia Claxton (Toronto: Coach House, 1976); *L'Amèr* has been translated as *These Our Mothers, or The Desintegrating Chapter*, trans. Barbara Godard (Toronto: Coach House Press, 1983).

25. Nicole Brossard, *Broadside*, 2, No. 8 (June 1981), 11.

26. Nicole Brossard, *L'Amèr, ou le chapitre effrité* (Montréal: Quinze, 1977), p. 43.

To write: I am a woman is full of consequences.

27. Nicole Brossard, "La Tête qu'elle fait," in "Les Corps, les mots, l'imaginaire," *La Barre du Jour*, p. 89.

My rigorous women, I want us to undertake the necessary steps, to coincide in seeing ourselves politically propitious for affirmation. To feel that the eye is undertaking to nourish from the inside of what it fixes upon, the vital form of the feminine. By extending fiction, *in reality*, I am looking things in the face.

28. *Les Stratégies du réel/The Story So Far* (Montréal: La Nouvelle Barre du Jour, 1979; Toronto: Coach House Press, 1979).

13

A Québécois and an Acadian Novel Compared: The Use of Myth in Jovette Marchessault's *Comme une enfant de la terre* and Antonine Maillet's *Pélagie-la-Charrette*

Micheline Herz

Myth has played a highly significant role in the novels of the *Québécoise* Jovette Marchessault and the Acadian Antonine Maillet. A striking example of this is the subversive genealogy that one finds in Jovette Marchessault's *La Mère des herbes*, or one might cite the example of Antonine Maillet's *Mariaagélas* where the chief protagonist makes herself a legendary figure as smuggler extraordinaire battling against customs officials, priests, rumormongers, and the like. Indeed, this sort of discourse crops up so frequently in the two authors' work that one might easily argue that it is the essential unifying aspect of their work. But this is making too general a concept out of myth. We have to recognize distinctive categories of myth and mythology.

In the novel there are three categories of myth and mythology. First there is the myth that plays the part of an ornament: it can be easily delineated, and its function is often that of the descriptive per se. Second is the myth that is not obvious to the reader; its hidden existence has to be construed through critical effort. Third, one can distinguish those myths and mythologies that are the very stuff of the novel and constitute a permanent structure which articulates the temporal dimensions of the narrative. I will concentrate here on Jovette Marchessault's *Comme une enfant de la terre* and Antonine Maillet's *Pélagie-la-Charrette*, two novels which handle mythology as if it were indigenous to the venture of fiction.[1]

In both cases, the mythologies are etiological. Both recount stories of mitigated triumph over historical fortune involving epic and sometimes heroic elements. Both succeed in linking past to present, thus opening up the future; the cycle, however, is never totally completed so that the tale can always, or could always, be picked up where it left off. The realist illusion is skillfully weighted and woven into the whole by combining the possible and the imaginary in micro—

or macro—sequences or, to the contrary, by subduing them in a hidden transition. Leitmotifs are sometimes employed to the same end. Reliance upon the mythological generates if not a cosmic at least an extended exploitation of space. We might also note that in this sort of mythology the code becomes clearly more important than the message, or, more succinctly, the signifiers exceed the signified.

Let us first consider the reader of the two books. We can envision a common aficionado. One major requirement: the reader, he or she, reads and probably speaks French, although the works of Jovette Marchessault are in the process of being translated (with one play already published in English), and *Pélagie-la-Charrette* has recently (1982) appeared in an English translation. Both in Quebec and in Acadia, as Michel Roy writes in *L'Acadie perdue*, "[a]re we not all reunited through the same yet infinite French idiom?"[2] This is not to deny the existence of important idiolectical differences, but the language of these two texts does not present insuperable difficulty. Under the circumstances in which these novels were written, French is more than a native tongue. It connotes a long struggle with the dominant English elite: survival is at stake, the survival of two people, the survival of their personae. The cultural referents are almost identical in the two books: a long history of more or less accepted frustration which, only lately, is being pushed aside; a change from the Apollonian to the Dionysiac vision of self and of the surrounding world! The *Québécois* and the Acadians have been suffering in common, and their past bears the marks of three imperialisms: French, English, and American. The needed identity of development is similar even though the fate of the *Québécois* and the Acadians was not exactly the same: "The first generation of French Canadians from lower Canada seemed to have had a different impression concerning the ups and downs resulting from British rule."[3] The point being made here is that the *Québécois* did not suffer from the same degree of uprooting as the Acadians. There is no *québécois* parallel to the *Grand Dérangement*. Two different orientations, different in their psychology, different in their eschatalogy of the conquest in question, can thus be ascribed to *Québécois* and Acadians. But there is a common brutality, although it was crueler for the Acadians, who were obliged to find the qualities that would help them survive their own alienation. The *québécois* reader and the Acadian reader alike will not, therefore, encounter problems of "decoding." Both, too, have lived with the Indians, be they Algonquins, Micmacs, or Abenaquis. But the French reader might experience difficulties with the components of the myths. This is, of course, not to say that he or she would be deprived of the sheer literary enjoyment of these texts. In fact, an empathy, coupled with a poetic distance, will be experienced. As for the American-born Francophone, he or she will derive pleasure from a familiarity with the myth.

One must next discuss the subject. Jovette Marchessault and Antonine Maillet are involved in the mythology they create. Jovette Marchessault speaks in the first person when she keeps company with Indian spirits or sucks at the breast of the primeval mother: "Quand j'ai soif, je peux en sortant ma langue, en prenant mille précautions, mille reptations, en faisant mes battements d'ailes,

téter les mamelles de la Grande-Oursonne, celle qui habite le pays blanc du
mangeur d'arbres.''[4] Antonine Maillet, in the prologue and in various chapters,
will also speak indirectly in the first person, since it appears that the tale told
was related to her by a storyteller of her kin. In Jovette Marchessault's novel
the narrator is most of the time in the story, while in Antonine Maillet's work
the narrator is near the story: "L'hiver a des griffes et des dents comme les bêtes
des forêts, que dit mon cousin Louis. . . . C'est ainsi que ni moi, ni Pélagie-la-
Gribouille, ni même Pélagie-la-Charrette, première du nom, n'aurons jamais
connu le nombre des victimes de l'ours ou du loup-cervier en forêt.''[5] Both
subjects and narrators have cosmic dimensions; both are women: "Je dis que
toute sorte de motivation est métaphysique, qu'elle tombe en ligne directe du
Grand-Esprit, de la mamelle de la Grande-Oursonne avec toutes sortes de signes
admirables, de miracles de mutation et cette source unique nous féconde.''[6] For
Maillet, the genealogical and the "national" are stressed as well:

> Elle continue encore dans la bouche de mon cousin Louis à Bélonie, qui la tient de
> son père Bélonie à Louis qui la tenait de son grand-père Bélonie—contemporain et
> adversaire de la Gribouille—qui l'avait reçue de père en fils de ce propre Bélonie, fils
> de Thaddée, fils de Bélonie premier qui, en 1770, fêtait ses nonante ans assis au fond
> de la charrette même de Pélagie, première du nom.
> Après ça, venez me dire à moi, qui fourbis chaque matin mes seize quartiers de charrette,
> qu'un peuple qui ne sait pas lire ne saurait avoir d'Histoire.[7]

One of the most interesting features of these mythologies is their female
characteristic. Both titles make this clear: *Comme une enfant de la terre*, with
Le Crachet solaire as a subtitle, and *Pélagie-la-Charrette:*

> Sa fille Madeleine n'avait point connu les moeurs anciennes d'avant le Dérangement. La
> plupart des chefs de famille avaient péri dans la tourmente, emportant au fond des bois
> ou des mers leur bâton d'autorité reçu au paradis terrestre. Les femmes avaient dû par
> la suite se dresser seules face à l'ennemi et à l'adversité, et ramasser elles-mêmes le
> sceptre de chef de famille. Madeleine en avait été témoin, enfant posthume de son père
> et de ses aïeux. Pélagie pouvait compter sur sa fille pour continuer sa lignée.[8]

One could venture that both books recount the saga of a woman—Maillet's as
that of a mother figure and Marchessault's as the aspiration to the aggrandizement
of one. Thus Jovette Marchessault indicates the female nature of the earth, the
yang, but she does not want to deprive woman of her part of sun, of her *yin*,
where woman shares in solar glory: "Et si je veux prendre la parole, il ne me
reste qu'une chose à faire: me mettre en route et m'expliquer avec l'univers.''[9]
La charrette, or its more reputable cognate, the chariot, also points to the sun.
It is the symbol of a dynamic, resourceful, and overriding mind. It is also
associated with self-control, courage, progress, and victory. Pélagie, she who
came from the sea or near the sea, will go back to what was her home, in her
wagon drawn by oxen. Both titles imply a victory of life over death. In both

novels, an ardent desire is invested in the work (''Rappelez-vous! Souvenez-vous du roucoulement du grand désir! Souvenez-vous du poids de la grande colère!''),[10] a desire comprehended and assimilated by the reader who answers with her or his own phantasm: ontologic freedom in the case of Jovette Marchessault; national pride and belief in a collective realization in Antonine Maillet. Each novel suggests its own form of ''consciousness raising.''

Think mythology, think ordeal! Mythological narration supposes a hero or heroine who conquers obstacles. Jovette Marchessault fights with a host of obstacles: from the thoughts of her traveling companion, Francine, to the technocratic excess of the State; from her own anguished moods to the story of Quebec; from the joys of her childhood, and particularly the difficulty of heydays, to her encounter with a self-taught culture; from the oppression inflicted by the other to the small joys that she learned to nurture and cherish; from the love and sense of humor of her grandmother, who would sketch hens, to the tavern of Joe Beef, who reveled in senselessly killing animals numbed with fear. The struggle or the fight is universal, or cosmic, in nature: Catholicism is defeated by the old Amerindian gods, and a female principle of peace ultimately emerges triumphant.

For Antonine Maillet, the obstacles and the ordeals are several. From an objective point of view we might note the hunger, the needs of all sorts, the hatred of and the contempt for an antagonistic people, the English. The road is long that follows the massive deportation from Georgia back to the homeland; it is a laborious and winding road and often lonesome, rich in fear and dread. In the course of the journey, wagons have been hitched to wagons, wagons of all sizes, small and large, which Pélagie has vowed to lead to safety, seawards to what is now the promised land, once the cradle of her people. At stake is a continuity of life, a permanence, a reaching beyond the limitations of woman as a fragment towards her integration into a whole.

Both works unfold as a journey. In mythologies, the hero is always a traveler. Ascendant or descendant schemes in space are typical in mythological tales. The traveler is restless. Here she aspires to discovery, to change, and also to a self-fulfillment, a new kind of knowledge or a new kind of happiness. Traveling is a rite of initiation, a flight from the mother or even a return to the mother. One might note a return to the mother in both works, an Ur-mother in the case of Jovette Marchessault and the motherland, the lost paradise of Acadia, in Antonine Maillet: ''Veuve d'un homme, d'une famille, d'un peuple. Veuve de toute l'Acadie qu'elle avait entrepris de ranimer et de rebâtir.''[11]

In *Comme une enfant de la terre*, Jovette Marchessault uses vertical and horizontal schemes. The horizontal schemes follow her trip across the Amerindian continent and back to her native Quebec. The vertical schemes are those of the fall, the descent into hell, the trauma of birth. They are also the schemes of an ascent towards celestial life: she who goes down knows that she can go up again. She will climb to the planets of sidereal creation and bathe in the solar energies that will allow her to decipher a system of correspondences many times renewed. As she writes, she assumes her planets and cells. She is a bird, she is a cloud, her very hand is the sun with which she writes:

Je suis comme l'oiseau kiwi: je palpe, je sonde avec mon bec. Je prends et j'entreprends. Je me déporte dans l'exil; je finirai par me conquérir sur l'angoisse.... J'écris avec cette main radieuse afin que la nuit où me seront comptées mes années, je sois en mesure de prononcer les paroles de la lumière. Avant que je commence ce récit, plusieurs soleils sont morts en moi. J'ai appris peu à peu à faire sauter les amarres du raisonnement, à faire table rase des théories.[12]

This cosmogony gone wild illustrates the transcendence of growth, the power of imagination contrasted with arid reason or theoretical logic. The motions in the work are sometimes so rapid that we might think of them in terms of a spiral progression where transition, transformation, and regeneration unite opposites. The solar eye acts as a center watching on those cosmic forms in motion that generate metamorphosis and continuity. The sun, star, and fire are symbols which accompany such patterns of motion. In the final analysis they are analogues of the female *écriture*, creating or transcribing its own genesis: "Il me semble important de créer de nouvelles constellations de mots qui seront comme des comètes: après métamorphose les mots mineurs deviendront des mots majeurs."[13] One should note here the importance of the female discursive, radical ferment in which there is an outcry against enforced silence and an eagerness to speak against all repressive powers. The very act of female speech is presented as a seminal transgression which opens onto uncharted lands to be spoken and written about: "Avec cette main glorieuse, j'écris avant que le cancer du doute et de la résignation ne dévore l'organe créateur, ne lui colle une étiquette de prix."[14] Jovette Marchessault proclaims the deployment of this new *parole* and of this new written word: "Qui d'autre qu'un être humain de sexe féminin ... qui d'autre qu'une femme pourrait apaiser ces flots, ce déluge en rupture de contenance et autres bonnes manières. Qui d'autre que la grande femelle de l'humanité pas encore parlée, pas encore racontée car elle est muette comme la vérité."[15]

For Jovette Marchessault, writing the female myth must create the form of the myth. This contributes to the differentiation of her text, at least in *Comme une enfant de la terre*, from a simple prophecy preaching a revolutionary creed with expected lyricism. Her *écriture* must be understood as an attempt to break down the old nuclei of constricted structures in order to attain a liberated structure of community. In other words, she is aiming at a coherence. In *écriture*, new origins lead to a new telos through a decentered meaning.

Travel in *Pélagie-la-Charrette* is a horizontal one. It leads Pélagie from South Carolina back home, but this return takes twenty years. The mythological element is underlined first by the death of the heroine, once her task of shepherdess of her people has been accomplished: "Son peuple. Pour la première fois, Pélagie s'aperçut que sa famille sortie de Géorgie dans une charrette, rendue en Acadie était devenue un peuple. En dix ans, elle avait raflé à la terre d'exil des tribus entières de ses pays et payses et les avait ramenées à leurs terres par la porte d'en arrière.''[16] Utilizing a typical characteristic of this sort of historical trajectory, Pélagie's journey borders on the fabulous, picaresque or baroque, tragic or pathetic. It is a tale of giants who put their strength at the service of Pélagie and her people, of miraculous and unexpected encounters, of colorful characters who steal now and then, even of a black man rescued from slavery, or of a spinster who is familiar with herbs, has a club foot, and falls in love at the age of fifty:

Elle avait trouvé la P'tite Goule, ce géant de la race des Gargan et Gargantua qui avaient parcouru les vieux pays sur l'entrepremier, abattant des montagnes sur leur passage, creusant des lacs de leurs sabots, et se balançant les pattes, à califourchon sur les églises, en pissant sur la foule en guise de bienvenue. La P'tite Goule sortait de ce genre de lignage, au dire de Pierre à Pitre dit le Fou, son compère depuis le sauvetage du cachalot.[17]

The journey is full of the most unusual events: bogged-down carts are saved with makeshift repairs, and the whole wagon train makes its way slowly through the Eastern states, more or less unseen and unheard of across a path of the back country. Bearers of all the old Acadian patronyms, by chance or by providence, find and join the march. Marriages occur, sometimes blessed by errant priests; children are born, and some die. Pélagie, a widow, falls in love with a legendary boat captain, Beausoleil Broussard: "Pélagie posa une main sur l'avant-bras de Beausoleil, et de l'autre caressa le bois rugueux de sa charrette. Huit ans déjà? C'était coûtume en Acadie d'apporter en dot une charrette à son homme, la charrette signe de pérennité.''[18] They have vague appointments, but neither Broussard nor Pélagie will be able to keep the last one. It is understood that he will take his boat and his Acadians to Louisiana, "entrant debout par la grande porte dans la légende de son pays.''[19]

The long march of *charrettes* seems to identify the essential mission of the Acadians: to fight, to acquire absolute reality and pride, to link the lost landscapes of Acadia with inner bonds to the spirits of the wanderers, to overcome abandonment and fear. Through a *surdétermination* of the symbol, the wagon also becomes a motherly image of intimacy; an earthly vehicle is transformed into a messianic device under a charismatic leader. We may contrast Beausoleil's ship and Pélagie's *charrette*. Both are linked to the Acadian wood, a mother symbol. The wagon and the ship are saviors like Noah's ark during a cataclysmic period. Both provide the means of a renaissance after they have been a temporary home: one connotes the earth and its toils, while the other, perhaps more poetically, connotes new discoveries and bountiful horizons.

We find in Antonine Maillet an inversion of *écriture*: her style is at once popular and very elaborate. Myth and history combined provide the dynamic of this novel. One can speak of a female *écriture* only in as much as Antonine Maillet puts mythology in a privileged position over history. Hence her novel illustrates a necessity to imagine and use that imagination to fuse history and myth. This results in an *écriture* which creates an Acadian communal sensibility rather than a strictly female one.

Both authors amplify the ordinary and the extraordinary, especially in the form of quantitative elaboration which dominates their literary composition. They are inclined to decorate the myth or the legend they are creating by adding elements, and they are openly expressionistic. All that is depicted is transfigured by the storyteller because of the urgency of a vision which has to strike the reader. The vitality of the scenes or of the events depicted is, by design, over-powering. Thus allegories multiply, and symbols are heaped over symbols. The logic here is not rational but almost biological: it allows for surpluses, reinforce-ments and reiterations; it practises juxtapositions and ellipses and cares little for the beauties of transitions. There is an aesthetic of excess often relieved, at least in the case of Antonine Maillet, by a healthy sense of humor. Cruelty rubs elbows with a feeling for joy, very often the joy of tricking one's persecutors.[20] In Jovette Marchessault's work, there is a global perception of the whole. Short sequences, often ironic in tone, provide respite for the reader:

Quel beau cadeau ils [the Indians] nous ont fait là! Sûr et certain qu'après la conquête, nos ennemis nous auraient donnés des noms d'allure plus britannique, victorienne. *"Mais sans doute ils pensèrent, eux aussi, que les mots Kébec, Kanada tenaient à la nature même des choses, des lieux puisque les Indiens les avaient eux-mêmes appliqués à ce pays."*[21]

When there is humor, it is more acid than that of Antonine Maillet. Analytical sequences contrast with the poetic explosion of a polyphonic nature.

The modern mythological hero or heroine belongs to the people. That is perhaps why the language of these works, while highly metaphorical, is not new. It does not create words but uses old ones, either as they were used in former times in Acadia and Quebec or in original combinations. The works are highly polysemic. Rich layers of images and lyrical motifs lend to the texts a savor of oral literature: "L'air se déchire de chaque côté; il neige du sel, du soufre, du phosphore, du mercure, des plumes, des cornes, des dents, des noeuds, des épines, des vieux cennes."[22] Antonine Maillet has the verbal powers of a Rabelais—whose works she happens to know well—and she obviously enjoys the Acadian language and the play element that they afford her: stories within stories, such as the evocation, made one evening by a storyteller near the earth, of a ship made of ice. Mythological and oral literature demand an authentic language, as in this beginning of an Acadian-Rabelaisian tale:

C'est l'histoire vraie d'un de ses aïeux, l'un des premiers de la race, qui vivait avant la tour de Babel, du temps que les hommes parlaient la même langue. Le héros, qui n'était point un méchant homme mais qui portait le nom de Tit-Jean Quatorze à cause des quatorze tours qu'il avait déjà joués à son père, décida un jour de prendre femme.[23]

The most important support of such literature is rhythm. We said earlier that in these books the signifiers exceeded the signified. A wealth of sound carries a wealth of rhythm which vary from the insidious to the throbbing:

Et les Landry, et les Cormier, et les LeBlanc se frottaient à leurs cousins Godin, Godin dit Beauséjour, Godin dit Bellefontaine, Godin dit Godin. Tous descendants d'une ancienne famille de France dont les prétentions remontaient à Godefroy de Bouillon. Des Godin qui auraient pu s'appeler Godfri, Godfrei, Godfrain, Godfrin, ou Godain avant de se fixer chez les Godin d'Acadie: ceux-là mêmes qui s'enfuirent dans les bois à l'heure du Grand Dérangement, qu'y s'y cachèrent durant la tourmente, et qui rescapèrent les charrettes prêtes à rendre le dernier soupir, englouties sous les neiges du terrible hiver 1780.[24]

The rhythm, in both books, blurs whatever might awaken the over-realist consciousness of the reader: "Et j'ai du grain de mil, et j'ai du grain de paille, et j'ai de l'oranger, et j'ai du tri, et j'ai du tricoli, et j'ai des allumettes, et j'ai des ananas, j'ai de beaux ... j'ai de beaux ... j'ai de beaux oiseaux."[25] Many narrative shortcuts are marvelously camouflaged under the music of the texts. This manner appears to us typical of mythological or legendary strategies in the modern French novel.

To conclude, we must point out that Jovette Marchessault's novel develops more in accordance with a paradigmatic axis, while Antonine Maillet follows a syntagmatic axis. Less ponderously, the *récit* gathers and departs from a nominal extension in one case and along the syntax of the story in the other. Both show the need to recreate roots for women in general and two people in particular. Jovette Marchessault and Antonine Maillet contribute to the return and the revival of their origins: the French word is probably more eloquent in this case when we speak of a *ressourcement*. Finally, beyond the two mythological treatments, we could sketch a simultaneously playful and political activity which would give them a baroque character, but we would have to define baroque as the opposite of an abstemious, deliberate style. It would be an appeal to the imaginary, an affair with the decorative, an embracing of the festival, and an inclination towards the individual. The particular way in which myth is used tips the balance of these texts into a revolutionary activity: a new reality is created; the liberation of woman is swept clean of bourgeois ideology and other established ideologies; and the cultural returning of a people is still under threat.

Recent Quebec literature represents, to paraphrase Philippe Sollers, the experience of bounds and the effort to break bounds. Does not Roland Barthes—so well known to the *Québécois*—say: "The text is (or should be) that unconstrained person who shows his backside to Father Politician"?[26]

NOTES

1. Antonine Maillet, *Pélagie-la-Charrette* (Montréal: Leméac; Paris: Grasset, 1979). All further references in these notes will be to the Grasset edition. Jovette Marchessault, *Comme une enfant de la terre: Le Crachat solaire* (Montréal: Leméac, 1975).

2. Michel Roy, *L'Acadie perdue* (Montréal: Editions Québec/Amérique, 1978), p. 168.

3. Roy, p. 80.

4. Marchessault, Premier Chant, p. 11.

Whenever I am thirsty, if I hang out my tongue and take endless precautions; if I crawl ever so carefully and flutter my wings, I can suck at the breast of the Great Mother Bear, she who dwells in the vast whiteness which devours the trees.

5. Maillet, ch. xiv, p. 287.

Like the beasts of the wild, winter has its claws and its teeth, as my cousin Louis says. . . . Thus not I, nor Pélagie-la-Gribouille, nor even Pélagie-la-Charrette, first of that name, will ever have known the number of victims claimed by the wolf or the lynx in the great forest.

6. Marchessault, Douzième Chant, p. 347.

Let me tell you that all motives are metaphysical, that they derive directly from the Great Spirit, from the breast of the Great Mother Bear, and are filled with marvelous signs, with miracles of mutation, and that this unparalleled well-spring makes us fruitful.

7. Maillet, Prologue, pp. 13-14.

The story goes on and on, repeated by my cousin Louis, son of Bélonie, who heard it from his father Bélonie, son of Louis, who got it from his grandfather Bélonie—contemporary and adversary of la Gribouille—to whom it was handed down, from father to son, from that very Bélonie, son of Thaddée, son of the first Bélonie who in 1770 celebrated his ninetieth birthday crouched in the cart of Pélagie, first of that name.

And now try to tell me, I who each morning dust off my coat of arms handed down through sixteen generations of cart drivers, that a people who cannot read have no history.

8. Maillet, ch. xii, p. 219.

Her daughter Madeleine had no knowledge whatsoever of the old customs before the Dispersion. Most of the heads of family had perished in the depths of the forests or seas during the upheaval, relinquishing there the reins of authority given them in the earthly paradise. Later on, women had to stand alone before the enemy and in the face of adversity; by themselves they had to take up the scepter of command. Being a posthumous child, Madeleine could bear witness to this. Pélagie could count on her daughter for the continuation of her lineage.

9. Marchessault, Cinquième Chant, p. 106.

And if I choose to speak, there is only one thing I would do: I would set forth and have it out with the universe.

10. Marchessault, Douzième Chant, p. 327.

Remember! Remember the cooing of the ardent desire! Remember the burden of the great wrath!

11. Maillet, ch. vii, p. 123.

She is left widowed by her man, by her family, by her people. All of Acadia has left her a widow—this Acadia which she had tried to bring back to life and to rebuild.

12. Marchessault, Sixième Chant, p. 137.

I am like the kiwi bird: I feel and probe with my beak. I take things and undertake others. I banish myself into exile: and I will end up by conquering anguish. . . . With this radiant hand I write so that when night comes and all my years are counted, I will be capable of emitting words of light. Several suns have died within me before I begin this narrative. Little by little I have learned to cast off the moorings of reasoning, to wipe the slate clean of all theory.

13. Marchessault, Sixième Chant, p. 136.

I think new constellations of words have to be created, which will then be like comets; and in the metamorphosis lesser words will become greater words.

14. Marchessault, Sixième Chant, p. 137.

I write before the cancer of doubt and resignation can consume the creative organ, before it can attach a price tag.

15. Marchessault, Douzième Chant, p. 335.

What human other than one of the female sex . . . who else but a woman could calm these raging waters, this flood threatening our demeanor and our social behavior? Who else but humanity's great female, she who has not yet spoken, has not told her tale, because like truth she is mute?

16. Maillet, ch. xvii, p. 304.

And her people. For the first time Pélagie realized that her family, come from Georgia into Acadia by cart, had become a people. Over a period of ten years she had gathered up in this land of exile whole tribes of her compatriots and had brought them home through the back door.

17. Maillet, ch. v, p. 93.

She had found la P'tite Goule, this giant of the race of Gargan and Gargantua who had roamed the countryside, knocking down mountains as they passed, forming lakes with the imprint of their wooden shoes, dangling their feet astride churches as they pissed on the crowds below as a welcoming gesture. According to Pierre à Pitre, alias the fool, her crony since the rescuing of the sperm-whale, la P'tite Goule was a descendant of this lineage.

18. Maillet, ch. xiv, p. 269.

Pélagie placed one hand on Beausoleil's forearm, and with the other stroked the rough hewn wood of her cart. Eight years already gone by? It was an Acadian custom for women to bring their men a cart in dowry, a sign of the everlasting.

19. Maillet, ch. xvii, p. 308.

Standing erect at the greatdoor he will pass into the legend of his country.

20. See Maillet, ch. ix, p. 169.
21. Marchessault, Septième Chant, p. 153. Italics in original text.

What a wonderful gift they [the Indians] gave us! We were more than sure that after the conquest our enemies would have imposed English-sounding names, Victorian names. *"But they must have reasoned that the words Kebec and Kanada belonged to the very nature of things in that place, since the Indians themselves had found them in keeping with the country."*

22. Marchessault, Dixième Chant, p. 291.

The air splits on every side; it is snowing salt, sulphur, phosphorous, mercury, feathers, antlers, teeth, tangles, pins, and pence.

23. Maillet, ch. xv, p. 274.

This is the true story of his forebears, one of the first of the race, who lived before the tower of Babel, when men all spoke the same language. The hero, although he was called Tit-Jean Quatorze because of the fourteen tricks he had played on his father, was in no way a bad man; and he decided one day to take a wife.

24. Maillet, ch. xvi, p. 292.

And the Landrys, the Cormiers, the LeBlancs rubbed elbows with their cousins Godin: Godin called Beauséjour; Godin called Belle-fontaine; Godin called Godin. They were all descendants of an ancient family of France which claimed ancestry back to Godefroy de Bouillon. Godins who might have been named Godfri, Godfrei, Godfrain, Godfrin or Godain, before coming to settle among the Godins of Acadia: the same Godins who had fled to the forests at the time of the great

Dispersion; who hid there during the upheaval, and who recovered their decaying carts from under the snows of the terrible winter of 1780.

25. Maillet, ch. xvii, p. 300.

And I have millet seeds, and seeds of straw, and orange pips; I have herbs, matches, pineapples; and I have beautiful ... beautiful ... beautiful birds.

26. Roland Barthes, *Le Plaisir du texte* (Paris: Editions du Seuil, 1973), p. 84.

14

Madeleine Gagnon's Po(e)litical Vision: Portrait of an Artist and an Era

Karen Gould _____

"J'ai toujours su que l'histoire m'écrivait. Mais que je sois écrite, avec d'autres et à travers les autres, s'est matérialisé ici en cette rencontre."[1] So begins Madeleine Gagnon in her opening remarks at the international conference on "La Femme et l'écriture," held in Montreal in October of 1975. Midway through an explosive decade for women writers in Quebec, Madeleine Gagnon's prophetic comment marks a personal as well as a collective turning point in the development of female texts and in the feminist movement as well. Even the most cursory glance at women's writing in Quebec during the early 1970s reveals a persistent preoccupation with patterns of sexual domination, repression, and estrangement, while the texts themselves often appear as nightmarish hallucinations or as mutilated fragments of a discourse that is yet to be born.... To be sure, reverberations from the angry political turmoil in Quebec during the late sixties can be traced throughout a diverse and significant number of feminist texts, including Michèle Mailhot's *La Mort de l'araignée* (1972), Hélène Ouvrard's *Le Corps étranger* (1973), Nicole Brossard's *Un Livre* (1970) and *Sold-out* (1973), and Marie's *Journal d'une folle* (1975). Moreover, for feminist writers on the left, the Quebec nationalist movement's explicit critique of the political subjugation and linguistic colonization of francophone Quebecers frequently became coupled with Marxist analyses of class struggle and the dialectics of alienation, as was the case with Madeleine Gagnon's own *Pour les femmes et tous les autres* (1974) and *Poélitique* (1975) and with much of France Théoret's early writing as well. Perhaps the most influential feminist newspaper during the early seventies, *Québécoises deboutte!* (1972-1975), also emerged out of the wake of the Independence movement with a decidedly Marxist-feminist orientation; its title became a rallying cry in numerous feminist circles.

With the swift rise to power of the Parti Québécois (P.Q.) in 1976, however, came the disturbing recognition for feminist activists and leftists in general that the political projects of the P.Q. would, in fact, do little to alter radically either class or sexual politics on L'Euguélionne's "planète négative."[2] At the same time, a number of leftist political groups were experiencing increasing discord among their members, especially over feminist issues such as abortion and child care. In part as a response to the widening political schisms on the left and the growing solidarity of the feminist movement in Quebec, many of Quebec's women writers who shared the concerns of the left began to look elsewhere for creative inspiration and political wisdom, and particularly to other women, both past and present, as their alienation gave way to a mounting solidarity, and the female text began to reconstruct itself, grounded in a new sense of cultural, psychological, and corporeal *différence*. Indeed, since 1976 the writings of Louky Bersianik, Denise Boucher, Nicole Brossard, Jovette Marchessault, and Madeleine Gagnon herself have increasingly resonated with the voices of other female artists and historical figures who speak to one another across cultural boundaries and across history in an orchestrated dialogue of female desires, accomplishments, and revolt.[3] Nicole Brossard's lead essay, "La Vie privée est politique," which appeared in the April 1976 issue of the radical feminist newspaper, *Les Têtes de Pioche*, published from 1976 to 1979, also attests to the beginnings of a new feminist current in Quebec. Much of the discourse emanating from this new phase of feminist activity and literary production has largely abandoned traditional Marxist analyses and the rhetoric of independence for a more subjective expression of the female condition, while at the same time calling for a considerably more probing critique of patriarchy and its attendant institutions.

Madeleine Gagnon's literary activity over the last decade reproduces many of the inner struggles of Quebec's feminist movement during the same period, primarily because of the political sophistication and underlying contradictions that have formed the essential framework of her artistic enterprise. Torn between issues of class and gender concerns, between a strong sense of collective allegiance and the necessity for personal exploration, Gagnon has been chastised by some feminists for her critique of radical feminist support groups, occasionally dismissed by male critics as a meandering voice lost in her own solipsistic labyrinth, and heralded by others still as one of Quebec's leading theoretical spokeswomen for the female "body text." And while some feminist critics, such as Lucie Lequin, have chosen to place Madeleine Gagnon alongside Nicole Brossard as two of the foremost leaders of feminist writing in Quebec,[4] surprisingly little criticism—feminist, Marxist, or otherwise—has emerged in recent years that seriously considers the dramatic evolution and unique character of Gagnon's work.

Overall, Gagnon has not enjoyed the resounding critical acclaim of Nicole Brossard nor the artistic notoriety of her friend and *collaboratrice*, Denise Boucher, yet her name is more internationally known than most of her Quebec counterparts, since she is regularly referred to in France and even in the United States, along with Hélène Cixous, Annie Leclerc, Chantal Chawaf, and Luce Irigaray, as one of the important new theorists and practitioners of corporeal writing. She is, for example, the only writer from Quebec to be included in the recent anthology on *New French Feminisms*,[5] which is surely the best introduction in English to date to the literary activity of recent French feminists. Quebec critic Jean Royer has cited the publication of Gagnon's *Lueur* as one of the key events in the history of women's writing in Quebec during the past decade.[6] Certainly, the verdict is not yet out on the impact of Madeleine Gagnon's literary contributions to women's writing in Quebec and to Quebec literature in general. Still, there is little doubt that she has been and will quite probably remain closely associated with the very heart of the debate over the significance and vitality of current experimentations in feminist discourse both on this continent and abroad.

TEXTUAL MILITANCY

Gagnon's early texts, particularly *Les Morts-vivants* (1969), *Pour les femmes et tous les autres* (1974), and *Poélitique* (1975), have received considerably less critical attention than her later work, and there is some reason to believe this is as it should be. The respectable (and conservative) *Dictionnaire pratique des auteurs québécois* comments on her work up to 1970: "Her poetry and especially her stories ... are tinted with a revolutionary color displayed in the rejection of the world her characters inhabit and also in writing which, to be honest, is for the author nothing more than the search for a style that she has not yet found herself."[7] While the evaluation may seem overly harsh, the critique is, in some respects, correct. And yet, for our purposes, the reasons behind Gagnon's initially groping style and somewhat obscured voice are no doubt more interesting than all the critical reactions to the work of this early period.

Appearing in 1975, *Poélitique* presents us with a radical collage of poems, quotations, and political analyses, written and assembled by the author from June 1972 to May 1974. Here, we read snatches of Brecht, Mao, and Maïakovski on Marxist aesthetics in striking juxtaposition to excerpts from the first issue of *Le Québec Littéraire* (1974), in which the editors self-righteously claimed their literary paper's right to exist outside of ideology, concluding in a somewhat contradictory fashion that all art is, inevitably, "a bourgeois fact a minority phenomenon." Interspersed amid this ideological debate are Gagnon's own poems and political reflections on a decade and a half of progressive struggle in Quebec. At their best, her poems act as a political conjuration, as she invokes the names, historical events, and mass demonstrations that so profoundly marked the people of Quebec from 1960 on:

> dans les chantiers de construction
> grève des employés d'hôpitaux
> grève du rail grève de la faim
> pour la reconnaissance du crime

politique grève à Air-Canada
à la Dominion Ayers Wood
et grève à la Manic
juillet 66 chaleur au Québec
quarante-cinq-mille grévistes
des intellectuels se prennent pour
une classe à part 1962: grève
des étudiants de l'U. de M. au nom
de la solidarité syndicale appelons
les choses par leur nom la poésie
c'est l'histoire en souffrance[8]

Indeed, the mission of poetry in *Poélitique* is to transmit the suffering of history. Furthermore, if history is the inquisitorial subject (''Sujet inquisiteur'') that inscribes itself in both the events and delirium of human experience, as Gagnon would have us believe, the poet is the artist whose literary projects seek to obliterate all barriers between language and action, ideology and desire:

le DESIR inscrit non plus au creux de nos cervelles
mais de nos actes inscrits dans les mémorables
j'écris c'est ce qu'on m'a appris à l'école
j'écris pour déchirer la poésie tordre les alphabets
rompre les codes jusqu'aux formes sonores de la carte
c'est derrière un discours que se noue le désir oui[9]

Heavily influenced at this particular stage of her artistic and political development by Marxist theories of cultural production, Gagnon views language not only as a tool of bourgeois oppression, but also, and perhaps more importantly, as a key to the radical transformation of reality through praxis: ''Lutter jusque dans les mines profondes et obscures du code grammatical.''[10] Subverting the dominant lexical, grammatical, and syntactic order calls for an uncompromising militancy toward the text that is both disruptive and creative in nature. The act of writing, like Marxist philosophy itself, thus becomes a revolutionary activity that engages in the struggle to construct a new and rebelliously authentic collective identity. The necessary bonding of the word and the collective social body is precisely the relationship Gagnon establishes in the final lines of *Poélitique*:

une longue trace descendait rue Papineau
une lettre pour l'inscrire à l'Histoire
20,000 bouches des millions de paroles
tapageuses et signifiantes
ler mai 1974[11]

Although the theoretical project underlying *Poélitique* is forcefully presented, Gagnon relies far too heavily on the voices of ''authority,'' albeit Marxist in perspective and therefore revolutionary, to ensure the political rigor she demands of her text. In fact, at times it would seem that the all too frequent intrusion of these extratextual sources unwittingly serves to widen the gap between intellectualism and the popular culture Gagnon strives so clearly to address in most of her own poems. In the final analysis, *Poélitique* is more manifesto and less poetry than even the author might have wished. Be that as it may, the imbalance in *Poélitique* is to a large degree corrected in the much more complex textual development of *Pour les femmes et tous les autres*.

Pour les femmes et tous les autres is, on the one hand, a disquieting people's portfolio, filled with working-class portraits of struggle and despair. The characters in Gagnon's poems speak in *joual*, the language of the common folk. And as was the case in much of Quebec's nationalist literature in the 1960s, the use of *joual* in *Pour les femmes et tous les autres* focuses the reader's attention on the political nature of language, and, more specifically, it serves as a source of linguistic solidarity or alienation between the reader and the fictional voice. The family concerns and work-related problems of Gagnon's characters reflect both the social burden and psychological damage of economic hard times and class exploitation. Like *Poélitique*, *Pour les femmes* ... is also a collage, mixing theory and poetry, fiction and everyday life, "literature" and journalism, in an attempt to ground the work of poetry more concretely in the hopes and deceptions of the common people:

> Pi moè chus ben écoeurée ma p'tite à soère
> nous autres y faut écrire on a trouvé l'aut'
> jour le titre (ça s'appelera REELLEMENT) c'est
> l'temps qu'y arrêtent de nous faire chier
> avec leurs beaux poèmes polis[12]

Gagnon's young family portraits are poignant depictions of human tragedy in capitalist society, particularizing the insidious effects of economic misery on the stability of the family unit, on a working man's pride, and on the confused mental state of an abandoned young mother. These poetic accounts also reveal the way in which the cycle of oppression invariably repeats itself from one generation to the next, crushing all hopes for an exit out of poverty and humiliation:

> Pi là a sait pus trop
> c'qui s'est passé dans l'temps
> Pourquoi Raoul pi elle
> y en sont arrivés là
> c'est comme si y s'retrouvaient
> pareils comme leux parents
> les fois qu'y parlent c'est pour chiâler
> on dirait qu'à c't'heure
> y peuvent même pus se r'garder
> la chicane est pognée
> y peuvent pus l'arrêter

a' souvient pus pantoutte
comment tout ça ça commencer[13]

But Gagnon does propose a way out of this vicious circle of rising expectations and invariable deceptions: the exit is through socialism, and her vehicle toward that end is a language of resistance and revolt. In the second in a series of three poems entitled "POEMES TRES LISIBLES (also subtitled, "NOS POETES ET LES AUTRES"), the author urges the voices of the many to cry out loudly enough to drown the official discourse of Capital, the State, and those poets who have failed to speak with and through the people: "MAIS LES POETES EUX-MEMES VOUS ASSOMMENT ET LEURS VAINES RECHERCHES D'E-CRITURES INSONORES SONT ECRANS ENTRE VOS PAROLES ET LA MIENNE PARLEZ PLUS FORT ENCORE. . . . "[14] Thus, Gagnon's revolutionary poet refuses to envision the act of writing as a privileged act or as the golden fruit of an educated elite who has privatized artistic expression and human experience as well. On the contrary, the poet's task in *Pour les femmes* . . . is to bear sober witness to the collective will of the working class and to reject the cultural domination of intellectual elites. "NOUS NE POUVONS PLUS RIEN SI VOUS NE PARLEZ PAS," concludes Gagnon,[15] thereby underscoring the tie that binds her own artistic production to the concrete realities of the daily lives of others. No longer the sacred realm of the individual imagination, poetry is first and foremost the realm of the people, the realm of the real.

Yet if *Pour les femmes* . . . is on one level a text that attempts to fuse the voices of working people with the words of the poet, it is also a text about women, as the first part of the title indicates. Although fragmentary at best, Gagnon's reflections on the female experience quite clearly bare the early seeds of her later feminist development. Hence we note, for example, how female friendship can assuage women's sense of loneliness and provide the only authentic communication in an otherwise mute and alien environment. Gagnon also makes ironic use of the advertising of feminine apparel in *La Presse* in order to emphasize the critical gulf that exists between bourgeois recipes of feminine beauty and the markedly different self-perceptions of working-class women:

Quand j'regarde des revues
j'me trouve ben laide
j'me r'connais pus chus toute perdue
ça s'peut pas comme y sont belles les
      femmes par là
La mode on dirait c'est pour eux autres
      qu'est faite[16]

The alienation depicted in the poem above is no less real, if we are to believe Gagnon, and no less pernicious than the specific forms of alienation experienced by workers in the existing division of labor and in the capitalist mode of production in general.

In the concluding pages of *Pour les femmes et tous les autres* Gagnon conjoins theories of class conflict and gender politics in a powerful blending of sexual pleasure and terrorism, revolutionary love and social justice:

> vagin fleuri fleurdelysé sexe et médecine nos sexes
> débouchent dans le ventre amour et terrorisme
> contradictoires vérités de nos jouissances leur sexe
> n'a rien à voir avec un ventre ouvert.... [17]
>
> Cela n'empêche pas le désir et la fête multiple
> cela ne refoule plus le délire enfin qui rompt les
> amarres coule libre et puis trace nous sommes amants
> camarades nous sommes nombreux cela n'est pas facile
> et pour le dire il faut creuser des mots de tous les
> jours.... [18]

What Gagnon posits here is a new kind of loving: the unrepressed, unashamed sexual love of male and female equals that literally becomes a subversive act, uniting male and female bodies in a mannerr wholly at odds with the dominant capitalist order. Ultimately, she assures us, the all too familiar rhythms and outworn images of the bourgeois ballade will, of necessity, yield to the visionary love poetry of a revolutionary era. *Pour les femmes et tous les autres* is, above all, an attempt to chart the possible directions of a poetic writing capable of breaking up the symbolic order of bourgeois discourse. Although the challenge is a formidable one, the prospect for change is a thing of beauty: "[C]omment devenir en armes nos caresses en combats nos amours."[19]

WRITING AND REPRESSION: "I AM MY OWN VOLCANO"

Among those who attended the 1975 Montreal conference on "La Femme et l'écriture," a number of female participants were drawn together through common political concerns and a growing sense that women's issues had been and would probably remain marginal issues in most of Quebec's political circles on the left. During the year that followed, these women began initiating a program of consciousness-raising groups that included the generation of small feminist "cells," comprised of five or six women who met regularly to share their thoughts and feelings about the myths and realities of womanhood. Madeleine Gagnon and Denise Boucher participated in one such cell, and they have recorded the aspirations and failures of their group experience in an unusual and admittedly controversial text entitled *Retailles: Complaintes politiques*, which appeared in 1977. Some feminists, like Jovette Marchessault, immediately denounced *Retailles* as an irreverent attack against female solidarity,[20] while others saw in it further evidence of the widening schism between heterosexual and "radical" or lesbian feminists. Despite the political debate it unleashed, or perhaps in some measure because of it, *Retailles* remains a crucial historical and literary document of the mid-1970s. The collaborative effort in *Retailles* adds to the book's bold frankness of spirit, subject matter, and intent. Most important, the text serves as a liberating confession of disillusionment that frees the authors from their own censorship. Gagnon admits that without such honesty, she would be unable to continue writing:

Il n'y a plus de mots tabous. Cette confusion qui à la fois me hante et me séduit. Toute ma vie passée et mon histoire récente avec nous cinq m'aura appris que parfois la plus profonde vérité du fond de soi, lorsque proférée, peut être reçue par l'autre comme violence, comme aggression. De là les nombreuses censures pour tous ces textes— littéraires ou politiques—qui dans le cours des siècles n'étaient pourtant que des cris isolés de vérité.[21]

This uneasy confrontation with previously *un*spoken truths is what gives *Retailles* its sense of urgency and persuasive strength. Ironically perhaps, it is also this surfacing of the unstated that links *Retailles* to so many of the feminist and radical feminist works that have appeared in Quebec since 1975. Both Gagnon and Boucher carefully weave the politics of repression into their poetry/prose fragments in order to expose the abuse of power, whether in the hands of men or radical feminists. In so doing, their dialogue of deception reveals the risks women continually run of duplicating male history and male culture, which Gagnon insists are dominated by Thanatos rather than by Eros: "Je les ai vues vouloir vous tuer une à une comme on tue trop d'amour quand on souffre du manque. Si au moins j'avais vu leur souffrance se dire."[22] Refusing all pacts with power, Gagnon denounces the growing cleavage between heterosexual and lesbian feminists as a destructive act that is shattering the illusion of a collective female voice and a collective love: "Etouffer la parole n'a jamais été et ne sera jamais un geste de tendresse."[23]

Gagnon's imagery in *Retailles* reflects her deep preoccupation with the necessity to undo male history through the invention of a new female language, a political and artistic concern that is still apparent in her more recent texts and in the texts of a number of other writers as well. Images of knotting and unknotting, knitting and unknitting, or unraveling all previous depictions of women permeate her writing from beginning to end: "Eux à nouer les stratégies dont je suis. Moi à découdre les fils de l'intrigue où ils se trouvent."[24] Her use of the infinitive and present participle explodes all temporal boundaries while at the same time she creates a kind of textual immediacy by drawing the reader into a verb that is seemingly subject-free:

Essayer de presser si fort l'orange
du désir qu'il en sortira de la tendresse.
Presser si fort l'orange, faire le défi qu'à
la limite du désir, dans l'absolu du

sexe, jusqu'à la lie: c'est là que
le jus de la tendresse peut le mieux
sortir. Entrer sur le terrain du pouvoir
et du désir pour me défaire de l'intérieur.
Pour le découdre jusque dans ses
doublures les plus cachées. C'est
pénétrer jusqu'à la moelle là où le
désir dit mieux la puissance d'être.
C'est vouloir détruire le pouvoir sur
le terrain même de la puissance de
vivre.[25]

The tone and structure of *Retailles* intentionally obliterate genre distinctions, as the text alternates between poetry and prose, political contexts and personal musings, and between Gagnon's oftentimes philosophical discourse and the more satiric humor of Denise Boucher. Deconstructive strategies such as these have, in fact, become the trademark of an entire generation of feminist writers in Quebec during the last decade, a fact Gagnon herself does not ignore. This may explain why Gagnon slips so easily into the *nous* pronoun throughout many of her portions of the text:

Que l'on nomme fiction ou poésie, ou encore philosophie ces venues de nous dans l'écriture, importe peu. Seule nous emporte, avec les formes qu'elle génère, cette libre course qui doit plonger dans la pénombre des symbolismes introjectés pour enfin remonter aux vérités étrangères que, seules, nous pouvons divulguer. Nous savons qu'un jour, grâce à tous ces risques passionnés d'actions, de paroles et d'écritures, nous aurons transformé, non seulement le poétique, en apportant au texte son corps à corps censuré, mais aussi le politique en nous plaçant, non plus comme objet dans la phallocratie mais comme sujet d'une nouvelle histoire de partage entre les femmes et les hommes.[26]

Whatever one's feminist leanings may be, it is difficult to dismiss either the originality of presentation or the powerful challenge to "male" politics and aesthetics that *Retailles* embodies. Skeptical of a discourse that would incite women to wage war indiscriminately on their male compatriots, Gagnon and Boucher look to the future, to the slow engendering of a discourse that will unsilence the voices of preceding generations of women and, perhaps most importantly, will reeducate future generations of male children so that one day men and women need no longer shape their identity at the expense of the other:

La nuit suivante, il me fut donné
de vivre un si grand bonheur. Calme,
allongée sur un plateau gazeux de
lumineuse obscurité, je donnai la vie
comme indéfiniment. Des dizaines de
bébés sortirent de mon ventre.
Aucun effort, aucune douleur; ILS

venaient, de moi, prendre leur
place dans l'histoire.[27]

In the final analysis, *Retailles* invokes the need for a new female discourse, based on Eros rather than Thanatos, on the release rather than the repression of women's words. But it is Gagnon's ground-breaking essay, "Mon corps dans l'écriture," that presents us with a blueprint for the fashioning of such a discourse. Published the same year as *Retailles*, "Mon corps dans l'écriture" immediately gave Madeleine Gagnon greater international recognition when it appeared in a French edition of critical essays alongside texts by Hélène Cixous and Annie Leclerc.[28] Like her French counterparts, Gagnon views women's writing as an act of self-possession and survival: "Je revendique ma place de sujet dans l'histoire. Je revendique mon pouvoir de représentation et de nomination."[29] Once again, Gagnon raises the problem of language, which she originally placed in a materialistic context in earlier works, in order to emphasize the immense power of *naming*.

"Mon corps dans l'écriture" argues for an approach to women's writing that would put female sexuality and desire back at the very center of discourse. For the historic repression of female sexuality in phallocentric discourse must be understood, Gagnon contends, as the intentional repression of the feminine form and of female creativity itself. Hence, we witness the birth of "body writing," which is gender-marked as well as intimately personal. Echoing American feminist Adrienne Rich, who urges women to "touch the unity and resonance of our physicality, our bond with the natural order, the corporeal ground of our intelligence,"[30] Gagnon considers the link between textuality and corporeality as essential to revolutionizing our sexual consciousness. As women write the female body, so will they write the female form. Moreover, by writing through the desiring body, Gagnon hopes to subvert and eventually dismantle altogether the false binary opposition between reason and sexuality that has long dominated traditional male discourse.

Given this more recent emphasis on the corporeality of the text, it is not surprising that Gagnon should choose to focus an important part of her discussion on the maternal body, since the act of giving birth is surely the most profoundly creative act in human life. Like Adrienne Rich, Hélène Cixous, Annie Leclerc, and others who have found parallels in their own lives between the act of giving birth and the act of writing, Gagnon shares with her readers grotesque scenes from her own childbirth experiences in order to underscore the severity of male repression:

C'était dans un petit hôpital de Provence où le gynécologue ressemblait à s'y méprendre au boucher de mon ancien village. Tablier blanc rempli de sang, manches de chemises retroussées pour la besogne, cigarette à la main. Il ne manquait que le couteau. Assis à l'autre bout de la salle, juste en face de moi, les yeux centrés sur mon vagin béant, c'est tout ce qu'il voyait de moi. Moi, allongée, tête en arrière, les pieds attachés aux étriers, mes mains bloquées par la sage-femme, essayant de reprendre mon souffle, pendant qu'il criait "poussez" "poussez" et que la sage-femme exécutait ses ordres. Montée sur moi comme un cavalier, ses genoux sur mes épaules et les deux mains qui pressaient sur le ventre pour que ça descende enfin. Ils étaient fatigués d'attendre. Cette scène grotesque m'a semblé durer des heures. . . . [31]

Indeed, the analogy she constructs between the struggling female artist and the woman in labor is painfully clear: men have controlled the birth process in much the same way that they have controlled women's language. Of course, for the contemporary female writer, such an analogy must have a stirring effect since it suggests the potential subversiveness and power of women who resist male domination when giving birth to children and to a language of their own.

In "Mon corps dans l'écriture," Gagnon's collective revolution has in fact become a revolution of bodies. And for women, this means reaching out of their isolation and corporeal separation toward union with other female bodies. Since no models for themselves exist in the dominant male discourse, women will need to recapture the lost female form through their own words:

Nous n'avons été pour nous longtemps d'aucun secours. Comment pouvions-nous nous aimer sans imaginer, sans représentations, sans modèles de nous à nous? Nous n'étions même pas référence de l'autre. La science de l'autre. L'amour de l'autre. Celles que l'on chantait dans les ballades. Mais nous, entre nous? Nous sommes encore atrophiées dans les ordres de leurs discours. Au stade du fantasme, nous n'avions même pas accès à l'ordre symbolique. C'est ça la castration féminine et pas autre chose. Pas l'envie du pénis dont on a tant parlé: l'exclusion pure et simple du discours c'est-à-dire du symbole et de l'abstraction. [32]

For Gagnon, the construction of a female discourse grounded in the uniqueness of woman's physicality would thus become not only an act of self-possession, but also, and concomitantly, an act of collective recuperation.

IN SEARCH OF PRIMAL BEGINNINGS

Since the publication of "Mon corps dans l'écriture," the texts of Madeleine Gagnon have focused increasingly on the female body as a primary poetic and political generator. Gagnon's textual search for the female body carries the author back to her own birth and the beginning of her own language, as well as to the initial sites of conflict and repression from her past. These primal visions constitute a kind of psychological journey backward to those initiatory experiences that have presumably molded female development throughout history. The "archeological writing" Gagnon develops in recent texts such as *Antre* and *Lueur* presents an unusual mixture of feminist psychoanalysis, autobiographical description, and critical theorizing on the creative process. To underscore her theme of creative unearthing, Gagnon has given *Lueur* the subtitle of "roman archéologique," evoking the long, slow, internal excavation of the writer's own depths while also commenting on the laborious and painstaking nature of the creative undertaking. The result of Gagnon's textual experiment is the emergence of a language that does in fact resemble an unconscious writing from the body, where linguistic constructions have been intentionally devised to reveal the backward and inward movements of a female consciousness who is actively tracing the outlines of her own corporeal and linguistic development. Such recent narrative experiments have bewildered some readers for whom Gagnon's latest texts have become unnecessarily opaque and introspective. And yet, perhaps because of the complex, fragmentary, and at times enigmatic nature of this archeological writing, both *Antre* and *Lueur* offer the diligent reader a poetic realm far richer than could be found in Gagnon's earlier texts.

In *Antre* and *Lueur*, Gagnon probes for her body and for the body of other women, both past and present, amid the warm recesses of the maternal womb, the symbolic den of female births, or in the dark corners of ancient caves, the physical sites of life's earliest beginnings. Moving back in time, she rediscovers her own physical shape emerging from a fluid world of rivers, lakes, oceans, and amniotic waters, feeling her way through strangely familiar landscapes of shadows and darkness. Gagnon's search for origins, and for a language in which to convey it, is unmistakably mythic in nature, linking personal sensations and physical desires to a collective female past that has been shrouded in cheerless mystery for centuries. As a feminist, her mythologizing has a dual purpose: to destroy or unravel male myths about women's bodies and to construct in their place a new site for discourse that allows her to speak of *le corps féminin* from the inside. And here Gagnon joins with a number of other Quebec feminists, such as Louky Bersianik, Nicole Brossard, and Hélène Ouvrard, who have also made use of the female body as a primary textual generator.

The prelinguistic state to which Gagnon attempts to return in *Antre* and *Lueur* requires a poetic journey backward in order to relocate her birthplace, which is where her own language began. At the same time, Gagnon's personal archeo-logical search will also transport her back to the ancient beginnings—to the primordial den of all female births. Once there, the author describes a dark and protected world where both the body and the mouth's initial sounds are still in a state of flux, not yet formed, nor solid: "Que dit d'abord ce corps d'elle? Des morphèmes, des sèmes, sans paroles. Un corps qui coule, une écriture qui suit, s'écoulant avec lui, s'insinuant partout où celui-ci le porte."[33] As the title sug-gests, *Antre* beckons us to journey backward into the damp darkness of the womb-earth, to the den of our beginnings, to the mute and eclipsed mother whose body speaks to us across time:

Ancrée au sol en pleine lune phosphorescente. Je cherche à retrouver l'antre, pour l'instant. Sur les parois ambrées toutes les lézardes, fausses issues, où suintent les sueurs froides de l'univers ambiant. Comment dans cette crique fabriquer l'âtre, où sortir, ou bien absolument dépossédée de sons et d'images, ma mère s'est endormie recroquevillée sous sa mante de poils d'ours, attendant que les bourrasques cessent, comptant le temps à ne plus dormir, à ne plus jamais pouvoir fermer ni yeux ni oreilles, ni bouches du dedans ni bouches du dehors. Elle sue.[34]

Gagnon's fascination with formlessness is the result of her conviction that women must reinvent their bodies in order to *reform*ulate a language of their own: "Laisser parler le corps, juste le corps, tout le corps sans fragments, sans morcellements. Laisser couler les paradigmes pulsionels d'avant l'image."[35] Thus, the narrative in *Lueur* originates in the darkest recesses of inner life as an *écriture de nuit*, during which Gagnon struggles to decipher the obscured traces of "la première page de ma première nuit."[36] Archaic liquids seem to ebb and swell throughout the narrative, while the eye moves slowly inward, in half-darkness, catching only glimpses of fleeting images from ancient and personal female pasts that somehow speak to one another outside of time. The written text of *Lueur* is interspersed with photographs of ancient Algonquin petroglyphs inscribed on early cave dwellings. They suggest the prelinguistic symbols of Gagnon's "new-ancient" language that can only be transcribed in the shadows of darkness, where the words themselves no longer adhere to any previous set of conventions. Instead, they are set free to form new meanings, explore new terrain, and render desires that are truly different:

Un pré de blé. En plein milieu de la forêt touffue, un pré de blé. Immense. Je ne l'aurais pas cru possible. Elle est allongée de tout son long dedans, une femme, comme endormie, la tête sur une ardoise plate où c'est écrit, hiéroglyphes. Des lettres sont gravées dont elle ne comprend ni la disposition ni le sens. Elle se repose et ne semble pas vouloir chercher; de son index, elle balaie la poussière de blé sur hiéroglyphes. Elle souffle sur l'ardoise. Emergent des mots signifiants jamais appris nulle part. Et comment, si ces mots ne furent pas appris, peut-elle prétendre au sens? Justement, elle n'a aucun préjugé, elle tend à tout sens, dans ce pré.[37]

Only in this state of openness to new meanings can the woman in the field and the writer of the text uncover words no longer spoken and as yet unimagined.

The central focus in *Antre* and *Lueur* insists on the fluid-like coalescence of body and text, a fusion that has dramatic consequences for the pace and direction of Gagnon's textual explorations. On the one hand, the more traditional linear development has been replaced by a meandering and, at times, halting narrative progression that allows the body's pulsations to function as initial catalysts for the production of poetic images and central thematic concerns. The frequent changes in narrative direction in *Lueur* also reflect Gagnon's desire to bring a sense of constant discovery to the body/text. And as we noted in her earlier Marxist texts, Gagnon continues to undermine the structures of conventional grammar in order to encourage the generation of new, "liberating" phrases and sentence groupings. The net result of these stylistic innovations is a highly personalized punctuation and syntax that enable the committed reader to flow with previously uncharted female rhythms. Writing the female body thus becomes both a creative celebration of what Cécile Cloutier has termed "la liturgie du corps''[38] and a recuperative act, laying claim to a new discourse capable of unearthing the primordial female body which, like women's language, has been historically devalorized and too long forgotten.

Throughout her literary career Madeleine Gagnon has been an iconoclast continually working to sabotage traditional approches to the act of reading and writing. In a crucial sense, both her earlier and more recent texts are experiments in linguistic subversion and invention, as are so many of the writings by Quebec women in the 1970s. Clearly, Gagnon adheres to the belief that no revolution, socialist or feminist, is possible without a complete rupture with the dominant symbolic order. Hence, from *Poélitique* to *Lueur*, writing functions first and foremost as resistance to power. There are, however, several levels to Gagnon's texts, and while the disruption of traditional discourse does play a substantial role in her artistic enterprise, it is also apparent that Gagnon's linguistic odysseys constitute the radical pursuit of a new center from which to affirm the self and the collective body politic.

Gagnon's double focus on self and collectivity may at times cause some vacillation in allegiances on her part, yet this fluctuation in emphasis is characteristic of a number of women writers in Quebec since the mid-seventies. On the whole, Gagnon's current effort to personalize the collective struggle expresses the direction undertaken in the most recent phase of feminist literary production. Among the vanguard of feminist writers in Quebec, some, such as Louky Bersianik, Nicole Brossard, and Jovette Marchessault, have gone even further than Gagnon in their search for a female body and discourse that are radically separate from traditional male discourse and the male body. Others, such as Denise Boucher and France Théoret, continue to focus persistently on the construction of a female subject without abandoning altogether a commitment to the elimination of class exploitation and social injustice in their own discourse. Gagnon remains more comfortably allied with the latter group, and yet she does not refrain from sharing with us her own bouts with uncertainty. As she notes here, Gagnon has been markedly influenced by the lesbian body/text. But in the final analysis, she cannot break with the male body and with the suffering of those men who also fight to break loose from the chains of social oppression and political injustice:

Tu avais vu défiler toutes ces grandes écritures du corps lesbien, tu les aimais, tu voyais les visages, les mains, le sexe, en train de les produire, tu les aimais, tu avais pour un temps tenté le miroir, le pastiche, mais avant même que tu puisses déchiffrer ce que tu avais inscrit, les feuilles t'étaient revenues déchirées de tes propres mains, la nuit pendant ton sommeil, ainsi que ton désir t'avait porté. Et tu étais passé à nouveau de la mort à la vie.

Tu avais revu cet homme d'amour étrange, la nuit suivante, la cicatrice de lui à sa joue, que tu aimais, à tout son corps, à la blessure immense que tu avais su reconnaître, malgré la violence, il ne t'avait pas dépossédée, la brèche d'incertitude devenait maintenant cratère illuminé du plaisir retrouvé, d'un temps non perdu à tout jamais.[39]

This kind of candid and often painful introspection has become one of the hallmarks of Gagnon's work and certainly contributes to the originality of her po(e)litical vision: "Je suis double sexe, double histoire, amour multiplié. Je suis mâle à force de me reconnaître et de m'affirmer femelle."[40]

Gagnon's contention that the new physicality of feminist writing will have a compelling effect on men and women alike is infused with an idealism that some readers may find untenable. It would seem, nevertheless, that her most enduring contribution thus far has in fact been this poetic binding together of a double-voiced discourse on female *différence* and socialist solidarity. As she herself explains, the historical and political specificity of Quebec itself may help us understand how this problematic coupling has come about:

Je viens d'un pays où tous les mots doivent être décousus avant que ne s'amorce le moindre combat; où l'on sait en naissant la mort de tout. Les hommes sont ici plus doux qu'ailleurs. Nos combats s'écrivent au jour le jour, partout s'affichent sur les murs de nos villes, aux portes de nos usines; des solidarités se tissent entre nous et nos frères; du sud noir, du nord rouge et de l'ouest étrange, nous commençons à peine à comprendre pourquoi les maîtres du pouvoir nous avaient divisés et nous divisent encore.... La vie est lutte pour la vie et non pour toutes ces morts, sexistes, colonisatrices et impérialistes; il faut savoir la mort pour vivre et tracer les frontières de ses alliances.[41]

Since the early 1970s the writings of Madeleine Gagnon have sought to mirror the social conscience of Quebec society, and already they have begun to shape a new vision of the future. After she writes to see, we read to discover.

NOTES

1. Madeleine Gagnon, "La Femme et l'écriture," *Liberté*, 18, Nos. 4-5, année 1976, Nos. 106-07 (juillet-octobre 1976), 250.

I always knew that history wrote me. But that I am written, with others and through others, has become apparent at this meeting.

2. See Louky Bersianik, *L'Euguélionne* (Montréal: La Presse, 1976).

3. See Karen Gould, "Setting Words Free: Feminist Writing in Quebec," *Signs*, 6, No. 4 (Summer 1981), 617-42.

4. Lucie Lequin, "Les Femmes québécoises ont inventé leurs paroles," *The American Review of Canadian Studies*, 9, No. 2 (Autumn 1979), 115.

5. Isabelle de Courtivron and Elaine Marks, eds., *New French Feminisms* (Amherst: University of Massachusetts Press, 1980).

6. Jean Royer, "Regards sur la littérature québécoise des années 70," *Le Devoir*, 21 novembre 1981.

7. R. Hamel, J. Hare et P. Wyczynski, eds., *Dictionnaire pratique des auteurs québécois* (Montréal: Fides, 1976), p. 269.

8. Madeleine Gagnon, *Poélitique* (Montréal: Les Herbes Rouges, 1975).

in the construction yards
strike of hospital employees

> strike of railroads hunger strike
> for the recognition of political
> crimes strike at Air Canada
> at the Dominion Ayers Wood
> and strike at the Manic
> July 66 heat in Quebec
> forty-five thousand strikers
> intellectuals take themselves as
> a class a part 1962: strike
> of students at the U. of Montreal in the name
> of union solidarity let's call
> things by their names poetry
> is history in suspense

There are no page numbers in this text. *Le Québec Littéraire* published two issues, one in 1974 and one in 1976. It was published in Montreal and edited by Yvon Boucher.

    9. Gagnon, *Poélitique*.

> Desire inscribed no longer in the hollow of our brains
> but in our actions inscribed in the memorable
> I write it's what they taught me at school
> I write to tear up poetry to bend the alphabets
> break the codes down to the sonorous forms of the map
> it's behind a discourse that desire is formed yes

    10. Gagnon, *Poélitique*.

Struggle even into the profound and obscure mines of the grammatical code.

    11. Gagnon, *Poélitique*.

> a long trail was coming down Papineau Street
> one letter to inscribe it in History
> 20,000 mouths millions of words
> noisy and significant
> the first of May 1974

    12. Madeleine Gagnon, *Pour les femmes et tous les autres* (Montréal: Editions de L'Aurore, 1974), p. 16.

> An' me I'm real sick lil' sister
> we folks got to write found the other
> day the title (it'll be called REALLY) it's
> time they stop shittin' on us
> with their pretty polished up poems

    13. Gagnon, *Pour les femmes et tous les autres*, p. 18.

> An' so she don't know no more
> what happened back there
> Why Raoul an' she
> got to that point there
> it's like they found themselves
> just like their parents
> the times they'd talk was for cryin'
> seems like these days

they can't even look at each other no more
the squabble gets goin'
they can't stop it no more
she don't remember neither
how all that got started

14. Gagnon, *Pour les femmes et tous les autres*, p. 45. Capitalization in original text.

BUT THE POETS THEMSELVES BEAT YOU TO DEATH AND THEIR VAIN SEARCHES FOR SOUND-PROOF WRITING ARE SCREENS BETWEEN YOUR WORDS AND MINE SPEAK LOUDER STILL....

15. Gagnon, *Pour les femmes et tous les autres*, p. 45. Capitalization in original text.

WE CAN'T DO ANYTHING ANYMORE IF YOU DON'T SPEAK OUT.

16. Gagnon, *Pour les femmes et tous les autres*, p. 34.

When I look at magazines
I feel real ugly
I don't see myself an' I feel lost
can't get over how pretty those
        women there are
the styles I reckon it's for them there
        that they're made

17. Gagnon, *Pour les femmes et tous les autres*, p. 42.

flowery vagina fleur-de-lised sex and medicine our sex organs
emerge in the womb love and terrorism
contradictory truths and our pleasures their sex
has nothing to do with an open belly....

18. Gagnon, *Pour les femmes et tous les autres*, p. 46.

That doesn't hinder desire and the multiple celebration
that no longer represses the ecstasy that breaks
adrift flows free and then traces we are lovers
comrades we are numerous that's not easy
and in order to say so we must dig for everyday words

19. Gagnon, *Pour les femmes et tous les autres*, p. 14.

How to become in arms our caresses in combat our loves.

20. See Jovette Marchessault, "'Retraite' par Soeur Madeleine Gagnon et Soeur Denise Boucher," *Les Têtes de Pioche*, 2, No. 6 (October 1977), 6.

21. Denise Boucher et Madeleine Gagnon, *Retailles: Complaintes politiques* (Montréal: Editions de L'Etincelle, 1977), p. 24.

There are no longer any taboo words. This confusion which at the same time haunts me and seduces me. All my past life and my recent history with the five of us will have taught me that sometimes the most profound truth from our inner depths, when uttered, can be understood by the other as violence, as aggression. From there the numerous censures which in the course of centuries were nothing but isolated cries of truth.

22. Boucher and Gagnon, *Retailles*, p. 44.

I saw them wanting to kill you one by one like killing too much love when one suffers from its absence. If only I had seen their suffering expressed.

23. Boucher and Gagnon, *Retailles*, p. 67.

Stifling the word has never been and will never be a gesture of tenderness.

24. Boucher and Gagnon, *Retailles*, p. 42.

For them to knot the strategies from whence I am. For me to unstitch the threads of the intrigue in which they find themselves.

25. Boucher and Gagnon, *Retailles*, p. 112.

> Trying to press so strongly the orange
> of desire that tenderness will come out of it.
> Pressing the orange so firmly, making the challenge that at
> the limit of desire, in the absoluteness of
> sex, to the dregs: it's there that
> the juice of tenderness can most easily
> come out. To enter onto the terrain of power
> and desire to undo me from the inside.
> In order to unsew it even in its
> most hidden linings. It's
> penetrating to the very marrow there where
> desire says better the power of being.
> It is wanting to destroy the power over
> the very terrain of the strength of
> living.

26. Boucher and Gagnon, *Retailles*, pp. 8-9.

Whether one calls it fiction or poetry, or even philosophy, these advents of ours in writing, matters very little. What transports us ultimately, along with the forms it generates, is the unhampered course that plunges introjected symbolisms into semi-darkness in order to reach far back to the strange truths that only we can divulge. We know that one day, thanks to all these passionate risks of actions, words, and writing, we will have transformed not only the poetic realm by bringing to the text its censored body, but also the political realm by no longer placing ourselves as objects in the phallocractic system but rather as subjects in a new history of sharing between women and men.

27. Boucher and Gagnon, *Retailles*, p. 147. Capitalization in original text.

> The following night, I was given the chance
> to live such a great happiness. Calm,
> stretched out on a gaseous plateau of
> luminous obscurity, I gave life
> as if indefinitely. Dozens of
> babies emerged from my womb.
> No effort, no pain: THEY
> came, from inside me, to take their
> place in history.

28. Madeleine Gagnon, "Mon corps dans l'écriture," in *La Venue à l'écriture*, Collection 10/18 (Paris: Union Générale d'Editions, 1977), pp. 63-116.

29. Gagnon, "Mon corps dans l'écriture," p. 64.

I reclaim my place as subject in history. I reclaim my power of representation and of naming.

30. Adrienne Rich, *Of Woman Born: Motherhood as Experience and Institution* (New York: Norton, 1976), p. 21.

31. Gagnon, "Mon corps dans l'écriture," p. 73.

It was in a little hospital in Provence where the gynecologist could have been taken for the butcher from my old town. White jacket covered with blood, shirt sleeves rolled up for the job, cigarette in hand. Only the knife was missing. Seated at the other end of the room, right in front of me, eyes centered on my open vagina, that's all he saw of me. Stretched out, head back, feet attached to the stirrups, my hands pinned down by the mid-wife, trying to catch my breath, while he yelled "push" "push" and the mid-wife executed his orders. Climbed up on me like a horseman, his knees on my shoulders and two hands that pressed on my abdomen so that it would finally move downward. They were tired of waiting. This grotesque scene seemed to last for hours. . . .

32. Gagnon, "Mon corps dans l'écriture," pp. 104-05.

For a long time we had been of no help to one another. How could we love ourselves without imagining, without representations, without models of ourselves for ourselves? We were not even a reference of the other. The science of the other. Love of the other. Those whom one sang of in ballads. But us, among ourselves? We are still atrophied in the orders of their discourse. At the level of phantasm, we didn't even have access to the symbolic order. That's what female castration is and nothing else. Not the penis envy which has been talked about so much: the pure and simple exclusion from discourse that is to say from the symbol and the abstraction.

33. Madeleine Gagnon, *Antre* (Montréal: Les Herbes Rouges, 1978), p. 46.

First what does this body say about her? Morphemes, semes, without words. A body that flows, a writing that follows, flowing with it, creeping everywhere that the latter takes it.

34. Gagnon, *Antre*, p. 26.

Anchored to the earth under a full phosphorescent moon. I am trying to find the den again, for the moment. On the amber walls all the cracks, false escapes, where the cold labor of the surrounding universe sweats. How to create a hearth in this crack, where to get out, or rather completely dispossessed of sounds and images, my mother fell asleep curled up under her mantle of bear skins, waiting for the squalls to end, counting the time so as to sleep no more, to no longer ever be able to close eyes or ears, mouths from the outside or mouths from the inside. She sweats.

35. Madeleine Gagnon, *Lueur: Roman archéologique* (Montréal: VLB Editeur, 1979), p. 59.

To let the body speak, just the body, the whole body without fragments, without cutting it up. To let the pulsionary paradigms flow before the image.

For a more complete discussion of *Lueur*, see Karen Gould, "Unearthing the Female Text: Madeleine Gagnon's *Lueur*," *L'Esprit Créateur*, 23, No. 3 (Fall 1983), 86-94.

36. Gagnon, *Lueur*, p. 13.

The first page of my first night.

37. Gagnon, *Lueur*, p. 58.

A field of wheat. Right in the middle of a thick forest, a field of wheat. I would never have thought it possible. She is fully stretched out in it, a woman, as if asleep, her head on a flat piece of slate on which there is writing, hieroglyphics. Letters are engraved whose placement and meaning she fails to understand. She relaxes and doesn't seem to want to search further; with her index finger, she brushes off the wheat dust on the hieroglyphics. She blows on the slate. Meaningful words emerge never before learned anywhere. And how if these words were never learned, can she lay claim to their meaning? But in fact, she has no prejudices, she leans toward all meanings, in this field.

38. Cécile Cloutier, "UTINAM!," *La Barre du Jour*, Nos. 56-57 (mai-août 1977), p. 107.

The liturgy of the body.

39. Gagnon, *Lueur*, p. 146.

You had seen on parade all those great writings of the lesbian body, you loved them, you saw the faces, the hands, the sexual organs, in the process of producing them, you loved them, for a while you tried the mirror, the pastiche, but even before you were able to decipher what you had inscribed, the pages returned to you torn by your own hands, at night during your sleep, just as your desire had wished it. And you had passed once again from death to life.

You had seen again that man with a strange love, the following night, the scar on his cheek, that you loved, over all his body, the immense wound you had known how to recognize, despite the violence, he had not dispossessed you, the injury of uncertainty was now becoming a crater illuminated with rediscovered pleasure, from a time that was not forever lost.

40. Gagnon, "Mon corps dans l'écriture," p. 67.

I am double sex, double history, multiple love. I am male by virtue of recognizing and affirming myself as female.

41. Gagnon, "Mon corps dans l'écriture," p. 113.

I come from a country where all the words must be unsewn before enticing the smallest battle; where we know at birth the death of everything. The men here are softer than elsewhere. Our battles are written from hand to mouth, they are postered everywhere on the walls of our cities, on the doors of our factories; solidarity is woven between us and our brothers, from the black south, the red north and the strange west, we are just beginning to understand why the owners of power have divided us and still divide us.... Life is a struggle for life and not for all these deaths, sexist, colonialist and imperialist; we must know death in order to live and trace the boundaries of its alliances.

15

Louky Bersianik: Feminist Dialogisms

Maroussia Hajdukowski-Ahmed _____

Louky Bersianik published *L'Euguélionne* in 1976, but she had been writing for some time before that, to wit, the short texts of *Maternative* (1980), three of which were written in 1954 and in 1966. Was the female word not worth the trouble to have it understood, or did she fear the norm's censorship, since at first glance it is evident that her writing, or rather her sayings, are concerned with transgression. *L'Euguélionne*, feminized version of the Greek "Evangue-lion," is a vast feminist anti-Bible, structured in chapter and verse, that de-mythifies/demystifies phallic power and its popes, papal bulls, and sacred writings. With each publication, however, the texts of Louky Bersianik tend to decrease in size. *Le Pique-nique sur l'Acropole* (1979), shorter by half, is aerated with multiple windows that frame citations and aphorisms, with grey or black pages/ pauses and with the fine etchings of Jean Letarte. It debases the sacred and parodies Plato's *Banquet*. Xanthippe (illustrious unknown wife of the illustrious Socrates), Ancyl, and Aphélie, having shared sandwiches and drinks, discuss the mutilations inflicted on women and talk of their sexualities. *Maternative*, even shorter and again illustrated by Jean Letarte, is comprised of poetic texts and dialogues (telephone and theater) that were published between 1977 and 1980 in various journals and which abandon parody in favor of feminist writing, the writing with "a difference." (And even shorter is *Les Agénésies du vieux monde*, 1982).

It seems, in these three publications, that Louky Bersianik has rid herself of her angers against the mutilation of women, be it physical, ontological, or linguistic, and has then recreated feminist sayings in an explosion of words/ utterances of the woman. She has perforated and stripped away the strata of phallic lies in order to find the source, the mother/alternative to which she comes to slake her thirst. She executes this archeological "dig" in concert with her radical feminist contemporaries around the planet—the American Mary Daly

(*Gyn/ecology*), or the French writer Françoise d'Eaubonne (*Le Féminisme ou la mort*), or the *Québécoise* Nicole Brossard, to cite just a few—and, while rediscovering this source, puts together the female universe and its history so that they are somewhat less utopian. Louky Bersianik echoes the stated intentions of Mary Daly: "Although I am concerned with all forms of pollution in phallotechnic society, this book [*Gyn/ecology*] is primarily concerned with the mind/spirit/body pollution inflicted through patriarchal myth and language at all levels." This cognitive process consists of "unweaving the web of deception," and this exorcism—or the "writing/journeying [as this book] passes/spins through the phallocratic maze"—has as its aim the "[m]oving from the state of anesthesia to empowering gynesthesia [multiform power of sensing and perceiving]."[1]

Louky Bersianik, too, traverses time, denouncing the referential phallic system from which monolithism has hidden the female: mythically (Oedipus, Agamemnon, Zeus); philosophically (Plato, Thomas Aquinas, Marx); psychoanalytically (Freud, Lacan); religiously (Judeo-Christian religions); historically (the Middle Ages, witch-hunts, and contemporary genital mutilations in Africa); and even linguistically (the sexism of the French language, the dissymmetries and the "langue du mépris" [language of contempt] attached to the female). On this framework that involves a dense intertextuality (dialogisms), she weaves a solid chain, in solidarity with the female universe, in the creation of an exuberant text-tact/ile.[2]

Louky Bersianik and her female narrators read the phallic texts/monuments in reverse and in parody fashion, using the words (or the texts) indicated by preceding contexts in an inverse function.[3] They divert these texts from their initial sense, making the speculative phallic universe and the language that underlies it explode in the bursts of laughter of L'Euguélionne and her readers: "The feminist content of feminine art is typically oblique, displaced, ironic and subversive."[4] In *L'Euguélionne* Bersianik proceeds to deconstruct the Bible and biblical discourse. The title is already a subversion of the word "evangeion" (in Greek: good news), and the text debases uniqueness, monosemy, and phallic verticality, while it feminizes them according to the principles of multiplicity, of horizontalness, of multi-direction of polysemy, and of openness.

L'Euguélionne comes from elsewhere: "Elle chante, danse et tournoie, change de visage et de forme";[5] she resembles Eva-Maria ("ni vierge ni putain"),[6] and shepherds/witnesses/reporters from the four corners of the earth hurry to note her arrival. Quickly she begins her quest to liberate the species, "[c]ar c'est elle qui annoncera la bonne nouvelle de la fin d'un certain esclavage sur la Terre."[7] Along the way she encounters those oppressed, some of whom become her evangelists and among whom are Louky Bersianik and Omicronne, whom she commands: "'Laisse-là ton torchon et suis-moi.'"[8] The crowd of women swells and joins with her, gathering momentum for the assault on the phallic "tables of the law." Omnipresent and omniscient as God, "[e]lle voit tout par transparence."[9]

At the end she dies, as did Christ, murdered by enemy soldiers and riddled

with bullet holes. Again like Christ, she rises from the dead, not as a unidirectional verticality but as showers of joy that fall on the spectators. In this subversion of Christ's life, one finds even other biblical episodes that have been
carnivalized, often in a blasphemous street vocabulary. In Chapter 24, entitled
"L'Emasculée Conception," for example, the archangel Evangéline pays a visit
to Nopal, fiancé of Nopaline, and announces to him that he will be "porteur
d'un ovule divin qui se fécondera à son insu ...," to which he answers: "Je
suis le serviteur de la Très-Haute Wondjina, qu'il en soit fait selon sa Sainte
Volonté ..."; so "le vrai père de l'Euguélionne resta puceau."[10] In this way
all the mysteries are demystified. The parodoxical reversal of roles distanciates
Christian dogma and thus relativizes it while subverting the sacred biblical language specific to the description of each mystery.

   Some sequences begin with "[E]n ce temps-ci de notre Préhistoire,"[11] up-
setting the evangelical "At that time." The "In the beginning was the Word"
from Genesis becomes "Au commencement sur ma planète était le mâle,"[12] a
denouncement in L'Euguélionne, and "Au commencement était la Chair. Et la
Chair s'est faite Verbe," utterance in Maternative.[13] Louky Bersianik overturns
the biblical maxims as well: "Demandez et vous ne recevrez pas,"[14] or "Pré-
tendez et vous serez."[15] She deconstructs prayers so that they appear as feminist
credo: "Je crois en Moi.... Je crois aux Autres.... Je crois qu'il n'y a personne
au-dessus de Moi et personne au-dessous de Moi.... Je crois à mon corps
entier"[16] (an affirmation of identity and of the body, of otherness and a rejection
of hierarchical verticality). Transgression supreme, she overturns the supreme
sign of Christianity, the sign of the Cross. It becomes "the sign of the Hole"
that transforms the dead wood of the cross of sacrifice into a tree of life full of
vigor, "the tree with holes." This new feminist sign becomes: "Au nom du
Trou accueillant, et du Trou pénétrant et du Trou évacuant, Amen,"[17] a sign
that restores life and fullness to the hole/absence/lack/emptiness/and silence in
which the female had been interred. Feminism perceives the Cross as a symbol
of necromancy in a sadomasochistic society, "whereas the tree belongs to the
cult of all Great Mothers and like them is sacred."[18]

   The same biblical structure serves to demystify Freudian psychoanalysis, considered a part of global phallic religion. "Saint Siegfried," "prophète du phal-
ludisme," preaches his religion on the mountaintop, flanked by his successor
and apostle, Saint Jacques Linquant,[19] according to the reiterative structure of
the Beatitudes: "Bienheureux les individus qui naissent avec un phallus."[20] A
New Moses, he compiles "the tables of the Law" from which the commandments
are "gravés sur deux monuments de pierre qui avaient été plantés dans la terre
et qui s'élevaient verticalement dans le ciel sur la crête de la montagne."[21] (One
recognizes the sacred mountain/verticality and the mono/lithism of phallic law.)
Ancyl, who has undergone psychoanalysis, makes a point of demystifying, in
the form of puns, "le complexe des Dupes,"[22] and in Le Pique-nique sur
l'Acropole, the same Ancyl exhorts her sisters to attend the "Jeux Zolympiques,"
presided over by Jacques Linquant in person, the theme of which is to be "Divan

le Terrible.''[23] Freud (and the neo-Freudian, Lacan) has long been a major target for feminist attacks (from Mary Daly and, especially, Luce Irigaray), as L'Euguélionne says: "Pas une femme de la Terre ne devrait ignorer le discours psychanalytique sur elle-même."[24]

In effect, Freudian theory is unacceptable. In establishing the primacy of the phallus, it defines the female in reference to the male, as she "who is not" or "who has not," she who must be content with substitutes (clitoris, breasts, child), all expressions of her "penis envy." Freudian theory erects the masculine libido ("*libida; lit-bidon*," according to L'Euguélionne) into the norm. The latter makes ironic Freud's statements: "Hors du Phallus, point de salut. . . . L'individu qui naît sans phallus est handicapé. . . . [I]l devra construire sa vie autour d'un manque."[25] She also parodies the Lacanian idiolect: "Ce dernier . . . étant ontologiquement shakespearien (ETRE OU NE PAS ETRE LE PHALLUS), très possiblement boulevardier (EN AVOIR OU PAS) . . . eu égard à la dialectique basale de toute contradiction inhérente à la condition spatio-temporo-humano-masculonoïde."[26] Finally, she relativizes, like Zazie, "cette envie du pénis—mon cul," by reversing the roles in a parody on the birth of Eve who, at the sight of Adam, cries out: "Ce n'est pas possible! C'est le monde à l'envers! Mon père-mère est un estropié! D'abord, il n'a pas de seins. Et ensuite, je crois qu'il est en train de perdre sa vulve et tout ce qui s'ensuit."[27]

Oedipus's murder of his father and subsequent punishable act of incest are situated at the base of Freudian psychoanalysis. They consist of an enormous trickery that hides the female—in particular the mother—and has acted as a guarantee for all subsequent mutilations (literal and figurative), from the clitoridectomy to the "language of contempt"[28] of the wife/mother and her daughters. Luce Irigaray attacks this myth head on: "When in *Totem and Taboo* Freud theorizes about the murder of the father, the founder of the primitive horde, he omits a more archaic murder, that is of the woman-mother called for by the institution of a certain order in society. . . . The father forbids any bodily contact with the mother." It is then the navel that is the scar of the initial wound, and it is the murder of Iphigenia by her father, Agammemnon, that is the significant murder.[29]

Three stories by Louky Bersianik wholly subscribe to this theory of Luce Irigaray. Having assailed the power of the Father in *L'Euguélionne*, she lays claim to that of the mother in *Le Pique-nique sur l'Acropole* and in *Maternative*. Xanthippe, referring to the making of the unconscious, declares against Freud's presupposition: "Voilà ce qui s'est d'abord gravé dans chaque inconscient issu d'un utérus, le Corps maternel, seul mémorable et signifiant fondamental."[30] The murder of Iphigenia recurs, in fact, as a complaint/leitmotif punctuated by the tormented cry of Iphigenia herself (the cry of a feminist Christ on the Cross): "Père! Père!"[31] In chorus the women take up the story of the repeated murder of the daughters: "Ces six femmes. Ces six cent femmes. Ces six mille femmes. Ces six-cent mille femmes. Ces six millions de femmes."[32] They weep; they moan, and wail, and cry "No" to Adizetu (Ah! disais-tu?), the little mutilated

African girl who asks, "Est-ce qu'Aga m'aime? Non!,"[33] subverting the *nom* (name) *non* (no) of the Father, and whose picture of suffering appears on one of the pages.[34] Louky Bersianik thus knots a dialogical solidarity, both diachronic and synchronic, between the daughters/victims, from one era to the next, from one continent to the other, and from one book to another, since the characters of Ancyl and Adizetu as well as other textual similarities reappear in each text.

The last daughter/victim is Ortygia in *Maternative*:

> Ortygie étant l'ancien nom de Delos, la plus petite île des Cyclades. Selon la légende, Zeus tomba amoureux d'Asteria qui, pour l'éviter, se transforma en caille. Alors, Zeus se transforma lui-même en aigle.... Dans son désespoir, Astoria se métamorphosa en pierre qui tomba dans la mer en formant de la sorte l'île d'Ortygie.[35]

In the end the *mer/mère* brings Ortygie to life again, shielding her from a state of *pierre/père*/father.

In "La Natte et la hutte" Avertine (*avertit/subvertit*), aged twenty-one years and shut away in an asylum, is visited by the six-and-a-half-year-old Adizetu. They play at being mother and daughter who are "looking for one another" and exchange roles saying: "Je te cherche comme une inconsolable Mater-Demeter,"[36] referring to Korê-Persephone, daughter of Demeter, goddess of fertility, whom Hades/Pluto had kidnapped and brought to the infernos: Demeter said that she would not bear fruit until her daughter returned—Zeus decided that Korê would live three months (winter) with Hades and nine months with Demeter, who compromised and ordered the soil to bear fruit again.[37] Bersianik's dialogue consists of a revolting description of the clitoridectomy that Adizetu has to undergo and of the Freudian doctrine which reduces the clitoris to a negligible substitute for the phallus (thus implicitly justifying this barbaric practice). Adizetu plays the role of the mother, of Korê, and of Iphigenia, and is responsible for the suffering of the daughters, who denounce the father/executioner/Agamemnon: "C'est son masque mortuaire qui continue à faire la loi, la loi sans amour. Loi du meurtre chez les filles, de femmes, loi du meurtre des mères. Et loi du meurtre des fils à la guerre."[38] But Adizetu announces that women will put an end to this State/male-controlled violence: "J'en connais qui commencent à être des femmes devant leurs filles." Avertine finally orders Adizetu: "[V]a brûler la hutte de tes pères."[39]

The end of "Ortygie l'inapparente" terminates on the same note, with the union of the mother/daughter in rebirth: "Je te donne à boire les mots de ma langue.... Je suis ton lieu d'origine et ton signe fondamental. Et ta Grande Déesse renaissance inapparente—Toi utérus de mon utérus, toi ma vivante,"[40] the *mer/mère* says to Ortygia. And in *Le Pique-nique sur l'Acropole*, the Caryatid awakens to the sound of the words of love addressed to her by Avertine, who "s'endort dans les bras de la Cariatide qu'elle a mise au monde,"[41] thus subverting the Sleeping Beauty. This rebirth, the passage from the Law of the Father to the Love of the Mother, is marked by the change from solid to liquid state.

"Descendez de l'Erechteion. Descendez de cette érection pétrifiée,"[42] Avertine commands the Caryatids.

The love of the mother as creator and the law of the father as destroyer are, in fact, central themes in the radical feminism expressed by Mary Daly who echoes Françoise d'Eaubonne's "eco-féminisme": "Patriarchy is itself the prevailing religion of the entire planet and its essential message is necrophilia."[43] Thus in *L'Euguélionne* under the reign of the law of the father, the universal Uterus manufactures canon fodder (the boys) and the flesh of slaves (the girls) and proceeds to "ce carnage qui commence à la sortie du ventre."[44] As for the menu for the "Banquet" in *Le Pique-nique sur l'Acropole*, however, it is one gynophagy that offers, among other things: "Cailles en timbale à la sauce Asteria" and "une jument au jus Demeter."[45] In order to have the love of the mother/Goddess rule, therefore, it is necessary to return to the prepatriarchal era, source of future generations, where "the planet ruled by the female principle would become green again for all to enjoy."[46] Gloria Orenstein remarks:

Thus to-day the image of the Goddess that is appearing in women's literature is often the result of a conscious search on the part of the writer who has engaged in readings about archeological and anthropological documents or religious traditions related to prepatriarchal cultures.

And she continues: "Feminist spirituality proclaims wholeness, healing, love and spirited power not as hierarchal, as power over, but as power for, as enabling power."[47] Louky Bersianik, like Madeleine Gagnon, Yolande Villemaire, and Madeleine Ouellette-Michalska does the work of archeologists in rediscovering the paths of the female. It is thanks to them that "[o]n commence seulement à se rendre compte que pendant les trente derniers siècles, on a rendu à César ce qui appartenait à Cléopâtre et à Dieu ce qui appartenait à la Grande Déesse."[48] Louky Bersianik's texts end in touching scenes of reunion, in sisterly equality, and not in the fear the Father inspires in the hierarchy of his law; and so Margot ends the telephone conversation with her mother, Aphélie: "Oh! M'mam! tu es une vraie soeur! La soeur de moi!"[49]

In the origin of Judeo-Christian belief is found the Platonic philosophy that validates the reproduction of Self (the Cave Myth). Luce Irigaray has given a remarkably demystifying and feminist reading of this philosophy in *Speculum* where the initial model, being a phallic one, draws up a hierarchy of human preoccupations which goes from the love of women (low and vile) to the love of the Ideas (high and noble). This philosophy serves as an implicit guarantee of phallic power, Pope of the Unique and of its reiteration and Grand Inquisitor of Difference.[50] Louky Bersianik directly subverts *Le Banquet* in *Le Pique-nique sur l'Acropole* and implicitly subverts the Platonic discourse in all of her books.

Plato's *Le Banquet* or *Discours sur l'amour* comprises a series of speeches held at the banquet given by the poet Agathon, in 426 B.C. Various orators one after the other (among them Aristophanes and Socrates), having dismissed the entertainment of the flute player (women, decor, diversion, metaphor), tender their definitions of love. They develop the traditional paradigm: official speech/ the serious/men/official commemoration/love of ideas. The text of Louky Bersianik, on the other hand, carnavalizes *Le Banquet*, transforming it into a picnic with food and drink, in an open area, and shared by women who discuss their sexualities. Furthermore, the writing is not delivered by *beaux esprits* but lies across the page like the imprint of the body. It is the fist (*le poing*) that traces the dots/points, making its point known: "Ecrire est une expression corporelle."[51] Louky Bersianik subverts the principal of literary *avertissement* to "A l'ami lecteur" that invites and guides the reader; conversely, she excludes him, just as the female had been excluded from "ce petit souper historique."[52]

The text is presented as a concerto grosso, with each female a soloist and a member of the choir. The women proclaim their "femaleness" wholeheartedly in concert, against the annihilating phallic powers. The concert (concert = those in accord and having the same goals) begins ironically with a "Prélude en 𝄡 mineur[e]" (A minor) on the subject of body-writing, followed by a first concerto, "le pique-nique," reuniting Aphélie, Ancyl, and Xanthippe, in which they discuss the importance of the senses (in particular the sense of touch) and of the blood of the female. Xanthippe does not even fail to mention those remarks of the cooks for the banquet about Zeus's scabrous love affairs. She thus debases even further the superlative value of the phallic power.

Each participant recounts a "farce" (*farce* signifying both the popular comic play and the stuffing that is food). They talk about their sensual pleasures and about their plural sexualities (heterosexuality, lesbianism, onanism, bisexuality, pansexuality) which Ancyl summarizes in these terms: "Je suis un être sexuel, sensible aux autres êtres sexuels qui m'entourent."[53] Thus they subvert the definition of the two types of love (the two Aphrodites) that Socrates gives and which is quoted in the epigraph of the second concerto, "The Saying of Sexualities":

L'Eros de l'Aphrodite populaire ... c'est l'amour dont aiment les hommes vulgaires.... L'amour de ces gens-là s'adresse d'abord aux femmes aussi bien qu'aux garçons, aux corps de ceux qu'ils aiment plutôt qu'à l'âme, enfin aux plus sots qu'ils puissent rencontrer, car ils n'ont en vue que la jouissance. L'autre au contraire, l'Aphrodite céleste, ne procède que du sexe masculin, à l'exclusion du féminin. De là vient que ceux que l'Eros céleste inspire tournent leur tendresse vers le sexe masculin, naturellement plus fort et plus intelligent.[54]

This amorous hierarchy, excluding the female, the body, and pleasure, has permeated Judeo-Christian thought, Catholicism, and particularly Thomist philosophy preached in Quebec ever since it has existed. The book ends with a "Fugue en [la] Majeur[e]" (fugue—musical and kinetic term) which tells of the woman who, like the Caryatid delivered from the weight of Erechteion/ erection, finds both her voice and her desire for mobility at the same time.

Louky Bersianik has taken up the theme of feminist anti-Platonism, articulated by Luce Irigaray and introduced in the following passage by Shoshana Felman:

Already in the Platonic metaphors which dominate western discourse and carry meaning, Luce Irigaray decodes a strategy which excludes woman from the production of discourse: woman and the Other as such are subjected to the philosophical principle of sameness . . . in itself a property of man. The Platonic text institutes the repressive logic of identity with its components: the primacy of oneness, the reproduction of similarity, the repetition of sameness, along with the methodology which supports it: correct determining, analogy, the comparison, symmetry, dichotomic oppositions, theological project (or projection?).[55]

Those principles that constituted the grounds for existence of the "Maries" of the traditional Quebec novel, Louky Bersianik refutes in her writing with her whole bodily being. In the Platonic/Judeo-Christian system, the Being alone has the monopoly of the (re)production of Self, reducing *L'Autre/L'Antre* (the other/ cave) to *le Néant* (nothingness), a procedure which necessitates the phasing out of the *différence*, that is, of the passage or vagina of the female. The texts of Louky Bersianik decapitate all the "isms" of the system: Thomism, Taoism (*Ying*/active/male and *Yang*/passive/female), capitalism, Marxism, Sartrism, Péquisme, surrealism, and "Barthisme,"[56]—"isms" which neglect or mutilate the female.

In order to keep within her logic of deconstruction, L'Euguélionne subjects her own discourse to the same relativity, saving it from the phallic Manichean dichotomy: "transgressez mes paroles et les paroles de tous ceux qui vous parlent avec autorité."[57] In all phallic "thought" the female is only worth noticing in that she goes unnoticed. She is obliterated or silenced literally and figuratively if she transgresses the law of silence and nonexistence. It is therefore urgent to return the female to her story (history) and to reality. Giving her own meaning to L'Euguélionne, Ancyl contends:

Nous sommes considérées, nous les femmes, comme des personnes fictives de l'histoire, cette histoire "sainte" et barbare que les ci-devant hommes ont arrangée scientifiquement pour leur plus grande gloire et profit. Indésirables, mises en marge de l'espace et du temps (sauf dans la fiction), nous sommes irréelles, anachroniques et extra territoriales, nous sommes des extra-terrestres sur notre planète. Il nous reste à débarquer sur la terre.[58]

It is a work of reweaving that these women-historians have set for themselves, a work that consists of "remembering ourselves,"[59] of creating an historic bridge between Xanthippe, Iphigénie, the witches, and the contemporary Adizetus, in order to retrace their blood/silence and denounce "le génocide, présent aujourd'hui aux quatre coins de la terre."[60] Louky Bersianik's multiple solidarity crosses these eras and continents outside of hierarchy, outside chronology, beyond frontiers, beyond fences/limits, in an antagonistic dialogue with phallic power and a sisterly dialogue with the feminist writers who bring information and testimony, who open up knowledge of and about women. This collective text is like "une embouchure plutôt où se rejoignent les eaux multiples, souvent tumultueuses,''[61] the place of confluence for the voices of Luce Irigaray, Françoise d'Eaubonne, Shere Hite (extracts of her report on female sexualities and clitoral pleasures punctuate *Le Pique-nique sur l'Acropole*), of Virginia Woolf, of Simone de Beauvoir, of her sisters, of her mother, of the women of the planet who speak to her, to whom she speaks, and who speak to us. This dialogism is woven from the cloth of dedications, epigraphs, and quotations that abound in the three texts of Louky Bersianik.

At the same time as she denounces the occidental system of thought, Louky Bersianik subverts the language which communicates it. She undermines this language from within by parody, irony, and distortion of the linguistic forms which identify it. She comes thus to question the language itself, as happens in other feminist writings, where the "terms of language itself, as well as the terms of psychoanalysis and of literary criticism are called in question and subverted from within.''[62]

Sooner or later, however, the feminist writer becomes aware that language itself is a trap, committing woman to self-mutilation, if she uses the language as it is, or to silence, since "the word is not only a tool but also an outlet, a form of action, a way to assert oneself as a social being.''[63] If "Au commencement était le Verbe,'' this Word killed woman's speech—which Louky Bersianik undertakes to recover—as much on the level of reality as on that of pleasure, of enjoyment. One must appropriate the language and palliate its dissymmetry to create the discourse of "difference''/woman—an oral discourse, fluid, corporeal, multiple, playful, one whose characteristics Suzanne Lamy defines:

It should be firmly rooted in the community of women. It has themes: the body, experiences and gestures which are specifically female. A feminist bias, whether implicit or not . . . texts which give an account of a differenciation which can manifest itself in a polymorphous way, appearing as an exploding, rupturing, plurality, as the absence of a closed structure.[64]

It becomes more and more difficult in Louky Bersianik's writing to separate the utterance from the enunciation, the body/theme from the body/text. In that/ this time of history, the mutilating signs that power had traced/traces on woman's body (scarifications, the wearing of heavy jewelry restricting speech and mobility, marks of the branding iron and of fire) become in feminist writing the body-tracing signs and signs/body: "Il faut redonner valeur à cette peau qui avait été épinglée, trouée, crucifiée, palpée par tous . . .'' for woman who had "aucun mot sur la langue, que des signes dans le corps.''[65]

These are no longer the signs inspired by the breath of the Almighty but those inspired by the respiration of the body. Respiration dethrones inspiration: "La bouche et le nez sont des ajours majeurs dans tout corps qui parle et qui écrit la nuit comme le jour.''[66] Thus, on the textual level, "il faut ouvrir des bouches d'aération dans son texte . . .''[67] in order to make it breathe and communicate with others. This is the origin of the unwritten pages/pauses and the windows in Louky Bersianik's texts. On a number of the grey or black pages of *Le Pique-nique sur l'Acropole*, for example, she draws the contour of various sorts of openings—transoms, a skylight, a small round window—within which are hand-written (traces of the body) her words, the concerted or unconcerted words of others. Minds no longer give birth to beautiful speeches, but the hand, the skin, the mouth, the uterus do, as the title (a subversion of Socrates) of the appendix to *Le Pique-nique sur l'Acropole* indicates: "Maïeutique et la voix comme utérus" (Maieutics and the voice as uterus).

The narrators/characters/author/critic disappear—along with the creative/fic-tive/interpretive hierarchy: there are only women—breathe and touch themselves through all the pores of the skin, just as sense circulates and multiplies through all the pores of the words radiating in all directions, with all their senses, like irradiating female pleasure. Creation is born of the holes and the meaning and textual chasm/opening. The holes are the principle of pleasure which manifests itself in polysemy and word play, as in this play on the sense of touch/touching, on voice and emotion: "Toutes touchantes et de n'être pas touchées. Toutes chantantes. Et toutes sachant toucher."[68] Xanthyppe praises those of our senses "qui nous collent à la peau. Ce sont les sens propres. Les sens du corps à corps . . . mais toucher d'abord."[69] Touch is the original sense since we were touched all over in the uterus. This sense was hidden by sight when the Father/God eliminated the Mother/Goddess. The body was then submitted to the avoidance of touch and to the overabundance of sight, to the look of the voyeur who uncovers/rapes the woman spectacle. All the women with multiple hands now touch themselves (themselves and others—"se touchent") with all their fingers in all directions: "Les formes se déforment et s'inventent autour des doigts en éventail. Touche-moi dans toutes les directions dans tous les sens."[70] Xanthyppe, Aphélie, and Ancyl discover their bodies by touching themselves: the Caryatids and Ortygia are reborn under their caress. Significantly, the first text of *Mater-native* which modulates touch is entitled "Me tangere"—touch me.

The exploration of the body/space is an isomorph of the exploration of writing/ space, both open and multidirectional, sidereal and stupefying, vast, black con-tinents of women which woman dis-covers/covers little by little. L'Euguélionne appears as a multiple body, which in pirouetting takes on the corporeal forms of fictive or real Quebec women. She is space/body/exuberant sex, text: "Elle marchait sur l'eau, nue et noire . . . ouvrant les estuaires, élargissant les côtes. . . . L'amplitude de ce pas émanait du sexe en mouvement."[71] Even her brain "a la forme d'un archipel d'utérus, avec des circonvolutions et des invaginations."[72] She travels in all directions, on all continents, in all possible ways, exhorting women to the radiating mobility: "'Soyez des roues de plaisir lancées sur l'autoroute.'"[73] Space (especially in *L'Euguélionne*), the body (especially in *Le Pique-nique sur l'Acropole*), and writing (particularly in *Maternative*) are sites of revolutions.

At the same time as her texts unveil this body/pleasure space of woman,

Bersianik gives woman the voice and immanent communicative speech which the transcendent imperative word had stifled. "Et la loi c'est la loi, parce que la loi c'est moi.... Le reste est Histoire sans Parole,"[74] says le Verbe-Mâle in *Maternative*, a text that rejects the paradigm, Law/Word/Power/Male, and subscribes to the paradigm, Transgression/Spoken Word/Marginality/Female. Many of Bersianiks's terms express and qualify, in addition, the multiplicity of voices. L'Euguélionne has a strong voice but does not prevent anyone from speaking. She sings and laughs a lot: "[s]a voix se répand comme une cascade de rires."[75] *Le Pique-nique sur l'Acropole* is presented as a musical work whose "Prélude en 𝄡 mineur[e]" is entitled "Le Chant des statues vives," the aim of these expressions being to give voice/the spoken word to women petrified by the power of the phallus (the Caryatids, Ortygia).

All these *parlantes* are more interlocutors than narrators. The texts are filled with words of the enunciation of dialogue ("says she"; "she replies"). *Le Pique-nique sur l'Acropole* gathers the words of Xanthippe and the "dits des sexualités" into a concert of women's voices. The "I" of *Maternative* always addresses herself to "you": "J'ai prémédité de te parler, orange invisible et suscitée par le poète."[76]

Louky Bersianik modulates the voices on all tones, all registers, all timbres— songs and cries, complaints and cascades of laughter. The discourse of the voice eliminates *le discours de l'oeil* (of sight) as in the stage direction regarding "La Natte et la hutte," according to which "on entend leurs voix, sans les voir."[77] This spoken word/voice unveils the sufferings and the enjoyments of woman whom Bersianik makes a sorceress, an agent of transformation, since, according to Jacques Derrida, "he/she who acts vocally penetrates more easily into the disciple's soul so as to produce ever unusual effects ...," the logos having the "power of an alchemical transformation which links it to witchcraft and magic."[78]

In this speech of woman, rhythm has particular importance and fulfills specific functions. The parody of litany-like reiteration and the series of exhortations which L'Euguélionne addresses to women certainly subvert the Bible and psychoanalysis, but they also subvert the sacred form of discourse and the imperative mode traditionally reserved for men—women being relegated to prayer, to petition, or to silence. Elsewhere the anti-litanies, like the Rabelaisian enumerative lists (insults against women, the list of holes, etc.) are a way of occupying the scriptural space which is outside the normative order, in the overflowing of excess. In *Maternative* the reiteration manifests itself in a spiraled writing which consists of returning to the same word in order to take it further or in another direction; the text then dialogues with itself, makes itself an echo, and also echoes other texts. These echoes can be semantic: "Mais le Pénis-Verbum mettait un mur opaque entre lui et le tact";[79] and later "le Pénis-Verbum n'est pas un trait-d'union, mais un trait de distanciation";[80] or they can be phonic: "hier ... délier ... relier ... lieux ... recueillir."[81] As Suzanne Lamy notes, reiteration permits the exposure of difference and resituates us in the primary rhythms, those of early childhood (babble, rocking), when the spoken word was still pure enjoyment, when order and the Word had not yet intervened to bridle it.[82]

Children's word games, this infantile babble, therefore, also appear in *Maternative*: "cott cott cott . . . cocorico . . . Atla atla atla les Québécois sont là! Ah! Ah! Ah! Ah!"[83] The function of such sounds, according to Lamy, is to give preeminence to the senses over understanding and intellect and, according to Mary Jacobus, to return to "what Julia Kristeva would call semiotic, the pre-oedipal phase of rhythmic, onomatopeic babble which precedes the symbolic. . . ."[84] Pushing to an extreme, one would come to pure sounds, but Louky Bersianik stops at the edge of the abyss, where woman's discourse would cease to make sense, would fall into madness or infantilism, ending its communicative function.

The coming and going of words and sounds also create a marine-like flux and reflux of waves which unfurl on the white *plage/page*, always the same and always different, since "a woman never speaks in the same way. What she utters is fluctuating, befooling,"[85] Bersianik pours out the flow of her repressed words in *L'Euguélionne* and *Le Pique-nique sur l'Acropole* and the sounds of *mer/mère* which speak of her difference in *Maternative*. In this last text one reads, for example: "Je te donne à boire les mots de ma langue . . . ,"[86] passing from the fluid of the signifier to that of the signified. Women writers situate their writing in the physics of fluids since water is the first element known by the human being and unites with the ink of the writers to express the blood, the milk, and the tears of women, to speak for the "[m]ère libérienne et textuelle empoisonnée de sève écrite à l'encre rouge à l'eau de roses à l'eau de vaisselle ou lacrymale et même à l'eau d'érable . . . mais omise sur le papier."[87]

This multiple, fluid, female universe subverts lapidary, phallic monolithism, since Louky Bersianik constantly associates man with stone ("You are the rock and on this rock I shall build my Church"), from the "Le Caillou de Barbarie" of *L'Euguélionne*[88] to Ortygie and the Caryatids, all works of men. In addition, the shiftings of the text make Louky Bersianik's writing modernist in that it bursts the phallic scriptural universe (the order of discourse), petrified in its vertical erection. Furthermore, the names of the narrators who encompass Louky Bersianik and the women of the world have little importance: "In women's speech, there is no subject which posits an object ahead of it (uttering/utterance). . . . There is a sort of continuous coming and going from the other's body to her own. It is not linked with any gender."[89] The texts circulate from multiple "I" to multiple "you," from one body to another, from one word to another, from one mode of discourse to another (pastiche, poem, pamphlet, theater, documents, a musical score, accounts, reflections of philosophers and cooks, a telephone conversation), from one language level to another (popular Quebec French, the intellectual language of psychoanalytic, linguistic, or mythological treatises, poetic esoterism), as does all feminist writing (or modernist writing).

Feminist writing also rejects the opposition of theory versus fiction, truth versus art because "it is a hierarchical opposition of absolutely decisive importance in the institution of metaphysics,"[90] every attempt at an ordering signifying phallic power. What counts is communicating and touching, an essential desire of Louky Bersianik who explores all possible forms of graphic and typographic communication: photographs, etchings, advertising posters, white, grey, and black pages, dedications, quotations, window frames, capital letters which affix power, italics and handwriting, spaces, notes, and bibliographies.

Finally, Bersianik makes the very tool of communication—language itself—burst, radiate outward. Language is "a symbolic system involved in social relations. It cannot be neutral. It is a cultural mirror."[91] It is evident that French, the language of genders, "sustains collective unconscious representations,"[92] submitting the feminine to the masculine. Originally in the Indo-European language, the sun's gender was feminine. It became masculine when God the Father replaced the Mother-Goddess.[93] In her characteristic manner, therefore, Louky Bersianik will denounce/renounce the language of dictionaries, a language polluted by the phallic language/ideology and filled with grammatical and semantic dissymmetry, in order to complete and enrich the language, to make of it a re-creation/recreation so that it can speak of woman and her enjoyment without mutilating her. In *L'Euguélionne*, the women thus demonstrate against the Academy, brandishing signs which demand "[l]a révision des règles de syntaxe et une étude approfondie de la sémantique et de l'usage courant de la langue, basée sur la discrimination sexuelle, selon laquelle l'animal, l'objet inanimé, l'emportent sur la femme dans les accords."[94]

Bersianik clearly denounces "the great misunderstanding" (practiced even by surrealists and the left) which confuses gender with species ("man" is also "human being") and which leads to shifts of meaning that hide woman. Xanthippe acts and reforms the dictionary by creating, in place of the word, "man" ("homme"), the words, "anthropos, andre et vir."[95] She pillories the sexism of dictionaries which perpetuates "la langue du mépris" in their references, examples, and definitions (effeminate = of woman, weak, and without energy). L'Euguélionne exhorts women not to ask but to act, to make "des fautes volontairement pour rétablir l'équilibre des sexes."[96] In Chapter ix, she constitutes a long diatribe against French in which "[l]e féminin ne figure que comme une redondance du masculin. A ce genre noble, l'e muet n'est qu'un ajout modeste."[97] She repairs the semantic dissymmetries, like *garçon/garce* (boy/bitch) and *cuisinier/cuisinière* (professional cook/cook-housewife),[98] by offering lists of occupational titles in the feminine form where only the masculine form exists. To do this, she uses Jacqueline Picoche's etymological dictionary, which she recommends to her readers/listeners. In this re-creative/recreative process she traverses the strata of linguistic discrimination, stating that "[l]es dictionnaires étymologiques m'en ont plus appris sur la différence entre les sexes et la discrimination qui en a résulté, que tous vos manuels de psychologie et de psychanalyse."[99] So that women may return to the source, to the word-mother, she teaches us that originally *motus* meant both word and silence, and that modesty (*pudeur*) means shame, but also that penis (*verge*) and comma (*virgule*) share the same etymology.[100]

The "grammatical silencing technique" which Mary Daly, Marina Yaguello, and numerous feminist linguists also denounce either projects an image of woman as receiver/object/adjective/metaphor, as an object of scorn, or it projects nothing.[101] Louky Bersianik likewise attacks the presuppositions and aphorisms (fixed petrified language) which perpetuate this image, as well as the double standard by which "si une femme a du génie, on dit qu'elle est folle. Si un homme est fou, on dit qu'il a du génie."[102] She returns to woman her "gynergy" by rectifying these false mental representations (woman as passivity, lack), by reminding women that the monthly course of the ovum is longer than that of the sperm (agitation is not movement), that immobility can also be active and creative (the sun), and that holes have a vital function of communication. While denouncing "la langue du mépris" and subverting its sacred texts, she gives back language's creative power by introducing new significations, by creating neologisms and humorous wordplay ("l'Emasculée Conception," "la josephté," "Déesses merci," "la gynilité,"[103] "le Famour,"[104] "clitorivage").[105] She returns words back to their infancy, as testify the childlike wordplay (ditties, phonic games)[106] and the numerous plays on words scattered throughout her texts ("lapidaire/lapidé";[107] "enfermement/le fer me ment";[108] "d'ores et de jeu"; "Lacan, roi des calembourgeois").[109]

Above all, Louky Bersianik's writing, like that of other radical feminists, discovers/unveils the body of woman and her speech, long contorted by texts and textiles. This veil/metaphorization/distanciation, in fact, hid the desire for the mother, since "it is the prohibition of incest—Derrida has stressed it enough—which necessitates the opening up of replacement, of metaphoricity, and of the whole chain of language substitutes."[110] Herein lies the fundamental significance of this return to origins, to all mothers. But this return is a trap in that it is necessarily accomplished by means of the existing language (and therefore by means of the existing system), a paradox which Michel Foucault, Shoshana Felman, and Jacques Derrida have not failed to note, since "is not archeology, be it the archeology of silence, a logic, that is structured language, an order?"[111]

The desire to communicate, to dialogue, drives Louky Bersianik—and other feminist authors—therefore, to a paradox: the more she speaks the phallic language, the better understood she makes herself (L'Euguélionne); the more she speaks in the female (fluidity, polysemy, etymologies, babble), that is, the more she subverts the normative code (especially in Maternative), the more restricted becomes the group to whom she addresses herself and who understands her. Nevertheless, Louky Bersianik seems to be aware of this danger, to the extent that she always gives her references, explains myths and esoteric terms, and thus creates, at the same time, a code and its key. She remains confident in the intelligence of the woman to whom she is returning her text, her body, and her mind.

NOTES

1. Mary Daly, *Gyn/ecology* (New York: Beacon Press, 1976), pp. 9, 33, 316. See Françoise d'Eaubonne, *Le Féminisme ou la mort*, Collection Femmes en Mouvement (Paris: Les Editions Pierre Horay, 1974).

2. Marina Yaguello, *Les Mots et les femmes* (Paris: Payot, 1978), Chapter iv. We prefer "dialogism" over "intertextuality" because it encompasses all forms of dialogues in the text and because of its oral connotation. Dialogism is a Bakhtinian concept. See Tzvetan Todorov, *Mikhail Bakhtine: Le Principe dialogique*; *Ecrits du cercle de Bakhtine* (Paris: Editions du Seuil, 1981), p. 8.

3. Oswald Ducrot et Tzvetan Todorov, *Dictionnaire encyclopédique des sciences du langage*, Collection Points (Paris: Editions du Seuil, n.d.), p. 328.

4. Elaine Showalter, "Towards a Feminist Poetics," in *Women Writing and Writing about Women*, ed. Mary Jacobus (New York: Barnes and Noble Books, 1979), p. 35.

5. Louky Bersianik, *L'Euguélionne* (Montréal: La Presse, 1976), p. 18.

She sings, dances, and whirls, her face and shape everchanging.

6. Bersianik, p. 55.

Neither a virgin nor a whore.

"Ni vierge ni putain" is an expression borrowed from a song written and sung by Pauline Julien in her feminist record, *Femmes de paroles*.

7. Bersianik, p. 54.

Because it is she who will announce the good news about the end of a certain slavery perpetrated on this Earth.

8. Bersianik, p. 84.

Leave your dustcloth here and follow me.

9. Bersianik, p. 20.

She sees everything as if it were transparent.

10. Bersianik, p. 53.

The bearer of a divine ovum which will be fecundated in spite of him.
I am the servant of the Highness Wondjina, may Her Holy Will be done....
The natural father of the Euguelionne remained a virgin.

11. Bersianik, p. 14.

At this time of our Prehistory.

12. Bersianik, p. 45.

In the beginning on my planet was the Male.

13. Louky Bersianik, *Maternative: Les Pré-Ancyl*, Acides de Jean Letarte (Montréal: VLB Editeur, 1980), p. 11.

In the beginning was the Flesh. And the Flesh became the Word.

14. Bersianik, *Maternative*, p. 77.

Ask and you will not receive.

15. Bersianik, *L'Euguélionne*, p. 263.

Pretend and you will be.

16. Bersianik, *L'Euguélionne*, p. 383.

I believe in Myself.... I believe in Others.... I believe that there is nobody above Me and nobody below Me.... I believe in my whole body.

17. Bersianik, *L'Euguélionne*, p. 397.

In the name of the welcoming Hole, and the penetrating Hole and the evacuating Hole, Amen.

18. Daly, p. 79.

19. Bersianik, *L'Euguélionne*, p. 84. This is a pun on the name of Jacques Lacan. "L' Obélisque" (pp. 214–16) and "Le Sermon sur la montagne" (pp. 218–20) are the two chapters devoted to Freud's theory.

20. Bersianik, *L'Euguélionne*, p. 218.

Blessed are the individuals born with a phallus.

21. Bersianik, *L'Euguélionne*, p. 221.

Engraved on two monuments of stone which were set in the ground and were standing vertically in the sky on the mountain ridge.

22. Bersianik, *L'Euguélionne*, p. 333.

The Dupes' complex.

This is a pun on the Oedipus complex, *le complexe d'Oedipe*.

23. Bersianik, *Le Pique-nique sur l'Acropole* (Montréal: VLB Editeur, 1979), p. 171. These are puns on the Olympic Games and Ivan the Terrible.

24. Bersianik, *L'Euguélionne*, p. 332.

Every single woman on this earth should be aware of the psychoanalytical discourse on herself.

See also Daly, p. 174; Luce Irigaray, *Le Corps-à-corps avec la mère*, entrevue, 28 mai 1980 (Montréal: Les Editions de la Pleine Lune, 1981), p. 43.

25. Bersianik, *L'Euguélionne*, p. 213.

Outside of the Phallus there is no salvation.... The individual born without a phallus is handicapped.... He/she will have to build a life around a gap.

"Lit-bidon" literally means "bed-cheat."

26. Bersianik, *L'Euguélionne*, p. 214.

The latter one ... being ontologically Shakespearian (TO BE OR NOT TO BE THE PHALLUS), very possibly an amateur of light comedy (TO HAVE OR NOT) ... taking into consideration the basic dialectics of every contradiction which is inherent to the time-space-humano-masculonoid condition.

27. Bersianik, *L'Euguélionne*, pp. 217, 42–43.

Penis-envy—my ass.
This is impossible! This is the world upside-down! My father-mother is a cripple! First of all, he has no breasts. And then, I think he is losing his vulva and all the rest.

28. Yaguello, p. 149.

29. Irigaray, pp. 16, 24.

30. Bersianik, *Le Pique-nique sur l'Acropole*, p. 48.

Here is what was first engraved on each unconscious born of a womb, the motherly Body, the only memorable one and the fundamental signifier.

31. Bersianik, *Le Pique-nique sur l'Acropole*, pp. 90, 100, 101.

Father! Father!

32. Bersianik, *Le Pique-nique sur l'Acropole*, p. 101.

These six women. These six hundred women. These six thousand women. These six hundred thousand women. These six million women.

33. Bersianik, *Le Pique-nique sur l'Acropole*, p. 101.

Does Aga love me! No!

This is a pun on the name, "Agamemnon."

34. Bersianik, *Le Pique-nique sur l'Acropole*, p. 146.

35. Bersianik, *Maternative*, p. 129.

Ortygia is the former name of Delos, the smallest island of the Cyclades. According to the legend, Zeus fell in love with Asteria who in order to avoid him, transformed herself into a quail.... Then Zeus transformed himself into an eagle.... In her despair, Asteria metamorphosed herself into a stone which fell in the sea, thus creating the island of Ortygia.

36. Bersianik, *Maternative*, p. 98.

I am searching for you like an unconsolable Mother-Demeter.

37. Daly, p. 40.

38. Bersianik, *Le Pique-nique sur l'Acropole*, p. 102.

It is his death mask which continues to rule, to impose its loveless law. Law of the murder of daughters, of women, of mothers. And law of the murder of sons at war.

39. Bersianik, *Maternative*, pp. 116-17.

Some of them I know have started to be women in front of their daughters.
Go and burn your forefathers' hut.

40. Bersianik, *Maternative*, p. 157.

Ortygia the inconspicuous.
I give you the words of my tongue to drink.... I am the space from which you originated and your fundamental mark. And your Great Goddess' inconspicuous rebirth. You, womb of my womb, you, my living one.

41. Bersianik, *Le Pique-nique sur l'Acropole*, p. 227.

Falls asleep in the arms of the Caryatid to whom she has given birth.

42. Bersianik, *Le Pique-nique sur l'Acropole*, p. 225.

Get down from the Erechteion. Get down from this petrified erection.

See also Luce Irigaray, *Ce sexe qui n'en est pas un* (Paris: Les Editions de Minuit, 1977), p. 106.

43. Daly, p. 39.

44. Bersianik, *L'Euguélionne*, p. 26.

This carnage which starts once one is out of the womb.

45. Bersianik, *Le Pique-nique sur l'Acropole*, p. 70.

Timbals of quails in an Asteria gravy.
A mare in Demeter sauce.

46. D'Eaubonne, p. 252.

47. Gloria Orenstein, "The Goddess as Symbol: A Gynocentric Vision in Modern Women's Literature," unpublished manuscript, pp. 2, 4.

48. Bersianik, *Le Pique-nique sur l'Acropole*, p. 190.

We have started to become aware that during the past thirty centuries, we have given back to Ceasar what belonged to Cleopatra and to God what was owed to the Great Goddess.

49. Bersianik, *Maternative*, p. 94.

Oh! Mom! You are a true sister! Mine!

50. Irigaray, *Speculum de l'autre femme*, Collection Critique (Paris: Les Editions de Minuit, 1974).

51. Bersianik, *Le Pique-nique sur l'Acropole*, p. 16.

To write is a corporeal expression.

52. Bersianik, *Le Pique-nique sur l'Acropole*, p. 10.

This small historical supper.

53. Bersianik, *Le Pique-nique sur l'Acropole*, p. 181.

I am a sexual being, sensitive to the other sexual beings who surround me.

54. Bersianik, *Le Pique-nique sur l'Acropole*, p. 111.

Eros of the popular Aphrodite . . . is the love known to vulgar men. . . . The love of this kind of people is directed first to women as well as to boys, to the bodies of the beloved ones rather than to their souls; finally it addresses itself to the most foolish ones they could meet, because pleasure is their only purpose. The other one on the contrary, the celestial Aphrodite, emanates only from the male sex and excludes the female. Consequently the ones inspired by the celestial Aphrodite turn their fondness toward the male sex, which is inherently stronger and more intelligent.

55. Shoshana Felman, *La Folie et la chose littéraire* (Paris: Editions du Seuil, 1978), p. 140.

56. Bersianik, *L'Euguélionne*, p. 240 (surrealism), p. 41 (Sartre's philosophy), p. 164 (nationalism), p. 241 (Marxism), p. 266 (capitalism), p. 337 (racism). See also Claudine Herrmann, *Les Voleuses de langue* (Paris: Editions des Femmes, 1976), p. 16.

57. Bersianik, *L'Euguélionne*, p. 385.

Transgress my words and the words of all who speak to you with authority.

58. Bersianik, *Le Pique-nique sur l'Acropole*, p. 75.

We, women, are treated like fictitious beings in history, this "holy" and barbarous history which the men from before have scientifically concocted for their own utmost glory and interest. Undesirable, pushed aside in the margin of time and space (except in fiction), we are unreal, anachronistic and extra-territorial. We are the extra-terrestrials on our own planet. What remains to be done is to land on earth.

59. Daly, p. 39.

60. Bersianik, *Le Pique-nique sur l'Acropole*, p. 164.

Genocide, perpetrated today in the four corners of the earth.

61. Suzanne Lamy, *D'elles* (Montréal: L'Hexagone, 1979), p. 56.

The mouth of a river where multiple, often tumultuous waters meet.

62. Mary Jacobus, "The Difference of View," in *Women Writing and Writing about Women*, p. 12.

63. Yaguello, p. 24.

64. Lamy, p. 64.

65. Bersianik, *Maternative*, p. 14.

Importance has to be given back to this very skin which has been pinned, pierced, crucified, palpated by all.

Not a word on her tongue, but only signs in her body.

See also Madeleine Ouellette-Michalska, "Rituels d'appropriation scripturale: Le Découpage des signes," in *L'Echappée du discours de l'oeil* (Montréal: Nouvelle Optique, 1981), pp. 125–52.

66. Bersianik, *Le Pique-nique sur l'Acropole*, p. 29.

The mouth and the nose are most important openings in every body which talks day and night.

67. Bersianik, *Le Pique-nique sur l'Acropole*, p. 26.

Air vents need to be opened in one's text....

68. Bersianik, *Le Pique-nique sur l'Acropole*, p. 15.

All of them touching for not being touched. All singing. And all knowing how to touch.

69. Bersianik, *Le Pique-nique sur l'Acropole*, p. 46.

Which stick to our skin. They are the proper senses. The senses of body to body contact ... but to touch first.

70. Bersianik, *Maternative*, p. 22.

Shapes are being distorted and created around the fan-shaped fingers. Touch me in all directions and in all senses.

71. Bersianik, *L'Euguélionne*, p. 19.

She was walking on the water, naked and dark ... opening estuaries, widening coasts.... The span of her stride was an extension of her moving sex.

72. Bersianik, *L'Euguélionne*, p. 36.

Was shaped like a uterine archipelago, with its convolutions and "invaginations."

73. Bersianik, *L'Euguélionne*, p. 385.

Also be wheels of pleasure dashing on the highway.

See also Maroussia Ahmed, "Transgresser, c'est progresser," *Incidences*, 4, Nos. 2-3 (mai-décembre 1980), pp. 119-27.

74. Bersianik, *Maternative*, p. 12.

And the law is the law, because I am the law.... The rest is Wordless History.

This is the same as "Wordless Cartoon" in French.

75. Bersianik, *L'Euguélionne*, p. 18.

Her voice spreads like peals of laughter.

76. Bersianik, *Maternative*, p. 25.

I intend to talk to you, invisible orange created by the poet.

77. Bersianik, *Maternative*, p. 97.

We can hear their voices, but we cannot see them.

78. Jacques Derrida, *La Dissémination* (Paris: Editions du Seuil, 1972), p. 131.
79. Bersianik, *Maternative*, p. 14.

But the Penis-Verbum built an opaque wall between himself and tact.

80. Bersianik, *Maternative*, p. 12.

The Penis-Verbum does not hyphenate but it distanciates.

81. Bersianik, *Maternative*, p. 21.

Yesterday ... to unbind ... to bind ... places ... to gather.

82. Lamy, p. 64.
83. Bersianik, *Maternative*, p. 89.

Cock-cock-cock ... cock-a-doodle-do ... Atla atla atla the Quebecers are there. Ah! Ah! Ah!

84. Jacobus, p. 12.
85. Irigaray, *Ce sexe qui n'en est pas un*, p. 110.
86. Bersianik, *Maternative*, p. 152.

I give you the words of my tongue to drink.

87. Bersianik, *Maternative*, p. 35.

Liberian and textual mother poisoned with sap written in red ink in rose water in dishwater or in teardrops and even in maplesap . . . but omitted on paper.

88. Bersianik, *L'Euguélionne*, p. 47.
89. Irigaray, *Le Corps-à-corps avec la mère*, p. 49.
90. Irigaray, *Le Corps-à-corps avec la mère*, p. 45.
91. Yaguello, p. 7. This also represents a Bakhtinian concept of language.
92. Yaguello, p. 106.
93. Yaguello, p. 106.
94. Bersianik, *L'Euguélionne*, p. 226.

The revision of syntactical rules and an indepth study of semantics and of the everyday use of language, based on sexual discrimination according to which, in the agreements, the animal and the inanimate object prevail upon the female.

95. Bersianik, *Le Pique-nique sur l'Acropole*, p. 44. See also Bersianik, *L'Euguélionne*, p. 242.
96. Bersianik, *L'Euguélionne*, p. 230.

Mistakes on purpose in order to reestablish the balance between sexes.

97. Bersianik, *L'Euguélionne*, p. 235.

The feminine appears only as the superfluity of the masculine. The silent ''e'' is nothing but a modest addition to this noble gender.

98. Bersianik, *L'Euguélionne*, pp. 227–34.
99. Bersianik, *L'Euguélionne*, p. 230.

Etymological dictionaries have taught me more about the difference between the sexes and about the discrimination that has resulted from it than all your psychological and psychoanalytical manuals.

100. Bersianik, *Le Pique-nique sur l'Acropole*, p. 177.
101. Daly, p. 16.
102. Bersianik, *L'Euguélionne*, p. 252.

If a woman has genius, she is called mad. If a man is mad, he is called a genius.

103. Bersianik, *L'Euguélionne*, pp. 53, 54, 373, 381.

The Emasculate Conception.
Josephty.
Thank Goddesses.
Gynility.

104. Bersianik, *Le Pique-nique sur l'Acropole*, p. 180. This is a pun on the the words, ''femmes'' (women) and ''amour'' (love).
105. Bersianik, *Maternative*, p. 59. This is a wordplay on ''clitoris'' and ''rivage'' (shore).
106. Bersianik, *L'Euguélionne*, pp. 126-32.
107. Bersianik, *L'Euguélionne*, p. 225.

Lapidaries/lapidated.

108. Bersianik, *Maternative*, p. 79.

Confinement/the fire is lying to me.

109. Bersianik, *Le Pique-nique sur l'Acropole*, p. 79.

From now and a game.
Lacan, king of the bourgeois puns.

These plays on words are to be found in all three books, but there are more puns in *L'Euguélionne* and *Le Pique-nique sur l'Acropole*, which imply the existence of a "referent" and of a greater intertextuality.

110. Sarah Kofman, *Le Respect des femmes*, Collection Débats (Paris: Editions Galilée, 1982), p. 100.

111. Jacques Derrida, "Cogito et histoire de la folie," in *L'Ecriture et la différence* (Paris: Editions du Seuil, 1967), pp. 57-58. See also Michel Foucault, *L'Ordre du discours* (Paris: Gallimard, 1971); Felman, p. 155.

16

The Development of a Lesbian Sensibility in the Work of Jovette Marchessault and Nicole Brossard

Marthe Rosenfeld ———————————————————

Until the rise of the women's liberation movement, lesbianism as a theme had no real existence in the history of literature. From the age of Sappho in the sixth century B.C. to the beginnings of a lesbian culture in the Paris of the early twentieth century, a silence of two thousand five hundred years bears witness to the long war which the patriarchy waged against lesbianism. In Quebec the literary expression of lesbian love would be censored for an even longer period of time due to the misogyny of the Catholic Church and the sexism of the State. In this essay, I shall try to answer the following questions: Does a relationship exist between lesbianism as a way of life and as a form of writing? What audiences are the lesbian books of Jovette Marchessault and Nicole Brossard addressing? Are the experimentations of Brossard and Marchessault affecting the contemporary literature of Quebec?

Jovette Marchessault is a self-taught person. Born in Montreal in 1938, she is of mixed ancestry, having both French and Indian forbears. Although she describes her early childhood as a time of joy and growth, she experienced despair at the age of five after her impoverished family had moved from the country to the slums of Montreal. She left school as an adolescent, worked for many years in factories, and continued to learn at night by borrowing books from the public library. Having come of age during the dark and bigoted Duplessis era, Jovette Marchessault felt isolated as a lesbian. Indeed her main reason for wishing to become a writer was to break the silence. But years would pass before she would finally overcome the self-censorship which society imposes on its outcasts.[1]

Since Jovette Marchessault came out as a lesbian only in 1979, she could not openly express her chosen way of life in the early seventies when she first wrote *Comme une enfant de la terre*. This book, however, clearly foreshadows the themes and sensibility which will ripen and bloom in her later works. Even at this early stage of the author's career, the lesbian spirit shines through the heroine's total identification with other amazons of Quebec.

Having eschewed woman's traditional roles of marriage and motherhood, Jovette Marchessault sought to express her feelings and her goals. She wanted, above all, to expand her horizons through readings and travel. With Francine, an old friend, the female protagonist of this work leaves her home in April on a sumptuous journey through North America. But the object of the voyage is neither sightseeing nor pleasure; rather, it is an amazon's quest for the promised land in which women can live in harmony with each other and with their natural surroundings. Similarly, during her nonstop journey from Quebec to Mexico, the young female warrior discovers new relationships between words and culture, between language and her amazonian identity. To Francine, her traveling companion, she expresses her faith in the power of words: "Les mots," she tells her, "m'apparaissent comme des escaliers en spirale qui aboutissent à une porte. Qui s'ouvre!"[2] Jovette Marchessault would continue to write five more years before discovering those particular words that communicate the spirit of a lesbian culture.

Between 1976 and 1977, while the author was writing *La Mère des herbes*, her most explicitly autobiographical novel, she brought out some of the factors which prompted her to become a lesbian and a feminist. Having grown up in a predominantly female setting, the protagonist felt drawn at an early age to the women and girls who inhabited the world of her youth. She loved the Pépin sisters and the happiness which the latter built after the death of their tyrannical father. She also admired the schoolgirls who worked collectively during the summer to write a play. Unlike the prosaic males in charge of the scenery, the young girls used their imagination to express in beautiful language their feminist vision of the past. The protagonist's feelings of love toward women go back, however, to the close relationships which existed between grandmother and grandchild, between mother and daughter. Both women helped one another to raise the child in a warm and caring atmosphere; both of them spoke to her about their work in the store or the factory. It was the grandmother's system of values, however, her empathy with the living creatures of nature, and her rebellion against all forms of oppression, which later would give the protagonist/Marchessault the insight as well as the courage to fight against the patriarchy. With its marvelous descriptions of the mother spirit in plant, beast, and grotto, *La Mère des herbes* may be interpreted as a mythopoetical evocation of the ancestral goddess culture. Indeed, the beautiful images which illuminate this autobiographical novel bring out the closeness of the protagonist/Marchessault to her natural environment as well as her gynocentric vision of the world:

En visite dans la terre, sous la terre, nous sommes une somme inouïe de possibles, tout est possible à l'embryon qui descend dans la mine pour se mettre au monde dans son rayon d'élection, s'installer dans le ventre de sa mère retrouvée et s'en extraire ainsi qu'une pépite d'or après un temps raisonnable de mûrissement, d'incubation.[3]

Written two years after *La Mère des herbes*, *Tryptique lesbien* is Jovette Marchessault's most openly lesbian text.[4] Through the use of myth and allegory, this book illustrates the long history of patriarchal violence against women. Indeed, a major theme of the first panel of the work, "Chronique lesbienne du moyen-âge québécois," is the lesbian heroine's journey from the dark ages of religious bigotry to the bright and joyous realm of a woman-centered culture. Appearing now as a real person, now as a legendary character, the child protagonist of this section is both a prophet who foretells the coming of a new feminist era and a fighter against the heterosexual ideology of male supremacy. Thus, Jovette Marchessault shows the immense grief which the female protagonist experiences as an adolescent when her beloved cousin leaves her for the sake of a man.

"Les Vaches de nuit" begins appropriately with the radical critique of a culture that robs women of their sexuality and freedom. But the mythical mother cow and her daughter remember a pre-patriarchal world, and this remembrance stimulates them to travel at night far from the daily drudgery. As mother and daughter leave the old kitchen behind, they begin to experience long-forgotten feelings of closeness towards one another. Having joined their sister mammals in a region of jubilation and desire, the mother is now able to initiate her daughter to the mysteries of lesbian love in a way that would have been taboo under the patriarchy.

Similarly "Les Faiseuses d'anges," the last panel of *Tryptique lesbien*, portrays a mother who is both a midwife and a goddess. Indeed the abortionist appears as a revolutionary figure, one who defies the norms of the heterosexist culture, and as a healer who helps her sisters to break the cycle of the ever increasing family, the endless toil, the self-sacrifice. Mother and daughter give birth metaphorically, to their new identities as women making conscious choices for personal freedom and for the quality of life on this planet.

By using analogies, myths, and symbols from a feminist perspective, Jovette Marchessault here tries, as in her earlier texts, to show the courage, the capacity for love, the solidarity of women. But the writer's growing militancy has given her an immediate awareness of the difficulties of expressing herself in a language molded predominantly by men. Writing now as a lesbian, Jovette Marchessault can proudly ignore the sexist rule which has legislated the priority of the masculine over the feminine in French grammar. The pronouns, "ils" and "elles," for example, refer in this text either to men only or to female creatures exclusively. Instead of being complementary to masculine third persons, absorbed in the dominant language, feminine third persons are, in addition, strongly present in *Tryptique lesbien*. Other ways of interfering with the rules of the inherited language include such techniques as the fracturing of the autobiographical "I" which in turn represents a variety of female types (the independent girl-child, the rebellious adolescent, the prostitute, the separatist) and the periodic repetition of the "nous" form to emphasize, for example, the author's identification with the other lesbians who resisted the indoctrination of a hateful Catholic upbringing:

En ce temps-là du moyen-âge québécois, toutes les petites lesbiennes tiraient la langue et bavaient sur le plancher ou sur les images du petit catéchisme. Dès la fête des rois mages, ils avaient décidé de nous faire subir un entraînement intensif. Nous étions les fétiches de l'année, têtes de cochon, anneau d'or dans le groin, les monstres! Du planifié! Du prémédité! Du déchaîné! Jusqu'à l'épuisement complet de cette résistance qui n'en finissait pas de résister.[5]

But Jovette Marchessault's rebellion against the patriarchal language transcends issues of grammar and stylistics. In order to express her rage against a culture which has severed women from their bodies, from the memory of their foremothers, from themselves, Marchessault had to unmask the taboos and the apparent logic of the dominant language as hypocritical veneers which hide the confusion and the pain of the oppressed. Ignoring the double standard of taste which has influenced literary critics to scoff at women writers for using words that would be accepted in texts written by men, Marchessault attaches strong particles such as "Super mâle" and "sperme" to the most exalted religious figures. The following passage is one example of a blasphemous description of the sacred and sadistic ceremonies of Christianity which rape the mind and spirit of the young lesbians: "A genoux les petites filles! C'est l'heure exquise de la fellation divine. A genoux! Ouvrez la bouche! Grande! Plus grande encore! Recevez la giclée de sperme du grand mâle eucharistique."[6]

To subvert the traditional bourgeois language of its facade of rationality, the author also experiments with the sound of words, the analogous formation of idioms, the emergence of the absurd. In fact, the power of the phonetic language to shape new perceptions is illustrated at the beginning of *Tryptique lesbien* when the young lesbian's discovery of the choke of a car produces a linguistic illumination. The words, "choke" and "chum," become so closely associated in her mind that a new truth dawns on her: the boyfriend is a strangler; heterosexual relationships are a trap. Similarly, the author's play on the sound and rhythm of idioms succeeds in communicating feelings of anger which might never surface in a purely rational discourse. The following passage describes men harassing young girls at the end of the school day: "Ils montent à l'assaut, les mâles, l'air hagard, leurs dents en tremblent, la salive dans la poussière de la genèse, à l'assaut, à la pinçade, à la rigolade, à la renverse."[7] Even more powerful than these word games are the passages in *Tryptique lesbien* which seem to arise from the subconscious. For example, when the lesbian is first confronted with the oppression of the working-class women of Quebec as prisoners in their own homes, as mothers of numerous children, as unwitting agents of the patriarchy, she cries out: "Cannibales, arrêtez le bal!"[8] Strange and dreamlike, this seemingly absurd little sentence expresses the chaos and the intensity of feelings as they are actually experienced.

In order to communicate women's true perceptions of reality, Marchessault felt the need to go even further: to reexamine the words, the very terms which shape our thinking and which mirror the prevailing attitudes of the class in power. Thus, while the word "fête" means public rejoicing to the dominant culture, the same term conveys notions of pain and sacrifice to the lesbian protagonist: "[Q]uand ils disaient: 'Fête,' moi j'entendais autre chose! J'entendais l'hiver du sang sur la Terre des hommes."[9] These semantic differences account for the author's desire to create other expressions and to give new meanings to a vocabulary which is incapable of expressing the feelings of minorities. In *Tryptique lesbien*, for instance, the words "rue" and "trottoir" come to mean the territories or gender roles in which the patriarchal culture imprisons both women and men.[10] Likewise, the word "relique," which evoked the remains of a saint, now symbolizes the suffering and the appropriation of female bodies under patriarchal law.[11] Other recurring expressions in *Tryptique*, such as "la Terre du sacrifice permanent," "le troupeau des ténèbres," and "l'ordre-des-castrants," are suggestive of women's bondage in the world of the fathers.[12]

These syntactic and lexical experimentations would not have changed the medium of expression sufficiently, however, to transport us into a female space had not Jovette Marchessault also rejected the lifeless and univocal discourse of the mainstream. The deep feelings which she brings to her text are not watered down by the necessities of an antiquated narrative form. On the contrary, thoughts and emotions succeed one another so swiftly that the words, liberated from the restrictions of pause and period, go beyond the traditional sentence with its main and subordinate clauses, its finished character, its closed appearance. In the following passage, heart-gripping regrets over the lost childhood of the young lesbians produce the uninterrupted flow of a new language:

Je vous dis qu'ils nous ont volé notre temps quotidien.
Notre précieux temps de tous les jours pour jouer dehors, dedans, dans la verdure de la tendresse mutuelle. Notre temps à nous autres, temps de feu, de passion dans le velours rouge des bercements d'extase, des embrassements du corps.[13]

Boundless and flowing, this new language is like a large river. The energy that emanates from this text helps to break down the old order, to challenge the powers that be. As a matter of fact, these passages with their rhythmical patterns, their pulse, their movement suggest, better than any specific ideas, the world of female creatures, the Utopia in which mother and daughter, memory and insight, struggle and sisterhood are brought together:

Le lait coule! Le lait gicle! Le lait coule à flot! Beauté, beauté, bonté blanche. Le lait neige! Le lait goutte, le lait odore! Le lait poudre! Le lait rafale! Le lait ouragane! Le lait nuage, le lait est maculé d'images![14]

The exuberant language of "Les Vaches de nuit" has become a paradigm for the liberation of all women.[15]

While Jovette Marchessault began to write in her thirties, and while she struggled for a long time to develop a style that would convey her lesbian/feminist vision of the world, Nicole Brossard revealed a passion for the modernistic expression of thought from the very outset of her literary career in the 1960s. By the mid-1970s, however, her personal life began to change dramatically. She read, in rapid succession, Simone de Beauvoir, Kate Millett, and Ti-Grace Atkinson, gave birth to a daughter, and fell in love with another woman.[16] Although Brossard had always shared Quebec's aspirations for sovereignty and independence, her feminist consciousness and her quest for a non-patriarchal language also led her, during this same period of time, to turn away from the phallocentric vocabulary of the nationalist writers.[17] In 1976, as a co-founder of *Les Têtes de Pioche*, she became politically active, penning incisive articles, many of which unmasked the oppressiveness of the heterosexual ideology. In *L'Amèr* (1977), *Le Sens apparent* (1980), and *Amantes* (1980), she takes the reader on a long journey from the hell of patriarchal censorship to the glorious vision of a lesbian Utopia.

Brossard's ability to reconcile her lesbian/feminist perceptiveness with her original interest in new writing accounts for the depth of feeling which emanates from a book such as *L'Amèr*. This work deals with both the theory of writing and a woman's daily experience of her fragmentation as the lesbian mother of a young child. The narrator's anger over the erasure of the female self enables her to reveal the frightful conflict between her yearning for autonomy and her painful awakening to the endless responsibilities of motherhood. *L'Amèr* begins, appropriately, with words of defiance: "C'est le combat."[18] The woman's struggle to free herself from this millennial bondage is a violent one. Although she loves her daughter, she totally rejects society's image of the mother as a paragon of virtue, a selfless drudge, a breeder and nurturer of children. While woman has been preoccupied with the survival of the young, man has appropriated to himself the symbolic order, the indispensable tool of language—hence his ideological control over the silent one, the stranger, the other. To take this language back, woman must challenge all of society, including its principal means of perpetuating itself: discourse. This questioning of the traditional language looms as a vital interrogation, a challenge which deals with the root causes of female oppression.

In *L'Amèr*, Brossard brings to light the arbitrariness of French grammar, and she shows in what way it has limited woman's self-expression. For example, the narrator, in the park with her young daughter, is unable to speak with the other mothers, the patriarchal mothers, devoted to men. Not only opposite attitudes towards life, but also language hampers communication: "Tout gravite autour d'une grammaire insensée."[19] The narrator of *L'Amèr* condemns this senseless grammar as a symbolic system which has institutionalized the subordination of feminine persons to masculine persons. While Jovette Marchessault circumvented this grammatical sexism by refusing to describe mixed groups in *Tryptique lesbien*, Brossard takes the issue a step further, for she recommends a genderless tongue. Speaking to a woman friend, the narrator of *L'Amèr* thus expresses her wish: "[M]ais je te veux immense et chaude du corps saches nos énergies autrement que dans ton ventre mais des yeux. Asexu( ) ou peut-être invariable."[20] The ending of the adjective has disappeared, just as gender will disappear in a society of equals.

Rebelling against the traditional idea of woman's subordination to the species and yearning to assert her own individuality, the narrator of *L'Amèr* writes: "J'ai tué le ventre et fait éclater la mer."[21] But like Marchessault, Brossard comes up against the limitations of a vocabulary which has been contaminated by centuries of patriarchal rule. As an enthusiastic proponent of modernism, however, Brossard is the more innovative writer. Not only does she play with the meaning and the sound of words as Marchessault has done in *Tryptique lesbien*, she experiments also in *L'Amèr* with syntax and orthography. This method of interfering with the traditional language appears, for instance, in the changing physiognomy of the word "mère," a term full of ambiguities. Having acquired an *A*, the A of Alpha, the beginning of all things, and having lost its powerless, mute *e*, *L'Amèr* symbolizes a woman whose creativity and assertiveness enable her to assume her identity as "fille-mère-lesbienne," the desirable mother, the autonomous person whose energy circulates among women. When written in two words, *L'A Mèr* connotes a radical questioning of female reproduction, the absence of the mother. Spelled with a final *e*, *l'Amère* acquires the bitterness of female dependency, while yet in another context *la mer* signifies the sea, powerful and uncontrollable, the very antithesis of domesticated motherhood. A text which reduces the gap between fiction, theory, and reality, this book marks the end of an old order and promises a new beginning.[22] It announces the coming of another world, of a non-patriarchal space in which women will relate to one another as independent creatures of desire and strength.

While *L'Amèr* transmits glimpses of lesbian love, *Le Sens apparent* tells the story of a deep friendship between Adrienne, Gertrude, Yolande, and the narrator, four women writers, who meet in restaurants and cafés traveling to and from New York and Montreal. Unlike the nameless character of *L'Amèr* who must first destroy the myth of woman's "biological destiny" before she can begin to write, however, the authors in *Le Sens apparent* possess the artistry, the leisure, and the love to support each other in their creative projects. As a matter of fact, one of the major themes of this novel is the narrator's protracted search for an amazon language: "Le temps tel que décrit par les amazones contemporaines."[23]

The narrator's dual aim—to evoke the spirit of the island of Lesbos and to discover new forms of writing—accounts for the twofold character of the book itself. On the one hand a series of poems celebrates the relation between two lesbian writers; on the other hand a feminist manifesto recalls the long history of women's oppression and identifies the qualities that will enable them to recreate, through their writing, the greatness of their amazonian past. This quest for a lesbian literature is of the utmost importance not only because of the millennia of erasure and censorship, but also because the limited concept of reality in patriarchal societies compels women to seek their own reality in the realm of fiction. In *Le Sens apparent* Brossard tries to reclaim words and forms in order to call an oppressive order into question and to produce a new environment for the women writers who circulate in the twilight zone between fiction and reality. Eschewing the photographic portrayal of everyday life as a two-dimensional and linear narrative that perpetuates an obsolete vision of the world, Brossard now writes in an open-ended and circular manner. The book ends as it began with the narrator reflecting on love and on the text itself: "J'avais pensé follement le grand amour car je voulais à tout prix écrire un livre.... J'avais pensé follement le grand amour car je voulais à tout prix écrire un livre de manière à ne pas exagérer cette folle tentation, ce fol incident qui parcourt l'échine à mon insu et qui me fait écrire *toutes ces choses*...."[24]

While *Le Sens apparent* shows women exploring together the relationship between fiction and reality, *Amantes*, as a lesbian continent, illustrates the link which exists between female eroticism and the development of a new form of writing. Divided into five parts by means of black and gray pages, illustrated with photographs of the modern world, and printed with a variety of types—capital letter, small letter, italics—this book immediately challenges the unidirectional character of patriarchal systems of thought. The vision of a rotating space and of a circular time in *Amantes*, however, is connected not only to the artist's search for new forms, but also to her lesbian passion which enables her to invent a version of reality outside of patriarchal censorship. That is why physical love between women, as a path leading to wholeness and integrity, forms the major theme of this volume of poetry. While the heterosexual view of woman's otherness leads to the erosion of the female self, erotic relationships between lesbians are conducive to the rediscovery of a new and multidimensional language.

Nowhere in Brossard's work is the rapport between lesbianism on the one hand and language on the other hand more evident than in *Amantes*, for the large number of grammatical feminines, in this book, constitutes a potent visual reminder of the separatist nature of this continent. Moreover, the recurrence of the "nous" form, plural and collective, expresses, as it does in *Tryptique lesbien*, the solidarity of a world of lesbians. But while Marchessault obeys the grammatical rules, Brossard does not hesitate to transgress them, omitting parts of the sentence, disrupting the subject-predicate sequence, altering punctuation and gender:

> ma continent, je veux parler l'effet
> radical de la lumière au grand jour
> aujourd'hui, je t'ai serrée de près,
> aimée de toute civilisation, de toute
> texture, de toute géométrie et de braise,

délirantes, comme on écrit: et
mon corps est ravi[25]

Amantes, Brossard's most avant-garde work, not only describes the touching, the embraces, the physical union of the lovers; it also brings out the omnipresence of words. Implicit in these pages is the existence of the subtle relationship which exists between Sapphic love and the writer's ability to create a new space or territory where lesbian women can be together. One of Brossard's principal methods for suggesting such an environment is the verbal spiral. Repeating the same words at intervals, but in so doing advancing a step each time, Brossard's twirling is related to her lesbian concept of love. The first spiral shows the lovers sharing the meaning of their nocturnal dreams:

la nuit décline ses relais. explorer:
l'ultime intime ailleurs

la tête tourne, enlaçons le détail de notre science, nouées
(l'ultime intime ailleurs)....[26]

The second spiral brings out in a rhythmical flow of words the joy of yielding to temptation:

j'ai succombé à toutes les visions
séduite, surface, série et sérieuse

j'ai succombé à la vision claire
des végétations et des événements
matinales,...

j'ai succombé à l'écho, au retour,
à la répétition. *au commencement
des vertèbres* était la durée
une réplique essentielle à tout instant
dans la joie que j'ai de toi,...[27]

In the third spiral, we see the connection between the texture of the words and the taste of a kiss:

et nous imaginons de nou-
velles moeurs avec ces bouches mêmes qui savent tenir un
discours, les nôtres au goût des mots au goût du baiser....

les faits sont tels que le projet du texte et le texte
de projet s'accomplissent au goût des mots, au goût du
baiser. je sais que tu m'es réelle / alors[28]

A subversive style which breaks the monotony of traditional and linear writing, the spiral signifies openness, continuity and the perpetuation of life. In the words of Brossard: " '[The spiral is] a very dynamic form . . . which is related to lesbian sensibility.' "[29]

Jovette Marchessault and Nicole Brossard, two lesbian/feminist writers of Quebec, have had the courage to explore the world of their dreams and to translate their experience into language. What distinguishes these two authors is their emotional honesty combined with their quest for a non-sexist idiom—fresh, daring, and uninhibited. Refusing the very thought of male domination, these women-identified-women are not afraid of venturing into the unknown, of taking chances with new modes of writing and new forms.

A careful reading of *Tryptique lesbien* and particularly of *Amantes* shows that there is a rapport between lesbianism, as a rediscovery of woman's desire, and writing outside of the heterosexual hegemony. As lesbian/feminists, Jovette Marchessault and Nicole Brossard address themselves primarily to women; as innovators, questioning the very nature of fiction, they are beginning to change the character of literature in Quebec.[30] In spite of the differences between these two writers—Brossard, an enthusiast of the big city, is urbane and modernistic; Marchessault, a devotee of the land, is an adherent of the earth goddesses, a friend of the mammals—both of these authors have undoubtedly made great contributions to the development of a lesbian sensibility in the literature of Quebec.

NOTES

1. I discovered certain aspects of Jovette Marchessault's difficult beginnings during a personal interview with the writer in Montreal, 7 July 1980.

2. Jovette Marchessault, *Comme une enfant de la terre: Le Crachat solaire* (Montréal: Leméac, 1975), p. 105.

"Words," she tells her, "appear to me like spiral staircases which lead to a door. That opens."

3. Jovette Marchessault, *La Mère des herbes*, pref. Gloria F. Orenstein (Montréal: Quinze, 1980), p. 78.

As visitors inside the earth, under the earth, we are an extraordinary sum of possibilities, everything is possible for the embryo who descends into the mine to give birth to herself in her favorite kingdom, to settle in the womb of her rediscovered mother and to spring up like a nugget of gold after a reasonable time of ripening and incubation.

4. Jovette Marchessault, *Tryptique lesbien*, postface Gloria F. Orenstein (Montréal: Les Editions de la Pleine Lune, 1980).

5. Marchessault, "Chronique lesbienne du moyen-âge québécois," *Tryptique lesbien*, p. 36.

At that time of Medieval Quebec all the young lesbians put out their tongues and slavered on the floor or on the pictures of the little catechisms. Ever since the holiday of the Three Wise Men, they had decided to make us go through an intensive training. We were the fetishes of the year, pig's heads, golden ring in the snout, monsters! Planned! Deliberate! Unfettered! Until the complete exhaustion of this resistance which never stopped resisting.

See also the reiterated condemnation of the Catholic Church and of the past terrorism of a strict Catholic education in such other lesbian prose works as *Georgie* by Jeanne d'Arc Jutras (Montréal: Les Editions de la Pleine Lune, 1978), and Reina Ha-Milton's *Lettre d'amoure de femmes* (Montréal: Les Editions du Remue-Ménage, 1981).

6. Marchessault, "Chronique lesbienne du moyen-âge québécois," *Tryptique lesbien*, pp. 38-39.

On your knees little girls! It is the exquisite hour of divine fellatio. On your knees! Open your mouth! Wide! Wider still! Receive the squirt of sperm of the great eucharistic male.

7. Marchessault, "Chronique lesbienne du moyen-âge québécois," *Tryptique lesbien*, p. 62.

They go over the top, the males, haggard, their teeth chattering, their saliva in the dust of genesis, on the assault, on the pinch, on the spree, on their backs.

8. Marchessault, "Chronique lesbienne du moyen-âge québécois," *Tryptique lesbien*, p. 55.

Cannibals, stop the ball.

9. Marchessault, "Chronique lesbienne du moyen-âge québécois," *Tryptique lesbien*, p. 31.

When they said: "Holiday," I heard something else! I heard the winter of blood on the land of men.

10. Marchessault, "Chronique lesbienne du moyen-âge québécois," *Tryptique lesbien*, pp. 33-35.

11. Marchessault, "Chronique lesbienne du moyen-âge québécois," *Tryptique lesbien*, pp. 63-64.

12. Marchessault, "Chronique lesbienne du moyen-âge québécois," *Tryptique lesbien*, pp. 61, 66, 68, 69, 71, 72, 75; "Les Vaches de nuit," *Tryptique lesbien*, p. 83.

The World of permanent sacrifice.
The herd of darkness.
The order-of-the-castrators.

13. Marchessault, "Chronique lesbienne du moyen-âge québécois," *Tryptique lesbien*, p. 41.

I tell you that they have stolen our daily time.
Our precious everyday time to play outside, inside, in the vigor of mutual love. Our very own time, time of fire, of passion in the red velvet of rapturous lullings, of embracements of the body.

14. Marchessault, "Les Vaches de nuit," *Tryptique lesbien*, p. 87.

The milk flows! The milk gushes forth! The milk flows in torrents! Beauty, beauty, white goodness. The milk snows! The milk drips, the milk is fragrant! The milk powders! The milk squalls! The milk storms! The milk clouds, the milk is tinted with pictures!

15. *La Saga des poules mouillées* (Montréal: Les Editions de la Pleine Lune, 1981), Jovette Marchessault's highly acclaimed drama about the *québécoise* heritage, dwells on the difficulties of women's creativity more than on lesbianism. For this reason, I felt it would be best to omit that work from a discussion on lesbian sensibility in the literature of Quebec.

16. Jean Wilson, "Nicole Brossard: Fantasies and Realities," *Broadside*, 2, No. 8 (June 1981), 11.

17. Louise H. Forsyth, "The Fusion of Reflexive Writing and Theoretical Reflection:

Nicole Brossard and Feminist Criticism in Quebec," Workshop No. 514, New Directions in Feminist Critical Theories in France and the Francophone World, Modern Language Association Convention, New York City, 29 December 1981, p. 14.

18. Nicole Brossard, *L'Amèr ou le chapitre effrité* (Montréal: Quinze, 1977), p. 6.

This is combat.

19. Brossard, p. 24.

Everything revolves around a senseless grammar.

20. Brossard, p. 73.

But I want you to be huge and warm of the body know our energies differently than in your womb but from your eyes. Genderless or perhaps invariable.

21. Brossard, p. 12.

I have killed the womb and have exploded the sea.

22. Caroline Bayard, "Nicole Brossard et l'utopie du langage," *Revue de l'Université d'Ottawa*, 50, No. 1 (1980), 87. In this article, Caroline Bayard makes a rapprochement between Nicole Brossard's writing in her later books and Roland Barthes's idea of the Utopia of language.

23. Nicole Brossard, *Le Sens apparent* (Paris: Flammarion, 1980), p. 23.

Time as it has been described by the contemporary Amazons.

Brossard also refers to the amazons as "le grand cercle des déviantes" [The great circle of deviants] (p. 22).

24. Brossard, *Le Sens apparent*, pp. 5, 76.

I had foolishly imagined the great love because I wanted at all costs to write a book.... I had foolishly imagined the great love because I wanted at all costs to write a book so as not to exaggerate this mad temptation, this crazy incident which sends shivers through my spine, without my knowledge and which makes me write *all these things*....

25. Nicole Brossard, *Amantes* (Montréal: Quinze, 1980), p. 109.

> my continent, I want to speak of the
> radical effect of the broad daylight
> today, I have clasped you close,
> loved you with all my civilization,
> with all my texture, with all my geometry with all my embers,
> frenzied as they write: and
> my body is overjoyed

26. Brossard, *Amantes*, first spiral, pp. 96, 100.

> the night draws to a close. explore:
> the ultimate friendship elsewhere

> the head spins, together let us clasp the essence of our knowledge
> (the ultimate friendship elsewhere)....

27. Brossard, *Amantes*, second spiral, pp. 67, 69, 72.

> serious and seduced, I have succumbed to all the visions
> whether on the surfaces or in series
> I have succumbed to the clear vision
> of early morning vegetations and events

I have succumbed to the echo, to the return
the repetition. *In the beginning*
of *the vertebrae* there was duration
an essential reply to every moment
of joy that I get from being with you,...

28. Brossard, *Amantes*, third spiral, pp. 13, 21.

and we imagine new ways of living
with those very mouths which know how
to express themselves in accordance with the taste
of words in accordance with the taste of a kiss....

the facts are such that the project of the
text and the text of the project are
fulfilled in accordance with the taste of words,
in accordance with the taste of the kiss.
then I know that you are real to me

29. Brossard, as quoted in Wilson, p. 11.

30. André Roy, "La Fiction vive: Entretien avec Nicole Brossard sur sa prose," *Journal of Canadian Fiction*, 25-26 (1977), 39. In this interview, Nicole Brossard mentions the changes that are taking place in the literature of Quebec as a result of women's writings. Her own influence can be seen in the 29 October 1982 colloquium, *Traces*, devoted to her works and published in *La Nouvelle Barre du Jour*, Nos. 118-119 (novembre 1982).

17

Women's Theater in Quebec

Jane Moss

One of the most notable aspects of the phenomenal growth of theater in Quebec over the last decade has been the emergence of women's theater. Women's theater groups, both amateur and professional, have sprung up not only in Montreal and Quebec, but also in smaller towns. Women poets and novelists as well as feminist activists have turned to the theater in search of a more public and more political forum for their work. Professional theater women, dissatisfied with the roles assigned to them on stage and behind the scenes, have taken the initiative in creating plays for women characters and for female audiences. While plays by Françoise Loranger, Anne Hébert, Marie-Claire Blais, and others prove that women playwrights have not been denied access to the stage in the past, the new *théâtre de femmes* is distinct in that it is written, produced, and performed by women with little or no male participation.

Primarily, dissatisfaction with the traditional roles of women motivates women's theater. Given theater's function as a stylized representation of society, what better place to attack the exploitation of women and demand changes? This is what collectives like the Théâtre des Cuisines of Montreal and the Commune à Marie of Quebec have done in plays on abortion, rape, and housework. What better place than the theater to undermine the image of women as weepy, resigned virgins, overworked martyr-mothers, and prostitutes? This is what Denise Boucher has done in *Les Fées ont soif* (1978). Women have started writing for the theater to replace unacceptable female stereotypes. Luce Guilbeault, an experienced middle-aged actress, has explained that her need to work with other women stems from her uneasiness with the female characters created by male playwrights and directors. Pol Pelletier, an actress and co-founder of theThéâtre Expérimental des Femmes, has complained that the female characters she wants to play are simply not in the traditional dramatic repertory. Michelle Rossignol, an actress and director of the Ecole Nationale de Théâtre, has echoed Pelletier, complaining that in order to keep working in the theater she has had to play roles which, as a feminist, she found repugnant. Louisette Dussault, an actress and author of the play *Moman*, has said that in order to discover true images of women, one must kill the stereotypes.[1]

Other women dramatists have used the theater for various purposes. Elizabeth Bourget's popular plays take a good-humored look at the efforts of women to reconcile liberation with life as part of a couple. Historical plays by Michèle Lalonde, Madeleine Greffard, and Marie Laberge remind contemporary Quebec women that some of their mothers, grandmothers, and great-grandmothers struggled valiantly (if vainly) against the political, religious, economic, and educational institutions which oppressed them. The poetic dramas of Jovette Marchessault seek to renew the mother-daughter relationship, to create a female (matriarchal) mythology, and to establish links between women writers of the past and present.

While it is very difficult to draw conclusions about a movement as recent and widespread as Quebec women's theater, we can make a few general observations. First of all, much of the female theatrical activity of the 1970s takes the form of *spectacles de femmes*, based on improvisation techniques and collective creation. Secondly, women's plays rely heavily on the monologue form, whether they are one-character or multiple-character plays. In both instances, plays by women tend to depend on the verbal and visual expression of a limited number of recurring themes rather than on plot and character development. Now that Quebec women's theater is well into the 1980s, several new trends seem clearly established: conventionally structured plays are reexamining the roles of women in Quebec's past and present, while poetic dramas glorify female culture.

The *spectacles de femmes*, collective works written and produced by groups of women, are examined by a special issue on women's theater published by the Quebec theater review *Jeu* in 1980. Although the women's groups differ greatly in degree of militancy, they share the basic goal of dramatizing the real situation of women in Quebec. Inevitably, certain themes recur from play to play: the repressive sexual stereotypes imprinted on young girls; the fears which reduce women to submissive silence or madness; the legal and economic injustices of a male-dominated social system; women's need to express themselves and communicate with others.

The first *spectacle de femmes*, entitled *Un Prince, mon jour viendra*, was performed in 1974 by Paule Baillargeon, Suzanne Garceau, and Luce Guilbeault. This modest production presented a specifically female universe on the Quebec stage for the first time. In the first part, it examined the relationships between mothers and children, women friends and acquaintances. The second part attacked the sexual stereotypes and lack of female perspective in the folktales still told to children.[2]

For the development of women's theater, 1974 marked another event of far greater importance: the first production of the Théâtre des Cuisines. With its avowed Marxist feminist orientation, the Théâtre des Cuisines uses the stage for propagandistic and didactic purposes. It is a non-professional group, appearing in town halls, parish and school auditoriums, or wherever it can to spread its message to a wide popular audience. In its initial play, the group took on the issue of abortion on demand in a work entitled *Nous aurons les enfants que nous voulons* (1974). The following year, they denounced another form of exploitation in a play dealing with the question of payment for housework. *Môman travaille pas, a trop d'ouvrage* (1975) presents three women exhausted by their household chores. The first is a working mother of two children whose husband refuses to help around the house. The second, a welfare mother abandoned by her husband, is humiliated, tired, and angered by her struggle to raise her children. The third housewife devotes herself totally to four demanding children and a passive husband. When the women unite and go on strike, the bosses and the politicians conspire to force them back to their household work. But the women hold firm in their demands for day care centers, school lunches, health clinics, equal job opportunities, equal pay for equal work, and help with housework. In the end, all three women have improved their lives by renegotiating their familial duties and establishing solidarity with other women. A more recent creation of the Théâtre des Cuisines, *As-tu vu? Les Maisons s'emportent!* (1980), examines how difficult it is for women to liberate themselves when they are held responsible for the emotional and material well-being of the family. The play's message is that, while women have come out of the home into the political arena and into the work place, they are still carrying the burden of the home on their backs, just as the actresses carry cardboard houses on their backs.[3] Inspired by Nicole Brossard's delcaration, "La vie privée est politique,"[4] *Les Maisons s'emportent!* presents the troubled private lives of various women and concludes: "Faut en parler. Faut agir. Toutes ensemble!"[5]

Other amateur theater groups turned to collective dramatic creation to express their feelings about their common female experience. A women's group from Thetford Mines performed *Si Cendrillon pouvait mourir!* in 1975.[6] In a series of tableaux, songs, monologues, and variety numbers, the show presents the oppression and exploitation of women engendered by the family, the schools, and the mass media. From the Bible's version of the creation of Adam and Eve through fairy tales to modern advertising, everything seems to tell girls, adolescents, and women that their role in life is to be pleasing and subordinate to men. Generations of Cinderellas have waited passively for Prince Charming because women have always been afraid. A group of women from Saint Bruno dramatized the disappointing reality behind the dream of life in the suburbs in *La Vraie Vie des masquées* (1977).[7] The *masquées* of the title are the suburban housewives who hide their boredom, frustration, and solitude behind the masks of their social and sexual roles. Despite their comfortable homes and life styles, they need to come together, throw off their masks, and talk about themselves. And the vehicle they have chosen is the play itself.

In the mid-1970s, a number of women writers and professional theater women began to feel the need to work exclusively with women. From time to time, groups have joined together to work on special projects. One of these special projects, the 1976 production of *La Nef des sorcières*, was the first major event in Quebec women's theater reaching a large popular audience during its successful run at the Théâtre du Nouveau Monde. *La Nef* is composed of eight monologues written by seven women: Luce Guilbeault, Marthe Blackburn, France Théoret, Odette Gagnon, Marie-Claire Blais, Pol Pelletier, and Nicole Brossard. All of the monologues deal with the alienation of women in a male-dominated society, the desire for self-possession, independence, and sexual liberation. The Actress is tired of being a pretty mouthpiece, repeating other people's words, being overprotected and stifled. The Menopausal Woman, just learning to talk, declares her resentment of men, doctors, and the Church who denigrate her body. It is time to put an end to discrimination and myths and to assume her existence as a woman. Talking about her monotonous, lonely life as a forty-year-old single working woman, the Sample Dressmaker reveals the heavy price of independence. The Whore's monologue deals with sex games men and women play: in exchange for being a sex object and for gratifying the male sex drive, women (wives, girl friends, and prostitutes) receive food, shelter, money, and gifts. Two voices reveal the two faces of the Lesbian: a woman in angry revolt against male-dominated society and passionately moved by the tender sensuality of lesbian love. In the final piece, the Writer declares that women must write about themselves as a political gesture of liberation, even though the task is difficult.

Thanks to the success of *La Nef des sorcières*, feminist writers found a broad audience for their message that women must appropriate a language of their own, a language to express what has been in the past unspeakable. In the "Préface" to the published play, Nicole Brossard and France Théoret insist that the official discourse of male society does not allow women to talk about themselves or their bodies, so they must invent a new form of discourse.[8] Brossard's monologue of the Writer expresses the belief that feminist discourse will liberate women from the fears, silence, and solitude of their private lives. Writing becomes a sexual act by which the writer takes possession of her own body and, as if she were giving birth to herself, creates a text:

Petites contractions. Détente. Petites contractions. J'ai la langue sèche. Fait chaud. Je suis humide. Ça coule. Poussez. Poussez. Respirez bien. Détends-toi. Fait chaud. Encore. Jouis. Jouis. Poussez. Poussez. C'est une fille.[9]

Writing is also an act of solidarity by which women enter into a political pact aimed at recuperating their place in history:

Je parle dans la perspective d'un pacte politique avec d'autres femmes. Touchez-moi. La vie privée est politique.... Je reprends mon droit, mes dûs. Les mots font surface.... J'exhibe pour moi, pour nous, ce qui nous ressemble. J'écris et je ne veux plus faire cela toute seule. Je nous veux. Faire craquer, grincer, grincher l'histoire. La vie privée est politique.[10]

One important aspect of women's private lives which became public and political through its presentation in *La Nef des sorcières* is lesbianism. Marie-Claire Blais's monologue (''Marcelle I'') expresses the desire for a literature which would speak for lesbians about the joy of love shared by women and the pain of proclaiming that love in a cruelly uncomprehending society. Pol Pelletier's monologue (''Marcelle II'') declares that lesbianism allows women to act aggressively against the society which oppresses them:

[C]haque fois qu'une femme couche avec une autre femme, c'est une merveilleuse gifle qu'on lance à la tête de notre monde pourri. Un magnifique acte de subversion. ''On n'a pas besoin de vous autres, vous entendez? Regardez-nous jouir toutes seules, l'une de l'autre.'' Chaque fois qu'une femme couche avec une femme, elle affirme l'amour de son propre sexe, donc d'elle-même.[11]

By raising the issue of lesbianism in front of a vast public audience, *La Nef* made it possible for other women to write and talk about homosexuality.

In the 1970s, collective works were also performed by the women's cell of the Eskabel, by a counter-culture troupe known as Trois et Sept le Numéro Magique, and by other groups of authors and actresses. A 1978 play by a feminist cell of the Organisation Ô, for example, was titled simply *E*,[12] a reference to the grammar rule whereby the feminine is formed by adding a mute *e* to the masculine. *E* gives us a scenic image of women's subservience to men: the three female characters are all tied by red cords to a phallic structure in the center of the stage. They reveal by anecdotes the distress endured during their apprenticeship for womanhood in a male-dominated society. From early childhood through adolescence to maturity, they are conditioned to believe that their happiness and personal value are dependent upon men. The three women also reveal the strength of their dreams and their desire to be what they want to be. They revolt, and by pulling at the cords that tie them, they succeed in breaking loose, giving us hope for the future of a new, nonsexist society.

Rebellion against sexual stereotypes and determination to overcome fears, powerlessness, and silence have also been the motivating factors behind the Théâtre Expérimental des Femmes, founded in 1979 by Pol Pelletier, Nicole Lecavalier, and Louise Laprade. Before 1979, these women, working with others, had produced three feminist plays for the Théâtre Expérimental de Montréal, plus *Trac femmes*, a collection of reflections on women's theater. *Essai en trois mouvements pour trois voix de femmes* (1976) and *Finalement* (1977) were efforts to recreate the sensation of life in the uterus, the moment of birth, and the explosion of female speech. *A ma mère, à ma mère, à ma mère, à ma voisine* (1978) presented the violent revolt of daughters against a powerful mother figure who tries to force them into the mold of the domesticated, fearful, repressed woman. Although they succeed in destroying the formidable mother, the daughters realize that through education and conditioning, society has stacked the deck against them. They must take possession of their own bodies, prove their physical capacities, and rally other women to their cause in order to abolish sex roles. The 1979 production *La Peur surtout* was a virulent denunciation of all the fears that male society has imposed on women. In this play, which relies heavily on litanies, a chorus of women exorcize their fears by exposing them.[13] The Théâtre Expérimental des Femmes has established itself as a major force in Montreal women's theater by continuing to produce innovative collective creations and works by individual women dramatists, as well as by sponsoring the Festival de Création de Femmes (Spring 1980, June 1982, and November 1983), lecture series on heroines (1980-1981), and women's art (1981-1982).

In Quebec City, a prolific group of professional theater women has been working together since 1977, first as the Centre d'Essai des Femmes and since 1978 as the Commune à Marie. *Le Fleuve au coeur* (1977),[14] written by Danielle Bissonnette, Léo Munger, and Manon Vallée, dealt with women's fears: fear of rape, fear of their own sexuality, fear of revealing their emotions. It also dramatized the violence and humiliation inflicted on women by sexist men. The play centers on two women, their friendship, their relationships with men, and their growing female consciousness. To convey its message on sexual violence, it includes monologues by a secretary who was raped, ridiculed by the police, and mutilated by doctors; a young women traumatized by an incestuous relationship with her father; and a middle-aged, middle-class woman unable to admit that she is a victim of conjugal rape. The title refers to the river of words and feelings pent up for so long which flow from the heart of women just learning to communicate. The Commune à Marie has produced several other collective creations, including *Mascarade* (1978) and *La Mer à boire* (1979).

Like *Le Fleuve au coeur*, *Où en est le miroir?* (1978) by Louise Portal and Marie-Louise Dion focused on two women friends and their relationships with men. The two women (hardly distinguishable) are tired of the self-effacing, protective roles their mothers played; they are tired of doing things to please others. They are also tired of their fear of being rejected by men and of their fear of being close to other women. The play's message of liberation through lucidity, self-understanding, and self-love implies that good relationships between women and between men and women are possible.[15]

The structures of these *spectacles de femmes* reflect the fact that they are dramatically the products of Quebec's *jeune théâtre* and politically the products of the women's movement. Because they are collective creations, the individuality of the female characters is overshadowed by the common experience which the play seeks to depict. There is often little differentiation between characters (who may even remain nameless) and little character development. Another striking feature is the lack of conventional linear plots. Francine Noël has observed that these plays are frequently constructed by the association of metaphors or ideas.[16] Like poetic discourse or interior monologue, women's collective creations tend not toward logical demonstrations but toward composite, disparate structures. Avoiding hierarchical discriminations while allowing for digressions, the plays can be series of tableaux, sketches, songs, improvisations, or monologues held together by certain recurring themes or dramatic devices.

A number of women's groups have described the process of collective creation.[17] Once the group is formed, the first step is choosing themes or subjects dealing with the female experience. Then the topic is researched or explored through group discussions. After this point the process varies. Some groups decide on a basic scenario, assign the task of writing the text to one or more members, then edit the final version together. Other groups improvise scenes on the chosen themes, saving what they agree to be good and discarding the rest. The improvisations of the professional groups tend to be more sophisticated, using the psychotherapy techniques of free association, exploring the subconscious through *rêves éveillés* (awake dreams), working around symbolic props (for example, the phallic structure of *E* or the laundry ball of *A ma mère*). Given these creative procedures, it is not surprising that the plays often seem to be unstructured, repetitive variations on a few themes.

While the *spectacles de femmes* bear witness to a strong desire for solidarity, the importance of the monologue form in Quebec women's theater reminds us of the loneliness and estrangement of many women. A number of writers have commented on this tendency toward the theatrical monologue. Although Michel Tremblay has asserted that women choose the monologue because they do not talk to each other very much (an assertion vehemently denied by Suzanne Lamy's essay on gossip in *D'elles*), Michelle Rossignol has called the monologue "our first form of expression," a first step towards self-affirmation.[18] According to Rossignol, female discourse, denied or diminished for so long, must take place within a restricted circle before it is ready for the dialectic of dialogue. In their preface to *La Nef des sorcières*, France Théoret and Nicole Brossard insisted that the monologue form was necessary to convey a sense of isolation and alienation:

Chacune isolée dans son monologue, comme elle l'est dans sa maison, dans son couple incapable de communiquer du projet à d'autres femmes, inapte encore à tisser les liens d'une solidarité qui rendrait crédible et évidente l'oppression qu'elles subissent et qui les fissure sur toute la surface de leur corps.[19]

Théoret has said that the monologue form responds to women's need to talk about themselves, to appropriate a language for themselves, to provoke others to talk about themselves.[20] Brossard has compared the theatrical monologue to the *journal intime*, noting that they are narcissistic, autobiographical forms through which women come to know themselves as both object and subject.[21]

Unlike the comic monologues of male performers such as Yvon Deschamps and Reynald Bouchard, women's monologues are intimate, personal insights into private lives and emotions. They represent a *prise de conscience* and a *prise de parole*. The narcissistic act of writing about oneself becomes a daring political gesture for some and a necessary act of self-creation for others. Often these dramatized forms of the *journal intime* use poetic language, songs, and litanies to convey feelings and self-perceptions which cannot be translated by ordinary discourse. We see this special female dramatic speech in works by Marie Savard, Cécile Cloutier, Denise Boucher, and Anne-Marie Alonzo, and in *La Nef des sorcières*. In her essay on litanies in *D'elles*, Suzanne Lamy suggests that female writing takes this frequently fragmentary, angry, repetitive poetic form because women are just learning to speak out.[22]

From the beginning of women's theater in Quebec, the monologue has been the preferred form since it gives women the opportunity to express their fears, disappointments, dreams, and emotions. The first play considered a woman's play by the feminists was Marie Savard's *Bien à moi*, written in 1969 and staged in 1970.[23] It is a poetic monologue interspersed with songs, letters, and telegrams, in which the female character, talking about her body, her fear of madness, and her need for her own language, seems to bury her life as a married woman. Tired of being treated as an object or a misloved statue, she claims her right to subjectivity and tries to narrow the distance between herself and the image others have of her. Isolated by her aristocratic status (she is a Marquise) and ignored by her husband, she fights her loneliness and frustration by talking to herself about herself. The monologue, a personal psychodrama, becomes a form of liberation.

Cécile Cloutier's "*UTINAM!*" (1977) also used the dramatic monologue to express the need for liberation.[24] In four brief speeches, a thirty-year-old woman denounces and refuses the roles, stereotypes, and institutions which restrict the freedom of women: maternity, femininity, Catholicism, and marriage. At the same time she rejects the chains which oppress her, she demands both the right to silence and the right to a sexually liberated language. But although Cloutier's woman succeeds in throwing off the symbols of her oppression (an aborted fetus, lipstick, lace, bra, communion wafer, wedding ring), for her the process of self-affirmation and liberation is not yet complete. The play's ending implies that only a future generation will achieve happiness and freedom.

The desire for liberation from traditional roles, by now a standard motif in Quebec women's theater, reappeared as the major theme of Denise Boucher's *Les Fées ont soif* (1978). *Les Fées* became a *succès de scandale* when the Greater Montreal Arts Council tried to block its performance. Despite the loss of a $15,000 subsidy from the Arts Council, the Théâtre du Noveau Monde decided to go ahead with the production, refusing to give in to what it considered an attempt to censor artistic expression. Writers, artists, civil libertarians, and feminists supported Boucher and the TNM with demonstrations, petitions, and protest letters to newspapers. Although the Arts Council claimed that its decision was based on objections to the play's language and depiction of *québécois* culture, many people believed that it was motivated by the presence on stage of a living statue of the Virgin Mary.

In fact, the play's three characters—the statue of the Virgin, Marie the Mother, and Madeleine the Prostitute—are simply three faces of the same archetypal woman, the Virgin Mary. The play then is essentially a monologue by three voices with an occasional dialogue. Boucher wrote *Les Fées* to exorcize the terribly repressive model of the Virgin, the woman who cannot enjoy sex. This archetype is the product of man's (especially priests') fear of sexuality, according to Boucher. All three characters feel imprisoned by their roles. "Moi, je suis une image. Je suis un portrait / J'ai les deux pieds dans le plâtre. / Je suis la reine du néant," says the statue.[25] "Entre le poêle et le réfrigérateur / Entre le réfrigérateur et le poêle / je t'attends et je prends ma pilule / . . . . Les murs se resserrent sur moi," says the mother.[26] "Moi, je comprends Marilyn Monroe. . . . / Je suis comme elle. . . . / En quête de toutes les qualités de la / séduction. . . . / Et en même temps il faudrait que je sois inatteignable. . . . / transpa- / rente. / Virginale," cries the Prostitute.[27] Together in the "Chanson d'errance," they proclaim their status as silenced, beaten, alienated, violated, demented, lost women.[28] Together they express their fears of madness, solitude, ugliness, emotions, and sexuality.[29] But finally they decide they have had enough: the time of victims is over. Marie drops her apron and leaves her kitchen; Madeleine drops her whore's boots and leaves her alcove; the Statue drops her rosary beads and breaks out of her plaster cast. Having exorcized the stereotypes and accepted their own carnality, the women are now ready to love and be loved by men.

Although the ending of *Les Fées ont soif* implies that women are ready for dialogue with each other and with men, women's theater is not yet ready to abandon the monologue completely. The last several years, in fact, have seen a vogue of one-women shows by Pauline Harvey, Sonia Côté, Francine Tougas, Louisette Dussault, Jocelyne Goyette, Louise Roy, and others. While some of these still express women's isolation and alienation, others present female characters finding their own way in life with tenderness and humor. *Bachelor*, written by Louise Roy and Louis Saia, is the funny but sad story of a twenty-eight-year-old window dresser used and abused by a spoiled young man with expensive habits and no scruples.[30] Despite her colorful, amusing banter, she cannot hide her pain and her fear of growing old alone. Louisette Dussault's *Moman* is also a bittersweet mixture, but here the message is more positive. *Moman* is the very touching, very funny monologue of an unmarried, working mother taking her toddler twin daughters to their father by bus during a blizzard. The main character, Moman, remembers her own mother as a typical self-effacing housewife who manipulated and policed her children. Moman wants to kill what she calls "la mère-police"; she wants to break down the barriers between mother and daughter; she wants to be loved for herself instead of for what she does for others. Jocelyne Goyette's one-woman show, *Ma p'tite vache a mal aux pattes*,[31] follows her through a normal day in her life as she tries to balance her roles as mother, stepmother, lover, and writer. The anger, despair, and alienation which color so many women's plays are missing in Goyette's work, where the expression of love for her son, her "chum," and her writing far outweigh the anxieties of womanhood.

Several other women dramatists have tried to reintegrate newly liberated female characters into their conjugal and familial roles. In order to depict male-female relationships, therefore, they have written plays for men and women characters. This inclusion of male characters signals a departure from the militant feminism of much of women's theater and a desire to attract a larger popular audience. These plays about couples are also different in that they are more traditionally structured with plots and character development. Elizabeth Bourget has had remarkable success with two plays, *Bernadette et Juliette ou la vie, c'est comme la vaisselle, c'est toujours à recommencer* (1978) and *Bonne Fête Maman* (1980).[32] *Bernadette et Juliette* focuses on two women flower children of the sixties and their efforts to reconcile their desire to be liberated with their need for male partners. It picks up standard women's themes: female friendship and solidarity, the mother-daughter relationship, fear of rape, the double burden of housework and job, the difficulty of believing in oneself. With humor and sensitivity, Bourget presents the pressures (sexual, educational, professional, and familial) that liberation imposes on individuals and couples. In *Bonne Fête Maman*, Bourget creates the character of Estelle, who seems to be the model woman for her generation. She has a nice home, a good job, nice children, and a husband who loves her. Yet, as she approaches her fifty-fourth birthday, she feels an inexplicable need for something else, a need to do something that will satisfy her own needs rather than the needs of others. Since Bourget prefers light comedy to serious feminism, there is an easy solution to Estelle's dilemma: she takes a young lover.

Janette Bertrand also studies the personal, professional, societal, and sexual pressures brought to bear on the modern couple in her play *Moi Tarzan, toi Jane* (1981).[33] In this play, Gaby is a hockey star who starts sleeping with Jeanne to prove to himself and his teammates that he is not gay. For her part, Jeanne is frigid and an alcoholic, having been psychologically damaged by an incestuous relationship with her father which resulted in an aborted pregnancy. After seven years of married life, Gaby and Jeanne finally stop soliloquizing and take the first step toward true dialogue! In a society obsessed with sexuality, this first step consists of admitting feelings of sexual inadequacy.

While some women playwrights continue to focus on themselves and their close personal relationships, others have broadened their vision in time and space. A number of plays by women use history and myth in a conscious effort to recuperate the past and explore the female imagination. Historical plays by women tend to see the oppression of their own sex as part of the general oppression of the *québécois* people by economic, political, and religious forces. Michèle Lalonde's *Dernier Recours de Baptiste à Catherine* (1977)[34] traces the humiliation of Quebec between 1760 and 1875 in five tableaux. The changing figure of Catherine represents the strong, proud, hard-working *habitante*. In the face

of English arrogance and the Church's submissiveness, Catherine takes a rebellious patriotic stance, suggesting that someday, with the help of future Cath-
erines, Quebec will rise above its colonial status. True relationships between
Quebec men and women will only be possible after the rejection of their colonial
mentality. The plays of Marie Laberge also depict strong women characters from
Quebec's past. Despite their inferior political, economic, and social status, Laberge's women maintain their dignity and their personal freedom. In *Ils étaient
venus pour* and *C'était avant la guerre à l'Anse à Gilles*,[35] we see women who
had the courage to reject the traditional wife/mother role accepted by Maria
Chapdelaine. Laberge's women do not hate men, but they respect themselves
enough to refuse marriage and motherhood. Madeleine Greffard's "Pour toi je
changerai le monde" (1981)[36] chronicles the efforts of the first Quebec feminists
to improve the position of women in the province. Based on the life of Marie
Lacoste Gérin-Lajoie between 1870 and 1940, the play presents (somewhat
didactically) the long struggle to undo the injustices and relieve the hardships
imposed on women by the patriarchal Quebec power structure.

By writing historical plays, Greffard, Laberge, and Lalonde seek to establish
links between the women of Quebec's past and present. Jovette Marchessault,
an artist and novelist who has recently started writing for the theater, shares this
goal, but her vision is more global, mythic, and poetic. In "Les Vaches de nuit"
(1979), a solitary woman speaker describes a nocturnal flight of fancy away
from daytime domesticity to a place where mothers and daughters are reunited
in beauty and tenderness. There, they recall a distant past when women reigned,
a joyful time cut short by the coming of a male order. Although at dawn the
women must return to their confinement and submissiveness, Marchessault expresses confidence that someday women will return to the promised land to
establish a new matriarchal order.[37] In *La Saga des poules mouillées* (1981)
Marchessault envisions another nocturnal gathering, this time a meeting of four
Quebec women writers: Laure Conan, Germaine Guèvremont, Anne Hébert, and
Gabrielle Roy. Talking about their lives, works, fears, isolation, and frustrations,
they reveal how difficult it has always been to create a female culture in a
patriarchal society. But the time of solitude, silence, censorship, or madness is
over. *La Saga* ends when the four authors take off on a mission to recuperate
the lost culture of women, to rehabilitate neglected women writers and artists,
to write the first page of what will be "the great book of women."[38] In her 1981
play, *La Terre est trop courte, Violette Leduc*, Marchessault continues establishing spiritual links between past and present women writers. In the tormented
figure of the lesbian French writer Violette Leduc, Marchessault sees the plight
of many women for whom the price of artistic creation is persecution and humiliation. But they continue to pay the price willingly, knowing that they belong
to a tradition of female culture which will eventually claim its rightful place in
history.[39]

In Quebec women have already gained a firm foothold in the theater at all
levels, be it popular, experimental, or amateur theater. As it enters its second

decade, women's theater also seems to have found acceptance among the critics. While it is difficult to foresee future developments, several trends seem clear. There is a growing presence of lesbian writers and actresses determined to speak out about their sexuality and equally determined to explore the richness of female culture and creativity. There is also a group of heterosexual feminists intent upon examining the problems and possibilities of women in the context of the male-female couple. As they continue to explore new dramatic forms and create their own dramatic language, women playwrights have proven by their talent that they will be a permanent part of the theater in Quebec.

NOTES

1. Luce Guilbeault, *La Barre du Jour*, 50-51 (Winter 1975), 58-61; Pol Pelletier, "Histoire d'une féministe," in *Trac femmes* (Montréal: Les Publications Trac Enr., 1978), pp. 97, 102; Michelle Rossignol's comments were made during the 1979 Vanier Conference, round-table on "L'Image de la femme dans le théâtre québécois," *Revue de l'Université d'Ottawa*, 50, No. 1 (janvier-mars 1980), 151; Louisette Dussault, "Itinéraire pour une moman," in *Moman* (Montréal: Boréal Express, 1981), p. 26.

2. See Pol Pelletier, "Petite Histoire," *Possibles*, 4, No. 1 (1979), 175-87, for a description of this and other women's plays.

3. Le Théâtre des Cuisines, *Môman travaille pas, a trop d'ouvrage* (Montréal: Les Editions du Remue-Ménage, 1976); *As-tu vu? Les Maisons s'emportent!* (Montréal: Les Editions du Remue-Ménage, 1981); see "Justement! oui encore!: Entretien avec le Théâtre des Cuisines," *Jeu*, 16 (1980), 97-115.

4. Nicole Brossard, "L'Ecrivain," in Brossard et al., *La Nef des sorcières* (Montréal: Quinze, 1976), p. 74.

Private life is political.

5. *As-tu vu? Les Maisons s'emportent!*, p. 86.

We must talk about it. Must act. All together.

6. Le Show des Femmes de Thetford Mines, *Si Cendrillon pouvait mourir!* (Montréal: Les Editions du Remue-Ménage, 1980).

7. Le Théâtre du Horla, *La Vraie Vie des masquées ou ça finit comme ça commence* (Montréal: Les Editions du Remue-Ménage, 1979).

8. Nicole Brossard et France Théoret, "Préface," in *La Nef des sorcières*, pp. 7-13. See Karen Gould, "Setting Words Free: Feminist Writing in Quebec," *Signs: Journal of Women in Culture and Society, 6, No. 4 (1981)*, 617-42.

9. Brossard, "L'Ecrivain," in *La Nef des sorcières*, p. 78.

Small contractions. Release. Small contractions. My tongue is dry. It's hot. I'm damp. It's dripping. Push. Push. Breathe deeply. Relax. It's hot. Again. Enjoy. Enjoy. Push. Push. It's a girl.

10. Brossard, "L'Ecrivain," in *La Nef des sorcières*, pp. 74-75.

I speak in the perspective of a political pact with other women. Touch me. Private life is political. . . . I reclaim my right, my due. Words come to the surface. . . . I display for myself, for us, that which resembles us. I write and I no longer want to do it alone. I want us. Crack, scratch, gnash history. Private life is political.

11. Pelletier, "Marcelle II," in *La Nef des sorcières*, p. 70.

Each time a woman sleeps with another woman, it is a marvelous slap in the face of our rotten world. A magnificent act of subversion. "We do not need you, you hear? Watch us enjoy sex by ourselves, each giving pleasure to the other." Each time a woman sleeps with a woman, she affirms the love of her own sex, thus of herself.

12. L'Organisation Ô (Johanne Fontaine, France Labrie et Danielle Proulx), *E*; videotape available at the Université de Montréal's Médiathèque; review of *E* in *Jeu*, 7 (Winter 1978), 99-100.

13. See the discussion of these works in *Trac femmes*, pp. 6-40; Dominique Gagnon, Louise Laprade, Nicole Lecavalier et Pol Pelletier, *A ma mère, à ma mère, à ma mere, à ma voisine* (Montréal: Les Editions du Remue-Ménage, 1979); see review of *A ma mère* in *Lettres Québécoises*, No. 11 (septembre 1978), p. 47, and of *La Peur surtout* in *Lettres Québécoises*, No. 16 (hiver 1979-1980), p. 31.

14. Danielle Bissonnette, Léo Munger et Manon Vallée, *Le Fleuve au coeur* (Montréal: Leméac, 1981).

15. Louise Portal et Marie-Louise Dion, *Où en est le miroir?* (Montréal: Les Editions du Remue-Ménage, 1979), pp. 68-70.

16. Francine Noël, "Plaidoyer pour mon image," *Jeu*, 16 (1980), 46.

17. For insights into the process of collective creation, see the published versions of *A ma mère*, *Le Fleuve au coeur*, *Où en est le miroir?*, *Si Cendrillon pouvait mourir!*, *As-tu vu? Les Maisons s'emportent!*, and *Trac femmes*.

18. Suzanne Lamy, *D'elles* (Montréal: Hexagone, 1979) pp. 15-35; Tremblay and Rossignol's comments are cited in "L'Image de la femme dans le théâtre québécois," pp. 150-51.

19. Brossard et Théoret, "Préface," in *La Nef des sorcières*, p. 7.

Each one isolated in her monologue as she is in her house, in her couple incapable of communicating her intentions to other women, still inept at forming the bonds of solidarity which would make believable and credible the oppression which they undergo and which cracks the entire surface of their bodies.

20. France Théoret's comments were made during a round-table discussion on "La Femme et la tradition théâtrale," *Revue de l'Université d'Ottawa*, 50, No. 1 (janvier-mars 1980), 19.

21. Nicole Brossard, "Rencontre avec Nicole Brossard," *Voix et Images*, 3, No. 1 (septembre 1977), 12.

22. Lamy, pp. 61-99.

23. Marie Savard, *Bien à moi* (Montréal: Editions de la Pleine Lune, 1979).

24. Cécile Cloutier, "*UTINAM!*," *La Barre du Jour*, Nos. 56-57 (mai-août 1977), pp. 93-115.

25. Denise Boucher, *Les Fées ont soif* (Montréal: Les Editions Intermède, 1978), p. 91

Me, I am an image. I am a portrait / I have my two feet in plaster. / I am the queen of nothingness....

26. Boucher, p. 97.

Between the stove and the refrigerator / Between the refrigerator and the stove / I wait for you and I take my pill / .... The walls close in around me....

27. Boucher, p. 98.

Me, I understand Marilyn Monroe.... / I am like her.... / in search of all the qualities of / seductiveness.... / and at the same time I must be unattainable.... / transpar- / ent. / Virginal....

28. Boucher, p. 86.

29. Boucher, pp. 104-07.

30. Louise Roy et Louis Saia, avec Michel Rivard, *Bachelor* (Montréal: Leméac, 1981). Male collaboration notwithstanding, this is essentially a woman's play.

31. Jocelyne Goyette, *Ma p'tite vache a mal aux pattes* (Montréal: Québec/Amérique, 1981).

32. Elizabeth Bourget, *Bernadette et Juliette ou la vie, c'est comme la vaisselle, c'est toujours à recommencer* (Montréal: VLB Editeur, 1979); *Bonne Fête Maman* was performed first by L'Escale (Summer 1980) and then by the Campagnie Jean Duceppe (Winter 1981-1982).

33. Janette Bertrand, *Moi Tarzan, toi Jane* (Montréal: Inédi Raffi, 1981).

34. Michèle Lalonde, *Dernier Recours de Baptiste à Catherine* (Montréal: Leméac, 1977).

35. See Noël, pp. 52-54; Marie Laberge, *Ils étaient venus pour* (Montréal: VLB Editeur, 1981); Marie Laberge, *C'était avant la guerre à l'Anse à Gilles* (Montréal: VLB Editeur, 1981).

36. Madeleine Greffard, "Pour toi je changerai le monde," *La Grande Réplique*, 11 (1981).

37. Jovette Marchessault, "Les Vaches de nuit," in *Tryptique lesbien*, postface, Gloria F. Orenstein (Montréal: Editions de la Pleine Lune, 1980), pp. 83-94. The monologue was first performed as part of *Célébrations* at the Théâtre du Nouveau Monde in 1979.

38. Jovette Marchessault, *La Saga des poules mouillées* (Montréal: Editions de la Pleine Lune, 1981), p. 177.

39. Jovette Marchessault, *La Terre est trop courte, Violette Leduc* (Montréal: Editions de la Pleine Lune, 1982) was performed at the Théâtre Expérimental des Femmes, November 1981.

Bibliography

Bersianik, Louky. *Les Agénésies du vieux monde*. Montréal: L' Intégrale Editrice, 1982.
———. *L'Euguélionne*. Montréal: La Presse, 1976.*
———. *Maternative: Les Pré-Ancyl*. Acides de Jean Letarte. Montréal: VLB Editeur, 1980.
———. *Le Pique-nique sur l'Acropole*. Montréal: VLB Editeur, 1979.
Bertrand, Janette. *Moi Tarzan, toi Jane*. Montréal: Inédi Raffi, 1981.
Bissonnette, Danielle, Léo Munger et Manon Vallée. *Le Fleuve au coeur*. Montréal: Leméac, 1981.
Blais, Marie-Claire. *Les Apparences*. Montréal: Editions du Jour, 1970.*
———. *La Belle Bête*. 1959; rpt. Montréal: Le Cercle du Livre de France; Pierre Tisseyre, 1978.*
———. *David Sterne*. Montréal: Editions du Jour, 1967.*
———. *L' Exécution*. Montréal: Editions du Jour, 1970.*
———. *Fièvre*. Montréal: Editions du Jour, 1974.
———. *L' Insoumise*. Montréal: Editions du Jour, 1971.*
———. *Un Joualonais sa joualonie*. Montréal: Editions du Jour, 1973.*
———. *Le Jour est noir*. Montréal: Editions du Jour, 1970.*
———. *Une Liaison parisienne*. Montréal: Alain Stanké; Quinze, 1975.*
———. *Le Loup*. Montréal: Editions du Jour, 1972.*
———. *Manuscrits de Pauline Archange*. Montréal: Editions du Jour, 1968.*
———. *Les Nuits de l'Underground*. Montréal: Alain Stanké, 1978.*
———. *L'Océan*, suivi de *Murmures*. Montréal: Quinze, 1977.*
———. *Pays voilés; Existences*. Montréal: Les Editions de L'Homme, 1967.
———. *Pierre: La Guerre du printemps 81*. Collection L'Echiquier. Montréal: Primeur, 1984.

*An asterisk after a bibliographical entry indicates that an English translation of that particular work has been published.

————. *Une Saison dans la vie d'Emmanuel*. Montréal: Editions du Jour, 1965.*

————. *Le Sourd dans la ville*. Montréal: Alain Stanké, 1979.*

————. *Tête blanche*. Montréal: Editions de L'Homme, 1969.*

————. *Visions d'Anna*. Montréal: Alain Stanké, 1982.

————. *Vivre! Vivre!* Montréal: Editions du Jour, 1969.*

————. *Les Voyageurs sacrés*. Montréal: Editions Hurtubise HMH, 1969.*

Boucher, Denise, *Cyprine*. Montréal: L'Aurore, 1978.

————. *Les Fées ont soif*. Montréal: Editions Intermède, 1978.*

———— et Madeleine Gagnon. *Retailles: Complaintes politiques*. Montréal: Editions de L'Etincelle, 1977.

Bourget, Elizabeth. *Bernadette et Juliette ou la vie, c'est comme la vaisselle, c'est toujours à recommencer*. Montréal: VLB Editeur, 1979.

Brossard, Nicole. *Amantes*. Montréal: Quinze, 1980.

————. *L'Amèr ou le chapitre effrité*. Montréal: Quinze, 1977.*

————. *Le Centre blanc: Poèmes 1965-1975*. Montréal: L'Hexagone, 1978.

————. *Double Impression: Poèmes et textes, 1967-1984*. Montréal: L'Hexagone, 1984.

————. *French Kiss: Etreinte/exploration*. Montréal: Editions du Jour, 1974.

————. *Journal intime: ou Voilà donc un manuscrit*. Montréal: Les Herbes Rouges, 1984.

————. *Un Livre*. Montréal: Editions du Jour, 1970.*

————. *Picture Theory*. Montréal: Nouvelle Optique, 1982.

————. *Le Sens apparent*. Paris: Flammarion, 1980.

————. *Sold-out: Etreinte/illustration*. Montréal: Editions du Jour, 1973.*

————, ed. *Les Stratégies du réel/The Story So Far*. Montréal: La Nouvelle Barre du Jour, 1979; Toronto: Coach House Press, 1979.

————, Marthe Blackburn, Marie-Claire Blais, Madeleine Gagnon, Luce Guilbeault, Pol Pelletier et France Théoret. *La Nef des sorcières*. Montréal: Quinze, 1976.

Cloutier, Cécile, *Chaleuils*. Montréal: L'Hexagone, 1979.

————. "UTINAM!" *La Barre du Jour*, Nos. 56-57 (mai-août 1977), pp. 93-115.

Conan, Laure. *Angéline de Montbrun*. 1884; rpt. Bibliothèque canadienne-française. Fides, 1976.*

————. *Oeuvres romanesques*. Ed. Roger Le Moine. 3 vols. Montréal: Fides, 1974-1975.

Dussault, Louisette. *Moman*. Montréal: Boréal Express, 1981.

Gagnon, Dominique, Louise Laprade, Nicole Lecavalier et Pol Pelletier. *A ma mère, à ma mère, à ma mère, à ma voisine*. Montréal: Les Editions du Remue-Ménage, 1979.

Gagnon, Madeleine. *Antre*. Montréal: Les Herbes Rouges, 1978.

————. *Au coeur de la lettre*. Montréal: VLB Editeur, 1982.

————. *Autographie I: Fictions*. Montréal: VLB Editeur, 1982.

————. *Lueur: Roman archéologique*. Montréal: VLB Editeur, 1979.

————. *Les Morts-vivants*. Montréal: Editions Hurtubise, HMH, 1969.

————. *Pensées du poème*. Montréal: VLB Editeur, 1983.

————. *Poélitique*. Montréal: Les Herbes Rouges, 1975.

————. *Pour les femmes et tous les autres*. Montréal: Editions de L'Aurore, 1974.

————, Hélène Cixous et Annie Leclerc. *La Venue à l'écriture*. Collection 10/18. Paris: Union Générale d'Editions, 1977.

Goyette, Jocelyne. *Ma p'tite vache a mal aux pattes*. Montréal: Québec/Amérique, 1981.

Guèvremont, Germaine. *Marie-Didace*. 1947; rpt. Montréal: Fides, 1969.*

———. *Le Survenant*. 1945; rpt. Montréal: Fides, 1974.*

Hébert, Anne. *Les Chambres de bois*. 1958; rpt. Paris: Editions du Seuil, 1979.*

———. *Les Enfants du sabbat*. Paris: Editions du Seuil, 1975.*

———. *Les Fous de Bassan*. Paris: Editions du Seuil, 1982.*

———. *Héloïse*. Paris: Editions du Seuil, 1980.*

———. *Kamouraska*. Paris: Editions du Seuil, 1970.*

———. *Poèmes*. Paris: Editions du Seuil, 1960.*

———. *Les Songes en équilibre*. Montréal: Les Editions de L'Arbre, 1942.

———. *Le Temps sauvage; La Mercière assassinée; Les Invités au procès*. 1967; rpt. Collection L'Arbre, No. G-2. Montréal: Editions Hurtubise HMH, 1973.

———. *Le Torrent*. Montréal: Editions Beauchemin, 1950; rpt. Paris: Editions du Seuil, 1963; Collection L'Arbre, No. 1. Montréal: Editions Hurtubise HMH, 1974.*

——— et Frank Scott. *Dialogue sur la traduction: A propos du* Tombeau des rois. Collection Sur Parole. Montréal: Editions Hurtubise HMH, 1970.

Laberge, Marie. *Avec l'hiver qui s'en vient*. Montréal: VLB Editeur, 1982.

———. *C'était avant la guerre à l'Anse à Gilles*. Montréal: VLB Editeur, 1981.

———. *Ils étaient venus pour*. Montréal: VLB Editeur, 1981.

———. *Jocelyne Trudelle trouvée morte dans ses larmes*. Montréal: VLB Editeur, 1983.

Lalonde, Michèle. *Défense et illustration de la langue québécoise*. Paris: Seghers/Laffont, 1979.

———. *Dernier Recours de Baptiste à Catherine*. Montréal: Leméac, 1977.

———. *Speak White*. Montréal: L'Hexagone, 1974.

——— et Denis Monière. *Cause commune: Manifeste pour une internationale des petites cultures*. Montréal: L'Hexagone, 1981.

Lasnier, Rina, *Chant perdu*. Montréal: Ecrits des Forges, 1983.

———. *Matin d'oiseaux*. Montréal: Editions Hurtubise HMH, 1978.

———. *Poèmes*. 2 vols. Montréal: Fides, 1972.

Loranger, Françoise. *Double Jeu*. Collection Théâtre Canadien, No. 11. Montréal: Leméac, 1969.

———. *Jour après jour; Un Si Bel Automne*. Montréal: Leméac, 1971.

———. *Une Maison, un jour*. 1965; rpt. Poche Canadien, No. 16. Montréal: Le Cercle du Livre de France, 1968.

———. *Mathieu*. Montréal: Le Cercle du Livre de France, 1967.

———. *Médium saignant*. Collection Théâtre Canadien, No. 18. Montréal: Leméac, 1970.

———. *Théâtre 2: Encore cinq minutes; Un Cri qui vient de loin*. Montréal: Le Cercle du Livre de France, 1967.

——— et Claude Levac. *Le Chemin du Roy*. Collection Théâtre Canadien, No. 13. Montréal: Leméac, 1969.

Maheux-Forcier, Louise. *Un Arbre chargé d'oiseaux*. Ottawa: Editions de L'Université d'Ottawa, 1976.

———. *Amadou*. Montréal: Le Cercle du Livre de France, 1963.

———. *Appassionata*. Montréal: Pierre Tisseyre, 1978.

———. *Arioso*. Montréal: Pierre Tisseyre, 1981.

———. *Le Coeur étoilé*. Montréal: Pierre Tisseyre, 1977.

———. *En toutes lettres*. Montréal: Pierre Tisseyre, 1980.*

———. *Une Forêt pour Zoé*. Montréal: Le Cercle du Livre de France, 1969.

————. *L'Ile joyeuse*. Montréal: Le Cercle du Livre de France, 1964.

————. *Neiges et palmiers; Le Violoncelle*. Montréal: Le Cercle du Livre de France, 1974.

————. *Un Parc, en automne*. Montréal: Pierre Tisseyre, 1982.

————. *Paroles et musique*. Montréal: Pierre Tisseyre, 1973.

Maillet, Antonine. *Le Bourgeois Gentleman*. Montréal: Leméac, 1978.

————. *Cent Ans dans les bois*. Montréal: Leméac, 1981 (printed in France as *La Gribouille*. Paris: Gallimard, 1982).

————. *La Contrebandière*. Montréal: Leméac, 1981.

————. *Les Cordes-de-Bois*. Montréal: Leméac, 1977.

————. *Crache à Pic*. Collection Roman québécois. Montréal: Leméac, 1984.

————. *Les Crasseux*. Montréal: Leméac, 1974.

————. *Don l'orignal*. Montréal: Leméac, 1974.*

————. *Emmanuel à Joseph à Davit*. Montréal: Leméac, 1972.

————. *Evangeline deusse*. Montréal: Leméac, 1975.

————. *Gapi*. Montréal: Leméac, 1976.

————. *Gapi et Sullivan*. Montréal: Leméac, 1973.

————. *Mariaagélas*. Collection Roman acadien. Montréal: Leméac, 1973; rpt. Montréal: Editions Marabout, 1981.

————. *On a mangé la dune*. Montréal: Leméac, 1977.

————. *Par derrière chez mon père*. Montréal: Leméac, 1972.

————. *Pélagie-la-Charrette*. Montréal: Leméac; Paris: Grasset, 1979.*

————. *Pointes-aux-coques*. Montréal: Leméac, 1970.

————. *Rabelais et les traditions populaires en Acadie*. Québec: Les Presses de L'Université Laval, 1971.

————. *La Sagouine: Pièce pour une femme seule*. 1971; rpt. Montréal: Leméac, 1974.*

————. *La Veuve enragée*. Montréal: Leméac, 1977.

———— et Rita Scalabrini. *L'Acadie pour quasiment rien: Guide historique, touristique et humoristique d'Acadie*. Montréal: Leméac, 1973.

Marchessault, Jovette. *Comme une enfant de la terre: Le Crachat solaire*. Montréal: Leméac, 1975.

————. *Lettre de Californie*. Montréal: Nouvelle Optique, 1982.

————. *La Mère des herbes*. Pref. Gloria F. Orenstein. Montréal: Quinze, 1980.

————. *La Saga des poules mouillées*. Montréal: Editions de la Pleine Lune, 1981.*

————. *La Terre est trop courte, Violette Leduc*. Montréal: Editions de la Pleine Lune, 1982.

————. *Tryptique lesbien*. Postface. Gloria F. Orenstein. Montréal: Editions de la Pleine Lune, 1980.

Portal, Louise et Marie-Louise Dion. *Où en est le miroir?* Montréal: Les Editions du Remue-Ménage, 1979.

Roy, Gabrielle. *Alexandre Chenevert*. 1954; rpt. Montréal: Librairie Beauchemin, 1973.*

————. *Bonheur d'occasion*. 1945; rpt. Montréal: Librairie Beauchemin, 1973.*

————. *Ces enfants de ma vie*. Montréal: Alain Stanké, 1977.*

————. *Cet eté qui chantait*. Québec; Montréal: Les Editions Françaises, 1972.*

————. *De quoi t'ennuies-tu, Eveline?* Montréal: Editions du Sentier, 1982.

————. *Fragiles Lumières de la terre: Ecrits divers 1942–1970*. Collection Prose Entière. Montréal: Quinze, 1978.*

————. *Un Jardin au bout du monde*. Montréal: Librairie Beauchemin, 1975.*

————. *La Montagne secrète*. 1961; rpt. Montréal: Librairie Beauchemin, 1974.*

————. *La Petite Poule d'eau*. 1950; rpt. Montréal: Librairie Beauchemin, 1970.*

————. *La Rivière sans repos*. Montréal: Librairie Beauchemin, 1971.*

————. *La Route d'Altamont*. Collection L'Arbre, No. 10. Montréal: Editions Hurtubise HMH, 1966.*

————. *Rue Deschambault*. 1955; rpt. Montréal: Librairie Beauchemin, 1974.*

Roy, Louise et Louis Saia, avec Michel Rivard. *Bachelor*. Montréal: Leméac, 1981.

Savard, Marie. *Bien à moi*. Montréal: Editions de la Pleine Lune, 1979.

Le Show des Femmes de Thetford Mines. *Si Cendrillon pouvait mourir!* Montréal: Les Editions du Remue-Ménage, 1980.

Le Théâtre des Cuisines. *As-tu vu? Les Maisons s'emportent!* Montréal: Les Editions du Remue-Ménage, 1981.

————. *Môman travaille pas, a trop d'ouvrage*. Montréal: Les Editions du Remue-Ménage, 1976.

Le Théâtre du Horla. *La Vraie Vie des masquées ou ça finit comme ça commence*. Montréal: Les Editions du Remue-Ménage, 1979.

Théoret, France. *Bloody Mary*. Montréal: Les Herbes Rouges, 1977.

————. *Nécessairement putain*. Montréal: Les Herbes Rouges, 1980.

————. *Nous parlerons comme on écrit*. Montréal: Les Herbes Rouges, 1982.

————. *Vertiges*. Montréal: Les Herbes Rouges, 1979.

————. *Une Voix pour Odile*. Collection Lecture en Vélocipède. Montréal: Les Herbes Rouges, 1978.

Index

Abenaqui tribe, 174
Abortion, 241, 243
Acadia, 8, 143, 144, 147, 149, 151, 152, 174, 176, 178; culture, 174. *See also* Great Dispersion
L'Acadie perdu (Roy), 174
Adam and Eve, 16, 17, 243
Adizetu (*Le Pique-nique sur l'Acropole*), 208-9, 212
Adrien ("La Justice en Danaca at ailleurs"), 27-28
Adrienne (*Le Sens apparent*), 233
Agamemnon, 206, 208, 209
Agathon, 210
Agénésies du vieux monde, Les (Bersianik), 205
Agneli, Michel. *See* Mike (*Le Sourd dans la ville*)
Alain ("Les Petits Pas de Caroline"), 32-33
"A la lumière des sens" (Brossard), 163-64
Alexandre (*Visions d'Anna*), 134-35
Alexandre Chenevert (Roy), 27, 76-77
Algonquin tribe, 174
Alonzo, Anne-Marie, 7; use of monologue, 248
Alphonse (*Bonheur d'occasion*), 74
Amadou (Maheux-Forcier), 95-98, 99, 102, 103

A ma mère, à ma mère, à ma mère, à ma voisine, 245-46
Amantes (Brossard), 232, 234-36
L'Amer (Brossard), 232-33
Amyot, Geneviève, 7
Ancyl (*Le Pique-nique sur l'Acropole*), 205, 207, 209, 211, 212, 214
Angéline de Montbrun (Conan), 11-23
"L'Anesse et l'ânon des rameaux" (Lasnier), 57
Angelou, Maya, 141
"Angoisee" (Lasnier), 56, 58
Anna (*Visions d'Anna*), 134-36
Anne (*Amadou*), 95-98, 102
Anne ("La Source au désert"), 31-32
Anne (*Cet eté qui chantait*), 28
Anthologie de la nouvelle poésie nègre et malgache de langue francaise, 64
Antoinette, Grand-Mère (*Une Saison dans la vie d'Emmanuel*), 128-29, 130, 137
Antre (Gagnon), 195-97
"A Okko" (Roy), 32
Aphélie (*Le Pique-nique sur l'Acropole*), 205, 211, 214
Aquin, François, 88
"L'Arbre en feu" (Lasnier), 58
Aristophanes, 210
Asbestos, 134, 135

As-tu vu? Les Maisons s'emportent!, 243
Atkinson, Ti-Grace, 167, 232
Augustine, Saint, 13
d'Aulniéres, Mme (*Kamouraska*), 119
Aurélie (*Kamouraska*), 119
Authors, women: United States, 4
"Advantage pour" (Roy), 30
Avertine ("La Natte et la hutte"—*Mater-native*), 209
Avertine (*Le Pique-nique sur l'Acropole*), 209-10
Azarius (*Bonheur d'occasion*), 74, 77

Bachelor (Roy-Saia), 249
Baillargeon, Paule: *Un Prince, mon jour viendra*, 242
Balzac, Honoré de, 72
Banquet (Plato), 205, 210-11
Barbe-la-Jeune (*Les Cordes-de-Bois*), 146
Barnes, Djuna, 167
Barre du Jour, La, 158, 159-60, 161, 163, 164; "Femme et language," 161-62
Barthes, Roland, 160
Bataille, Georges, 160
Baudelaire, Charles, 55
Beatles: "She's Leaving Home," 88, 89
Beauchemin, Amable (*Le Survenant*), 38, 39, 41, 43, 45
Beauchemin, Didace (*Le Survenant*), 38, 39, 42, 43, 45, 47, 48
Beauchemin, Marie-Amanda (*Le Survenant*), 42, 43
Beauchemin, Nérée, 55
Beauchemin, Phonsine (*Le Survenant*), 38, 39, 41, 42, 43
Beauchemin family (*Le Survenant*), 38, 39
Beaulieu, Germaine, 163
Beauvoir, Simone de, 213, 232
Bédette ("La Grande Voyageuse"), 28, 33
Belle Bête, La (Blais), 125-27, 134
"Belles Histoires des pays d'en haut, Les" (Grignon), 49 n.9
Bélonie-le-Vieux (*Pélagie-la-Charrette*), 144, 148, 150, 151

Bélonie, young (*Pélagie-la-Charrette*), 150
Benamou, Michel, 64
Bernadette et Juliette (Bourget), 250
Berque, Jacques, 160
Bertrand, Janette: *Mon Tarzan, toi Jane*, 250
Bersianik, Louky, 8, 186, 196, 198-218; *Les Agénésies du vieux monde*, 205; *L'Euguélionne*, 205-8, 210, 212, 214, 215, 216, 217, 218; feminism, 205-6, 210, 212; *Maternative*, 205, 207, 209, 214, 215-16, 218; *Le Pique-nique sur l'Acropole*, 205, 207-11, 213, 214, 215, 216; *L'Euguélionne*, biblical structure, 206-7; language, 206, 213, 215-16, 217; "La Natte et la hutte," 209, 215; *Le Pique-nique sur l'Acro-pole*, female sexuality, 211; *L'Eugué-lionne*, speech rhythms, 215-16
Bessette, Gérard, 28
Bibeau, Rose-de-Lima (*Le Survenant*), 43, 44, 46
Bible, 205, 206, 215, 243
Bidoche (*Mariaagélas*), 148
Bien à moi (Savard), 248
Bissonette, Danielle: Le Fleuve au coeur, 246
Blackburn, Marthe: *La Nef des sorcières*, 244
Blais, Marie-Claire, 4, 8, 125; *La Belle Bête*, 125-27, 134; mother-daughter re-lationships in fiction, 125-26, 128, 129, 134, 136-37; *Les Nuits de l'Un-derground*, 125, 130-31, 133; *Le Sourd dans la ville*, 125, 131-34, 135; *Visions d'Anna*, 125, 130, 134-36; mother figure in fiction, 128, 132, 133, 134, 135-36, 137; *Une Saison dans la vie d'Emmanuel*, 128-29; female char-acters, 129, 130, 135; *Manuscrits de Pauline Archange*, 128, 133, 136; les-bianism in fiction, 130-31, 133, 136; *L'Insoumise*, 132; male characters, 133-35; feminism, 137; plays, 241; *La Nef des sorcières*, 244, 245
Bobinette ("A Okko"), 32
Boileau, Nicholas: *Le Lutrin*, 142

Boisvert (*Bonheur d'occasion*), 74
Bonheur d'occasion (Roy), 27, 28, 73-75
"Bonne à marier" (Roy), 30
Bonne Fête Maman (Bourget), 250
"Booz endormi" (Hugo), 55
Bosco, Monique, 6
Bouchard, Reynald, 247
Boucher, Denise, 186, 191, 198; *Retailles: Complaintes politiques*, 191-94; *Les Fées ont soif*, 241, 248-49; use of monologue, 248
Boudin, Eugène Louis, 134
Bourget, Elizabeth, 242; *Bernadette et Juliette ou la vie, c'est comme la vaisselle, c'est toujours à recommencer*, 250; *Bonne Fête Maman*, 250
Brecht, Bertolt, 187
Brochu, André, 74
Brossard, Nicole, 3, 5, 8, 157-69, 186, 196, 198, 206, 232, 243; non-traditionalism, 157-58, 160; approach to writing and language, 158, 160-61, 162-63, 164, 167-68, 232-33, 234, 236; career, 158, 159, 160, 161, 165, 167, 232; feminism, 158-69, 232; lesbianism, 158, 160-61, 164, 232; and Quebec nationalism, 159-60, 232; and *La Barre du Jour*, 160, 164; "Vaseline," 160; "Le Cortex exubérant," 161; "Femme et langage," 161-62; "E muet mutant," 162-63; "A la lumière des sens," 163-64; "Celebrations," 163; "Le Corps, les mots, l'imaginaire," 163; "La Femme et la ville," 163; and *Les Têtes de Pioche*, 165-67, 186, 232; political views, 166; fiction, 167-69; *La Nef des sorcières*, 167, 244, 247; *Some American Feminists*, 167; *Les Stratégies du réel/The Story So Far*, 169; *Sold-out*, 185; *Un Livre*, 185; "La Vie privée est politique," 186; *Amantes*, 232, 234-36; *L'Amèr*, 232-33; lesbianism in fiction, 232-36; mother figure in fiction, 232, 233; *Le Sens apparent*, 232, 233
Broussard, Captain Beausoleil (*Pélagie-la-Charrette*), 149-51, 178

Bruno (*Les Chambres de bois*), 113-14
Bulletin des Agriculteurs, Le, 27

Canada, xi; English-speaking and Quebec, 4
Canadian Broadcasting Corporation, 111
Capitalism, 212
Cart of Death (*Pélagie-la-Charrette*), 144, 148, 150
Cart of Life (*Pélagie-la-Charrette*), 143, 144, 148, 150, 151
Caryatids (*Le Pique-nique sur l'Acropole*), 209-10, 214, 215, 216
"Catalpa, Le" (Lasnier), 56
Catherine (*Derrier Recours de Baptiste à Catherine*), 250-51
Catherine (*Les Chambres de bois*), 112-13
Catherine (*Une Maison, un jour*), 83-84
Catholic Church, xi, 5, 211; in Quebec, 40, 45, 118, 159, 227, 229; in Blais fiction, 129, 133; in Maillet *Les Cordes-de-Bois*, 146, 147
Causse, Michèle, 167
"Cendrillon '40" (Roy), 30
Centre d'Essai des Femmes, 246
Césaire, Aimé, 64
Ces enfants de ma vie (Roy), 28
"C'est toi" (Lasnier), 58
C'était avant la guerre à l'Anse à Gilles (Laberge), 251
Cet eté qui chantait (Roy), 28, 71, 78
Chambres de bois, Les (Hébert), 112-14
"Chansons" (Lasnier), 54, 57-58
Chapdelaine, Madam (*Maria Chapdelaine*), 47
Charrette noire. *See* Cart of Death
Chateaubriant, François René, vicomte de, 13
Chawaf, Chantal, 187
Chemin du Roy, Le (Loranger), 85, 87-89, 91, 92
Chenal du Moine, 40, 44, 45, 47, 48
Chenevert, Alexandre (*Alexandre Chenevert*), 28, 76-77
"Cheveux, Les" (Lasnier), 58
Childbirth, 194-95
Chodorow, Nancy, 135, 137

Choquette, Adrienne, 6

Christine (*Rue Deschambault*), 29

Cinderella, 243

Cixous, Hélène, 3, 187, 194

"Claire fontaine" (Lasnier), 57-58

Clara, Aunt (*Mariaagélas*), 145

Class struggle, 5

Claudel, Paul, 54

Cloutier, Cécile, 197-98; use of monologue, 248; *UTINAM!*, 248

Colonialism, xi

Comédie Canadienne, 85, 89

Comme une enfant de la terre (Marchessault), 174, 179-80, 227-28; mythology, 173-77, 179-80; cultural referents,
174; language, 174, 179-80; woman as
subject, 174-75; ordeals of heroine,
176; structure, 176-77

Commune à Marie, 241, 246

Conan, Laure, 4, 7, 11, 251; *Angéline de
Montbrun*, 11-23

"Conversion des O'Connor, La" (Roy),
31

Cordes-de-Bois, Les (Maillet), 141-42,
145-47, 148-49; sea motif, 146; sexuality of Mercenaires, 147

Cordorai, Pierre (*La Montagne secrète*),
77-78

Corps étranger, Le (Ouvrard), 185

"Cortex exubérant, Le" (Brossard), 161

"Coteau, Le" (Lasnier), 56, 58

Côte, Sonia, 249

Cotnoir, Louise: "La Complicité," 163

Cross, James, 89

Culture, popular, 37

Curate (*Les Cordes-de-Bois*), 148-49

Daly, Mary, 4, 167, 208, 210, 217; *Gyn/
ecology*, 205-6

Damas, Léon-Gontran, 64-65; "Nuit
blanche," 64-65

Daniel (*Une Maison, un jour*), 83-84, 87

Darville, Maurice (*Angéline de Montbrun*), 12, 13, 23

Darville, Mina (*Angéline de Montbrun*),
14, 15, 21

Darwin, Charles, 65

Death: in Lasnier "Présence de l'absence," 58, 59

Death (*Pélagie-la-Charrette*), 143-44

DeFroi family (*Le Survenant*), 38

De Gaulle, Charles: 1967 visit to Quebec, 87-88, 90, 91

D'elles (Lamy), 247, 248

Demeter, 209

Dernier Recours de Baptiste à Catherine
(Lalonde), 250-51

Derrida, Jacques, 160, 215, 218

Deschamps, Yvon, 247

Désileux, Véronique (*Angéline de Montbrun*), 14-15

Desmarais, Angélina (*Le Survenant*), 41,
42, 46, 48

Desmarais family (*Le Survenant*), 38

Desroches, Marie (*Angéline de Montbrun*), 14-15

*Dictionnaire pratique des auteurs québé-
cois*, 187

Dinnerstein, Dorothy, 137

Dion, Marie-Louise: *Où en est le miroir?*, 246

Dominique (*Une Maison, un jour*), 83-
84, 87

Dorman, Lali (*Les Nuits de l'Underground*), 130, 131

Double jeu (Loranger), 85-87, 88, 89,
90, 91, 92

Duhamel, Roger: on poetry of Hébert, 63

Duplessis, Maurice, 38, 39, 40, 41, 46,
48, 49, 84, 164, 227

"Du port aux banques" (Roy), 73

Dürer, Albrecht: "Angel," 130, 133

Dussault, Louisette: *Moman*, 242, 249

d'Eaubonne, Françoise: *Le Féminisme ou
la mort*, 206, 210, 213

Ecole Nationale de Théâtre, 242

Elizabeth, Saint, 13

"Embobeliné" (Roy), 33

Emmanuel (*Une Saison dans la vie
d'Emmanuel*), 129

"E muet mutant" (Brossard), 162-63

Encore cinq minutes (Loranger), 83, 84-
85, 91

Enfants du sabbat, Les (Hébert), 112

England, xi
English language, xi, 5
Eskabel, 245
Essai en trois mouvements pour trois voix de femmes, 245
Estelle (*Bonne Fête Maman*), 250
Ethier-Blais, Jean: on poetry of Hébert, 63
Ethnopoetics, 64
L'Euguélionne (Bersianik), 205-8, 210, 212, 214, 215, 216, 217, 218; biblical structure, 206-7; speech rhythms, 215-16, 217
L'Euguélionne (*L'Euguélionne*), 206-8, 212, 214, 215; speech rhythms, 215-16, 217
Evangeline (Longfellow), 65
"Evanguelion," 205
"Eve" (Hébert), 65, 68

Family: in *Le Survenant*, 38-39, 48
Fanon, Frantz, 160
Father figure: in *Le Survenant*, 38-39, 40
Fées ont soif, Les (Boucher), 241, 248-49
Felman, Shoshana, 212, 218
Female relationships, 125, 127-28, 134, 136-37
Feminism, 7, 8, 141, 227; in Quebec, xi, 5-6, 158, 164, 165, 166, 185-86, 191; lesbian, 8, 158, 192, 198, 227; in *Le Survenant*, 41; in Loranger drama, 88, 90-91; in Quebec, internal conflicts, 166-67; Marxist, 185, 186, 243; and Freud, 208; and love of mother, 210; anti-Platonism, 212. *See also* Front de Libération des Femmes du Québec
Feminisme ou la mort, Le (d'Eaubonne), 206, 210, 213
Feminist literature. *See* Literature, feminist
Feminist writers. *See* Writers, feminist
"Femme et langage" (Brossard), 161-62
"Femme et l'écriture, La," international conference, 185, 191
Ferdinand (*Mariaagélas*), 148
Ferron, Madeleine, 6
Festival de Création de Femmes, 246

"Feuilles mortes" (Roy), 27
Filial devotion, 11, 12
Finalement, 245
Fleuve au coeur, Le (Bissonnette-Munger-Vallée), 246
Florence (*Le Sourd dans la ville*), 132, 133
Florentine (*Bonheur d'occasion*), 74, 75, 78
Flournoy, Oliver, 23
Forêt pour Zoé, Une (Maheux-Forcier), 95, 100-103
Foucault, Michel, 160, 218
Fous de Bassan, Les (Hébert), 3, 112
France, xi; and Quebec, 4
Francine (*Comme une enfant de la terre*), 228
François ("Le Torrent"), 110
Françoise (*Les Nuits de l'Underground*), 131
French language, xi, 5, 174, 206, 217
French Symbolist tradition, 7, 53
Freud, Sigmund, 11, 12, 206, 208; *Totem and taboo*, 208
Front de Libération des Femmes du Québec, 164
Front de Libération du Québec, 89, 164
"Fuite de Sally, La" (Roy), 31

Gaby (*Moi Tarzan, toi Jane*), 250
Gagnon, Madeleine, 3, 4, 5, 8, 185, 186, 210; *Poélitique*, 185, 187-89, 198; *Pour les femmes et tous les autres*, 185, 187, 189-91; reputation, 186-87, 194; *Lueur*, 187, 195-97, 198; *Les Morts-vivants*, 187; language, 188, 189, 190, 192, 194, 195, 196-98; poetry for working class, 189-90; feminism, 190, 192-93, 194; and socialism, 190; *Retailles: Complaintes politiques*, 191-94; and female body, 194-98; and female sexuality, 194, 195; and women's literature, 194; "Mon corps dans l'écriture," 194-95; *Antre*, 195-97
Gagnon, Odette: *La Nef des sorcières*, 244
Garceau, Suzanne: *Un Prince, mon jour viendra*, 242

Garneau, Saint-Denmys, 57
Gaspé Peninsula, 119
Gender roles. *See* Roles, gender
Genesis, 65, 207
Geneviève (*Encore cinq minutes*), 84, 85
Geneviève (*Les Nuits de l'Underground*), 131
Genital mutilations, Africa, 206
"Gérard le pirate" (Roy), 28
Gérin-Lajoie, Marie Lacoste, 251
Gertrude (*Encore cinq minutes*), 84-85, 87
Gertrude (*Le Sens apparent*), 233
"Gisants, Les" (Lasnier), 59
Gloria (*Le Sourd dans la ville*), 132-33
Gobineau, Jospeh Arthur, 64
Goldmann, Lucien, 126
Goyette, Jocelyne: *Ma p'tite vache a mal aux pattes*, 249-50
Grandbois, Alain, 57
Grand Dérangement. See Great Dispersion
"Grande Berthe, La" (Roy), 31, 33
"Grande Voyageuse, La" (Roy), 28, 33
"Grand Mariage, Un" (Hébert), 111
Grand Pré, 147, 152
Grand Vital (*Mariaagélas*), 148
Great Dispersion, 143, 147, 150, 174. *See also* Acadia
Greater Montreal Arts Council, 248
Green, André, 21
Greffard, Madeleine, 242; "Pour toi je changerai le monde," 251
Grignon, Claude-Henri, "Les Belles Histoires des pays d'en haut," 49 n.9
Grosskurth, Phyllis, 28
Guérin, Eugénie de, 13
Guèvremont, Germaine, 4, 7, 251; *Le Survenant*, 37-51; reputation, 37; feminism, 41, 44-45, 46-47; mother-daughter relationships in fiction, 127
Guilbeault, Luce, 241; *Some American Feminsits*, 167; *Un Prince, mon jour viendra*, 242; *La Nef des sorcières*, 244
Guislaine (*Visions d'Anna*), 130, 136
Gustave ("Un Vagabond frappe á notre porte"), 28
Gyn/ecology (Daly), 205-6

Hades/Pluto, 209
Harvey, Pauline, 249
Hébert, Anne, 3, 4, 7, 98, 251; career, 110, 111, 112; *Les Fous de Bassan*, 3, 112; poetry, interpretation, 63; *Le Tombeau des rois*, 63, 65-66, 68; "Eve," 65, 68; *Héloise*, 65, 112; *Kamouraska*, 65, 109-10, 114-21; *Les Songes en équilibre*, 65; "Le Mystère de la parole," 67-68; *Poèmes*, 67; use of the past, 68; *Kamouraska*, historical basis, 109; *Kamouraska*, related works, 110-14; short stories, 110-11; *Le Torrent*, 110-11, 127; drama, 111, 241; "Un Grand Mariage," 111, *Les Invités au procès*, 111; "La Maison de l'Esplanade," 111; *La Mercière assassinée*, 111; "Le Printemps de Catherine," 111; *Le Temps sauvage*, 111-12; *Les Chambres de bois*, 112-14; *Les Enfants du sabbat*, 112; *Kamouraska*, structure, 114-16, 118; *Kamouraska*, themes 116-17, 118-19
Héloise (Hébert), 65, 112
Héloise (*Une Saison dans la vie d'Emmanuel*), 129
Hémon, Louis: *Maria Chapdelaine*, 119, 127, 128, 251
Henderson ("Cendrillon '40"), 30
Henri á Vital (*Les Cordes-de-Bois*), 146-47
Henri (Encore cinq minutes), 84-85
Herrmann, Claudine, 75
Hite, Shere, 213
Hitler, Adolf, 64
Housework 241, 243
Hugo, Victor, 13; "Booz endormi," 55

L'Ile joyeuse (Maheux-Forcier), 95, 98-100, 102
"Il pleut" (Lasnier), 57-58
Ils étaient venus pour, 251
Improvisational theater, 85. *See also* Spectacles de femmes
Incarnation: in poetry of Lasnier, 57
l'Incarnation, Marie de, 4, 13
Incest, 7, 13; father-dauther, in *Angéline de Montbrun*, 12-13, 19-20, 23

L'Insoumise (Blais), 132
"Inutilité" (Lasnier), 60
Invités au procès, Les (Hébert), 111
Iphigenia: murder, 208, 209, 212
Irigaray, Luce, 4, 167, 187, 208, 212, 213; *Speculum de l'autre femme*, 210
Isabelle (*L'Ile joyeuse*), 98-100, 101
Isabelle-Marie (*La Belle Bête*), 125-26, 129
Isis (*Une Forêt pour Zoé*), 100, 101, 103

Jacob (*Manuscrits de Pauline Archange*), 129
Jacob, Suzanne, 7
Jacobus, Mary, 216
Jardin au bout du monde, Un (Roy), 28, 29
Jean, Michele: *Les Têtes de Pioche*, 166
Jean-Baptiste ("Bonne à marier"), 30
Jeanne (*Moi Tarzan, toi Jane*), 250
Jesus Christ, 16, 57, 206-7
Jeu, 242
"Joli Miracle, Le" (Roy), 27, 28, 32
Joncas, Agnès (*Le Temps Sauvage*), 112
Joual (language), 189
Journal d'une folle, 185
Judeo-Christian religions, 206, 210, 211
Judith ("Les Petits Pas de Caroline"), 32-33
Julie (*L'Ile joyeuse*), 98, 99, 100
Julien (*Amadou*), 96
Juliette ("Sécurité"), 31
"Jungle de feuilles" (Lasnier), 56-57, 58
"Justice en Danaca et ailleurs, La" (Roy), 27, 30

Kamouraska, 119-21
Kamouraska (Hébert), 65, 109-10, 114-21; historical basis, 109; related works, 110-14; structure, 114-16, 118; themes, 116-17, 118-19
Khan, Masud R., 21
Korê-Persephone, 209
Kristeva, Julia, 4, 216
Kumachuk, Elsa (*La Rivière sans repos*), 28

Laberge, Marie, 242; *C'était avant la guerre à l'Anse à Gilles*, 251; *Ils étaient venus pour*, 251
"Lac, Le" (Lasnier), 58
Lacan, 160, 206, 208
Lacasse, Rose-Anna (*Bonheur d'occasion*), 28, 75, 77, 78
Lacasse family (*Bonheur d'occasion*), 73
Lajeunesse, Mlle. ("Six Pilules par jour"), 33
Lalonde, Michèle, 5, 242; *Dernier Recours de Baptiste à Catherine*, 250-51
Lamarsh, Judy, 92
Lamontagne-Beauregard, Blanche, 55
Lamy, Suzanne, 215-16; *D'elles*, 247, 248
Land, importance of owning, 47
Lange, Judith (*Le Sourd dans la ville*), 132, 133-34
Language: and women, 158, 162-63, 217-18
Laporte, Robert, 89
Lamprade, Louise: *A ma mère, à ma mère, à ma mère, à ma voisine*, 245-46; *Essai en trois mouvements pour trois voix de femmes*, 245
Finalement, 245; and Théâtre Expérimental des Femmes, 245; *Trac femmes*, 245
Lasnier, Rina, 4, 7, 53; absence in "Présence de l'absence," 53, 56-57, 58; and Quebec, 53, 57; approach to life, love, nature, 53-54; "Présence de l'absence," 53-60; silence, use of in "Présence de l'absence," 53, 54, 58; "Chansons," 54, 57-58;"Présence de l'absence" (title poem), 54-55, 58; flight of birds in "Présence de l'absence," 55; "La Mouette," 55-56, 59; "Lune blanche et," 55; "Lune rousse," 55; *Miroirs*, 55-56; "Perdu en montagne," 55; "Plénitude," 55, 59; purity and evil in "Présence de l'absence," 55, 57; "Retrouvé par les eaux," 55; "Angoisse," 56, 58; "Le Catalpa," 56; "Le Coteau," 56, 58; "Jungle de feuilles," 56-57, 58; "Mensonge," 56, 59; "Le Pommier

d'Asie,'' 56; ''Le Temps,'' 56; ''L'A-
nesse et l'ânon des rameaux,'' 57;
''Claire fontaine,'' 57-58; ''Il pleut,''
57-58; incarnation in ''Présence de
l'absence,'' 57; ''Le Noël des animaux,'' 57; ''Les Palmes,'' 57; ''Le
Roi de Jade,'' 57; ''L'Arbre en feu,''
58; ''C'est toi,'' 58; ''Les Cheveux,''
58; ''Le Lac,'' 58; ''Mirement,'' 58;
''Noël de la mère vieille,'' 58; ''Prés-
ence de l'eau vierge,'' 58, 59; ''Le
Reflet,'' 58-59; ''Les Voix,'' 58; ''Les
Gisants,'' 59; ''L'Orme vieux,'' 59;
''Inutilité,'' 60
Lebrun, Father (*Le Survenant*), 40, 44-45
Lecavalier, Nicole: *A ma mère, à ma
mère, à ma mère, à ma voisine*, 245-
46; *Essai en trois mouvements pour
trois voix de femmes*, 245; *Finalement*,
245; and Théâtre Expérimental des
Femmes, 245; *Trac femmes*, 245
Leclerc, Annie, 3, 187, 194
Leduc, Violette (*La Terre est trop courte,
Violette Leduc*), 251
Le Maigre, Jean (*Une Saison dans la vie
d'Emmanuel*), 128
Lemelin, Roger, 37
Le Moine, Roger, 12, 17
Léonard, Germaine (*Manuscrits de Pau-
line Archange*), 130
Lequin, Lucie, 186
Lesbian feminism. *See* Feminism, lesbian
Lesbianism, 227, 245; in Quebec, 158,
277
Letarte, Jean, 205
Létourneau, Emmanuel (*Bonheur d'occa-
sion*), 74-75
Levac, Claude: *Le Chemin du Roy*, 87-89
Lévesque, Jean (*Bonheur d'occasion*),
74, 75
Levesque, René, 88, 91
Liberté: ''Recontre québecoise interna-
tionale des écrivains,'' 161
Life: in Lasnier ''Présence de l'absence,''
53
Liliane (*Visions d'Anna*), 136
Linqunt, Jacques, 207

Literature, psychoanalytic interpretation
of, 12
Literature, feminist, xi, 3-9, 216-17, 244;
Quebec, 185; language, 244. See also
Barre du Jour, La; *Nouvelle Barre du
Jour, La*; *Têtes de pioche, Les*; Writers
feminist
Livre, Un (Brossard), 185
Lizzie (''La Conversion des O'Connor''),
30
Longfellow, Henry Wadsworth: *Evangeline*, 65
Loranger, Francoise, 7; *Encore cinq minutes*, 83, 84-85, 91; *Une Maison, un
jour*, 83-84, 91; *Le Chemin du Roy*,
85, 87-89, 91, 92; *Double jeu*, 85-87,
88, 89, 90, 91, 92; improvisation in
drama, 85-87; psychodrama, 86-87; fe-
male characters, 87, 91, 92; feminism,
88, 90-91; *Médium saignant*, 89-91,
92; use of fear in drama, 90-91; male
characters, 92; *Mathieu*, 127; drama,
241
Loubka (''Le Joli Miracle''), 28, 32
Louise (*La Belle Bête*), 125, 126
Louisiana, 178
Love: in Lasnier ''Présence de l'ab-
sence,'' 53-55, 56, 57-58; in Hébert
Kamouraska, 116, 118-19, 121; in
Maillet *Pélagie-la-Charrette*, 151
Lucile (''Avantage pour''), 30
Lueur (Gagnon), 187, 195-97, 198
''Lune blanche et'' (Lasnier), 55
''Lune des moissons, La'' (Roy), 30
''Lune rousse'' (Lasnier), 55
Lutrin, Le (Boileau), 142

Madeleine (*Pélagie-la-Charrette*), 151
Madeleine the Prostitute (*Les Fées ont
soif*), 249
Maheux-Forcier, Louise, 7-8; *Amadou*,
95-98, 99, 102, 103; *Une Forêt pour
Zoé*, 95, 100-103; *L'Ile joyeuse*, 95,
98-100, 102; love in fiction, 96, 101;
homosexuality in fiction, 96-98, 102-3;
sensuality in fiction, 96, 97, 98, 99,
102-3; Catholic background, 97; fe-

male characters, 98; mother figures in fiction, 98, 101

Maïakovski, 187

Mailhot, Michèle, 6; *La Mort de l'araignée*, 185

Maillet, Andrée, 6

Maillet, Antonine, 3, 8; *Les- Cordes- de Bois*, 141-42, 145-47, 148-49; female characters, 141, 148, 151-52; *Maria-agélas*, 141, 142-43, 144-45, 148, 173; *Pélagie-la-Charrette*, 141, 142,143-44, 147-48, 149-51, 152; *Les Cordes-de-Bois*, sea motif, 146; *Les Cordes-de-Bois*, sexuality in, 147; male characters, 148-51; *Pélagie-la-Charrette*, sea motif, 148; myth in novels, 173; *Pélagie-la-Charrette*, mythology, 173-80; *Pélagie-la-Charrette*, cultural referents, 174; *Pélagie-la-Charrette*, language, 174, 179-80; *Pélagie-la-Charrette*, woman as subject, 174-75; *Pélagie-la-Charrette*, symbolism of cart, 175, 178; *Pélagie-la-Charrette*, ordeals of heroine, 176; *Pélagie-la-Charrett*, journey in, 177-78; *Pélagie-la-Charrette*, style, 178-79

Maine, 151

"Maison de l'Esplanade, La" (Hébert), 111

Maison, un jour, Une (Loranger), 83-84, 91

Mallarmé, Stéphane, 55, 59

Maman-Eveline (*Rue Deschambault*), 29

Manitoba, 27

Manuscrits de Pauline Archange (Blais), 129, 133, 135

Mao Tse-tung, 187

Ma p'tite vache a mal aux pattes (Goyette), 249-50

Marchessault, Jovette, 8, 163, 186, 191, 198, 227-31, 236; *Comme une enfant de la terre*, 173-77, 179-80, 227-28; *La Mère des herbes*, 173, 228-29; myth in novels, 173, 228-29; *Comme une enfant de la terre*, cultural referents, 174; *Comme une enfant de la terre*, language, 174, 179-80; *Comme une enfant de la terre*, woman as sub-ject, 174-175; *Comme une enfant de la terre*, ordeals of heroine, 176; *Comme une enfant de la terre*, structure, 176; lesbianism, 227-28; feminism, 228, 229-31; lesbianism in fiction, 228-31, 236; language, *Tryptique lesbien*, 229-31, 232, 233, 234, 236; *Tryptique lesbien*, 229-31, 236; mother daughter relationship in drama, 242; drama, 242; *La Saga des poules mouillées*, 251; *La Terre est trop courte, Violette Leduc*, 251; "Les Vaches de nuit," 251

Mariaagélas (Maillet), 141, 142-43, 144-45, 148, 173

Maria Chapdelaine (Hémon), 119, 127, 128, 251

Maria (*Mariaagélas*), 142-43, 144-45, 152

Marie (*Angéline de Montbrun*), 13-14

Marie (*Une Forêt pour Zoé*), 100, 101

Marie the Mother (*Les Fées ont soif*), 249

Mariette ("Le Monde à l'envers"), 32

Marriage, 30-31; in *Le Survenant*, 42-44, 46

Martin, Claire, 6

Martine (*Cet été qui chantait*), 78

Marx, Karl, 206, 212

Marxist feminism. See Feminism: Marxist

Marxism, 187

Mascarade, 246

Massé, Carole, 7

Ma-Tante-la-Veuve (*Les Cordes-de-Bois*), 142-43, 145, 146-47

Maternative (Bersianik), 205, 207, 208, 209, 214, 215-16, 218

Mathieu (Loranger), 127

Médium saignant (Loranger), 89-91, 92

Memmi, Albert, 160

Mennonite women, 30

"Mensonge" (Lasnier), 56, 59

Mer à boire, La, 246

Mercenaire, Catoun (*Les Cordes-de-Bois*), 149

Mercenaire, la Bessoune (*Les Cordes-de-Bois*), 141-43, 145-47, 148-49

Mercenaire, la Piroune (*Les Cordes-de-Bois*), 141-43, 145-47, 152

Mercière assassinée, La (Hébert), 111

Mère des herbes, La (Marchessault), 173, 228-29

Mexico, 228

Mia (*Une Forêt pour Zoé*), 100, 101

Michel (*Les Chambres de bois*), 112-13

Michel (*Une Maison, un jour*), 83, 84

Michelle (*Visions d'Anna*), 134, 136

Micmac Tribe, 174

Middle Ages, 206

Mike (*Le Sourd dans la ville*), 132, 133

Millet, Kate, 232

"Mirement' (Lasnier), 58

Miroirs (Lasnier), 55-56

Miron, Gaston, 160

Moi Tarzan, toi Jane (Bertrand), 250

Moman (Dussault), 242, 249

Môman travaille pas, a trop d'ouvrage, 243

"Mon corps dans l'écriture" (Gagnon), 194-95

"Monde à l'envers, Le" (Roy), 32

Monologue form: in Quebec women's theater, 9, 247-48

Montagne secrète, La (Roy), 28, 77-78

Montbrun, Angéline de (*Angéline de Montbrun*), 12, 14; and Maurice Darville, 12-13, 23; love for father, 14, 15, 21, 22; innocence, 16, 17; disfigurement, 17; sexual desire, 19-20, 21; narcissism, 21-22; loneliness, 21, 23

Montbrun, Charles de (*Angéline de Montbrun*), 12, 13; and women, 14, 15; narcissism, 15-16; sexual desire, 15, 19-20; love for daughter, 15, 22; death, 18, 20, 22, 23

Montreal, 27, 73, 227

Montreal World's Fair, 135

Moral example in literature, 12

Morin, Marie, Soeur, 4

Mort de l'araignée, La (Mailhot), 185

Morts-vivants, Les (Gagnon), 187

Mother-daughter relationship: Quebec, 125-26, 127; in Marchessault *Tryptique lesbien*, 229

Mother figure: in Quebec fiction, 5, 127; in Roy fiction, 28-29; in *Le Survenant*, 38, 42-43; in Blais fiction, 125, 128, 132, 133, 134, 135-36; in Marchessault *Tryptique lesbien*, 229; in Brossard fiction, 232, 233

Mother, Quebec, 39, 42, 43, 132, 133, 137, 230

"Mouette, La" (Lasnier), 55-56, 59

Munch, Edvard, 132

Munger, Léo: *Le Fleuve au coeur*, 246

"Mystère de la parole, Le" (Hébert), 67-68

Myth, 8; in Maillet novels, 173; in Marchessault novels, 173

Narcissism, 7; in *Angéline de Montbrun*, 14-16, 22, 23

Nathalie, (*Amadou*), 95-98, 101, 102

Nathalie (*Une Maison, un jour*), 83, 84, 87

National Film Board, 111

"Natte et la hutte, La" (Bersianik-*Maternative*), 209, 215

Nature: in Lasnier "Présence de l'absence," 53-54, 58, 59; in Roy fiction, 71

Nef des sorcières, La, 167, 244, 247, 248

Negritude poets, 64-65

Nelson, George (*Kamouraska*), 113, 118, 119, 120

New French Feminisms, 187

Nick ("La Lune des moissons"), 30

"Noël de la mère vieille" (Lasnier), 58

"Noël des animaux, Le" (Lasnier), 57

"Noël, en route, Un" (Roy), 28

Noël, Francine, 246

Nopal (*L'Euguélionne*), 207

Nopaline (*L'Euguélionne*), 207

North America, 228

Nous aurons les enfants que nous voulons, 243

Nouvelle Barre du Jour, La, 163; "Célébrations," 163; "La Complicité," 163; "Le Corps, les mots, l'imaginaire," 163; "La Femme et la ville," 163; "La Femme et l'humour," 163; "La Femme et l'humour," 163; "La Mer-

mour,'' 163. See also *Barre du Jour,*
La
Nuits de l'Underground, Les (Blais),
    125, 130-31, 133

October Crisis, 160. *See also* Quebec,
    nationalism
Oedipus, 23, 206, 208
Olivier (*Médium saignant*), 90
Omicronne (*L'Euguélionne*), 206
Orenstein, Gloria, 210
Organisation Ô: *E*, 245
Original sin, 17
''L'Orme vieux'' (Lasnier), 59
''Orphée noir'' (Sartre), 63
Ortygia (''Ortygie l'inapparente,'' *Mater-*
    native), 209, 214, 215, 216
''Ortygie l'inapparente'' (Bersianik-*Ma-*
    ternative), 209
Ottawa, 87
Ouellette-Michalska, Madeleine, 7, 210
Où en est le miroir? (Dion-Portal), 246
Ouvrard, Hélène, 7, 196; *Le Corps*
    étranger, 185

Pagé, Pierre, 37-38, 66
''Palmes, Les'' (Lasnier), 57
Paradis, Suzanne, 6
Paris, 112, 227
Parizeau, Alice, 7
Parti Pris, 159-60, 165
Parti-Québécois, 185-86
Pascale (*Médium saignant*), 92
Passion, sexual, 7
Patrice (*La Belle Bête*), 125, 126
Paul (*Angéline de Montbrun*), 13-14
Pauline (*Manuscrits de Pauline Ar-*
    change), 129-30
Pearson, Lester B., 88-89, 92
Pélagie-la-Charrette (Maillet), 141, 142,
    143-44, 147-48, 149-51, 152; sea mo-
    tif, 148; mythology, 173-80; cultural
    referents, 174; language, 174, 179-80;
    woman as subject, 174-75; symbolism
    of cart, 175, 178; ordeals of heroine,
    176; journey in, 177-78; style, 178-79
Pélagie (*Pélagie-la-Charrette*), 143-44,

147-48, 149-51, 152, 175,176, 178;
    journey, 177-78
Pelletier, Pol, 241; *La Nef des sorcières*,
    244, 245; *A ma mère, à ma mère, à*
    ma mère, à ma voisine, 245-46; *Essai*
    en trois mouvements pour trois voix de
    femmes, 245; *Finalement*, 245; and
    Théâtre Experimental des Femmes,
    245; *Trac femmes*, 245
''Pension de vieillesse, La'' (Roy), 33
Péquisme, 212
''Perdu en montagne'' (Lasnier), 55
Péribonka, 119
Persephone. *See* Korê-Persephone
Peter (*Visions d'Anna*, 134, 135-36
''Petits Pas de Caroline, Les'' (Roy), 32-
    33
Peur surtout, La, 246
Picoche, Jacqueline, 217
Pique-nique sur l'Acropole, Le (Bersi-
    anik), 205, 207-11, 213, 214, 215,
    216; female sexuality, 211
Pitou (*Bonheur d'occasion*), 74
Plato: *Banquet*, 205, 210-11; Cave Myth,
    210
''Plénitude'' (Lasnier), 55, 59
Pluto. *See* Hades/Pluto
Poélitique (Gagnon), 185, 187-89, 198
Poèmes (Hébert), 67
''Pommier d'Asie, Le'' (Lasnier), 56
Popular culture. *See* Culture, popular
Portal, Louise: *Où en est le miroir?*, 246
Poudrier, Donalda (*Un Homme et son*
    péché), 47
Poulin, Gabrielle, 133
Pour les femmes et tous les autres (Gag-
    non), 185, 187, 189-91
Poverty: in Roy fiction, 73-75
''Présence de l'absence'' (Lasnier), 53-60
''Présence de l'absence'' (title poem-Las-
    nier), 54-55, 58
''Présence de l'eau vierge'' (Lasnier), 58,
    59
Prince, mon jour viendra, Un, 242
''Printemps de Catherine, Le'' (Hébert),
    111
Prix Fémina, 3, 4
Prix Goncourt, 3

Prix Médicis, 4
Provençal, Catherine (*Le Survenant*), 46
Provençal, Joinville (*Le Survenant*), 43, 44, 46
Provençal, Odilon (*Le Survenant*), 39, 44, 46
Provençal, Pierre-Côme (*Le Survenant*), 38, 39, 40-41, 44, 46, 47
Psychoanalysis, Freudian, 207-8, 215
Psychoanalytic interpretation, 12
Psychodrama, 86-87

Quebec, 4, 228; nationalism, xi, 5, 6, 8, 87-89, 90, 141, 152, 159, 160, 164, 174, 185, 232, 250-51; culture, 5, 174; educational system, 5; society, men in, 5; society, women in, 5, 6, 7, 9, 43-44, 45, 115, 242; society, 7, 39, 49, 110, 111, 118, 121, 126, 127; self-image, 37, 38, 174; transition to modern society, 45-46, 49, 127; traditions, 63; family structure, 83; 1967 De Gaulle visit, 87-88, 90, 91; language issue, 89-90, 91, 174; physical environment, 109-110, 111, 119, 120-21; colonial mentality, 118; family structure, in Blais fiction, 125, 127, 137; union movement, 164. *See also* October Crisis; Quiet Revolution; War Measures Act
Quebec City, 114, 119
Quebec in poetry of Lasnier. *See* Lasnier, Rina, and Quebec
Quebec Litteraire, Le, 187
Québécoises deboutte!, 185
Quiet Revolution, 5, 7, 49, 91, 92, 126, 128, 159

Rabelais, Francois, 179
Radio serials: Quebec, 37-39
Rape, 241
Rassemblement pour l'Independence Nationale, 88
Raymond, Nathalie ("La Source au désert"), 31
Raymond, Vincent, Dr. ("La Source au dèsert"), 31, 32

Raymonde (*Visions d'Anna*), 134, 135, 136
Realism, 72
"Reflet, Le" (Lasnier), 58-59
Renaud (*Encore cinq minutes*), 84, 85
René (*Les Nuits de l'Underground*), 131
Retailles: Complaintes politiques (Boucher-Gagnon), 191-94
"Retrouvé par les eaux" (Lasnier), 55
Révolution tranquille. *See* Quiet Revolution
Revue Moderne, La, 27
Ricard, François, 28
Rich, Adrienne, 4, 127-28, 136-37, 167, 194
Rinquet, 37
Rioux, Hélène, 7
Rita (*Visions d'Anna*), 134
Rivière sans repos, La (Roy), 28
Robert, Guy: on poetry of Hébert, 63
Rodin, Auguste, 131
"Roi de coeur, Le" (Roy), 30
"Roi de jade, Le" (Lasnier), 57
Roland, 142
Roles, gender, 5
Rolland, Elizabeth (*Kamouraska*), 113, 114, 116-18, 119
Rolland, Jérôme (*Kamouraska*), 118
Rosolato, Guy, 21, 22
Rossignol, Michelle, 241, 247
Rousseaux, André: on poetry of Hébert, 63
Route d'Altamont, La (Roy), 29
Roux, Eliette: *Les Têtes de Pioche*, 166
Roy, Gabrielle, 4, 7, 27, 28, 37, 72, 251; *Alexandre Chenevert*, 27, 76-77; *Bonheur d'occasion*, 27, 28, 73-75; "Feuilles mortes," 27; male characters, 27, 29-30, 31, 32-33, 75, 78; "La Sonate a l'Aurore," 27; "Le Joli Miracle," 27, 28, 32; "La Justice en Danaca et ailleurs," 27, 30; "Securité," 27, 31; and role of mother, 28-29, 127; *Ces enfants de ma vie*, 28; *Cet été qui chantait*, 28, 71, 78; female characters, 28-29, 30-32, 33, 75, 78; feminism, 28-29, 30, 33; "Gérard le pirate," 28; *La Montagne secrète*,

28, 77-78; "La Source au désert," 28, 31; "La Grande Voyageuse," 28, 33; *La Rivière sans repos*, 28; *Rue Deschambault*, 28, 29; *Un Jardin au bout du monde*, 28, 29; "Un Nöel en route," 28; "Un Vagabond frappe à notre porte," 28; *La Route d'Altamont*," 29; traditionalism, 29, 30, 33; 30, 33; "Avantage pour," 30; "Bonne à marier," 30; "Cendrillon '40," 30; "La Lune des moissons," 30; "Le Roi de coeur," 30; marriage in fiction, 30-31; and children, 31; "La Conversion des O'Connor," 31; "La Fuite de Sally," 31; "La Grande Berthe," 31, 33; "Le Monde à l'envers, 32; "Les Petits Pas de Caroline," 32-33; "Embobeliné," 33; "La Pension de vieillesse," 33; "Six Pilules par jour," 33; "Introduction," *Terre des Hommes/ Man and His World*, 71; characters and environment, 71-72; characters and nature, 72; city in fiction, 72-78; influence of Realism on, 72; "Du port aux banques," 73; poverty in fiction, 73-75; country in fiction, 77-78
Roy, Louise: *Bachelor*, 249
Roy, Michel: *L'Acadie perdue*, 174
Royer, Jean, 187
Rue Deschambault (Roy), 28, 29

Sabrini, Anna (*Médium saignant*), 91, 92
Saga des poules mouillées, La (Marchessault), 251
Saia, Louis: *Bachelor*, 249
Saint Bruno, 243
Sainte-Catherine, rue, Montreal, 73, 74
Saint-Henri, Montreal, 73-75, 77
Saint Lawrence River, 119
Saison dans la vie d'Emmanuel, Une, (Blais), 128-29
Salem, 143, 148, 150, 151
Salvail, Bedette (*Le Survenant*), 44-46, 47, 49
Salvail, Jacob (*Le Survenant*), 44
Salvail family (*Le Survenant*), 38
Sappho, 95, 227

Sartre, Jean Paul, 160, 212; "Orphée noir," 63
Savard, Marie: *Bien à moi*, 248; use of monologue, 248
Sea: in Maillet *Les Cordes-de-Bois*,146; in Maillet *Pélagie-la-Charrett*, 148
"Securité" (Roy), 27, 31
Senghor, Léopold Sédar: *Anthologie de la nouvelle poésie nègre et malgache de langue française*, 64
Sens apparent, Le (Brossard), 232, 233-34
Serials, radio. *See* Radio serials
Sexual repression, 5, 194; in *Angéline de Montbrun*, 20, 23
"She's Leaving Home" (Beatles), 88, 89
Si Cendrillon pouvait mourir!, 243
Sign of the Cross, 207
Silence: in Lasnier "Présence de l'absence," 53, 54, 58
Simoneau, Constantin ("Feuilles mortes"), 28
"Six Pilules par jour" (Roy), 33
Smith-Rosenberg, Carroll, 127
Socialism, 190
Socken, Paul, 71-72
Socrates, 205, 210, 211, 214
Sold-out (Brossard), 185
Sollers, Philippe, 180
Some American Feminists (Brossard-Guilbeault), 167
"Sonate à l'Aurore, La" (Roy), 27
Songes en équilibre, Les (Hébert), 65
Sophie ("Cendrillon '40"), 30
Sorel, 41, 43, 45, 46, 47, 48, 116, 120
Soubliere, Roger, 160
"Source au désert, La" (Roy), 28, 31
Sourd dans la ville, Le (Blais), 125, 131-34, 135
Spectacles de femmes, 9, 242; structures, 246-47; collective creation, 247. *See also* Improvisational theater
Speculum de l'autre femme (Irigaray), 210
Stanislas (*La Montagne secrète*), 77
Stein, Gertrude, 167
Stéphane (*L'Ile joyeuse*), 98, 99, 100

Stratégies du réel, Les/The Story So Far
(Brossard), 169
Subconscious: and conscious, in *Angéline
de Montbrun*, 11
Surrealism, 212
Survenant, Le (Guèvrement), 7; reviews,
37; radio version, 37-38, 39; reflection
of Quebec society, 38, 39, 49; absence
of mother figure, 38; father figure, 38;
male dominance, 38-39, 40-42, 43-44,
46-47, 48; Catholic Church in, 40; female characters, 40-47; male characters, 40, 41, 43, 48; motherhood in,
42-43; marriage in, 42-44
Survenant (*Le Survenant*), 37, 39, 40-41,
44, 45-46; independence, 47-49
Sylvia (*Amadou*), 95-98

Tagore, Rabindranath, Sir, 95
Taoism, 212
Tassy, Antoine (*Kamouraska*), 113, 117-
18, 119-20
"Temps, Le" (Lasnier), 56
Temps sauvage, Le (Hébert), 111-12
Terre est trop courte, La (Marchessault),
251
Têtes de Pioche, Les, 158, 159, 164-67,
186, 232
Theater, women's: Quebec, 9, 241-52
Théâtre des Cuisines, 241, 242-43
Théâtre du Nouveau Monde, 111, 167,
244, 248
Théâtre Expérimental de Montreal, 245
Thétre Expérimental des Femmes, 241,
245-46
Théoret, France, 7, 167, 185, 198; *La
Nef des sorcières*, 244, 247
Thérèse (*Une Forêt pour Zoé*), 100-103
Thetford Mines, 243
Thomas Aquinas, Saint, 206
Thomist philosophy, 211, 212
Tintoretto, 13
"Tombeau des rois, Le" (Hébert), 65-
66, 68
Tombeau des rois, Le (Hérbert), 63, 65-
66, 68
Tom Thumb (*Les Cordes-de-Bois*), 146,
148, 149

Torrent, Le (Hébert), 110-11, 127
Totem and Taboo (Freud), 208
Tougas, Francine, 249
Trac femmes, 245
Traditionalism, xi, 6, 7, 46, 47-49, 141
Tremblay, Michel, 247
Trois et Sept le Numéro Magique, 245
Tryptique lesbien (Marchessault), 229-31,
236; language, 229-31, 232, 233, 234,
236

United States, xi, 46, 127, 128; and Que-
bec, 4
Université de Montreal, 159
UTINAM! (Cloutier), 248

"Vaches de nuit, Les" (Marchessault),
251
"Vagabond frappe à notre porte, Un"
(Roy), 28
Valleee, Manon: *La Fleuve au coeur*,
246
Valriant (*Angéline de Montbrun*), 16, 22
"Vaseline" (Brossard), 160
Verlaine, Paul, 65
Veuve à Calixte (*Mariaagélas*), 142-43,
145
"Vie privée est politique, La" (Bros-
sard), 186
Villemaire, Yolande, 7, 210
Vincent (*Une Maison, un jour*), 83, 84
Virgin Mary, 16, 58
Virgin Mary (*statue-Les Fées ont soif*),
248, 249
Visions d'Anna (Blais), 125, 130, 134-36
"Voix, Les" (Lasnier), 58
Vraie Vie des masquées, La, 243

War Measures Act, 160. *See also* Que-
bec: nationalism
Westmount, Montreal, 74
Winnipeg, 72
Wittig, Monique, 167
Women: work outside home, 41, 43-44;
traditionjal roles, 127, 241, 243, 245,
246, 248; image of, 241
Women in Quebec society. *See* Quebec:
society, women in

Women's theater, Quebec. *See* Theater, women's: Quebec
Woolf, Virginia, 167, 213
Writers, feminist: Quebec, xi-xii, 3-9, 127, 158, 159-60, 165, 185-86, 191-92, 198

Xanthippe (*Le Pique-nique sur l'Acropole*), 205, 208, 211, 212, 214, 215, 217

Yaguello, Marina, 217
Yaramko, Martha (*Un Jardin au bout du monde*), 29
Yolande (*Le Sens apparent*), 233
Yourcenar, Marguerite, 3

Zeus, 206, 209, 211
Zoé (*Une Forêt pour Zoé*), 100, 101-3
Zola, Emile, 72

Contributors

MAURICE CAGNON is a Professor in the Department of French at Montclair State College (Upper Montclair, New Jersey). His fields of interest include twentieth-century French and *québécois* prose and poetry. He is the editor of *Ethique et esthétique dans la littérature française du XXᵉ siècle* and has published widely in the areas of both contemporary French and *québécois* literatures. He has recently completed two books, *The French-Canadian Novel* and *Idée principale/Style varié: Techniques de traduction, composition et stylistique*.

CARROL F. COATES is an Associate Professor in the Department of Romance Languages and Literatures at the State University of New York at Binghamton and an exchange lecturer at the Université d'Aix-Marseilles I in France. His interests lie in the fields of seventeenth-century French poetry, nineteenth-century French poetry and novel, and *québécois* literature, especially theater. Presently he is undertaking research on verse structuring in nineteenth-century French poetry and on the work of La Fontaine.

MARJORIE A. FITZPATRICK is an Associate Professor in the Department of French and Administrative Coordinator for Internships at Dickinson College (Carlisle, Pennsylvania). Her interests comprise both seventeenth-century French literature and *québécois* and francophone literature and civilization, and she has published in these two areas. She is presently doing research on Quebec novelists.

LOUISE H. FORSYTH is a Professor and Chair of the Department of French at the University of Western Ontario (London, Ontario, Canada). Her interests lie in the fields of women writers of Quebec and France, with a special interest in Nicole Brossard, and of Quebec theater history. She has published several articles in these fields. Currently she is working on a book-length study of the work of Nicole Brossard, with specific attention to language and ideology.

FRANÇOIS GALLAYS is an Associate Professor in the Department of French at the University of Ottawa (Ontario, Canada). His field of interest is *québécois* literature, with an emphasis on poetry and the novel, and he has published many articles in this field. Currently he is working on studies of Gaston Miron, Roland Giguère, and Anne Hébert.

JAMES P. GILROY is an Associate Professor in the Department of Foreign Languages and Literature of the University of Denver (Colorado). His fields of interest are eighteenth-, nineteenth-, and twentieth-century French literature, *québécois* literature, and black francophone literature. He is the author of *The Romantic Manon and Des Grieux: Images of Prévost's Heroine and Hero in Nineteenth-Century French Literature* and numerous articles on both French and *québécois* writers, and the editor of *Francophone Literatures of the New World*. He is currently doing research on *québécois* poetry and on Abbé Prévost.

KAREN GOULD is an Associate Professor in the Department of Foreign Languages and Literature at Virginia Polytechnic Institute and State University (Blacksburg, Virginia). Her fields of interest are contemporary French fiction, contemporary women writers in France and Quebec, and feminist criticism. She is the author of *Claude Simon's Mythic Muse*, is co-editor of *Orion Blinded: Essays on Claude Simon*, and has published articles on Simon and feminist *québécois* writers. Her current research project is a book on feminist writing in Quebec.

MARY JEAN GREEN is an Associate Professor in the Department of French and Italian and Co-Chair of the Women's Studies Program at Dartmouth College (Hanover, New Hampshire). Her interests include the twentieth-century French political novel, women's studies, and *québécois* literature. She is the author of *Louis Guilloux: An Artisan of Letters* and of many articles in her fields of specialization. She is currently working on a series of articles on Quebec women novelists.

MAROUSSIA HAJDUKOWSKI-AHMED is an Assistant Professor in the Department of Romance Languages at McMaster University (Hamilton, Ontario, Canada). Her interests lie in the fields of the *québécois* novel, social anthropology and literary theory, theory of feminist literature, and Bakhtinian studies. She has published several articles in these areas and is presently continuing research for a book on "Le Carnaval, la sorcière et l'écriture de la transgression."

JAMES J. HERLAN is a Lecturer in the Department of Foreign Languages and Classics and Interim Director of the Canadian-American Center of the University of Maine at Orono. His interests include Quebec studies and *québécois* literature, radio, and television. He has published several articles in these fields and is currently continuing his research in this same area.

MICHELINE HERZ holds a Chair in the Department of French at Douglass College of Rutgers University (New Brunswick, New Jersey). Her fields of interest include seventeenth- and twentieth-century French literature and civilization and *québécois* literature and civilization. She has published many articles in all of these areas and is currently working on a study dealing with the concept of Europe in the seventeenth century.

PAULA GILBERT LEWIS is a Professor in the Department of Romance Languages at Howard University (Washington, D.C.). Her fields of interest comprise Quebec studies and literature with an emphasis on women writers, women's studies, and nineteenth-century French literature, particularly Symbolist poetry. She is the author of *The Aesthetics of Stéphane Mallarmé in Relation to His Public* and *The Literary Vision of Gabrielle Roy: An Analysis of Her Works*, as well as numerous articles on Quebec women writers, *québécois* literature, and nineteenth-century French Symbolism. She is presently working on studies of American feminist theory as applied to texts by Quebec women writers.

JANE MOSS is an Assistant Professor in the Department of Modern Foreign Languages at Colby College (Waterville, Maine). Her fields of interest include seventeenth-century French theater, nineteenth-century French theater and novel, Quebec theater and novel, and women writers. She has published several articles in these fields and is presently doing research on French and *québécois* women novelists and dramatists.

MARTHE ROSENFELD teaches French and Women's Studies in the Department of Modern Foreign Languages at Indiana University-Purdue University, Fort Wayne (Indiana). Her fields of interest comprise women writers of France and Quebec, lesbian literature in France and the francophone world, and the twentieth-century French novel. She has published *Edmond Jaloux: The Evolution of a Novelist* and articles on lesbian/feminist writers. Currently she is working on the concept of feminist utopias in contemporary French and francophone literatures.

SUSAN L. ROSENSTREICH is a translator for Rosetta Foreign Language Communications (Cutchogue, New York). She is also Associate Editor for the Francophone Project at Cross-Cultural Communications (Merrick, New York). Her major field of interest is the problems in the translation of minority literatures. She has published her own poetry and translations of poetry, and she is now working on studies of *québécois* poets and on bilingual editions of that poetry.

MURRAY SACHS is a Professor and Chair of the Department of Romance and Comparative Literature at Brandeis University (Waltham, Massachusetts). His major interest is in fiction, both the novel and short story, with a concentration on nineteenth-century French fiction. He has published *The Career of Alphonse Daudet: A Critical Study* and *Anatole France: The Short Stories*, as well as numerous articles on nineteenth-century French writers. His current project is a book-length study of Gustave Flaubert.